John Coltrane

The Michigan American Music Series

Richard Crawford, Series General Editor

The Michigan American Music Series focuses on leading figures of American jazz and popular music, assessing both the uniqueness of their work and its place in the context of American musical tradition.

John Coltrane

His Life and Music

Lewis Porter

Ann Arbor

THE UNIVERSITY OF MICHIGAN PRESS

Copyright © by the University of Michigan 1998
All rights reserved
Published in the United States of America by
The University of Michigan Press
Manufactured in the United States of America
⊗ Printed on acid-free paper

2001   2000   1999   1998   4   3

A CIP catalog record for this book is available from the British Library.

Library of Congress Cataloging-in-Publication Data

Porter, Lewis.
    John Coltrane : his life and music / Lewis Porter.
        p.   cm.
    Includes bibliographical references, discography, and index.
    ISBN 0-472-10161-7 (alk. paper)
    1. Coltrane, John, 1926–1967.   2. Jazz musicians—United States—
Biography.   I. Title.
ML419.C645P65   1997
788.7'165'092—dc21
    [B]   97-41995
                                                                CIP
                                                                MN

To my brother Spence—my advisor and confidante during much of the work—and to my children, Matthew and Rachel, an ever-present source of joy.

Contents

Preface

When I began writing about Coltrane in 1980, my intention was to fill a need in the literature for a full-length survey of his musical accomplishments. I eventually realized that a new biography was also required. To date only two people—J. C. Thomas and C. O. Simpkins—have done extensive research on Coltrane's life. Their resulting books were both published in 1975. Both are sincere efforts that contain a great deal of information derived from firsthand interviews, and they are essential for the Coltrane devotee. However, neither is totally reliable. They contain uncredited statements and stories that do not jibe with common sense.

Since 1975 there have been no new biographies based on fresh research. The book by Bill Cole is a mixture of philosophy and a bit of musical analysis. Eric Nisenson and John Fraim base their works on published material, although Nisenson tries to present a biography while Fraim's self-published volume concentrates on his impressions of the music. A small volume by English pianist Brian Priestley is of value for his musical observations; he based his biography on previous books, with a few new interviews.

So, in 1994, after about fourteen years—on and off—working on musical analysis and discographical research (encompassing music recordings, films and recorded interviews), I decided to write a Coltrane biography from scratch. I interviewed many people who had been interviewed before and many key figures who had never been approached. I compiled a genealogy of Coltrane's family roots going back to the 1830s.

For Coltrane's own words I relied on tapes of him speaking, some never transcribed before, and a treasure trove of French print interviews not previously available in English. The photo section is comprised primarily of images not known to the public.

In discussing the music, I have concentrated on what seem to me essential insights into this astounding body of music, and on new information about the genesis of some of his compositions. Although Coltrane's music is commonly discussed in terms of periods—the early period, the Miles Davis period, the "classic" quartet, and the last period—I have purposely avoided using that approach because it obscures the fact that he was constantly developing and changing. There is a lot here about his composing, because he was just as brilliant on paper as he was on the saxophone. There are also several chapters that re-create what Coltrane practiced, in more detail than has ever been done for any jazz musician.

I have been able to date dozens of previously undated events in Coltrane's life—not only performances but also personal affairs—by collating information from printed sources, interviews, newspapers, and archives. The notes only begin to explain this laborious process. If I fully explained how I arrived at each sentence in the book, it would fill several volumes this size. I read literally hundreds of articles in English and French, and some in Italian, German, and other languages. The notes indicate the relevant ones, and the bibliography is a guide for further reading, not a complete list of my sources.

In the course of my research I came upon scores of performances and newspaper mentions never documented—not even in the 1995 Coltrane discography by Fujioka. This information is presented in the most detailed chronology of Coltrane's career ever compiled.

So, while this book presents the details of Coltrane's story for the novice, it is primarily composed of materials never before published. In the process it provides corrections to what has already been published. This project has been more exciting for me than any of my other publications, largely because it drew on so much of my background—as a researcher, as an educator, as a jazz pianist and composer. Even my training at seminars of the Jewish Genealogy Society, which I attended in order to uncover my own family history, turned out to be of tremendous relevance in uncovering Coltrane's.

I never did see Coltrane. I'm still kicking myself for passing up the "Titans of the Tenor" concert on February 19, 1966. I know now that Coltrane came out and played an intense set of "free jazz" with four other winds, and I wonder what I would have made of it—I was not yet fifteen.

A few notes:
There is no discography here (just a short listing) because most of Coltrane's music is readily available on individual CDs and in boxed sets. The reader who wants to pursue Coltrane's recording career in more depth is referred to the Fujioka discography, which came out in March 1995. (A second edition is planned for the middle of 1998.)

References to the books mentioned above are given by author and page number in the text. In many cases I cite them for material from interviews that seems significant. However, the reader should remain aware that wherever

Thomas or Simpkins is my *only* source for a statement, I cannot vouch for its accuracy although I have made a judgment that it is worth including. I have indicated numerous errors in the previous books, but I could not possibly cite all of them. Where there is a discrepancy the reader may assume that my version is more authoritative. I should also mention that my own previous writings on Coltrane need to be corrected, as they did not have the benefit of the research documented here.

Where references to short articles are given just by author, full publication details appear in the bibliography. The unpublished Blume interview is also cited this way. Wherever the text indicates that "Ray Bryant told me" or "Mary Alexander believes," or the like, the reader will know that I am drawing from the list of interviews in the acknowledgments. For the sake of space and clarity I have cut out most instances of "you know," "like," and "well" from the interviews I conducted. Other references are given in the standard note form at the end of the text.

Wherever the original tapes of Coltrane's interviews exist, I have transcribed his words anew. All translations from French periodicals are my own, but they are purposely rather literal. With the French version, after all, we are already two steps away from the original: whatever Coltrane said in English was edited the way all interviews are, and then translated into French. To guess at Coltrane's exact wordings would introduce one more possible level of inaccuracy. So instead I have been rather dry and literal to the French—and I apologize if it reads that way. I had helpful input from Carl Woideck and two of the authors, Postif and Mialy.

All music examples are in concert key and treble clef; Coltrane's tenor saxophone actually sounds one octave lower. (The examples would have to be written one whole step higher if they were to be read on tenor, because it is a B-flat instrument.) Chord symbols for transcriptions represent what is actually played by the rhythm section, even where it does not fit smoothly with what Coltrane plays. I also checked leadsheets against the recordings and corrected them from the published versions where necessary.

The reader will notice that, for all my efforts, there are still many points left open. It is a delight for me to learn what I can do better, and I welcome all comments and corrections. With your help, which will be acknowledged in print, any future editions of this book can continue to serve as a reliable repository of our knowledge about this great artist.

Lewis Porter
Associate Professor of Music
Rutgers University
Newark, NJ 07102
Office fax: 973-353-1392
E-mail: 73300.2264@compuserve.com

Acknowledgments

Beginning in May 1989, I assisted Yasuhiro Fujioka in preparing *John Coltrane: A Discography and Musical Biography* (Metuchen, N.J.: Scarecrow Press, 1995). Fuji—as he is called—and I made an agreement to share every Coltrane item that we uncovered in our research. Each of us came up with previously unknown items. Together, we studied all known audio- and videotapes of Coltrane playing and speaking (except for a few private collections to which we did not gain access), including many items not available to the public. Fuji also shared leads, phone numbers, and the results of his own interviews with musicians. He was a tremendous help in preparing this study, and I owe him a great debt for his generosity.

The finished manuscript was read carefully by Richard Crawford, Professor of Music at the University of Michigan and a specialist in American music, and Carl Woideck, jazz educator at the University of Oregon, author, and saxophonist, who also shared a number of leads. Critic and friend Ed Hazell worked through early drafts of chapters 5, 10, 14, and 19, and the beginning of 17, rewriting passages, suggesting quotes, and giving me some needed criticism. François Postif deserves a special mention here for his generosity in connecting me with a number of French critics who had tapes and interviews—he was always ready to help. My research assistant, jazz drummer Ken Yamazaki, was supported by a Rutgers University Research Council Grant for the 1995–96 and 1996–97 school years. Ken was a big help in preparing the chronology, among other things.

I had a wonderful experience meeting (often by telephone) and getting help from so many people that I hardly know where to begin. The text is built around the primary interviewees, and I thank each of them heartily. Special thanks go to Jimmy Heath, Mary Alexander (John's cousin and the family historian), Aisha Tyner, and Steve Kuhn for spending hours with me going over

little details. The interviewees and the dates of interviews are Ahmed Abdul-
Malik (12/23/92), Mary Alexander (3/1/95, 2/9 and 6/26/96, and 5/30/97),
Augusta Reid Austin (2/20/96), George Avakian (10/1 and 10/10/95), James
Boyd (3/30/96), Ray Bryant (2/16/96), Michael Cuscuna (1/23/96), Tommy
Flanagan (11/12/95), James Forman (5/20/96), Ira Gitler (3/13/96), John
Glenn (5/20/96), George Goldsmith (1/17/96), Bill Goldstein (2/11/96), Benny
Golson (1/5/96), Isadore Granoff (1/15/96), Kitty Grime (2/9/96), Carl Grubbs
(4/17/96), Chico Hamilton (4/17/96), Rosetta Haywood (3/27/96), Jimmy
Heath (3/3 and 3/4/95, 1/3/96, 11/30/96, 5/19/97, and 6/9/97), Billy Higgins
(11/11/95), Walter Hoover (5/19/97), Betty Jackson (3/27/96), Sy Johnson
(3/14/96), Steve Kuhn (10/13/95), Byard Lancaster (5/19/97), Peter Sims
LaRoca (10/19/95), Rufus Leach, Jr. (3/27/96), Al McKibbon (2/15/96), Louis-
Victor Mialy (3/14 and 6/15/96), Floyd Phifer (4/17/96), Norman Poulshock
(12/3/89), Benny Powell (2/1/96), Matthew Rastelli (5/22/96), Charlie Rice
(11/19/95 and 1/9/96), Dennis Sandole (1/15, 2/21, and 4/17/96), Shirley Scott
(3/14/96), Billy Taylor (9/29/95), Joe Termini (2/9/96), Aisha Tyner (1/9/96),
Georgetta Watkins (1/13/96), Bob Weinstock (2/2/96 and 3/15/96), Vance Wilson (3/15, 4/17, and 6/26/96), Reggie Workman (2/21/96), David Young
(3/27/96), Alvin Jackson (1/25/96), Willie Cook (1/25/96 and 5/19/97), Ellis
Marsalis (3/15/96), Hale Smith (2/2/96), and Atilla Zoller (1/23/96).

People who answered a few specific questions for me included Saeeda
Coltrane, Ravi Coltrane, Jamal Dennis, McCoy Tyner, Elvin Jones, Art Davis,
Archie Shepp, Joe Henderson, Johnny Coles, Phil Schaap, Kurt Mohr, John
Hicks, J. J. Johnson, Kenny Barron, the late Art Taylor, Nat Hentoff, Francis
Davis, Eddie Henderson, Alonzo White, Nellie Monk, Pat Martino, Zita Carno,
Kenny Burrell, Bill Carney, Bob Porter, Valerie Wilmer, Michael Futch, Don
Schlitten, Lenore Von Stein, Mrs. Gelatt (mother of the late Timothy Gelatt),
Alejandro "Sleepy" Stein, Bob Rusch, Ted Panken, Leo Johnson, Bob Blu-
menthal, Willie Smith of High Point, the late Bob Thiele, Rudy Van Gelder,
Don Friedman, David Liebman, David Wild, Bob Rusch, Gary Goldstein, Don
Manning, Herb Pomeroy, Andy McGhee, Ed Rhodes, Dr. C. O. Simpkins, Art
Zimmerman, Bill Miner, Andrew White, Jean-Claude Zylberstein (pen name
Dargenpierre), Michel Delorme, Anna Barrons, Bill Lowe, Kevin Whitehead,
Randi Hultin, Jim Patrick, Barry Marshall, Greg Downing, Franz Hoffman,
Paul Berliner, Tynie Clemons, J. R. Taylor, Chris White, August Blume, Jan
Lohmann, Thierry Bruneau, Mark Gridley, Frank Tiberi, Bob Belden, Steve
Allen, Andrew Homzy, Bob Blumenthal, Bill Smith (of *Coda*), Chris Albertson,
Steve Bloom, Ben Young, Henry Martin, Annette Wright, Jeff S. Coltrane Jr.
(no relation to John), Rev. Jackson and Eugene Dunlap of Hamlet, Phillip
Jacka, Harris Lewine, and Jim Doran. Those who volunteered information
included Francis Davis, Max Hoff, James Kelly of Hamlet, Bill Bauer, John
Szwed, Paul Hahn, Gregg Gelb, Ken Schaphorst, Chris Harlos, Mark DeVoto,
Rich Scheinin, Gerard Wiggins, and Gordon Blewis.

John Morton took the time to drive Fuji and me all over High Point; he helped with follow-up questions too. Dr. Fred McQueen showed us around Hamlet. Peter Keepnews shared information from his work in progress on Thelonious Monk, and Peter Pullman from his Bud Powell research. Bob Belden kept me posted on discoveries from the Miles Davis years.

Record producer Joel Dorn, with whom I worked on two Rhino Records sets that included rare and newly discovered Coltrane material, was a great help in connecting me with key people and unissued materials. Thanks to him I was able to study the extra takes of "Giant Steps" as soon as they were found, and it was he who first introduced me to Mary Alexander and Aisha Tyner. Rare and unissued materials also came from Steve Rowland (producer of radio documentaries), Toby Byron (producer of *The World according to John Coltrane*), Frank Turco, Thierry Bruneau, Michael Frohne, Axel Stumpf, Meg Hill, Louis LoCicero, Jan Lohmann, Phil Schaap, Alan Sukoenig, Reggie Marshall, Jean and Toby Gleason, Mark White, Tim Blangger, Joe Fitzgerald, Henry Martin, Joshua Berrett, and Michel Delorme. Norman Saks deserves a special mention for obtaining the interview tape directly from August Blume and for providing rare music on tape as well.

People who researched at libraries and archives included Dan Morgenstern, Director of the Institute of Jazz Studies at Rutgers, and his colleagues Ed Berger, Vince Pelote, and Don Luck and assistant Esther Smith; Jeanne Baptiste, Library Assistant, Dana Library at Rutgers; the staff at the Schomburg Center and at the National Archives, both in Manhattan; Mark Freundt, who dug around in North Carolina state archives; Susan Rountree, Register of Deeds, Chowan County, N.C.; Linda H. Cowan, Deputy Register of Deeds, Richmond County, N.C.; Katherine Lee Payne, Register of Deeds at Guilford County, N.C., and deputies Judy Johnson and Jackie Harrison; Michael Hill, a researcher with the Division of Archives and History in Raleigh; the Register of Deeds in Lee County, N.C.; Dr. William S. Crowder, Chair of Humanities and Fine Arts Division, Livingstone College; Rev. Willie Aldrich, Director of Heritage Hall, Livingstone College, and her assistant Thomasina Paige; Alan Parker and Dr. Joan Bishop, Guilford County schools; Sherri Simon, Director, John Marks, Curator of Collections, and Jane Willis, of the High Point Museum; Angie Patteson, North Carolina Collection at Chapel Hill; Wolfram Knauer and his staffperson Doris Schröder at the Jazz-Institut Darmstadt; Larry Applebaum, Samuel Brylawski, and James Wolf at the Library of Congress; Kevin Winkler, Assistant Curator of the Billy Rose Theatre Collection, New York Public Library; David Carp; Ernie Carmichael; and Gig Brown. Senior Naval Chief Orin Hatton, Director of Public Affairs for the United States Navy Band—and incidentally a former student of Jimmy Heath as well as Paul Jeffreys—deserves special mention for talking with people and digging up materials in his archives well beyond the call of duty.

People who provided information in their area of expertise included

Dr. David Weiser, Dr. Louis Buzzeo, Dr. John Morgan, George Weissblum (lawyer), Herb Cohen (tax expert), Lily Spencer (Military Personnel Records), Dr. Stuart Kahn, Dr. Milton Zaret, and Joan Berger of Campbell Soup (Camden, N.J.). Those who gave me leads—names, phone numbers, citations—included Bill Kirchner; John Morton, Director of the John Coltrane Cultural Workshop in High Point, N.C.; Kirby Kean; Don Manning; Kevin Fry; Eric Miller; Chuck Niles; Steve Lindeman; Gary Carner; Tim Lindeman; Bob Davis; Thomas Cassidy; Paul Brown; Mel Straus; John Riley; Hiroshi Matsunaga (Fuji's good friend); and Sandor Moss. Assistance in locating photographs came from Aisha Tyner, Michael Lang, Cynthia Sesso, Charlie Lourie, Photo Archives, and photographers Don Schlitten, Ray Avery, Esmond Edwards, Bill Spilka, Bill Smith, and Fuji again—in addition, of course, to those who are credited in the photo section.

I'm sure that my conversations and correspondence with the following found their way into my writing—Carl Woideck, David Demsey (who was also kind enough to submit some ideas in writing that appear within), Andy LaVerne, Bill Kirchner, Bob Belden, Paul Berliner, Bill Bauer, Paul Epstein, Henry Geisinger, Peter Kivy, Paul Cohen, Ingrid Monson, Eric van Tassel, Ken Wiley, Jan Evensmo, David Wild, Barry Kernfeld, Jim Patrick, Ross Bauer, Gerhard Putschögl, and Lee Lowenfish. My students Jason Varano and Frances Moore conducted an initial interview with Steve Kuhn, and Juan Carlos de Jesus worked hard to create an initial rough transcription of the poorly re-corded unpublished taped interview of Coltrane with August Blume. Woideck provided his own expert transcription that helped with several hard-to-hear passages, and he tracked down Blume for me so that I could request Blume's permission to use this material. To this Mr. Blume graciously agreed.

I'm sure some of these people have forgotten that they helped me. Conversely, it's possible that I forgot someone. If so, I apologize.

I take full responsibility for the accuracy of all music examples. I am indebted to Andrew White for permission to quote extensively from his monumental library of transcribed Coltrane solos. I based my versions of "Venus" and "A Love Supreme" closely on his, as well as the excerpt from "Little Melonae" and some of the examples from "Impressions." I used his for comparison while making my own transcriptions of some other pieces. Transcriptions of Coltrane's solos of 1946 were initially prepared by Ingrid Monson and John O'Gallagher. They contributed analytical observations as well. Regardless of the source, I edited every music example against the recording until I found it satisfactory. In many cases, among them "Giant Steps" and "Equinox," the resulting versions are new transcriptions. My friend Paul Cohen, a respected classical saxophonist, undertook the Herculean task of preparing all the examples that were typeset on computer, with assistance from Peter Lutkoski.

My first writing on Coltrane was an early version of chapter 17, "A Love

Supreme," prepared in September 1980 for a New England regional meeting of the American Musicological Society. It was also the beginning of my Ph.D. dissertation in music history at Brandeis University, completed in 1983, and my advisors Joshua Rifkin and Lawrence Gushee (of the University of Illinois) gave many valuable suggestions. I also thank my other two readers, Edward Nowacki and Conrad Pope. A different version of the chapter appeared in the *Journal of the American Musicological Society*, fall 1985, and the present version is thoroughly revised. This book is not in any sense a revision of my dissertation, but passages of musical analysis from it appear in chapters 11, 13, 14, 16, and 19. Some of the material in chapters 5, 10, and 14 appeared in different form in the booklets I wrote more recently to *Discovery! Live at the Five Spot* (Monk and Coltrane), *The Last Giant: The John Coltrane Anthology,* and *The Heavyweight Champion: The Complete Atlantic Recordings.*

This book would never have been completed without the support of Rutgers University, which gave me two semesters of sabbatical (FASP) leave, and the research assistant. Nor could I have produced this study without a year-long Governor's Fellowship sponsored by the New Jersey Department of Higher Education.

The teachers and mentors who started me on my academic career were, first and foremost, T. J. Anderson, Professor Emeritus of Tufts University; and Dean Robyn Gittleman of Tufts; Chuck Mangione and David Russell Williams, both formerly of the Eastman School; the late Martin Williams; and Eileen Southern, Professor Emerita of Harvard University, to name a few.

Thanks go to the people I have worked with at the University of Michigan Press—Colin Day, Joyce Harrison, Kevin Rennells, Richard Isomaki, Jillian Downey, and especially Susan Whitlock. My son Matthew, a budding jazz pianist at age 9, took a special interest in this project and did some photocopying and photographing for me. Finally, my brother Spence Porter has been my essential sounding board throughout the preparation of this book. His suggestions for writing style, for organization, and even for promotion and marketing were a great help.

1

Southern Roots

John William Coltrane, one of the great musical artists of the twentieth century, was born on September 23, 1926, in Hamlet, North Carolina. His mother's family, Blair, was prominent and respected; his father's family was less visible, and after his father's early death they played little part in his life.

Blair and Coltrane are both Scottish names, a reminder that—until voluntary movement from the Caribbean began after World War II—virtually without exception black families were brought here as slaves directly from Africa. Most American blacks are named after their ancestors' "owners," which is why they have English, Irish, and Scottish names. The black Blairs were former slaves of a family that had originally settled in Virginia and came to North Carolina with Daniel Boone (1734–1820) (Thomas, 3). The Boone family left Pennsylvania in 1750 and seems to have stopped over in Virginia for a year or more. They could have teamed up with the white Blairs, who settled early on in Williamsburg, before arriving in Davie County, west of Guilford County, North Carolina, around the beginning of 1752.[1] I do not know how soon after this the Blairs acquired African slaves. By the mid-1800s, the black Blairs are traceable to Chowan County, in the northeast, an area that once had big tobacco plantations worked by slaves. It is a rural area; Edenton is the only town of any size there, and its population even today is only 5,300.

Scots were prominent in colonial North Carolina; the southern tip was home to the earliest and largest settlement of Highlanders in America. During the short span between 1746 and 1776, about twenty thousand Highlanders—traditionalists—came there to escape persecution and violence from the pro-English Lowlanders. Inland North Carolina eventually had a county named Scotland. When the colony became a state in 1776, its population was about three hundred thousand, of whom nearly a third were Scottish, about a third were of English descent, and a full fifth were African slaves.

The African-American Blairs were a large family who valued the new-found opportunity to receive an education after the Civil War. But few of them had children of their own, and today John's first cousin Mary Alexander, childless as well, is the sole survivor among his direct relations. The story of the Blairs begins with William Wilson Blair and Alice V. (for Virginia, says Mary Alexander) Leary. Census reports suggest that Blair was born between February 18 and April 28, 1859, but Mary Alexander believes that his date of birth was January 11 and adds that Alice was born on July 25, 1859. They appear to have been free, but their parents had likely been slaves. Blair's parents were William D. Blair and Easter (this was in general use at the time, but it might be Esther) Blair, both of Edenton and living at the time of his marriage; Leary's parents, also living, were Thomas and Bettie Leary (whose maiden name was given as Willis on Alice's death certificate). Thomas had surely been a slave to one of the Learys of lower Edenton—Thomas H., who owned twenty-seven slaves, or John H., whose plantation housed forty-two.

W. W. Blair and Alice V. Leary were married by a Methodist preacher on December 27, 1882, in Pleasant Grove Church, in Yeopim township. (Yeopim was a section of the county, not a particular town or village; today the four parts of the county are simply numbered.) They raised a family in Edenton. Alice Blair reported on the 1920 census that she had given birth to eight children, of whom seven were still living. (In those days infant mortality was very high. It is very typical on this census to read such numbers.) The first one, says Mary, was Thomas, who died in infancy. "They always talked about him like he was living. 'When Thomas was born'—that's the way they would talk!" Effie Blair, the oldest who survived, had two children, Viola (born in 1902) and Mildred (born shortly after 1902). Minnie and Bettie were next, they were close in age, and it's unclear who was older. Minnie had a daughter, Sarah Elizabeth, who appears to have died somewhere around her late teens. (Mary, born in 1927, recalls that "I used to hear them talk about her and all, but I never saw her.") Bettie (apparently named after her grandmother),[2] was born November 8, probably in 1887; she was to be the mother of Mary Alexander. A daughter named Mary was born 1891 or 1892. Then, in 1895 or 1896, came William Wells Blair Jr., known as "Bud." Alice Gertrude Blair, born March 22, 1898, was to be the saxophonist's mother. The youngest, John Blair, was born April 4, 1902, according to Mary and to John's relation Georgetta Watkins.

Before September 1909, the family moved to Tampa, Florida. Mary Alexander suspects that the elder Blair may have been run out of Edenton for his activism. He was an outspoken preacher who she believes was also involved in local politics there. Simpkins states that he had been a state senator (2), but there is no record of such service. He could have been active in some other capacity—perhaps local rather than state politics—before he was married, but after 1890 a wave of backlash kept blacks out of office.[3] He must have been a

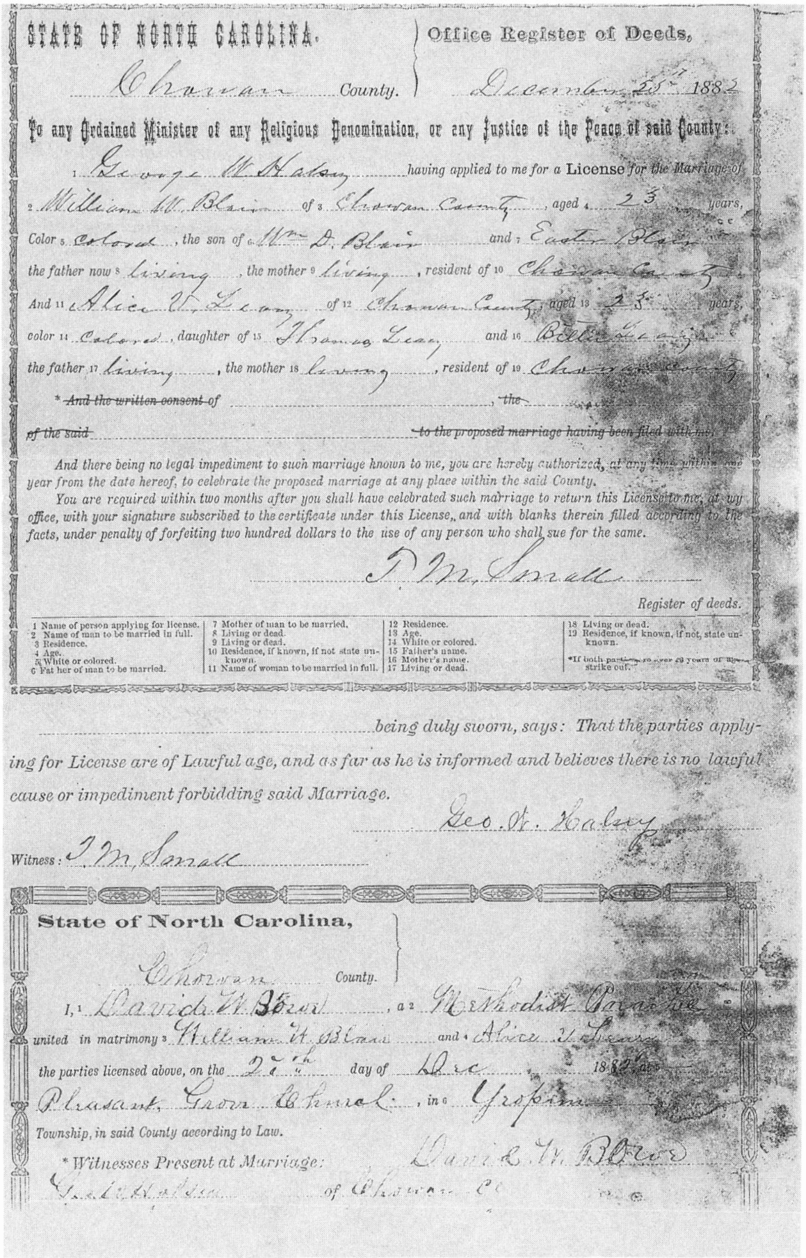

STATE OF NORTH CAROLINA. | Office Register of Deeds,

Chowan County. | December 25th 1882

To any Ordained Minister of any Religious Denomination, or any Justice of the Peace of said County:

1 George W. Halsey having applied to me for a License for the Marriage of 2 William W. Blair of 3 Chowan County, aged 4 23 years, Color 5 colored, the son of 6 Wm D. Blair and 7 Easter Blair the father now 8 living, the mother 9 living, resident of 10 Chowan County And 11 Alice V. Leary of 12 Chowan County, aged 13 23 years, color 14 colored, daughter of 15 Thomas Leary and 16 Bettie Leary the father 17 living, the mother 18 living, resident of 19 Chowan County

* ~~And the written consent of~~ ......, ~~the~~ ~~of the said~~ ...... ~~to the proposed marriage having been filed with me.~~

And there being no legal impediment to such marriage known to me, you are hereby authorized, at any time within one year from the date hereof, to celebrate the proposed marriage at any place within the said County.

You are required within two months after you shall have celebrated such marriage to return this License to me, at my office, with your signature subscribed to the certificate under this License, and with blanks therein filled according to the facts, under penalty of forfeiting two hundred dollars to the use of any person who shall sue for the same.

T. M. Small

Register of deeds.

1 Name of person applying for license. 2 Name of man to be married in full. 3 Residence. 4 Age. 5 White or colored. 6 Father of man to be married. 7 Mother of man to be married. 8 Living or dead. 9 Living or dead. 10 Residence, if known, if not state unknown. 11 Name of woman to be married in full. 12 Residence. 13 Age. 14 White or colored. 15 Father's name. 16 Mother's name. 17 Living or dead. 18 Living or dead. 19 Residence, if known, if not, state unknown. *If both parties ... over 18 years of age strike out.

...... being duly sworn, says: That the parties applying for License are of Lawful age, and as far as he is informed and believes there is no lawful cause or impediment forbidding said Marriage.

Geo. W. Halsey

Witness: T. M. Small

State of North Carolina,

Chowan County.

I, 1 David W. Brown, a 2 Methodist Preacher united in matrimony 3 William W. Blair and 4 Alice V. Leary the parties licensed above, on the 27th day of Dec 1882, at Pleasant Grove Church, in 6 Yeopim Township, in said County according to Law.

David W. Brown

* Witnesses Present at Marriage:

G. W. Halsey of Chowan Co

Fig. 1. Marriage license and certificate of Coltrane's maternal grandparents, William W. Blair and Alice V. Leary.

The Blair Family Tree

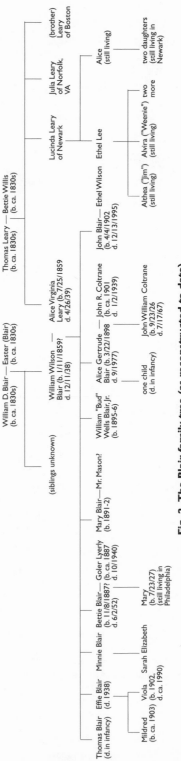

Fig. 2. The Blair family tree (as reconstructed to date)

Republican, as Mary recalls, because in those days the party wanted black support. The old-school Democrats were allied with the Ku Klux Klan.

In any case, her uncle John Blair told Mary that when he was a small child "the Klan came riding through the yard" and that "he heard the horses and all that stuff." That they moved in haste is suggested by Mary's memory of the Blairs owning land in Edenton that they never claimed; it was eventually sold.

The federal census taken on April 28, 1910, reports that the Blairs, all born in North Carolina, were living in Tampa in a rented house at 915 Third Avenue, an area inhabited mostly by African-Americans. The Blairs were all literate. William W. Blair reported that he was employed full time as a minister in a church. He was African Methodist Episcopal (AME) Zion. His wife Alice was a full-time homemaker. Effie was grown and moved out, eventually settling near Norfolk, Virginia; Minnie was also out of the house. Of the children still with their parents, Mary wasn't working, while Bettie was working at home as a dressmaker. William Jr., now fourteen, had started working part time that year as a servant at a club house, when he was not in school. The youngest children, Alice and John Blair, were also in school. Alice reported in 1921 that her grade school had been the Harlem Academy in Tampa, Florida. It may be that she, John, and William Jr. all went there.[4] The family spent time in Key West, too, probably for vacations. They often talked about how nice it was there, Mary recalls: "John and I always wanted to go down there because they talked about it so much."

I don't know if they stayed in Florida throughout the teens, but by 1920 the family was definitely back in North Carolina. From 1920 through 1923, Reverend Blair was the leader of the St. Stephen AME Zion Church on Price Street in High Point, a city of 35,000, one fifth black. The church history records that it "experienced significant improvements" under Blair: "A number of boards and clubs that are still operating in the present financial system were organized by Rev. Blair. These boards reported monthly and were known as the Blair-Henderson League."[5] Still an activist, Blair was involved in a drive to create a public school for black children that resulted in the building of a new brick structure adjacent to the church, known as the Leonard St. Elementary School, in October 1921. Simpkins also reports that this movement resulted in converting the Quaker school that had been used for black instruction into the William Penn High School (2). Actually, the Quakers who ran the High Point Normal and Industrial Institute for black students initiated the proposal to sell the property to the city in 1923, under the condition that it would continue to serve as a high school for black youth. As the High Point Board of School Commissioners debated the plan, they listened to notable members of the black community who spoke in favor of the idea, and it was finally accepted. At first known as the Normal High School, it was later named after the Quaker leader William Penn.[6] Blair could have been one of those who advocated for it.

Mary believes that he even received an honorary degree or some comparable recognition from one of the schools in the area, perhaps even from the black high school.

In the census taken February 1920, the Blair family was found residing at a rented house at 105 Price Street, a few doors from the church. The church at that time was a small frame structure affectionately known as "the hut," and its parsonage was not suitable as a home for the family.[7] Bud had left, probably initially to join the military during World War I, and Mary had also moved out. John was now 17, not working, and had attended at least some school since September 1919. Bettie and Alice, still home, didn't indicate that they were working.

In September 1921 Alice began studies at Livingstone College, a black college affiliated with the AME church, in Salisbury. Salisbury was a medium-size city (in the 1990 census its population was 23,087) with a main street and a pleasant campus. Livingstone was composed of a high school "prep" College Entrance program, with separate dorms for young women and men, and a college level that was primarily for men. In many parts of the state the black public-school systems went only through the elementary grades. To continue one's education, one had to attend one of the few private high schools for blacks.[8] Sometimes it took time to raise the tuition, which is why students were often in their late teens. It was common for girls of nineteen or twenty to enroll in the college entrance program. The tuition was twenty-five dollars a month; there were no scholarships but one could obtain a job in the dining room and elsewhere on campus. Most of the teachers were men, often well qualified; some were reverends (probably AME Zion), and one was from Africa.[9]

The College Entrance program's Class of 1925 included one Alice G. Blair, the person of great import to our story.[10] Alice was reportedly a fine singer who had interests in opera and played the piano accompaniment for the choir at Reverend Blair's services when she was at home (Simpkins, 2). At Livingstone there were music teachers and a chorus, so it's fair to assume Alice pursued her musical interests there.

After her graduation at the end of May 1925, Alice returned not to High Point but to Hamlet, a small town on the southern border of North Carolina. Perhaps as early as 1920, the Blairs had become acquainted with the family of another AME Zion minister, William H. Coltrane, who was at that time in Hamlet. Alice became close with the reverend's son, John Robert Coltrane, and she began spending time with his family; an undated page of her Livingstone record gives Hamlet as her home town. Within a few years, by early 1925 at the latest, Alice and John R. were married, not in Hamlet, but at an unknown location.[11]

Coltrane was the name of a leading white family of Guilford County and neighboring Randolph County, adjoining it to the south. (These particular

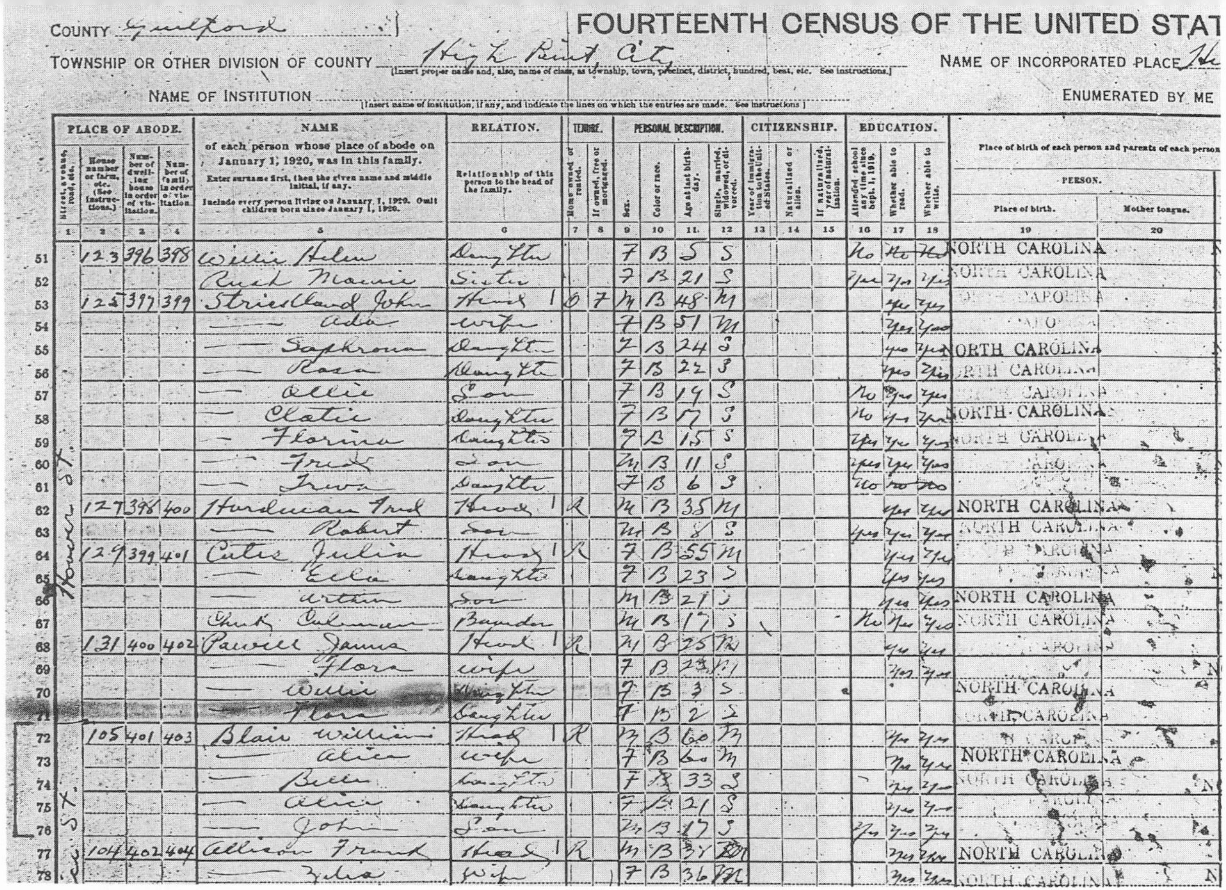

Fig. 3. Portion of a 1920 census page, showing the Blair family as resident in High Point, in Guilford County

county names have existed since about 1780 although Guilford has been divided into two counties since then.) Some Coltranes owned a few slaves, and John Coltrane's ancestors probably worked for and were named for this family.

Coltrane or "Coltran" is an old Scottish name, now uncommon, from the lowlands District of Galloway on Scotland's southwestern coast near the old royal burgh (borough) Wigtown. The earliest known Coltranes in America appear in the public records of Edgecomb County, in the northeast of North Carolina, in 1737. So they arrived shortly before the Boones and the Blairs.[12]

They became concentrated in Guilford and Randolph counties in the center of North Carolina, but the Coltrane clan has a presence throughout the state: to this day there are more Coltranes in North Carolina than in all the other states combined.[13] The 1937 city directory of High Point listed thirty-three Coltrane families, of whom four were black (denoted in the directory by (c) for "colored"). The name remains rare among black people. It's been noted that Guilford County was "never a large slaveholding or landholding area,"[14] but the area was not totally closed to slavery, despite a sizable Quaker minority who were vocal in their opposition to the practice.[15] Kelly Coltrane (1818–58) was a known slave owner. A family story of the post–Civil War period tells of black men of the community who helped with the threshing, including one Howard Coltrane and "Uncle Sandy" Coltrane, "who was eighty years old, but looked about sixty. Everyone, black and white, called him 'Uncle Sandy.'"[16] It seems reasonable to assume that African people must have received the name Coltrane as former slaves of the Coltrane family.

This does not mean that John Coltrane was a descendant of Howard or Uncle Sandy. All of the Coltranes' slaves would have received that last name, even though they were often unrelated African individuals. The practice of giving slaves their masters' names created some incongruous juxtapositions. For example, the famous newscaster Edward R. Murrow was a descendant of the white Coltranes.[17] This is very interesting, but it does not mean that John Coltrane and Edward R. Murrow are related!

The particular Coltrane family we are interested in here is difficult to locate. Apparently Reverend Coltrane traveled quite a bit without his wife and children, for they aren't recorded in any North Carolina census; they may have lived in one of the neighboring states. He was born in January 1858, and married Hellen, who was about five years younger, around 1880. They were both literate, and both they and their parents were North Carolina natives. The census taken in June 1900 found "Wm. H. Coaltrain" (one of many common misspellings) boarding by himself with the family of Monday Starnes (born in 1830), in a black farming community of Monroe, near the southern border to the west of Hamlet. Coltrane described himself as a "minister (gospel)." He would probably preach for a while in this area and then move on to another town.

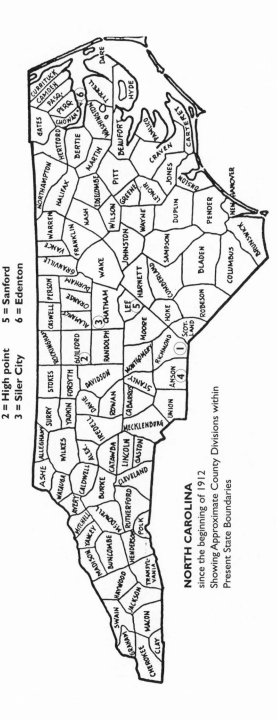

1 = Hamlet   4 = Wadesboro
2 = High point   5 = Sanford
3 = Siler City   6 = Edenton

NORTH CAROLINA
since the beginning of 1912
Showing Approximate County Divisions within
Present State Boundaries

Fig. 4. North Carolina counties today. Indicated on the map are the locations of (1) Hamlet, (2) High Point, (3) Siler City, (4) Wadesboro, (5) Sanford, (6) Edenton.

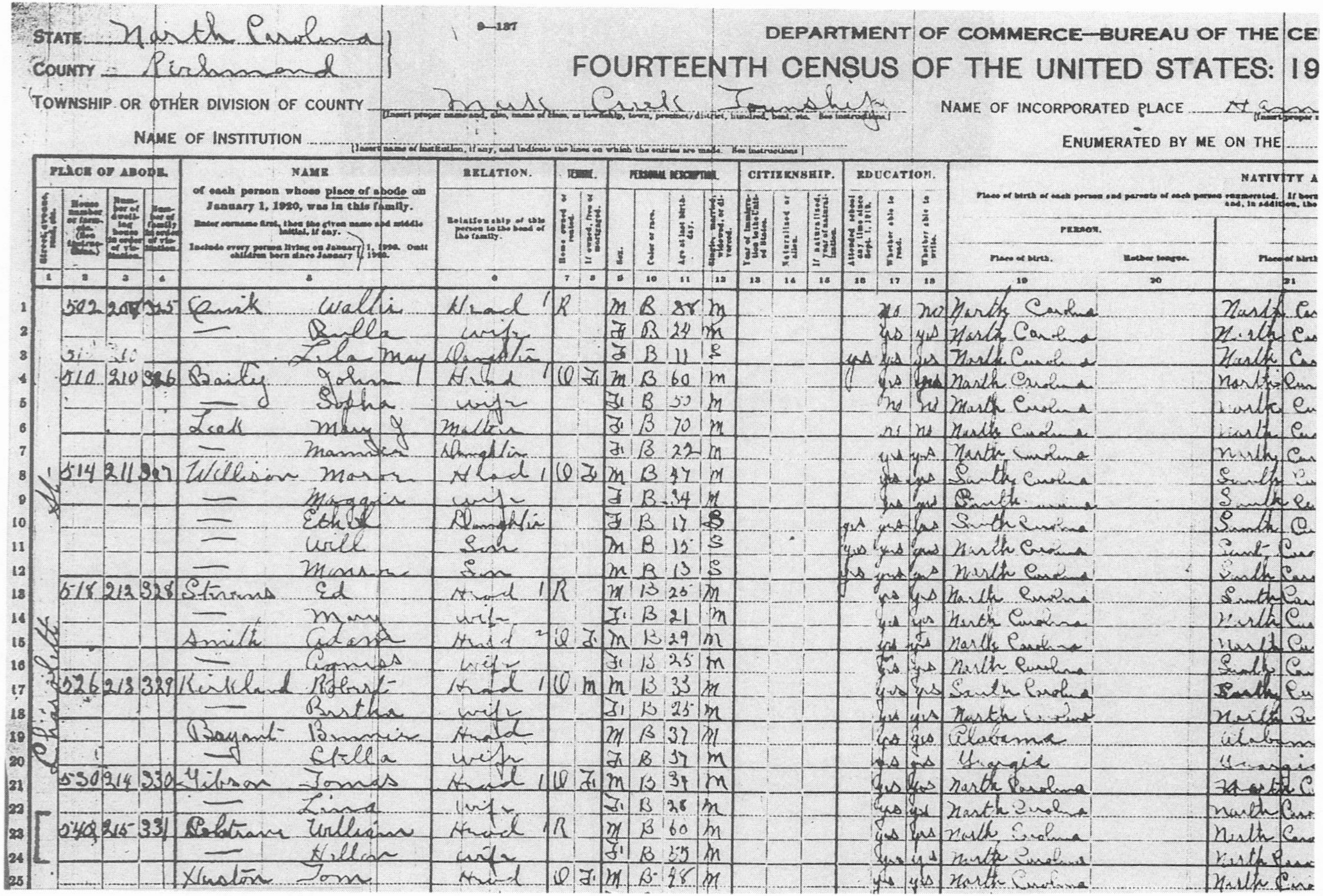

STATE North Carolina
COUNTY Richmond
TOWNSHIP OR OTHER DIVISION OF COUNTY Marks Creek Township [Insert proper name and, also, name of class, as township, town, precinct, district, hundred, beat, etc. See instructions.]
NAME OF INSTITUTION [Insert name of institution, if any, and indicate the lines on which the entries are made. See instructions.]

9—187

DEPARTMENT OF COMMERCE—BUREAU OF THE CE

FOURTEENTH CENSUS OF THE UNITED STATES: 19

NAME OF INCORPORATED PLACE

ENUMERATED BY ME ON THE

	Place of abode: Street, avenue, road, etc. (1)	House number or farm (2)	Number of dwelling in order of visitation (3)	Number of family in order of visitation (4)	Name of each person whose place of abode on January 1, 1920, was in this family (5)	Relation (6)	Home owned or rented (7)	If owned, free or mortgaged (8)	Sex (9)	Color or race (10)	Age at last birthday (11)	Single, married, widowed, or divorced (12)	Year of immigration (13)	Naturalized or alien (14)	If naturalized, year of naturalization (15)	Attended school (16)	Able to read (17)	Able to write (18)	Place of birth (19)	Mother tongue (20)	Place of birth (21)
1		502	208	325	Crisk Wallie	Head	R		M	B	38	M					no	no	North Carolina		North Ca
2					Bella	wife			F	B	24	M					yes	yes	North Carolina		North Ca
3					Lila May	Daughter			F	B	11	S				yes	yes	yes	North Carolina		North Ca
4		510	210	326	Bailey John	Head	O	F	M	B	60	M					yes	yes	North Carolina		North Ca
5					— Sopha	wife			F	B	50	M					no	no	North Carolina		North Ca
6					Leak Mary J	Mother			F	B	70	M					no	no	North Carolina		North Ca
7					— Mamie	Daughter			F	B	22	M					yes	yes	North Carolina		North Ca
8		514	211	327	Willison Moror	Head	O	F	M	B	47	M					yes	yes	South Carolina		South Ca
9					— Maggie	wife			F	B	34	M					yes	yes	South Carolina		South Ca
10					— Ethel	Daughter			F	B	17	S				yes	yes	yes	South Carolina		South Ca
11					— Will	Son			M	B	15	S				yes	yes	yes	North Carolina		South Ca
12					— Monroe	Son			M	B	13	S				yes	yes	yes	North Carolina		South Ca
13		518	212	328	Strouns Ed	Head	R		M	B	26	M					yes	yes	North Carolina		South Ca
14					— Mary	wife			F	B	21	M					yes	yes	North Carolina		North Ca
15					Smith Adam	Head	O	F	M	B	29	M					yes	yes	North Carolina		North Ca
16					— Agness	wife			F	B	25	M					yes	yes	North Carolina		South Ca
17		526	213	329	Kirkland Robert	Head	O	M	M	B	33	M					yes	yes	South Carolina		South Ca
18					— Bertha	wife			F	B	25	M					yes	yes	North Carolina		North Ca
19					Bryant Bennie	Head			M	B	37	M					yes	yes	Alabama		Alabama
20					— Stella	wife			F	B	37	M					yes	yes	Georgia		Georgia
21		530	214	330	Gibson Tomas	Head	O	F	M	B	37	M					yes	yes	North Carolina		North Ca
22					— Lina	wife			F	B	26	M					yes	yes	North Carolina		North Ca
23		540	215	331	Coltrane William	Head	R		M	B	60	M					yes	yes	North Carolina		North Ca
24					— Hillar	wife			F	B	55	M					yes	yes	North Carolina		North Ca
25					Houston Tom	Head	O	F	M	B	48	M					yes	yes	North Carolina		North Ca

Fig. 5. A portion of the 1920 census page regarding Coltrane's paternal grandfather

In January 1920, Reverend Coltrane and his wife were renting rooms at 540 Charlotte Street in Hamlet. The house was owned by a forty-eight year old minister named Tom Huston and his wife Mary. Huston and Coltrane both described themselves as Methodist, meaning AME Zion.

J. R. Coltrane was born, according to Mary and to his tombstone, in 1901. I don't know if he had any siblings. In any case, sometime after the January 1920 census he settled in Hamlet, and once Alice finished school in 1925, the married couple lived there in a second-floor apartment of a boarding house at 200 Hamlet Avenue, on the corner of Bridges Street.[18] J. R. was a tailor and pressed clothes, and Mary believes he already was working at that trade when he met Alice. In 1926, Alice gave her occupation as "domestic," which meant she was a full-time homemaker. (Sometimes *domestic* indicated maid's work, but I doubt the reverend's daughter was doing that.) Later, she worked alongside her husband as a seamstress. Alice had given birth once, but that baby had died in infancy. At the beginning of 1926 she became pregnant again: On September 23 of that year, John William Coltrane was born at home, in the afternoon.[19] His middle name was William, after his two grandfathers.

Within a few months of John's birth, around the end of 1926, his parents decided to move to High Point to be with the rest of the Blair family: Alice's mother (the senior Alice) and her sister Bettie and brother John. Perhaps Reverend Coltrane had moved on from Hamlet, or even died, so there was no reason to stay there. So, although Hamlet is renowned as the birthplace of Coltrane, High Point is actually where he grew up, where he was educated, and where he began to play music. The family was still at 105 Price Street.

Meanwhile, Mary believes that Reverend Blair, now past age 65, was appointed a presiding elder of the AME Zion Church, and that this required him to visit churches around the state. After a while he settled in Kannapolis. Sometime in the 1930s he moved to Wadesboro, down near Hamlet. In order for the children to have stability in a good environment, the rest of the family stayed in High Point. Even though Reverend Blair only visited two or three times a month, his presence was palpable, as Coltrane recalled in an interview conducted by August Blume.

> *Blume:* What faith were you brought up in, John?
> *Coltrane:* Methodist.
> *Blume:* Methodist? Did you have a very strict religious life or . . . ?
> *Coltrane:* Well, it wasn't too strict, but it was there. Both my grandfathers were ministers. My mother, she was very religious. Like, in my early years I was going to church every Sunday and stuff like that, being under the influence of my grandfather—he was the dominating cat in the family. He was most well versed, active politically. He was more active than my father, [who] was a tailor; but he [Coltrane's father]

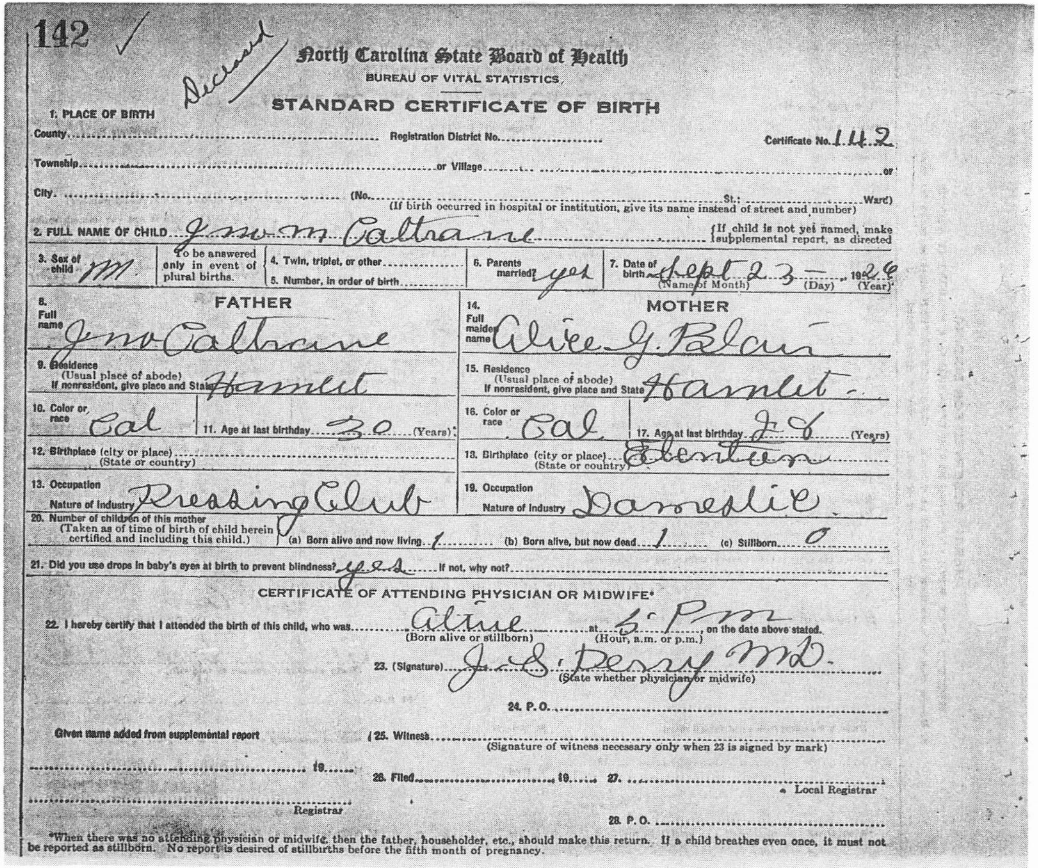

142 ✓ Deceased

North Carolina State Board of Health
BUREAU OF VITAL STATISTICS
STANDARD CERTIFICATE OF BIRTH

1. PLACE OF BIRTH
County .... Registration District No. .... Certificate No. 142
Township .... or Village .... or
City .... (No. .... St.; .... Ward)
(If birth occurred in hospital or institution, give its name instead of street and number)

2. FULL NAME OF CHILD Jno. W. Coltrane {If child is not yet named, make supplemental report, as directed

3. Sex of child M | To be answered only in event of plural births. | 4. Twin, triplet, or other .... 5. Number, in order of birth .... | 6. Parents married? yes | 7. Date of birth Sept 23 — 1926 (Name of Month) (Day) (Year)

FATHER
8. Full name Jno Coltrane
9. Residence (Usual place of abode) If nonresident, give place and State Hamlet
10. Color or race Col | 11. Age at last birthday 30 (Years)
12. Birthplace (city or place) (State or country) ....
13. Occupation Nature of industry Pressing Club

MOTHER
14. Full maiden name Alice G. Blair
15. Residence (Usual place of abode) If nonresident, give place and State Hamlet.
16. Color or race Col | 17. Age at last birthday 28 (Years)
18. Birthplace (city or place) (State or country) Edenton
19. Occupation Nature of industry Domestic

20. Number of children of this mother (Taken as of time of birth of child herein certified and including this child.) (a) Born alive and now living 1 (b) Born alive, but now dead 1 (c) Stillborn 0

21. Did you use drops in baby's eyes at birth to prevent blindness? yes If not, why not? ....

CERTIFICATE OF ATTENDING PHYSICIAN OR MIDWIFE*

22. I hereby certify that I attended the birth of this child, who was alive (Born alive or stillborn) at 5 P.m (Hour, a.m. or p.m.) on the date above stated.

23. (Signature) J. S. Derry MD. (State whether physician or midwife)

24. P.O. ....

Given name added from supplemental report .... 19 .... Registrar

25. Witness .... (Signature of witness necessary only when 23 is signed by mark)

26. Filed .... 19 .... 27. .... Local Registrar

28. P.O. ....

*When there was no attending physician or midwife, then the father, householder, etc., should make this return. If a child breathes even once, it must not be reported as stillborn. No report is desired of stillbirths before the fifth month of pregnancy.

Fig. 6. John Coltrane's birth certificate

never seemed to say too much. He just went about his business, and that was it. But my grandfather, he was pretty militant, you know. Politically inclined and everything. Religion was his field, you know. So that's where—I grew up in that.[20]

Mary recalls that the reverend's library included all sorts of religious titles, as well as books of black American history and black poets.

Alice's older sister Bettie had married after 1920, to a man named Goler Lyerly. The Lyerly family came from Granite Quarry, North Carolina, where Goler was born around 1887 (or the last half of 1886). Goler worked as a cook and butler for white families. Goler was seriously asthmatic, and he and Bettie moved several different places, for health reasons—even to Detroit to live with his brother, Mary states: "He couldn't take the climate there and he came back and then they went to Jacksonville, Florida, where I was conceived, and my mother came back to High Point so I was born around her mother." Goler and Bettie rented a house at 840 Hoover Street in High Point, and Mary Alice Elizabeth Lyerly was born there on July 23, 1927, at 2:35 P.M., with the help of a midwife.[21] "Then after that [at three months of age approximately] one of my aunts came and took me down to Jacksonville, and I stayed down there with them until I was about three years old." Since the Lyerlys were away so much during this period (the late 1920s), they had no reason to continue renting on Hoover Street. When young Mary returned, she found herself living with John's mother and father and "started calling them Mama and Daddy. That's how close those sisters were." Around 1931, Mary's mother Bettie "came back to get me," and she went back to Florida with her parents and attended a nursery school or kindergarten.

The family of Coltrane's father was never much of a presence. Mary believes that by the early 1930s they resided in Sanford, about fifty-five miles southeast of High Point, and that the Coltranes had ancestry in Siler City, in the same general vicinity. She recalls that John had a first cousin, James Martin Black, and the Coltranes would sometimes bring this boy with them when they visited High Point. The only person by this name I could locate is a James Martin Spruill Black born in Sanford on March 20, 1927. The mother was a Helen Black, age seventeen and born in Monroe, but living in Sanford. She supported herself by doing "housework," states the birth certificate. The father is not listed—the word "illegitimate" is written in—so it appears that the mother gave the child her own family name. So the father could be a brother of John R. Coltrane. James and John "looked just alike," recalls Mary. John when young had reddish hair, and his father had a ruddy complexion. Mary remembers meeting Hellen Coltrane only once, has no memory of the Reverend Coltrane and does not know whether he'd passed away.[22]

In High Point, Coltrane's father worked at several locations. He is said to have started off in Deacon Johnson's tailor shop (Simpkins 5). Rufus Leach Jr., a schoolmate of the son, thinks J. R. worked along with Leach's father at the High Point Steam Laundry at 228–232 North Wrenn Street. By 1937, the High Point city directory lists John R. Coltrane at the Piedmont Tailoring Company at 700 East Washington Drive, the main business street of black High Point.[23] Shortly after, J. R. had his own "pressing club" (as it was then called, since clothes were pressed there), where he also did dry cleaning. Walter Hoover told me that the pressing club shared a building with his Hoover Funeral Home, on 600 East High Street at the corner of Beaman. Hoover and the saxophonist's childhood classmate Rosetta Haywood both describe the pressing club as a small place—only one room big enough for a sewing machine, a few clothes racks, and a steam press. (He must have sent out the dry cleaning.)[24]

Around 1932 or 1933, with Mary and her parents back in town, the little house on Price Street began to feel awfully cramped. Reverend Blair, although living away, started building a larger house for the family, at 118 Underhill.[25] "So that meant that John and his mother and father and my mother and father and myself and Grandma moved into the new house. We slept right in the room with our parents. Everybody was close." The city directory for 1937 lists them at that address, and they had probably been there for a few years.

Underhill was at that time in the better black part of town, says Betty Jackson: "Professional people like teachers and doctors lived in that area— that's the type of people John grew up with." Mary agrees: "One of my teachers lived across the street, so did the dentist. Our next-door neighbor was a doctor; another teacher and the family of another minister also lived on the street."[26]

Mary recalls their lifestyle: "[Grandmother] Alice had rheumatism, so she was not very active, but stayed in the house all the time, although she did cook a lot of good food for us. [Grandpa] would come home two or three times a month, or something like that. He'd come and get us [in the summer], drive over to High Point—John and I would go down there [to Wadesboro] and spend two or three weeks with him during the summer. He had a housekeeper who took care of the parsonage [and helped with the children when they visited]."

The Blair family produced very few children. Coltrane had only two other cousins, Mildred and Viola, and they were twenty-five years his senior and didn't live nearby. Grandmother Blair had some grandnieces and grand-nephews who were the same generation as John and Mary, as shown in figure 2. But these were distant relations, and living elsewhere. So Mary was John's constant companion. She says they were so close that some people thought they were siblings. "Sometimes I was called Mary Coltrane, and we didn't make it any different [didn't correct them]. We went to the movies every Saturday." They also loved roller skating. John said in 1961, "I was raised with one of my cousins who's like a sister to me." Elsewhere he described her as "a very earthy, folksy, swinging person."[27]

John probably entered first grade at the Leonard Street School in September 1932, just before his sixth birthday; he graduated from the William Penn High School in May 1943, several months before his seventeenth birthday.[28] He must have been one of the youngest in his class throughout school. Mary started first grade a year behind him. She describes John as "basically a good child, but he was mischievous and he always had this dry sense of humor. Basically he was very quiet."[29]

Betty Jackson, born the same year as John, knew him even before first grade: "Our families were very close. I lived across the railroad on Hoover Street. Every weekend or so we would gather together and we went to the movies—like Shirley Temple—and ate together and did different things. We were all about the same age. My younger sister and Mary were about the same age. We'd often meet between houses. Monday was wash day but we girls went window shopping downtown and just did things together instead of washing."

Rosetta Haywood (born Cousar in 1926) started first grade with John. The school was a big building with a porch or addition for the sixth and seventh grade. There were two or three classes in each grade. There was a "high" first— for better students and for those who had to repeat the grade. "John was always kind of shy, and I guess he did his best work on paper, not performing before the class. He was real smart and in fifth grade we had a test at the end of the year and he and two more people, we all made the same high average for the year. They always had a test at the end of the year and they would announce [the results]."

Betty Jackson recalls: "He was a very neat child. All of his work was neat, all of his papers were exact. I would say he was meticulous with his work. He played rough with boys but—in those days the boys wore knickers, their socks would be one up and one down, but he was always neat." In the fifth grade, each student had to write a report in a notebook, making up a Negro History Book. He wrote about Marian Anderson, the concert singer, and Mary has that in his handwriting. He also copied out a poem by Langston Hughes.

Haywood continues: "We had a graduation program from grammar school. We girls wore our little white dresses with chartreuse ribbons. The boys wore suits or whatever." At that seventh-grade elementary school graduation on June 1, 1939, Betty Jackson remembers being valedictorian, and John was salutatorian. His short speech was entitled "Indian Life"; Jackson doesn't recall it, nor her own. Mary Lyerly, also a fine student, was valedictorian the following year when she finished seventh grade.

But during this seventh-grade school year of 1938 and 1939, Coltrane's family suffered a series of deaths that were to have disastrous consequences.

First Aunt Effie, oldest of the Blair siblings, died in 1938 in her little place outside of Norfolk, Virginia. Mary recounts: "That's where she passed away, and my grandfather and all of them went up to her funeral. They didn't take us. They wouldn't let us go to the funerals. And just a few months later, [Grandpa] was gone. And we *had* to go to his funeral. Plus, they brought the body home to the house and all that, and I had never seen anything like that before. Only one time before that had I been to a funeral, and that upset me." The reverend in fact died on December 11, 1938, at age seventy-nine. According to his death certificate, he had become ill with lobar pneumonia on December 5 and died at 2:50 A.M. on December 11 in Wadesboro, attended by a Dr. C. S. Massey.

Even more devastating to the young John, his father died at 9:00 P.M. on January 2, 1939. Doctor M. B. Davis, who filled out the death certificate, wrote that in 1937 John R. began to suffer from what turned out to be "carcinoma gastric," or stomach cancer. Davis first saw him on November 23, 1938, but it was probably already too late. The tumor can spread through the gastrointestinal tract. It is quite deadly once it has gone beyond the early stages, and even today it is usually not diagnosed very early.

Research in the 1980s by Barry Marshall and others showed that a leading factor in stomach cancer is a bacteria called Helicobacter Pylori, which is closely associated with ulcers as well. The bacteria thrives in a poor diet—high salt, low fiber, and low protein—and in food that is not completely fresh. Stomach cancer was the most common kind in the United States at that time; today it is seventh or eighth, mostly due to improved refrigeration, but it still flourishes in countries that are less technologically developed.

The family was very private about the death of the senior Coltrane. He went into the hospital "for an undisclosed illness" and died a few days later, wrote Thomas (8). Mary remembers that he was very sick, "but that's the one time I wasn't really that nosy" and the adults "never told us about any of them." None of the High Point residents I interviewed knew anything about John R. Coltrane's death. He was buried on January 5, near Reverend Blair in the Blair family plot at the Grew Hill Cemetery.[30]

Next, Reverend Blair's widow, Alice, died on April 26, 1939, of breast cancer. A Dr. Gaylord had attended her from December 8 (just before her husband died) until her death. Mary recalls that she hadn't been well: "They used to send me in a taxicab to the hospital for Grandma to have radiation treatment. I took care of my grandmother. I remember they used to say Grandma had a lump in her breast. But I never heard 'cancer' until many years after that." She was buried on April 30.[31]

"All of them passed at the same time," says Mary. It was devastating "because we had them all that time and then all of a sudden they were all gone, with only months in between. . . . John couldn't even remember what his father looked like. He would say to me, 'Mary, what did Daddy look like?' I would talk to him and I would tell him what he looked like." No photos of John's father are known to exist.

It was upsetting for him to think about his father. The support and love of his mother counted for a great deal: "John looked just like his mother. They were close," says Mary. But the loss of his father at the beginning of his teen years was critical. It was just at this time that he began to take up music, playing first the alto horn, then the clarinet, and from the beginning he is said to have practiced continuously, obsessively, as if practicing would bring his father back, or maybe help him to forget his father—as if, by succeeding in music, he could restore stability and control to his life. Perhaps, in a sense, music became his father substitute. And through music, he could both express and relieve the pain he felt about his father's death, a pain that he never seems to have allowed himself to fully explore.

"For a while," observed his high school friend David Young, "I don't think he had anything but that horn."

2

Life without Father

The family's troubles were not over. The 1940 High Point city directory lists Goler Lyerly as the head of the family at 118 Underhill; the entries for William Blair and John R. Coltrane have been removed. But a year later, in October 1940, there was one more death to cope with. Goler, Mary explains, "had chronic asthma, and it had enlarged his heart, so he had a heart attack."[1] His death certificate is incompletely filled out—the date of death is missing, for example—but it does report that he was buried on October 29, 1940. Goler's funeral, like those of the Reverend and Mrs. Blair and J. R. Coltrane, was handled by the Hoover Funeral Home, and he joined them in the Blair family plot.[2]

Meanwhile, Coltrane had begun high school in September 1939. His performance soon changed markedly—rather than being a top student, as he was in elementary school, he became an indifferent student, earning many Cs. He began playing music around this time, and it may be true, as Thomas surmises, that "perhaps music was too much on his mind" (18). But more to the point, his obsession with music was a way of dealing with the tragedies in his life.

Rosetta Haywood has positive memories of their high school experience: "We had some really good teachers and we had respect for them. Mr. Samuel Burford was a really good principal and he was real stern—he could just give you a look that would make you melt. Two or three teachers are still alive. T. B. Smith, who went into the [military] service, still comes to the reunions, and lives in Maryland. Smith was a great biology teacher—he taught all the sciences, chemistry and everything."

But we must not forget that Coltrane grew up under the constant presence of segregation. At that time life for an African-American in the southern United States was not much different from life under the apartheid system formerly practiced in South Africa. In High Point there was no fear of violence, but there were constant reminders of second-class status. Rufus Leach Jr., born in 1924, recalls: "If the white schools got new books one year, the blacks might have got them a few years later. They got used books from the white schools. But nobody spoke up at that time—even the principal had to go along with it." Leach remembers that they taught bricklaying, carpentry, and other manual skills in both black and white schools. "We had about three little machines down there. One day I went down to the white high school. It looked like a factory, with all the machinery lined up and down on both sides. If one didn't work right, they'd probably give it to us!"

John played football in his senior year, but because of the low budget at black schools, the football team was also poorly equipped. The school paper, the *Student's Pen*, of May 22, 1942 reports on a five-hundred-dollar drive for football equipment and band instruments. The football equipment used in the previous season "was ragged from several years of use. In fact some was in such deplorable condition that it was soon discarded. As a consequence our gridiron warriors were attired in (non-matching) uniforms of different color, and style." John resented these signs of their second-class status, notes Mary: "[A]ll the uniforms were handed down from the white schools. They had ragged uniforms that were handed down to them. In fact our books were too. And those things John didn't like at all. Every time he opened a book and it said [that it was] from the white school, that just got to him." In later years, "He didn't like to go down [South] and play because he didn't like the segregation. He didn't like playing for a segregated audience. Other people would say they went to New Orleans and had a ball. John just sat in his hotel room, went to the gig, and then went right back to his room."[3]

But High Point's black community was warm and supportive, and that got its residents through hard times. David "June" (for junior) Young, a high school friend of John and Mary, reflects, "That's one thing I liked about High Point. We were very close there, kind of like family. And everybody I meet from High Point up North, it's like I'm related to them. Although I don't even know them—the feeling's there. I came up with a bunch of fellows who were very poor, but they were all striving to make something and to better their lives, and quite a few have done quite well."

Meanwhile, Coltrane's decimated family—only he, Mary, and their mothers remained—worked desperately to better their own lives. They went from middle class to poor. Mary recalls that "after our fathers passed, things changed. Our mothers had to go to work, and my aunt and my mother worked together at a country club. John used to shine shoes there. Our whole thing changed. No one really knew how we lived, but we had to rent out our bedrooms and we all slept downstairs. My mother, John, and I all slept in the dining room. John's mother slept upstairs in the bedroom because she had arthritis and needed special attention.[4] We had cots. And John was sick there, he had some sort of—not asthma, but we had to sit up with him at night. . . . This went on for a long time."[5]

Probably in the fall of 1942, when Coltrane played on the football team, Mary recalls, "He was accidentally kicked in his back, and his mother really went off. In fact, one morning I thought John had died, because he couldn't walk. She came downstairs and said, 'Oh, my son!' so I ran out the back door because I thought he had died or something." It took him about a week to recover.[6]

They retained some connection with Hamlet because John Blair, the youngest uncle, settled there after attending North Carolina Agricultural and Technical State University (known as A and T) in Greensboro. Hamlet used to be a hub for the Seaboard Railroad, and Blair became a headwaiter with that railroad's dining room department. He married one Ethel Wilson, whose cousin, Georgetta Watkins, born as Haily in February 1924, is the only known relative of Coltrane still in the Hamlet area, and a distant one at that. Blair told Watkins that Coltrane loved trains as a boy. He would come down from High Point to go on a run with Blair.[7] Perhaps this contact helped temporarily to fill Coltrane's need for an older man in his life. During the summer of 1942 John also went to visit an aunt—probably a sister of his late father—in Philadelphia (Simpkins, 17).

It was to Philadelphia that John's mother decided to move, probably during his senior year (1942–43). She needed more of an income, and knew she could get work there. However, she ended up spending a lot of time in Atlantic City, New Jersey, partly because she found work there and partly because her older sister Mary had settled there and fallen ill.[8] Meanwhile, Mary and Bettie moved to Newark in February 1943 to live with one of Goler's brothers, and Mary attended high school there for a while. Her education had been interrupted by all the upheaval within the family. Mary and her mother also got to know Newark resident Aunt Cindy—born Lucinda Leary—a sibling of the late Grandmother Blair.

Alone in High Point for the rest of the school year, John continued to live with the boarders—the Fairs (Simpkins, 17), possibly the family of Thomas Fair, who had previously rented nearby on Underhill—until he finished high school. "He used to write postcards," Mary recalls. "In fact I kept that postcard for a long time: 'I sure wish y'all would come home. I miss you.' This kind of thing." He wasn't generally known as a letter writer, so he must have been very lonely. Mrs. Fair would also write, about once a month. She reported that John was constantly sitting in the dining room, practicing his "flute"—she didn't know it was a saxophone.

But John did have a life; he had developed a faithful circle of friends in High Point. Two of them remained part of his life after he left High Point:

Franklin Brower and James Kinzer, both of whom lived on Underhill.[9] Brower liked to write, and John liked to draw, so the two combined their talents to produce a homemade "big little book—those real thick books they had years ago," says Mary.

John liked a girl in his school with the unusual name of Doreatha Nelson.[10] Haywood recalls: "He was kind of shy. That was the only girl I'd ever known him to like. She was a very quiet girl. She was an A student—she was probably even smarter than he was." Nelson left high school before graduating, took a civil service job in Washington, D.C., married an African and moved there.

On the same page of the May 1942 school paper cited above, one finds a list of "The Junior Class Superlatives." Here we meet many of the people who have figured in our story so far: Coltrane is the "Best Dressed Boy." The accomplished Doreatha Nelson is "Best Actress" and "Most Polite Girl" and "Most Studious Girl." David Young had the "Best Physique," Betty Leach was the "Wittiest Girl," Rosetta Cousar (later Haywood) was "Shortest Girl," Franklin Brower was "Most Studious Boy," and James Kinzer was the "Most Active Boy."

Simpkins and Thomas both report that Coltrane worked as a soda jerk during high school.[11] He had time for social life as well. While Coltrane was on his own for the last few months of high school, he and his friends had parties every Friday night and drank lots of wine (Simpkins, 17; Thomas says it was bourbon [19]). This normal and socially acceptable way of fulfilling his needs would come back to haunt him, as he later became addicted to alcohol and heroin. He also smoked until the end of his life, cigarettes and then, in the 1960s, cigars and pipes.

Finally came John's graduation from high school, probably on Friday, May 28, 1943.[12] Significantly, the class superlatives this time listed him as "Most Musical." John was only sixteen at the time; that's because North Carolina schools finished at grade eleven.[13] Elementary school was comprised of grades one through seven, and high school offered seven (I suppose for those who needed an additional year) through eleven. Tenth graders were juniors and eleventh graders were seniors. Many of Coltrane's classmates—David Young (born 1922), Kinzer, Brower—were older than he, usually because they had taken time off to work and support their families.

Shortly after graduation, in June 1943,[14] Coltrane moved to Philadelphia, following the lead of his friend Brower. Brower's two older brothers there sent back positive reports of the city and its job prospects (Thomas, 21–22), and he decided to join them. Coltrane came along to rendezvous with his mother as planned, and Kinzer accompanied him. In Philadelphia, Brower lived in the same house as his brother George; he directed the other two to his aunt Mae Hillman, who helped them locate an apartment in her building at 1450 North 12th Street between Jefferson and Master.[15] They all found work, John at a sugar-refining factory,[16] Brower at the U.S. Signal Corps, Kinzer as a clerk in the grocery business. By November 1943, Kinzer was drafted. Probably in January 1944, Brower, who was not drafted due to a thyroid condition (Thomas, 27), enrolled at Temple University.

John revisited friends in High Point a few times soon after coming to Philadelphia (Simpkins, 29). After a while, Bettie and Mary moved into the apartment on Twelfth Street with John and Franklin.[17] A month or so later, Mary recalls, John made another visit to his High Point friends and stayed in the house with the renting family. During this visit, Coltrane caught the mumps from the children living there and ended up staying longer than he expected. Mary hadn't had the mumps, so for once she was glad he stayed away. Floyd Phifer believes John visited High Point once or twice more between late 1944 (when Phifer returned from the navy) and August 1945 (when John went into the navy). But after that John cut off all associations with High Point. In fact, Mary recalls that in the 1960s he was invited to perform at a High Point day in his honor and declined.

Coltrane much preferred the racial climate of Philadelphia, which, though it had its problems, was after all a northern city and less segregated than North Carolina. Rosetta Haywood says Coltrane was missed: "We kept writing him when we had our class reunions but he was always in Europe or something so he never came to our reunions. He never even mentioned anywhere that he lived in High Point. I don't know what he had against High Point. He always just said where he was born, in Hamlet." But High Point would always have negative associations for John: It was, after all, the place where he lost all the men in his life as well as his grandmother, when he was at a tender age.

Yet High Point was also the place where he spent his formative years, and it was in his blood. Mary went back there periodically, and Coltrane's mother apparently continued to visit High Point, according to Betty Jackson. The family kept the house and continued to rent it well into the 1970s and to use it when they were in town.[18] John was drawn to people with North Carolina connections: his first wife, Naima who was born there; Thelonious Monk, who had been born in Rocky Mount; Jimmy Heath, a Philadelphia native whose father and older siblings were from there and who attended high school there; McCoy Tyner, whose parents were from Murfreesboro; and Dizzy Gillespie, from Cheraw, South Carolina, just across the state line and twenty miles from Hamlet. Coltrane in 1958 wrote "Goldsboro Express" after a city in his home state (and perhaps for a railroad that went through there); in 1965 he wrote "Welcome" for the peaceful feeling it suggests, but that is also the name of a small town right near High Point. Consciously or not, the state of his birth always held a grip over Coltrane. In fact, another North Carolinian who grew up in Philadelphia, a drummer named Billy Kaye, says Coltrane "was always talking about Carolina," at least to those who would understand.[19]

David Young visited Coltrane in the late fall of 1944, so he is able to tell us a little about John's life in Philadelphia. Young traveled with Harry, a close friend and schoolmate from High Point, to Philadelphia, with no plans: "When we got off [the train] in Philadelphia, it was very cold. We were walking down the street—didn't know where we were going, trying to make up my mind what we were gonna do—and we met a fellow from High Point, Philip McCoy. We'd played football together. We met him on the street." McCoy told them that John lived around the corner, in the apartment on Twelfth Street. They walked over and found John by himself practicing his alto saxophone.

"He was glad to see us," Young recalls. "John talked very slow, you know, he was a quiet guy. He said, 'I wish you could stay here with me . . . I'm here by myself.' So I told Harry, 'You go to the train station and get our bags.'" They didn't pay rent but bought their own food. Bettie and Mary stayed most of the week at the house where Bettie worked, and Alice lived most of the week where she worked; they came home on Thursdays and Sundays. "I got a job, and Harry got homesick, so we had to send him home. I think after Harry left, James Kinzer came up. [He was back from the military in late 1944, after about a year of service.] He stayed there with us. I don't know what type of work he had, but Coltrane got James a job where he was working." Around this time, John had changed jobs and began working at the world headquarters of Campbell Soup Company in nearby Camden.[20]

> I remember John got beat up one night by some of the fellas who worked at the same place he was. It was black on black. Some of the gang figured that when they got paid off, they'd take their pay. They were standing in a dark alley waiting for him. John and James passed that alley too fast for them to stop them. They called them by name and told them to come there, and Kinzer said, "I'm not going back there," and John said, "Well, they work with me. I'll go back there." When James got home he said, "They got John!" I said, "Who got John?" He told me the story. I got my coat and hat on and I was going to try and find out about it. James—we called him Poshay—said, "No, we'll call the police." But just then John came in. He said, "I was a fool."

Coltrane wasn't badly hurt, but he'd learned a lesson. The level of crime in Philadelphia was frightening to Young—at the movies once a stranger stole his hat at knifepoint.

Then Mary's mother, Bettie, called and said Mary had to stay with them full-time until they could make some other arrangement. Young recalls that Bettie said, "'I know you will take care of her.' I didn't like that, because Mary was a very attractive girl, and I was kind of wild during that time myself. So Mary came down, and I think I stayed around about a month. It was too much pressure on me, so I had to leave. She was attractive, I was fond of her, and she was fond of me, and I didn't want to disappoint her mother. I left and went to Connecticut [for a short while]." He'd been in Philadelphia a few months. Young, who is an artist, does not remember showing John anything about painting, but maybe John saw him drawing. In any case, sometime during this period John finished two paintings, one a scene on the water with moonlight, the other an autumn scene.[21] "John could draw," Mary affirms.

John's mother, Alice, worked as a live-in domestic during the week, staying with her family only on weekends. Bettie took care of the apartment and was like a second mother to John, and Mary worked as a secretary. After a while they found a second apartment on another floor of the building on Twelfth Street and lived between the two floors.

John's mother had a piano—a tall upright that housed a working player-piano unit. The family had a few piano rolls that they played, Mary recalls. And John began to work toward becoming a professional jazz musician.

3

A Musical Education I

Coltrane's music with his quartet of the 1960s is thick with the deep soulful sound of the blues. It has often been said that he sounded like a Baptist preacher, and so he did, but contrary to popular lore he was not a Baptist. Coltrane's grandfather Reverend Blair was, as we have seen, a Methodist, and he was apparently a forceful speaker but not a shouter. Coltrane's cousin Mary explains: "It was good music, but not all that shouting and what not. It was more conservative." So while it's a bit of a mystery where he got that so-called Baptist feeling, the blues influence is no mystery. Mary doesn't recall hearing the blues during childhood, though blues artists such as "Blind Boy" Fuller were in the vicinity.[1] More important, the blues provided the soundtrack for Coltrane's early career. He toured for months, as we will see, with Eddie "Cleanhead" Vinson and Earl Bostic, two accomplished saxophonists whose music was drenched in the blues. He played with a number of rhythm-and-blues groups. And he performed alongside Thelonious Monk and Miles Davis, each of whom had a unique approach to the blues.

Surely in the course of his travels he could have also heard preachers of every variety. One might also imagine that he heard and appreciated the way Illinois Jacquet and even Coleman Hawkins played with a preacher's vehemence. Still, it would be difficult to illustrate how these experiences worked their way into his music. The way one absorbs those kinds of influences is subtle, subliminal, mystical. We're on surer ground when we look at technical aspects of Coltrane's music. We know that Coltrane spent most of his waking hours working on technical things, developing an astonishing mastery of his instrument. What did he practice? Let's look at his history as a musician, beginning with his home life in High Point.

As we've seen, Coltrane's mother was musical—she sang and also played piano—but she does not seem to have ever taught John. He may have picked up some knowledge of piano, perhaps of basic chords. Mary recalls: "John's mom played the piano, not professionally or anything. And my mother sang. John's father played instruments, but he did it to entertain himself within his own bedroom. I don't think Uncle John brought his violin or his ukulele outside of that bedroom.[2] And we had a big radio in the living room that stayed on all the time. We listened to everything. . . . We listened to Frank Sinatra, everybody, you name it. He and I would turn the radio up loud so that we could hear it in the kitchen."[3] Coltrane wrote in 1957 that his father also played clarinet,[4] and he told François Postif in 1961, "My family was passionate about music and my father played the violin very well."

According to Thomas, J. R. Coltrane's favorite song was "The Sweetheart of Sigma Chi" (7), a sentimental waltz by Vernor and Stokes that was popular as far back as 1912, when J. R. had been an impressionable teenager. It's the kind of romantic melody, played slowly, that Coltrane could pull off in later years with that intense, nostalgic calm of his.

Beginning of "The Sweetheart of Sigma Chi," by F. Dudleigh Vernor and Byron D. Stokes

I agree with Thomas that this highly chromatic tune has "an implied sadness, a strain of unadmitted melancholy" (8), at least when played slowly and purely, in the Coltrane manner, if you can imagine that. Somehow I think those ballads brought back his father for him. Benny Golson, the saxophonist, said John played such tunes in Philadelphia, too. Further, as Thomas notes (8), the song was a waltz, and Coltrane did beginning in 1960 make some powerful statements in triple meter. But I'm getting ahead of myself. What other music did he have around him as a child?

In elementary school the music teacher was Julia Hall. Betty Jackson remembers, "She was very well known. She could play, and she taught music. She taught practically everybody that wanted to play piano. She taught piano private lessons at her home after school and on the weekends." In elementary school, Rosetta Haywood explains, "We really didn't have a school band, but we had little musical groups, singing groups." Jackson amplifies this: "Every morning in elementary school we would have assembly and pray. We'd sing all kinds of songs, the whole assembly. And then the music teacher [Mrs. Hall] . . . would play a march and everybody would march to their rooms. The janitor had a drum—he'd drum us out, and she'd play. And we had assembly books, and we'd learn all kinds of songs. We had assembly songs—spirituals, hymns, we did all kinds of songs in the morning."

During the late 1930s, John and his cousin Mary would occasionally go to see big swing bands. The Kilby Hotel at 627 East Washington Drive is said to have presented Duke Ellington and Ella Fitzgerald, among others. According to Sherri Simon, director of the High Point Museum and Historical Society, Coltrane was quite familiar with the hotel and liked to sit outdoors in that area and practice after he began his musical studies.[5] Mary recalls that in High Point there was also "a park where they had a dance floor. They built that, and we used to go there and dance [to recordings] all the time." Jimmy Lunceford played there while on tour. Big bands also came to the theater in High Point: "They had all kinds of stage shows there. [Black people] sat way up in the balcony, somewhere like on the fourth story of the building, and we looked downstairs on that little stage—they looked like ants almost." Betty Jackson remembers Cab Calloway appearing in a hall between High Point and Greensboro, and James Boyd says there were dance parties at the local Paramount Theater with regional names such as one Fannie (Carwell) Parker.

Mary is certain that she and John never went to the larger cities near High Point to catch live music. But it is tantalizing to learn that Count Basie's band with Coltrane's early idol Lester Young on saxophone performed in nearby Winston-Salem on June 21, 1940. Basie returned there on June 20, 1941, with Don Byas, another astounding saxophonist.[6]

Probably beginning in the fall of 1939, around his thirteenth birthday, Coltrane received his first instrumental training in a community band—a wind and percussion group with no string instruments. Floyd B. Phifer, a friend born in 1925, recalls: "We started under a man named Warren B. Steele, who started a community band. At that time he was at least forty years old. We were boy scouts—Steele was our scoutmaster first. At that time you couldn't be a boy scout unless you were twelve years old." The scout group had started during the previous year at St. Stephen's AME Zion Church, the same church that Reverend Blair had pastored at until 1923.

James Boyd, who played trumpet in the band, says that Steele had played in military bands in World War I. "Mr. Steele was a community worker," Boyd explains. "He did more than he ever got any credit for." In addition to the Boy Scouts and the band, Steele played chamber music with a string group, and he taught local church choirs to read music. Although both Thomas and Simpkins call Steele a reverend, Boyd avows that Steele was not a reverend then, but "He got to *be* a reverend." Phifer agrees: "At this time he was not a preacher. He became a reverend when I became a grown man." Betty Jackson takes the middle ground: "Steele was a reverend, had trained as one, but he had a family to raise so he didn't go out to pastor. He just worked around in the boy scouts and the band." Tynie Clemons, the church historian, confirms that Steele was active part-time at St. Stephen's.

Coltrane began on an alto horn. A smaller relative of the tuba, it was common in wind bands—it had been Charlie Parker's first instrument too.[7] But very soon John was switched to the clarinet. Phifer continues: "John and I started out on a B-flat clarinet [the standard kind]. We had used clarinets we bought from Nash Jewelry store—that was a pawnshop.[8] Steele taught us the scales on the B-flat clarinet. He took us individually. I don't know if you would call him a skilled musician who could use a blackboard and charts and blow the horn himself. But he had the ability to tell you how to place your hands and to know if you are making the right notes. He was very talented." He rehearsed them once a week in the basement of St. Stephen's church with a pianist to accompany them.

Coltrane was rather more critical in his assessment of the experience: "I hadn't decided yet to become a professional musician. I learned a little bit haphazardly, without any system, just enough to play a song or two. . . . Besides, our school didn't have an orchestra, but, on the other hand, possessed a sort of community center where we would spend our free time. [Perhaps Coltrane means that Steele's band later rehearsed at the high school recreation center mentioned below.] This 'Youth House' was supervised by a minister who knew how to play a bunch of instruments but didn't give us enough time for us to learn. However, we formed an ensemble in which each of us played a piece that we knew well—each of us only knew one or two pieces. These were my first contacts—so to speak—with music."[9]

Boyd remembers that the band played easy marches—no Sousa. It was a small group; Phifer thinks they started with seven or eight, and Boyd thinks it may have grown to perhaps ten or twelve people. "John and I were playing clarinet together," says Phifer. "There were other [clarinetists] too. James Hill was one. We called him Juicy because every time he was blowing the high notes all that spit and stuff came out! . . . I believe John had the advantage because in his home they had a piano so therefore he was kind of familiar with notes. He really taught me a lot because even though we started out at the same time he was advanced."

According to another band member, John Ingram, a group from the band got together in John's basement to have beginners' jam sessions (Thomas, 17). He tells us that "John was not only practicing and running scales, he'd also learned several popular tunes and he could play them, note for note." When Coltrane began clarinet, he bought the music to "Blue Orchids" (Thomas, 14), a Hoagy Carmichael song that Glenn Miller, Bob Crosby, Benny Goodman, and Tommy Dorsey all recorded between June and August 1939.[10] The recordings were issued that fall; the Miller version was the biggest seller, and the song was a number-one hit. It makes sense that Coltrane would have picked it up since that was the season he began playing. The song is not an easy choice for a beginner; it spans a wide range and involves some chromatic notes:

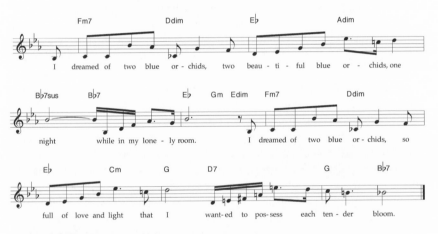

Beginning of "Blue Orchids."
Words and Music by Hoagy Carmichael. Copyright © 1939 (Renewed 1966) by Famous Music Corporation. International Copyright Secured. Reprinted by Permission. All Rights Reserved.

Probably in September 1940, the principal, Samuel Burford, encouraged by the success of Reverend Steele's community band, worked with the PTA to raise money and started a band at William Penn High School. The school paper of May 1942 states that the band was then two years old, which confirms that it started at the beginning of the 1940 school year.[11] The high school alumni booklet of 1968 states, "The famous William Penn band was started by the PTA which purchased six clarinets and a set of drums for the initial debut of the group." The high school band rehearsed in a building on the Penn campus that belonged to the school system. The building was used mostly for recreation—such as table tennis—and had a library at one end.

Coltrane was a founding member of that band, as were other Steele protégés. Phifer notes that the first director started with an advantage because she had a core of students who had trained under Steele. Rosetta Haywood recalls: "Grayce W. Yokely was John's music teacher. I think she taught John most of what he knew. I think she might have done some private lessons, but in the music room—that's where John was all the time—I think she taught him a lot. She was a trained pianist and had gone to Europe and different places with Dr. Nathaniel Dett." Dett (1882–1943), a noted black composer, taught from 1937 to 1942 at Bennett College in Greensboro, High Point's neighbor city, so that is likely where Yokely studied with him. The choir that he conducted there toured periodically and broadcast on CBS radio.[12] Yokely directed the band and choir for the elementary school as well. She was young when she started there, recalls Betty Jackson: "She had a tremendous job—it was too much of a job for one person."

Yokely told a reporter, "I remember John being a very fine little boy, a very conscientious type child. He was interested in wanting to learn, and he always showed great potential for music . . . [H]e showed great interest in wanting to get everything just right. He was a very rhythmic fellow, and he paid attention."[13]

Around this time—the fall of 1940—Coltrane became interested in the saxophone. He later recalled, "I chose the sax because Lester [Young] played it."[14] To Postif he said, "At the beginning, I played the alto—I don't really know why, since I admired [tenor saxophonist] Lester Young at that time." He had evidently heard Young on recordings, whether or not he heard him with the Basie band later in Winston-Salem. But the smaller alto is a traditional instrument to start on. Phifer remembers one Charlie Haygood who took up the saxophone and later led his own band locally. I'm not sure whether he was in the band. Thomas (20–21) and Simpkins (14) say he was an older man who owned a restaurant. In any case, both credit Haygood with helping Coltrane, and Thomas says Haygood loaned out his alto saxophone so John could get started on his preferred instrument. Phifer doesn't know if at some point John went to the pawnshop and got his own.

In any case, Phifer continues: "Now John wanted to play a saxophone, and at that time the tune 'Tuxedo Junction' came out." Trumpeter Erskine Hawkins recorded this original, which he coauthored, with his band on July 18, 1939. Although he has been little noted in the history books, when the black newspapers in the 1940s referred to Hawkins it was almost always Erskine rather than Coleman! "John could play that tune without any music—he played from ear. And he had the rhythm and everything." The tune begins as follows.

Beginning of "Tuxedo Junction," by Erskine Hawkins, William Johnson, Julian Dash and Buddy Feyne.
Copyright © 1939 (Renewed) by Lewis Music Publishing Company/Music Sales Corporation. International Copyright Secured. All Rights Reserved. Reprinted by Permission.

Ingram states that another early Coltrane specialty was "Margie" (Thomas, 17), which the Original Dixieland Jazz Band had composed and recorded back in 1920 and which had remained popular, having been recorded over two dozen times since by jazz bands alone. Benny Goodman had recorded it on September 14, 1938, but the most notable version of that era was Jimmy Lunceford's earlier recording from January 6, 1938. The song begins as follows.

Beginning of "Margie," by Benny Davis, Con Conrad and J. Russel Robinson, 1920.

Ingram doesn't specify what instrument John used for "Margie," and I would suggest that John could have been inspired as a saxophonist by the Lunceford version, which, while remembered for the vocal and trombone solo by Trummy Young, begins with a fine alto saxophone chorus by Ted Buckner.[15]

"So John was on the alto sax," Phifer recalls, "so therefore he was the number one man. John played his horn all the time; I just played mine during practice [rehearsal], because I was interested in other things. He played his horn in all his spare time, so therefore he was advanced. He had the rhythm, he knew how to make the tone mellow—his horn wasn't squeaking. He played as if he had been playing all the time."

Phifer explains that at the beginning they never even played for the football games because "we weren't that good. We played very simple band marches. Nothing fancy, because we didn't have no drums, no bass. It wasn't really a band—more like an ensemble, just a group of us. At the beginning we didn't have the right musical equipment." But the band grew in size and accomplishment. The school paper of May 22, 1942, announces that the "up-and-coming band, under the expert tutelage of Miss Grayce Ellner Forrell" would give a music recital on the school campus the Sunday morning before graduation.[16] "The band has been polishing up for the occasion during the past week and is expected to be well received." Elsewhere on the same page, after noting a fund drive to buy band instruments, the paper notes: "The band continues to grow in quantity and talent. After two years it has a wide repertoire of tunes that it can play almost flawlessly." Note the "almost"! It continues: "By gaining in popularity it has instilled a love for instrumental music in a number of pennites [Penn students]. Some are vowing to join next year. The personnel of this year's band numbers eighteen, of which only a small number will graduate." Since most of its members were returning, by the time Coltrane graduated in 1943 the band was probably more than eighteen strong. Thomas reports that Coltrane also played saxophone and clarinet in a dance band for the party at the end of the school year in late May 1943 (21).

The band was new, but the high school had had vocal groups for a while—an octet of girls (says Haywood), a mixed chorus, and a boys choir. It appears that Coltrane did some singing in the latter two groups. Betty Jackson says, "I was in the choir, and John was in the choir too. I remember we were singing 'Jesu Joy of Man's Desiring' [by J. S. Bach], and John used to hum the bass part. That made me decide I liked that part too. We used to sing a lot of those songs that people don't even know about nowadays. All those good songs that people used to do years ago."[17]

The boys' chorus was a more recent addition, and Mary says John sang with them: "They'd do beautiful things like college songs. It was directed by the principal, Burford. Even boys who could not sing, he had them singing." This fits with the account in the 1968 alumni booklet: "William Penn always boasted an excellent choral group but the newly organized Boys Chorus became popular. This group came about when several football players complained that they could not get into the chorus and that they wanted to sing. It was easy to see why they could not get into the chorus—most of them did not know one note from the other. . . . but the new principal, a lover of music himself, organized the group."[18] On the other hand, David Young, who says he was the athlete who, on a whim, suggested the boys chorus to the principal, doesn't remember if Coltrane was in it. But the consensus of his schoolmates seems to be that Coltrane did do some singing.

From the beginning John is said to have practiced constantly. Simpkins claims he had played the clarinet in his backyard at three or four in the morning (9). He was already noted for his ability to concentrate. Later in life, his ability to both practice and perform for hours at a time became legendary. As Rosetta Haywood recalls, "He kept that saxophone with him all the time, and you could hear him all the time [after school], from any other part of the building, back in the music room practicing by himself. I think it was jazz. He just loved that horn." Mary recalls: "Even as a child he would sit at the (dining room) table and practice all the time. He practiced *all* the time."[19]

By the end of high school John was already clearly on the way to a career in music. A teacher identified as Mrs. Hughes told Simpkins that Coltrane, "in any conversation, always expressed his desire to do something in music" (15). As John told Postif, "I wanted to progress quickly. . . . This was something new for me, and I threw myself into it headlong."

Franklin Brower wrote in 1949 that Coltrane "never owned a sax until he came here from High Point, N.C." Perhaps that's because John's High Point instruments had either been borrowed from the school or from a pawnshop. Soon after he moved to Philadelphia in June 1943, his mother bought him a used alto saxophone (Thomas, 28). Once Mary moved there, she was again surrounded by John's practicing: "We never looked at John as a genius, he was John. We all just lived in those two rooms, and he would just sit there all the time and practice and smoke cigarettes. He would sit at my vanity and look at himself in the mirror playing his horn. We were used to his practicing, but the neighbors weren't. When they complained, the minister of the church we attended gave John a key to the church. He could go there anytime he wanted and practice."[20]

Probably in 1944 and continuing for about a year, Coltrane began taking saxophone lessons and theory classes at the Ornstein School of Music on Spruce Street.[21] Leo Ornstein had been born in the Ukraine in 1892 and arrived in America in 1907. He was a virtuoso pianist whose experimental compositions aroused great controversy during the 1910s, but after he decided to retire from performing and concentrate on teaching in 1933, his innovative works were soon forgotten. (None were recorded until 1975.) He founded the Ornstein School around 1940, not to promote his compositional ideas but to offer traditional music training, so it is not likely that Coltrane was exposed to his compositions.[22] Coltrane studied there with Mike Guerra. Guerra was born in Philadelphia in 1888 and died in 1976. He was initially a clarinetist who played show music at the Earle and other theaters, and played classical music occasionally with the Philadelphia Orchestra. He took up the saxophone reluctantly when it became necessary for his pit band work, but by January 1941 he was doing so well on it that Rachmaninoff praised his work on the composer's "Symphonic Dances." During the 1940s Guerra became a very popular teacher, and Stan Getz and Gerry Mulligan studied with him for a time.[23] Matthew

Rastelli, a former student of Guerra, recalls that he used the standard method books, such as the one by Klosé.[24]

When David Young visited Coltrane in Philadelphia in the fall of 1944, he clearly remembers, "At that time he used to practice on Schubert's 'Serenade.' He worried me to death with that one. The first thing in the morning he'd get up and grab the horn—before he'd leave for work—and the first thing when he'd come in that afternoon. The last thing at night he'd have that horn and the only thing I really remember is Schubert's 'Serenade.'" This was a saxophone transcription of the melody line from Schubert's much-loved song (lied) "Standchen," part of the song cycle *Schwanengesang*.[25] It appears then that Guerra also recommended the *Universal Method for the Saxophone* by Paul de Ville, published in 1908, a standard compendium of saxophone exercises and repertory. On page 304 appears the Schubert. The saxophone version of the piece begins as follows:

Beginning of Franz Schubert's "Serenade," as it appears in *Universal Method for the Saxophone* by Paul de Ville (1908, p. 304)

Guerra apparently also taught a theory class for his students at the Ornstein School. Coltrane stood out: "I wrote out complex chord progressions and special exercises in chromatic scales, and he was one of the few who brought his homework back practically the next day and played it on sight. . . . He was always asking for more" (Thomas, 27).

Tenor saxophonist Vance Wilson also studied with Guerra at Ornstein, and he remembers other jazz players there, such as trumpeter Johnnie Splawn and fellow saxophonist Bill Barron (1927–89), who sat next to Vance in the concert (classical) band. Coltrane became friendly with both Splawn and Barron there. Barron recounts that Coltrane showed great interest in his tenor saxophone versus the alto John was then playing (Thomas, 28–29). So Coltrane began to be part of the circle of Philadelphia jazz musicians.

4

"Every Day Was an Adventure"

Coltrane unwittingly had landed in the perfect place to develop his art. Philadelphia nurtured a thriving jazz community in the 1940s. The older generation players were swing musicians such as Jimmie Tisdale, Jimmy Gorham, and trumpeter Charlie Gaines. Frankie Fairfax's was one of the first bands Dizzy Gillespie played with, in the mid-1930s. Aside from pianists Bill Doggett (who became a popular organist in the 1950s) and Jimmy Golden (who worked with the legendary Billy Eckstine band in 1946), few, if any, of them recorded, so they did not have an impact beyond that metropolitan area. But they were surely fine artists, as word of mouth attests. Pianist Ray Bryant recalls: "A lot of the guys were great; they could have gone anywhere and been anything they wanted to be, but they chose to remain around Philadelphia, so consequently their fame was limited."

There were segregated musicians unions, one black and one white (they merged in the 1960s). Most of the bands were segregated as well. Bryant recalls that there were many social clubs in the black community that sponsored cabaret parties and dances at such places as the Elate Ballroom, Elks Lodge, Bombay Gardens, and the O.V. Catto Lodge. A typical event was the Gala Jitterbug Contest held at the Town Hall on Friday March 3, 1944, from 9:00 P.M. until "whenever." Admission was $1.25, with cash door prizes of $12.50, $25, and $50. Two bands alternated sets—Jimmy Adams and His Swingsters and Mel Melvin's Music-Makers.[1]

Big bands were popular in Philadelphia, as they were nationwide, and they were a valuable training ground for young players. But World War II created great practical and financial difficulties for the big groups, not the least being the constant drafting of musicians into the military as bandsmen or soldiers. With audience tastes changing as well, after the war many of the bands gradually went out of business. The decline of the big bands, combined with the appearance of the radical new bebop style, amounted to a revolution in the jazz world. Many of the younger generation in Philadelphia were to join the bebop revolution, and the Philadelphia scene was to move from local notoriety to worldwide acclaim.

Right by Coltrane's apartment was a private after-hours (early morning) place, the Woodbine Club, at Twelfth and Master, where local musicians would jam on weekends. Mary Alexander says that such artists as Lester Young, Coleman Hawkins, and Duke Ellington would show up there after gigs elsewhere in town.[2] Saxophonist and composer Benny Golson (born January 25, 1929) exclaims: "Oh, it was so fertile, man! Every day was an adventure. We wanted to sleep fast so we could wake up and [start again]. We had so many jam sessions all over Philly, at everybody's house. Because there were so many of us, you know. We had the pictures of our heroes on the wall, 8 × 10 glossies, but we didn't know that we would come to know those guys, become peers with them. I told Dizzy how John and I came to get his autograph and he laughed years later. We didn't think we would come to know him and actually play with him and record with him. If somebody told us then, we'd be falling down on the floor!"[3]

Charlie Rice (born March 1, 1920), a superb and dynamic drummer,[4] remembers: "When I played at Spider Kelly's [as a leader], we'd play six nights, and three matinees—Monday, Friday, Saturday. . . . That was extra bread, and then you didn't mind playing them. I didn't think nothing of playing a matinee. . . . And we loved it. And then sometimes there were after-hours gigs that started around 12:30, after you got off. But those were good music days. I don't think you'll ever see it again—never." (Musicians like to use the word *gigs* for professional engagements because there is no other word that encompasses all the categories of work—nightclubs, concerts, private parties, weddings.)

"You had so many clubs in Philly at that time. The type of music that was going on then, everybody liked that. Like with the big bands—everybody was into that—especially up this way. You could go get a job yourself—you didn't need no agent or nothing like that locally. Just go by and see whoever was responsible, talk to them, and make a deal."

In 1945 Coltrane began picking up professional engagements, beginning with work in a trio. "I played with a pianist and a guitarist," he told François Postif—"a sort of cocktail music, but it offered me a living!" This would have been playing current pop songs, with one of the members contributing an occasional vocal. He also joined the musicians' union at this time.[5] Benny Golson told me that when he met Coltrane, "I was sixteen and he was eighteen," so this would have been early 1945. Golson recalls, "I lived on Page Street, and he lived on Twelfth Street. . . . We soon became very close friends and found ourselves playing together in a couple of local big bands playing stock arrangements." (Stocks are arrangements in general use as opposed to those commissioned for a specific group. Local bands used them, and well-known recording groups such as Fletcher Henderson's did as well.) The Jimmy Johnson band was one such group. Johnson was a very good drummer in the swing style, Rice recalls.[6] This was occasional work at dances, not a full-time job, and the Johnson band personnel varied from job to job, or from gig to gig, as musicians say.[7]

Golson continues: "We soon, thereafter, began to play in various small groups, which meant we had more opportunities to play extensive solos." They were trying to master the new language of bebop. A defining moment was their first opportunity to attend a concert of Dizzy Gillespie with Charlie Parker. The ad said "Nat Segall and Bob Horn present an All-Star Jazz Concert at the Academy of Music, Tuesday, June 5, 1945, 8:30 P.M., featuring 'Dizzy' Gillespie and his Quintet, Starring Charlie Parker," as well as Slam Stewart, Sid Catlett, Don Byas, Trummy Young, Buddy DeFranco, Sarah Vaughan, the Elliot Lawrence Orchestra (which may have included the teenagers Red Rodney and Gerry Mulligan), and others—quite a program![8] The accompanying press release said that the concert would feature "the nation's leading swing exponents"—remember, the word *bop* was not yet common knowledge, nor would it have been good marketing. One title from this concert, "Blue 'N Boogie," survives as a private recording. According to Parker expert Phil Schaap, the rhythm section was Al Haig, piano, Curley Russell, bass, and Stan Levey on drums.

Golson and Coltrane were familiar with Gillespie but not with Parker (Thomas, 36). After all, "Bird" had recorded only a little commercially, and only as a sideperson. From their seats in the next-to-last row of the balcony they were smitten by the electrifying altoist. They went backstage after the concert to get Parker's autograph and exchanged a few words. Jimmy Heath, another saxophonist and composer who was to become important in Coltrane's career, reveals, "I found out later that I was sitting downstairs and Trane and Benny Golson were upstairs."[9] This concert had a powerful impact on all three saxophonists. Coltrane wrote "The first time I heard Bird play, it hit me right between the eyes" ("Coltrane on Coltrane"). Heath was also impressed with tenorist Byas—"He knocked me to my knees!"

With World War II raging, the draft was a concern to every eighteen-year-old. Mary told me that John stayed at the Campbell Soup Company because he thought having a job would help keep him out of the army. She believes that Campbell's may have been providing food for the military and that Coltrane may have felt this would have qualified as a defense job.[10] Regardless, he ended up in the military, serving in the navy for a year, from August 6, 1945, through August 11, 1946.[11]

The armed forces were segregated and blacks in the navy had been allowed to serve only as messmen (kitchen help) and as the stewards who supervised them. After late 1942 limited numbers of black men were allowed in as seamen and black women as WAVES (the naval equivalent of WACS). They were accepted for general service in the navy, but only ashore. Initially they were only allowed in on reserve status, and in fact Coltrane's file does identify him as a member of the U.S. Naval Reserves.[12]

Coltrane entered the navy just as the war ended. Germany surrendered unconditionally on May 7, 1945; Japan surrendered on August 14 (after the U.S. dropped atomic bombs on August 6—the day Coltrane joined—and August 9) and formalized it on September 2. So Coltrane came in just when "there was a rapid and immediate downsizing," says Senior Naval Chief Orin Hatton. Coltrane appears to have joined too late to be sent to the training camps for black seamen that were active near Waukegan, Illinois, just north of Chicago, from 1942 through the end of the war. Several thousand musicians— including such notables as Clark Terry and Al Grey—went through these Great Lakes camps, played in bands there, and formed bands that were sent to bases around the country.[13] Instead, on August 7, 1945, Coltrane was classified as an apprentice seaman and was received for recruit training at the Sampson Naval Training Center in upstate New York. Bill Goldstein, a clarinetist and saxophonist who was sent to the white section of Sampson, recalls it as a big complex where everyone went through boot camp, standard military training— securing outfits, taking physical examinations and vaccinations; then platoon drills, rifle practice, classes in knots and splicing, naval customs, flags and insignia, first aid. However, even while in boot camp, bands were occasionally put together for special occasions that paired Goldstein with such stars as trombonist Lou McGarity. After training, Goldstein, like most musicians, black or white, became part of a newly formed band that was sent intact to its base.

On October 18, Coltrane completed his training and was upgraded to seaman second class. On November 1, 1945, he arrived at Camp Shoemaker (or Shumaker), a center next to Camp Parks, near Livermore, California (east of Oakland), where recruits were held until about twelve hundred men—enough to fill a troop ship—were assembled. On November 12 he officially began his "tour of duty outside the continental limits of the United States," as his record states. On November 28, 1945, he was routed for active duty through San Francisco to Pearl Harbor, then under the command of Admiral Chester W. Nimitz.

On Oahu, Coltrane began playing in a navy band known as the Melody Masters. This group was probably formed to replace its distinguished predecessor, the first all-black navy band, Unit Band Number One. Coltrane may have heard of this band, because it had been formed at Chapel Hill, North Carolina, in April 1942, when he was still in High Point. This group, known as the Cloudbusters, had been stationed in Hawaii from May 1944 until the end of the war. There has been some confusion as to just what instrument Coltrane played in the Melody Masters. Thomas (34) and Simpkins (21) write that he played only clarinet, but a photo of the band clearly shows Coltrane playing an alto saxophone, with a clarinet standing beside him (Simpkins, following p. 150). The group appears to be a big band of perhaps fourteen people (the piano and drums are not visible), but this may be a contingent of a larger group. The Cloudbusters had been a concert or marching band, with forty-four members in North Carolina but possibly fewer in the version that went to Hawaii.[14]

Once they finished their training and were placed in bands, navy musicians were in their own world. Goldstein recalls that they were told they had to learn to march, but even this they didn't take very seriously: "Everybody was walking in different directions—they were as clumsy as you can imagine." Typically they provided music for parades, awards presentations, and sporting events. The white dance band had few regular formal duties. One was to play "colors" in the morning—that is, to open the day with the "Star Spangled Banner" and other anthems—but Admiral Nimitz opened his window the first time they did so and, says Goldstein, was angry to have been woken up, so that was canceled. The only duty remaining was to play for about a half hour before each outdoor movie. During 1946 many of the musicians and other sailors were being discharged, so even that obligation was ended. They would simply practice and rehearse at their leisure, often outside in the sun. On occasion they would get a gig and perform elsewhere on the island. They were free to do so as time allowed.

As a black seaman, Coltrane did not have the leisure time available to the whites. Black band positions were apparently not full-time, at least after the war. There is no mention of music anywhere in Coltrane's naval record. He was classified as V-6, the category General Service and Specialists—apparently not unusual among blacks.[15] On March 1, 1946, Coltrane was upgraded again, this time to seaman first class; on March 18 he was transferred to the Second Battalion Company, and on April 4 he was transferred to security duty. These reports indicate that Coltrane was required to perform various functions in addition to playing music. In fact, pianist Norman Poulshock, who ended up playing on Coltrane's first recordings made there, thinks Coltrane had kitchen duties as well.

But apparently the Melody Masters did get to play gigs around the island, even for white audiences. Simpkins quotes an undated clipping, probably from July 1946, from a navy paper called *The Mananan* (21). *Manana* (which means "rabbit" in Hawaiian) appears to have been the location for the barracks where the black sailors resided separately from the whites, possibly on the small Manana Island off Makapuu Beach, on the eastern side of Oahu. The article notes: "This the last of Manana's bands, has done much to break down the racial barriers around the island. Lovers of fine swing are not prejudiced against who gives it to them, and the Melody Masters gave fine swing. Playing for dances all over the 'rock,' these music makers left a fine opinion of themselves and they also left pleased audiences."

As the "downsizing" of the armed forces progressed, it became clear that the bands were no longer needed, so they were decommissioned and their members were sent home. The quotation above indicates that this was the last black band left. The article continues with an indication that Coltrane had assumed some leadership in the band:

> Yes, we have witnessed the official decommissioning of the band, a band which has held on to the end and done their job well, even in the face of overwhelming circumstances. Much of this "carry on" spirit can be attributed to Coltrane who sought to keep the band together in the waning hours. It is with a feeling of loss that we bid "goodbye" to the last of Manana's bands; for the history of the bands on Manana has been a colorful one; one filled with true entertainment, not only for the Men of Manana but for everyone on the island of Oahu. (Simpkins, 21)

So it was time for Coltrane to be sent home as well. His discharge involved several steps through the military bureaucracy. A transfer to the receiving station of Pearl Harbor is noted on his record as early as May 22, 1946, but his discharge appears to have begun in earnest on July 25, when a note in his file indicates that he was in line to be sent "to the nearest . . . Ship or Station on the West Coast of the United States for a discharge from the United States Naval Service." The process took several more weeks. He was given certain standard decorations on his discharge, including the Pacific Theater Ribbon, the American Theater Ribbon, and a Victory Medal. He was also assigned the following marks on a scale of 1 to 4: Conduct 4.0, Leadership 3.6, Seamanship 3.6. Coltrane's term in the navy officially ended on August 11, 1946.

Despite whatever enthusiasm he had had for the Melody Masters, Coltrane was not fond of the service, as he later told James Forman and other musician friends. But, as we'll see, he took advantage of the veterans' benefits, which included free tuition and easy housing loans. And he returned to Philadelphia to pursue his musical ambitions with a renewed intensity, an intensity that would lead him into uncharted musical waters.

5

A Musical Education II

Since Coltrane eventually developed a new approach to music, it's imperative to try and trace how he got there. We are fortunate that Coltrane himself was very generous and very specific in acknowledging musicians from whom he learned. And I have managed to uncover a number of recordings that Coltrane knew, routines that he practiced with friends, exercise books that he studied, and other less tangible influences.

Before the navy, Coltrane had been under the spell of Johnny Hodges, the celebrated altoist from Duke Ellington's band: "Johnny Hodges became my first main influence on alto" ("Coltrane on Coltrane"). Benny Golson wrote that in early 1945 "a high school buddy of mine [named Howard Cunningham] introduced John to me as 'the next Johnny Hodges.'"[1] He continues: "Cunningham brought Coltrane over to my house one day. John had his alto, and he played with a fat, exquisite sound that I'd never heard before. It was even bigger and broader than Johnny Hodges'. He played 'On the Sunny Side of the Street,' a tune Hodges played quite often.[2] [John] played it so beautifully that the next time he came back, my mother asked him to play the same song again" (Thomas, 34–35). Golson told me that before they could start their jam sessions, "She would holler out, 'Is John down there yet?' And he had to play 'On the Sunny Side of the Street.'"

Hodges was also noted for his creamy sound on ballads. As we noted, Coltrane had a special penchant for romantic ballads that perhaps even dated back to his late father's taste. Many of the ballads Coltrane later recorded were popular before he entered the navy (Priestley, 16), so this may be an indication of his taste and listening habits at that time: "I Love You" (the one by Cole Porter), "Ev'ry Time We Say Goodbye," and "Like Someone in Love" were all popular in 1944, as was "Out of This World" in 1945. Billy Eckstine's version of "I Want to Talk about You" and Sarah Vaughan's vocal on "I'll Wait and Pray"

41

were the two sides of a Deluxe 78 that was recorded December 5, 1944, and released early in 1945. Coltrane could easily have owned this.

Golson and John would take turns playing piano to accompany each other in order to work on improvising over chord progressions. Golson notes, "He must have picked up piano by himself. Even then, I could tell that he knew harmony, and knew it well" (Thomas, 29). Coltrane's theory classes at the Ornstein School had surely helped with both piano and harmony.

One song Coltrane liked to play at such times, Golson recalls, was the romantic ballad "There's No You," which had become popular in 1944. The song begins as follows:

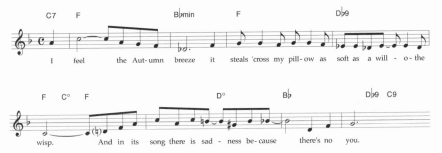

Beginning of "There's No You," by Tom Adair and Hal Hopper.
Copyright © 1944 Barton Music Corp. © Renewed 1972 by Hal Hopper and Tom Adair, assigned to Barton Music Corp. All Rights Reserved. Used by Permission.
WARNER BROS. PUBLICATIONS U.S. INC., Miami, FL 33014

Golson also wrote, "As a teenager he liked these kinds of melodies, the floating kind [like 'Greensleeves']."[3]

After Golson and Coltrane (and as they later found, Jimmy Heath) witnessed Charlie Parker in person in June 1945, they began to seek out his music with a passion, and Hodges became a thing of the past. "I stayed with alto through 1947 [actually until the end of 1948], and by then I'd come under the influence of Charlie Parker [and Dizzy Gillespie]. . . . It was through their work that I began to learn about musical structures and the more theoretical aspects of music" ("Coltrane on Coltrane"). Coltrane's entrance into the navy on August 6 would seem to have put a stop to those explorations. But we now know, thanks to the discovery of private recordings from Oahu, that he was pursuing bebop with a vengeance when he was not playing the more swing-oriented music of the navy band.

Bill Goldstein, the reedman from the white navy band, was a friend of the participants in the Oahu recordings. He was not there on the day of the session, but he did have a set of the four 78s that had been privately pressed for the participants. (Remember, recording tape was just being developed).[4] It was understood that black and white seamen were not to congregate together, but musicians, always open minded, would sneak over to the white side or the black side at night and get together and jam. Coltrane was developing a reputation, and he and a black singer were invited by a group of white musicians to come to an informal recording session. These men never performed in public together, and none of the musicians appears to have had any contact with Coltrane before or after the session except, probably, for trumpeter Dex Culbertson.[5]

As we have seen, by July the navy bands were decommissioned and Coltrane and others were waiting to be sent home, so they probably had lots of free time on their hands. The session was the idea of Joe Theimer, the drummer. He had a room at the YMCA, on the fourth floor, where the musicians liked to hang out, and it was he who brought Coltrane around. The drummer was later based in Washington, D.C. Now known as Joe Timer, he led the Orchestra, a big band that performed with Charlie Parker and others in 1953. (Timer died around 1955.) Writing on the paper sleeves of the 78s he sent to Goldstein, Theimer provided the following description of the session.

Prelude. These sides aren't as perfect as they might've been if time could have allowed rehearsing each one—2 bad sides (Sweet Lorraine & How High) are due to the extreme speed in which we cut the tunes one right after the other all in 1 hour's time. [They were] cut at Armed Forces Radio Station on Saturday, July 13th, 1946, from 1:30 sharp to 2:30 on the nose. Help. ["Help" because they had to work so quickly, explains Goldstein.] This session was inspired by John Coletrane [*sic*], a Bird disciple, whom 2 weeks after this session cut out of this "land of fools" to go home and make his way in life. . . . Here's Trane's address in case you're in Philly: John Coletrane, 1450 N. 12th St.

Notice that John is already known as "Trane." Theimer also identifies the other musicians and their home towns:

Trumpet—Dex Culbertson (L.A.)
Bass—Willie Stader (Detroit)
Piano—Norm Poulshock (L.A.)[6]
Joe (himself)—D.C.
vocal by Benny Thomas

Poulshock recalls Coltrane as a very reserved individual. The black vocalist, he thinks, may have been in the army, and not the navy. (Notice in the photographs that his uniform is different.) The bassist, a friend of Culbertson, was in a different outfit of the navy. He got into some drug trouble after the war and from 1948 on was not heard from.

Dexter Culbertson was a Miles Davis protégé as early as 1945—as revealed in his private letters to Goldstein—at a time when most people were barely aware of the nineteen-year-old Davis through his recordings and performances with Parker. Billy Eckstine recorded Culbertson's arrangement of "Prelude to a Kiss" on April 21, 1947, but he is not known to have been involved with any other recordings, and his whereabouts have been unknown since the early 1950s. Culbertson ordered by mail all the 78s that came out on Savoy and other small labels as soon as they were issued. Coltrane said, "I went overseas but we still heard Bird's records and I was copying like mad just to see what he was doing."[7]

Culbertson selected the titles for the jam session, apparently in consultation with Coltrane, and also wrote out whatever arrangements were used. The pieces they played reflected the most modern jazz repertory, including some that had been recorded as recently as March and just released. Four of the eight were pieces specifically associated with Charlie Parker. Theimer lists the tunes in this order, which may be the recording sequence. He also indicates the performer they associated with each one:

1. Sweet Miss (Kai [Winding])
2. Paper Moon (Nat ["King" Cole])
3. Sweet Lorraine (Nat)
4. "KoKo" (Bird & Diz)
5. Now's the Time (Bird)
6. Hot House (Diz & Bird)
7. Embraceable [You] (Nat)
8. Ornithology (Bird study)

Coltrane solos on every side, and the result of all this new aural information is to reshape our view of his development. He was not, as one might have thought, a great talent who took a long time to get recognized. He was, rather, someone who did not begin with obvious exceptional talent, and that makes his case all the more interesting—one can become one of the great musicians of all time and not start off as some kind of prodigy. These recordings illustrate that the *process* of development, of education, is the same for people of spectacular achievement—geniuses, if you will—as for everyone else. They too exchange ideas with friends and colleagues and begin to come up with ideas of their own. Coltrane was not some isolated genius coming up with brilliant flashes of inspiration, as in a Hollywood movie, but a normal person growing and developing in a fortunately inspired circle of musicians.

Maybe this is why few of Coltrane's Philadelphia colleagues remember him as having that touch of genius. He was always anything but self-promoting; he was quiet and self-effacing to the end. Besides, they knew him "when"—at that time, in the high standards of this crowd of musicians, he truly did not stand out above them. He was, like them, a fine young player with lots of room for growth. Golson told me, "During that time none of us knew where we were going with what we were trying to do. None of us knew that we would be successful. Nobody had an *idea* that he [Coltrane] would become the international icon that he turned out to be. Nobody! We were just scuffling, trying to get it together. He and I used to practice. Quite a few days he'd come over to my house and we'd practice all day, go out and eat a sandwich. We were trying to get it together! We were completely equal." And as they heard him improving month by month, it was like your own child growing—you're hardly aware of the growth while it's happening, because you're too close to see the incremental changes.

Coltrane only recorded on the alto again in 1958, 1966 and 1967, after he was thoroughly committed to the tenor saxophone as his main instrument. On these first recordings of 1946, although the repertory reflects an ardent pursuit of the Bird, Coltrane's tone on the alto differs from Parker's in its rather pure, ungritty sound and absence of vibrato. It sounds more like Benny Carter, an important predecessor of Parker. Coltrane tends to play short phrases with swallowed notes and woozy slides. It seems also that he may have been having some problems with his saxophone—some of his awkward rhythms are partly due to difficulty in getting the instrument to speak instantly. For example, on "Embraceable You," there are two places where his middle E doesn't speak, causing disturbing gaps in those phrases.

Coltrane uses certain figures or "licks," as musicians call them, repeatedly on this session. For example, his short chorus on "Sweet Miss" (which had been commercially recorded by its author, Kai Winding, on December 12, 1945) employs a little phrase-ending figure (marked *a* on the example) four times, and figure *c* is used to begin three phrases. In fact *c* and *a* are teamed up two of those times. The Parkerish formula *b* appears once. (*See following page.*)

Coltrane's solo on "Sweet Miss," unissued recording, July 13, 1946. The chords are as played by the rhythm section.

Music by Kai Winding and Hawley Garren.

© 1945 (Renewed 1973), SCREEN GEMS-EMI MUSIC INC. All Rights Reserved. International Copyright Secured. Used by Permission.

These licks are fairly generic—they do not establish a distinctive musical personality—and by Coltrane's next recording, in 1949, he had developed a more coherent and original vocabulary.

"Koko" had been recorded by Charlie Parker's Reboppers on November 26, 1945, and released shortly thereafter. Coltrane's "Koko" begins with an original introduction and ending—perhaps the recorded intro was just too hard for the group to manage and to transcribe. In addition, they play the wrong changes on the bridge, beginning in G-flat major instead of B major (as John O'Gallagher pointed out to me). Coltrane's solo is clearly informed by close study of the Savoy recording. He uses the Parker phrase b in four places and, more significantly, uses the bluesy licks from Parker's recording several times. Coltrane also uses the "High Society" lick (so called because it was derived from the opening of the piccolo solo on a piece by that name that was much played in New Orleans), part of the common fund of jazz licks, at the start of the second chorus, as does Parker. Coltrane uses it again at the start of the last A section.[8]

Parker's original recording of "Now's the Time" came from the same Savoy session that produced "Koko," and it was issued on a separate 78 probably around the same time. In the navy version, after the theme—one of Parker's most accessible (with words added, it later became a hit as "The Hucklebuck")—the altoist solos first. His first chorus vaguely reminds one of Parker's opening chorus on the same tune and on the other blues from that Parker session, "Billie's Bounce," which Coltrane almost certainly knew as well. But Coltrane is not necessarily aiming to become a Parker clone: There is no direct quotation of Parker, just a general resemblance in phrasing. The last eight bars of Coltrane's first chorus closely follow the shape, but not the actual notes, of Parker's solo on "Now's the Time." Both begin with a high bluesy run, then continue with some arpeggiation of a major seventh chord, and conclude with downward moving sequences of neighbor note ornaments. We find Coltrane's formula a here again, at the end of the first four-bar phrase.

The only item from the session to be issued is "Hot House," which was included on *The Last Giant*. This has one of the more flowing saxophone solos of the batch, although there is a jarring pause at the beginning of measure 4. The formula c is especially prevalent here, as in measures 5, 6, possibly 13 (does this phrase constitute an elongated version of c?), 25, and 30. A direct reference to Parker is heard in the first phrase after the bridge—measures 17 to 20 are a paraphrase of what Parker plays at the start of the second A (measure 8 to 12) in his solo recorded May 11, 1945. Toward the end of the chorus Coltrane uses the same lick that Parker used—from a 1942 song called "I Get the Neck of the Chicken."[9]

Coltrane's solo on "Hot House," recorded July 13, 1946. The chords are as played by the rhythm section.

HOT HOUSE, by Tadd Dameron.

Excerpt of Charlie Parker's improvisation on "Hot House" (1945)
HOT HOUSE, by Tadd Dameron.
© 1954 (Renewed) WB Music Corp.
All Rights Reserved. Used by Permission.
WARNER BROS. PUBLICATIONS U.S., INC., Miami, FL 33014

Coltrane seems comfortable with the minorish feel of the chords in the A sections (particularly the F minor), which is interesting in view of his later predilection for minor keys. On the bridge he produces a crude discord in measures 3 and 4, clearly misunderstanding the chord or expecting a different one. (The pianist plays a B-flat chord, while Coltrane begins in what appears to be D-flat and then moves to what sounds like B-natural minor.) On the other hand, he is ready for the last chord of the bridge with a phrase that utilizes the melodic shape of the theme at that point and exploits the higher intervals of the chord.

The vocalist, Benny Thomas, is clearly a disciple of Nat King Cole, and chose three numbers that Cole had recorded for Capitol Records on December 15, 1943: "(It's Only a) Paper Moon," "Sweet Lorraine" (which Cole had also recorded for Decca in 1940), and "Embraceable You." On Payne's version of "Paper Moon," Coltrane provides a counterpoint during the vocalist's first chorus, then takes a half-chorus solo where he reuses some of the same ideas. He doubletimes throughout most of his sixteen bars. However, he's not quite prepared, technically or melodically, to doubletime for that long. So he spends measures 9 to 12 tangled up in a turn, seemingly unable to pull away from it but wanting to keep the doubletime feeling going.

On the other hand, "Sweet Lorraine" is proof that at age nineteen Coltrane could play lyrically when he chose to. In one of the most impressive and secure solos from the date, Coltrane produces smoothly melodic lines. However, there is a clash with the pianist, which is why Theimer rated this as one of the bad takes of the day. Poulshock seems familiar and comfortable with the song, but uses different chords than what Coltrane seems to expect in the fifth measure of each A section. Still, this is perhaps the most relaxed example we get of Coltrane's abilities at this time.

The awkwardness of Coltrane's playing on most of the other numbers seems partly to be due to his desire to do highly technical things that he is not quite capable of executing—his mind is ahead of his fingers. Of course, at this stage in the bebop movement, young players all over the country shared this problem. All of them were confronted with this new and highly technical style and were trying desparately and with varying success to master it. Coltrane's 1946 solos are only slightly more awkward than the contemporary trumpet solos of young Miles Davis, or of the barely listenable solos of pianist Argonne Thornton (later known as Sadik Hakim). But as Theimer's annotations explicitly stated, Coltrane was admired and respected in his circle.

Miles Davis got to hear these discs. In a letter to Bill Goldstein on October 29, 1946, just a few months after the session, drummer Theimer reported that Culbertson had played these discs for Davis, and that Davis "was knocked by Coltrane's playing, isn't that mad!! Trane would flip, if he knew that *the* Miles Davis said that about him, huh! Too much!!"[10] This is by far the earliest reference ever found to Davis's hearing Coltrane. The connection that would eventually set Coltrane's career in motion had, unbeknownst to him, already been made.

Meanwhile, back home in Philadelphia, Coltrane probably resumed saxophone lessons with Mike Guerra, at least for a while—perhaps at Guerra's studio rather than through the Ornstein School (Thomas, 35). But his primary focus beginning probably in the fall of 1946 and continuing into the early 1950s was at the Granoff Studios at 2118 Spruce Street, where his veteran's benefits paid his tuition.[11] The director, Isadore Granoff, was born in Russia probably in 1898 and came to Philadelphia at the age of eleven.[12] His family was poor and illiterate, and Granoff completed sixth grade, but then began traveling to New York to study violin over a period of about seven years. He began teaching private violin students while in his late teens. He took over a small music studio around 1918 and gradually built it into one of the largest music schools on the East Coast. He expanded and moved his music studios into the building on Spruce Street in the early 1920s. Granoff believes his school was the third largest in the country at its height, after Juilliard in New York and the Curtis Insitute in Philadelphia. The school offered a traditional classical training, and students received a certificate of completion after four years—they graduated and received diplomas but no degree.[13] Although there is general agreement that Coltrane completed the four-year program, it must have taken him longer than that to do so because he was out of town quite a bit with bands, as the chronology shows.

Granoff opened up the school to GIs and wounded veterans, and Coltrane was one of many whose tuition was paid for by the military. The G.I. Bill of Rights (Public Law 346 passed by Congress in 1944) also paid the school for books and supplies, and provided a monthly allowance of $65 for single men or $90 for those with dependents. In return GIs were required to attend classes or lessons for twenty-five hours a week, much more than the typical student, who just took lessons once or twice a week.[14]

Granoff felt the jazz musicians had an inadequate music background. "I got some people who taught jazz. Then they themselves got together about three or four times a week, with music. I said, 'You must learn [to use sheet] music and you must learn the fundamentals [of theory, harmony, ear-training].'" He recruited Dennis Sandole and other teachers from a rival school, probably during the 1946–47 school year.

Sandole, a legendary figure, became a mentor for Coltrane. Born in south Philadelphia on September 29, 1913, Sandole was self-taught and toured as a guitarist and arranger in the bands of Ray McKinley (ca. July through December 1942),[15] Tommy Dorsey (February 1943 through May 1944), Boyd Raeburn (May and June 1944), and Charlie Barnet (ca. April through August 1946). During those years he also did "a lot of studio work," he says, such as film soundtracks in Hollywood. During his Hollywood days he began to develop original concepts for teaching guitar that became his unpublished method *Guitar Lore*. It was probably in the fall of 1946, just after leaving Barnet, that he began to devote himself to teaching, first at another school and then at Granoff. He still performed on occasion, for example, on Fifty-second Street in Manhattan.[16]

Sandole remembers Coltrane fondly: "He used to take two legitimate [classical] lessons a week, not one. He was superbly prepared for each one. He was superlatively gifted, you know. I mostly teach a maturing of concepts, and it involves advanced harmonic techniques you can apply to any instrument. Coltrane went through eight years of my literature in four years. And we became excellent friends—we had dinner together once a week."

"I used exotic scales—scales from every ethnic culture. Eventually I created my own scales, based on sharp contrasts, ultrachromaticism. I heard various abstract combinations. I began hearing all these principles. I have a volume called *Scale Lore*. It hasn't been published. Slonimsky's book [to be discussed later] is a very good book, but it's more of an intellectual approach— I didn't approach it from that premise. Mine is based on the aural approach [whether it sounds good]. *Scale Lore* is not a teaching procedure."

"I experimented with combining notes—not only seven-note scales but eight-note scales and nine. I called them nonatonic, decatonic, and so on. I had substitute chords based on dominant to minor in [Coltrane's] handwriting— he copied it. I found it in one of my old books, but I can't find it anymore." Sandole recalls that Coltrane also used to bring in original compositions.

Granoff recalls that after a while, probably by the early 1950s, Coltrane was writing more and more. He would rehearse his own music with such colleagues as bassist Percy Heath and drummer George "Butch" Ballard, and they would give recitals at the school.[17]

Coltrane and Sandole remained close. In fact, guitarist Pat Martino (born in Philadelphia in 1944) studied with Sandole for roughly two months, probably in August 1958 or May and June 1959, and he remembers that Coltrane stopped in several times when he was in town for a week.

Eventually Coltrane studied with a saxophone teacher at Granoff, a student of Guerra named Matthew Rastelli (born in 1911). Rastelli recalled, "He came in with the tenor. He worked [primarily] with the tenor sax." But he also played alto and other winds. Coltrane studied with Rastelli for two or three years, about once a week, then stopped when the government money ran out. These details lead me to believe that Coltrane continued with Guerra first. First of all, Coltrane was at Granoff for over four years (interrupted by stints on the road), and Rastelli thinks Coltrane was not with him all that time. Second, Rastelli clearly remembers the tenor, which suggests that he was Coltrane's teacher after late 1948, when Coltrane took up the tenor in earnest. However, it's not impossible that Coltrane was working on tenor a bit before that.

Rastelli is modest about his own contribution: "I was just an average musician making a living at it. I had studied mostly clarinet for four and a half years with Mike Guerra. I remember that [Coltrane] studied the average [method] books that were on the market—we used Klosé, and so forth. He was just a natural musician. When he started with me he couldn't read at all [that is, not well]. We started slowly, just went about it. He improved rapidly. He had that horn in his hands all day, I think. I think he slept with his horn. He did his usual homework, but he practiced a lot of jazz [on his own] and that's what he worked on."

There is absolute agreement that Coltrane practiced maniacally. Granoff says he would arrive at the school early and wait for it to open, then stay until evening. Several people say that he even liked to practice long into the night, just the fingerings, without blowing air into the instrument, so as not to wake anyone. Bill Barron points out that this is actually a very good exercise for finger and hand coordination (Thomas, 36); I'd add that it's also good practice for hearing the music in one's head. That is essential for improvisation, since one must hear music in one's head in order to produce it at will.

These stories—and there are scores of them—are told with apparent love, respect, and admiration. But there is often a suggestion that Coltrane's practicing was obsessive, that it was not a simple matter of working to improve, that there was an emotional desperation and drive in it that was somehow beyond the norm. It is this quality that I suspect may date back to his father's death at just the time that he was beginning to study music. It seems to me that at some level his musical activities got tied in for him with the breakup of his family. For musicians, music always represents a certain sort of constancy, an emotional support unlike any that human relationships provide. Perhaps for Coltrane it also became a replacement and a mourning for his lost family—a replacement that could never be fully satisfactory, for a loss whose magnitude may never have been fully acknowledged.

And as he built his career in Philadelphia this intensity helped him to reach audiences and to develop his talent. His career probably would have taken off sooner had he not wandered into the hazardous territory of substance abuse.

6

Philadelphia, 1946–48

Back from the navy in August 1946, Coltrane plunged into the heady excitement of the new music and the blossoming bebop scene in Philadelphia. It's
impressive how much artistry came out of this generation—Golson and Barron, Jimmy Heath and his older brother Percy, Ray and Tommy Bryant, Red
Garland, drummers "Philly" Joe Jones and "Specs" Wright, composer Cal
Massey, trumpeter Johnny Coles. Within a few years younger players coming
up included drummer Al "Tootie" Heath (Jimmy's younger brother), trumpeter Lee Morgan, saxophonist Odean Pope, and pianists McCoy Tyner and
Kenny Barron (Bill's younger brother), to name only a few. Philadelphia's jazz
scene had high technical standards in comparison with many local scenes
outside of New York. This clearly had an impact on Coltrane, who was fascinated with technical and theoretical matters. He both contributed to and
benefited from this aspect of the Philadelphia jazz life.

Aisha Tyner, formerly married to McCoy, recalls that there was also a lot
of Latin music in town. People were familiar with Machito, one of the pioneers
of fusing Latin music with bebop, and she says, "Everyone from Philly knows
the Merengue" and other Latin dances. This is significant because there is a
vital Latin influence on Coltrane's writing that becomes evident by at least
1959.

Philadelphia had a lively nightclub scene. Drummer Charlie Rice states
that his first "good jazz gig" was an extended stay with local saxophone star
Jimmy Oliver at the Downbeat on Market Street opposite such visiting stars as
Parker, Gillespie, and pianists Bud Powell and Hank Jones during 1945 and
probably into 1946 or even 1947.[1] Once Parker came with Gillespie, Al Haig,
and Max Roach. The Downbeat was a "nice club" says Rice, and owner Nat
Segal was a clarinetist who understood and respected musicians. The Earle

Theater was just a few doors down, and often the musicians appearing in the big stage shows at the Earle would drop by the Downbeat.

The Club 421 on Wyalusing Avenue also became one of the leading venues for jazz. Rice recalls: "I was the first band in [Club 421]. That was right around the corner from me. That place used to be a restaurant at first. We used to hang around there—it was called the Coffee Pot. Then a guy bought it and made a nightclub there—a gentleman named Mr. Roach. So they decided to have music, and I had the first band in there with [saxophonist] Vance Wilson, [William] "Reds" [later known as "Red"] Garland [on piano; 1923–84], [bassist] Bob Bushnell, and a good trumpet player, Johnny Hughes, who passed on some time ago."

Vance Wilson led groups there after Rice—sometimes it may have been the same group (minus Hughes) but with Wilson billed as leader. Wilson, born in Lancaster, Pennsylvania, on February 28, 1925, became one of the most popular tenor saxophonists in Philadelphia shortly after moving there around 1946. He got so much work that Coltrane would call him sometimes for leads "because I had most of the jobs sewn up." Once when he was driving home in his Cadillac after a haircut, he heard, "Hey Vance, get me a gig!" It was John, and they stopped and talked for a while. Wilson would have two jobs a night sometimes.

But Coltrane did begin picking up freelance work steadily. Ray Bryant recalls one instance among many: He and Benny Golson played regularly in late 1946 with the bassist Gordon "Bass" Ashford. They performed one night a week at Joe Pitt's Musical Bar, and weekends at the Caravan Republican Club, for as long as six months at a stretch. On one weekend Ashford said the quartet would feature an alto saxophonist who just got out of the navy. Bryant "recognized right away that he was a hell of a talent. It wasn't entirely Bird. He had his own directions and ideas. His own stuff was in there—very evidently." Coltrane played several gigs with them. They played bebop (recent compositions by jazz artists such as Parker and Gillespie) and standards (popular songs from Broadway shows and other sources)—no originals (compositions by members of the band) to speak of. From that point on, Bryant and Coltrane would occasionally meet on gigs, and around home because Bryant's family home was near Coltrane's.

Coltrane told Blume he felt his first job leaving Philadelphia and going on tour with a band marked a turning point. "[What] I usually call my first professional job was with a band from Indianapolis led by Joe Webb. . . . Big Maybelle was in this band, you know—Big Maybelle the blues singer. This was, I don't know, this was . . . I don't know what the hell we were, rhythm and blues or everything." Coltrane was hired when Webb played for dancers in Philadelphia's Elate Ballroom at 711 South Broad Street on Friday, September 13, 1946. Cal Massey (1928–72), a trumpeter from Pittsburgh, called "Folks" after his mother's maiden name, happened to walk by when the band was playing and he ended up in the trumpet section.[2] A lifelong friendship between Massey and Coltrane began as the two toured the country with the Webb band.

Big Maybelle's real name was Mabel Louise Smith. Born in 1924 in Tennessee, she had toured nationally with the International Sweethearts of Rhythm, an exciting big band of women musicians, from around 1936 into the 1940s. But the period of 1945–47 is relatively undocumented for her.[3] As of March 1945 the Webb band had featured pianist Lil Howard, Huey Woods on trumpet, and Curtis Young on drums.[4] The band made its "first Eastern appearance" in Philadelphia on January 11, 1946. By the September 1946 dance in Philadelphia, Young had been replaced by Rudolph Pitts, whom the ad hailed as the "Greatest drummer since the late Chick Webb."[5]

Coltrane was back in Philadelphia after the Webb tour. But by February 1947 he was out again with the King Kolax big band, probably playing lead alto. Born in Chicago as William Little in 1918, Kolax was a high-note player and also a fine soloist. He'd been in the Ernie Fields band in 1942[6] but had led his own groups before and after that. Saxophonist Yusef Lateef, born in 1921, recalls seeing fellow tenorist Gene Ammons with Kolax around 1943. The band put on quite a show: "I walked in and Gene Ammons was standing on top of the piano playing . . . so impressive."[7] This may have been the unique band with four alto and four tenor saxophones that Kolax brought to the Savoy Ballroom in Manhattan. Kolax recorded with Billy Eckstine's band during 1946, and around the end of that year he formed the band that Coltrane joined.[8]

Trombonist Benny Powell (born in 1930) worked with King Kolax just after Coltrane, from about the late spring of 1947 (joining in Texas) for eight months or so.[9] He remembers that the band was part of a show with several acts including female impersonators. Powell helps re-create the experience of touring with this band: "Kolax got stranded several times, for two or three days at a stretch. We were given 25 cents a day to live off of. . . . We were booked by a management company from Indiana, and many times we got to jobs and there were no bookings. We'd have to just stay around until Kolax got some money from the booking agency and we'd move on to the next town." The band did one-nighters, many in Texas and Oklahoma, and an occasional week at a theater like the Regal in Chicago or the Earle in Philadelphia. Kolax's group had about twelve to fourteen members: five reeds, two trombones, two or three trumpets, and a four-piece rhythm section. Powell's New Orleans mate Vernel Fournier was on drums; some of the other members that Powell recalls were trumpeters Walter Miller and Arnold Depass, George Crigler on the other trombone, Joe Houston on tenor, baritone saxophonist Lonnie Shaw from Philadelphia, and guitarist Ernest Butch Lockett.[10]

The Kolax band did some of the modern jazz repertory associated with the Eckstine band. It was exciting dance music, mostly instrumental. Coltrane told Postif: "We didn't play 'rhythm and blues.' I really liked this band, which was truly my 'school.' At this time I wanted to do some arranging. They even recorded one of my pieces, 'True Blues,' for a little label in Los Angeles!" Unfortunately this recording has never been found.[11]

Vocalist Earl Coleman remembered meeting Coltrane in Los Angeles, where he believes Coltrane was playing lead alto with Kolax. Coleman was recording with Charlie Parker on Wednesday, February 19, and Coltrane was among the spectators at the session. Coleman says Coltrane jammed some at Bird's invitation.[12] Other accounts, as in Thomas (43), say that Coltrane also jammed with Parker at Red Callendar's house near the ocean, either that night or on a Sunday afternoon. If this was a typical week-long engagement, Coltrane could have done it on Sunday; Wednesday night is less likely since he would probably have had to play with Kolax. In any case the story is significant because it indicates a continuing relationship between Parker and Coltrane over the years—first backstage at the June 1945 concert in Philadelphia, then in Los Angeles, and later with Jimmy Heath's band and then Dizzy Gillespie's. Parker performed regularly in Philadelphia as well.

When Coltrane returned from the Kolax tour, probably in April or early May the latest, he played Parker's piece "Relaxin' at Camarillo" to Golson and Barron (Thomas, 43). Parker had just spent six months at Camarillo State Hospital, by a court order, recovering from a physical collapse brought about by heroin addiction and alcoholism—the problems that eventually killed him. He recorded this blues a week after the Earl Coleman session, on February 26, and it may not have even been released at the time Coltrane came home. (*See following page.*)

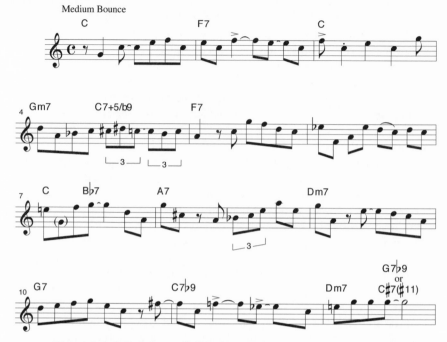

"Relaxin' At [The] Camarillo" by Charlie Parker (1946); the recording omits the word "The." The chords for the solos are a bit different than those shown here for the theme.
Written by Charlie Parker.

It seems that Coltrane was with Kolax for three or four months. He told Postif, "I didn't stay long with Kolax; I went immediately with Eddie 'Clean-head' Vinson, the blues singer." But my research clearly establishes that Coltrane spent the period after Kolax, from May 1947 through the end of 1948, freelancing around Philadelphia—and no doubt studying at Granoff with Sandole and others. Much of this work was with a man who is now a leading jazz saxophonist, composer, and educator—Jimmy Heath.

Born a month after Coltrane, on October 25, 1926 in Philadelphia, Heath had worked around Philadelphia with big bands led by trumpeter Calvin Todd and then percussionist Mel Melvin. He was rejected by the draft board for being under the weight limit—Heath is a short, thin man—so while Coltrane was in the navy, Heath toured from around the end of 1945 through most of 1946 with the Nat Towles band. There he picked up, on the fly, some basics about writing. Towles led a legendary "territory" band—that is, a group that toured the middle of the country but never developed a national reputation—that former members such as Buddy Tate rated the equal of many famous bands.[13] But the group never recorded.

Back home in Philadelphia, Heath founded his own big band at the end of 1946.[14] Heath's band performed on a occasional basis, rarely more than once a week, but in between engagements the group rehearsed and served as a workshop for new ideas. "The band would rehearse in my mother's living room," Heath told me. "Since my mother and father loved music so much, that was what was so nice about it. We'd be sitting on the sofa and on chairs out of the dining room, and I'd put the bandstands up and take the music up. We'd rehearse right in the house. And all the neighbors would be coming looking in the window and hanging out to hear us play."

The Heath group became a fixture of the city's jazz scene until 1949, the year when Heath joined the band of one of his role models, Dizzy Gillespie. Heath says, "I wanted my band to be like Dizzy's big band. I was transcribing some of the music that Dizzy would record. Even before that, I had heard the Billy Eckstine band—they were playing bebop arrangements before Dizzy. Eckstine gave him [Gillespie] copies of some of the arrangements." Heath and some of his musician friends would travel to Gillespie's performances in Manhattan and even to Wilmington, Delaware, and Washington, D.C. They would go backstage and got to know Gillespie and some of his band members. However, when asked about the band's music by a local newspaper columnist in March 1948, Heath avoided the controversial word *bebop* and said, "I don't know what 'Be-Bop' is, I play Modern Jazz."[15]

The original personnel of the band, as recalled by Heath, represented an integrated group of Philadelphia's finest young talent. Among the trumpets, Johnny Lynch had played with Gillespie's big band during 1946, and Johnny Coles made many fine recordings with Gil Evans and others during the 1960s; John Drew was a player of middling ability, but his family helped provide financial backing for the band. The trombonists included at times Willie Dennis, who later recorded with Charles Mingus, as well as Bill Leonard and Joe Steinberg. Heath played alto saxophone along with John Joyner. The main tenor soloist was James "Sax" Young, one of those fine local players who never became a national name.[16] The other tenor was sometimes Wilbur Campbell and sometimes Benny Golson. Joe Adams played baritone saxophone. Pianist James Forman and drummer Charles "Specs" (so named because he wore glasses) Wright later worked with Gillespie, while bassist Nelson Boyd recorded with Charlie Parker and others.

Musicians were in and out of the group. By mid-1947, the trumpet section included Cal Massey and his cousin Bill Massey. Heath believes that Bill had met Coltrane in the navy—if not in Hawaii then at Sampson or one of Coltrane's other stops—but in any case he was the one who brought Coltrane to Heath's attention.[17] Cal had toured with Coltrane in the Webb band and was to become a respected composer and intimate of Coltrane. Coltrane was in Heath's band from around the middle of 1947 through November of 1948; in the chronology I have assumed that Coltrane was on all the band's gigs during this period.

In the March 1948 newspaper profile of Heath, he gives the current personnel of the band, to which I have added a few notes:

> Trumpets: Bill Massey, John Drew, Calvin Massey, Johnny Coles. [John Burris, originally from Detroit, also played on occasion.][18]
> Trombones: William Leonard, Howard Scroggins [not "Scoggins" as in the newspaper], Willie Dennis
> Saxophones: John Coaltrane [sic; usually lead alto], John Joyner, James Young, William Barron, Joe Adams.
> Piano: James Forman [sometimes Ray Bryant]
> Bass: Percy Heath [sometimes Bob Bushnell]
> Drums: Charles "Specs" Wright
> Vocalist: Jimmy Thomas

Thomas was described as "the young man who has the girls swooning and the fellows grabbing their best girls when he gives out with his rendition of 'Don't Blame Me.'" Heath was conducting, writing some of the arrangements and taking occasional alto saxophone solos, but he was no longer playing in the saxophone section because it was too hard to direct as well as play. The article comments on the band's repertory, "Although he gives out with such fine pieces as 'Mam'selle[s],' 'Night and Day,' and more of that music he calls modern Jazz, 'Donna Lee' and 'Don't Blame Me' rate tops with Heath." The band also played transcriptions of charts recorded by Gillespie's band, including, for example, "Emanon," and also originals by Heath, multi-instrumentalist John Acea, and Leroy Lovett.

The Heath band offered Coltrane another opportunity to observe Parker close at hand. On December 7, 1947, the band played a benefit for an injured child, and Parker played with them. The event is memorialized by a photo, in which the seated Coltrane, obviously mesmerized by the music of Parker, who is playing just in front of him, is allowing a lit cigarette to burn dangerously close to his hand.[19] Heath always shows this picture to students who idolize Coltrane as the founder of jazz saxophone: "I say, 'Well, if it started with Coltrane, what is he doin' about to burn his hand lookin' at Charlie Parker play, with his mouth open?!'" Earlier that week Parker's group with Miles Davis had been in town at the Downbeat, and Heath believes he introduced Davis and Coltrane.

Around this time Heath began an association with trumpeter Howard McGhee, and he was out of town a few times playing and recording with McGhee's small group over the next year. During October and November 1948,

McGhee had a few engagements for a big band and chose to use Heath's band intact. This was the only opportunity they ever had to play outside Philadelphia. Heath recalls, "We played in the Apollo, and we played in the Paradise in Detroit, on a show with Illinois Jacquet and Sarah Vaughan, and some nice gigs." Coltrane was on those gigs and was excited to perform at the legendary Apollo in Harlem. A newspaper column probably from October 1948 reports that "John (The Train) Coltrain . . . tells me that gig at New York's Apollo was really a gone thing."[20] Coltrane told Postif, "We were part of an orchestra [perhaps in conjunction with some house musicians] that accompanied the blues singers and vocal groups, but I also got to play an occasional solo, and I must say that, when we played very modern, the audience reaction was very favorable. Bop was accepted very rapidly by the strictly black public." This is an interesting observation that may apply more to Harlem than to Philadelphia, where the local black press continued to debate the merits of bebop into the early 1950s.

Unfortunately, there are no recordings of the Heath band. Heath recalls doing some demos, but "they were done on acetate, and those things wore out. I don't have any records from the band." Equally disappointing is the fact that during the tour with McGhee, all the band's sheet music "got lost in the Inglewood Station in Chicago. It was checked, and I never saw it anymore!"[21]

Musicians were constantly getting together just to play: "We had many jam sessions at my house or at Johnny Coles's house. His mother would fix Kool Aid and sandwiches and stuff and we would go there—Trane and Bill Massey and Ray Bryant and [bassist] 'Sugie' Rhodes and Dolo Coker. And we would always get together. And once in a while Jimmy Oliver [would come], who was the noted saxophone player in Philly who we all used to go hear— 'Satin Doll' we called him, because he's a little guy with a dark, shiny complexion."

There were also regular open jam sessions held at nightclubs. Usually there would be a hired or "house" band that would host the young players by letting them come up and play along; sometimes the name artist of the week would be present as well. Golson and Coltrane used to "walk very quickly from one club to another" to sit in at the many matinee jam sessions held from 4:00 to 7:00 P.M. on Saturdays (and sometimes other days) at clubs along Columbia Avenue and elsewhere.[22]

Musically the jazz life of black Philadelphia was vital, but it carried certain dangers. Coltrane had been very much on his own ever since his father had died, and he was getting involved in self-destructive habits. He was drinking heavily (Thomas, 40, 47, 49), and when he developed toothaches because of his fondness for sweets and his dislike of dentists, he only drank more to mask the discomfort. He was smoking, perhaps as much as two packs a day. And by 1948, he was using heroin.

Charlie Parker had unwillingly become a role model for young musicians in this respect. He eventually made public statements denying that his heroin habit helped him to play so well, but young players insisted on giving it a try. In fact it got to the point that virtually every young player, white or black, who began professionally in the late 1940s and early 1950s could not escape the pressure to try heroin. And all too often it led to addiction. Many died as a result, direct or indirect, of the ravages of heroin on their health—not only Parker but also Wardell Gray, Fats Navarro, and other influential figures. Miles Davis, Stan Getz, Dexter Gordon, Chet Baker, and many others fell under the influence. By the 1950s the general public knew of the heroin problem in the jazz community—it was discussed in magazines, and in 1955 Hollywood dramatized the situation in a major motion picture, *The Man with the Golden Arm*, starring Frank Sinatra.

Coltrane imposed great pressure on himself. A driven man, he may have initially found in drugs a way to escape frustrations and depression. Jimmy Heath points out that Coltrane had a certain maniacal intensity of concentration while on heroin that actually helped him get through his extended practice sessions. Coltrane would often turn to alcohol during periods when he attempted to kick heroin. This cycle of drugs and alcohol sapped his creativity and health. Mary Alexander says, "His first wife and my mother and I knew. But his mother didn't know until much later."[23]

Musicians snorted it through the nose. Heath began in the summer of 1949, after Coltrane. Parker told him, "When you put it in your nose, you're still a gentleman; when you put it in your arm, you're a bum, exposed to all the world." As long as you kept it to yourself it was just considered your personal pleasure; you were not considered a junkie. But when you became hooked the fun left and, Heath says, "you became Dr. Jekyll and Mr. Hyde. Everybody thought it wasn't going to hook them—'Not me!'"

But Coltrane never became Mr. Hyde. Forman recalls that Coltrane never borrowed money, stole, or in any way became a problem for his associates: "Trane knew he was sick, and he knew he had the habit, but he controlled himself very beautifully. He didn't try to rip anybody off. He told me one time he was going to stop. He said, 'Man, I spent eighty dollars today. I gotta cut this out!' That was a lot of money back then." There is general agreement that Coltrane remained the quiet, likeable person that he had always been.

Perhaps because of his private nature, Coltrane never was arrested for drug use. But he was lucky: Philadelphia was tough on drug users, and many of Coltrane's colleagues ran into trouble with the law, most notably Heath.[24]

So this was Coltrane's circle, a source of brilliant talent and of self-destructive ways. He managed to avoid prison, but his addictions to heroin and alcohol were to haunt him for years to come, and to hold him back in his professional and personal life.

7

A Musical Education III

We are fortunate to have several reliable witnesses to Coltrane's practice routines during the years 1947 through about 1951. During this period he continued to investigate theoretical insights into music, and he changed to the tenor, which caused him to broaden his musical outlook.

Jimmy Heath and Coltrane were good friends—they used to double-date together and hang out together, and they would practice together fairly often at one or the other's house. This would have begun in 1948, when both were still playing alto. Heath recalls, "Trane and I used to go to the Philadelphia Library together and listen to Western classical music—they had the earphones, you know. We would play Stravinsky and people like that and listen to all this music that we could. We listened to the *Firebird Suite* and *The Rite of Spring* because we heard that Parker was carrying around miniature scores of Stravinsky. We were in tune with whatever was happening with Bird and Diz. We knew that that was what we were supposed to do!"[1] He said they also listened to Shostakovich. But he doesn't remember looking at scores in those days. As for method books, Heath notes, "We were practicing the altissimo notes in Ted Nash's book [*Studies in High Harmonics*, 1946], and a Sigurd Rascher book—probably the overtone book [*Top Tones for the Saxophone*, 1941]." Both books concentrated on extending the upper register of the saxophone past the high F, which is the top note obtained through normal fingerings. Heath continues, "I didn't get into Slonimsky's book until later and I know Trane wasn't into it then."

One of the most important methods for learning to play jazz, then and now, is transcribing phrases and complete solos from recordings. By learning these on one's instrument, one gets beyond a general sense of theory and improvisation into the details of style. Heath recalls, "We would write out transcriptions of some things that we heard, plus the lead saxophonist with Dizzy, Howard Johnson, had transcribed 'Don't Blame Me' [recorded November 4, 1947] and some other solos by Charlie Parker." Heath continues, "When Coltrane played in my band and took solos, he didn't know all the changes, but there was one thing that was noticeable to me—regardless of the tempo, his rhythm would always be good. The only thing he had to learn was the harmonies and the chords, because he had the rhythm. His rhythm was similar to Parker and the bebop style, but he wasn't playing Parker's clichés. He had that eruptive feeling that Parker had—a way of exploding in chords, where he'd have understated notes, or ghost notes, and he'd erupt into these lines. He had that before he really learned all the right notes to play."

Heath describes Coltrane's practice regimen:

> When I'd go to his apartment in the summertime, Trane would be stripped down to his boxer shorts. He'd be sweating and practicing all day. . . . Anything that Trane grabbed, he would work on it until he got it. See, that was the thing about Coltrane. When he started to play tenor, he and [drummer] Philly Joe [Jones] and Percy [Heath] were on gigs around Philly. We were talking about the fact that the older tenor players like [Coleman] Hawkins and [Ben] Webster played in the key of D-flat because it was the heaviest key for the tenor—gets the best sound. "Body and Soul," all those tunes were in D-flat. Duke wrote a lot of tunes in D-flat. Trane said, "I'm going to practice in D-flat." Being who he was, he would zoom in and practice in D-flat for the next six months. And when he later [with Miles Davis] played a solo in D-flat on "Two Bass Hit," nobody ever played that much in D-flat on a blues in the history of the saxophone. And it was fast. Sonny Stitt and others would rely on Lester's licks [when they were in D-flat]. They didn't finger that saxophone and play as much stuff as Trane did.
>
> Coltrane would be able to isolate everything and zoom in on anything that he didn't know that he wanted to know. He might pick out E-concert, or F-sharp [for tenor]. We all were trying to play in all the keys. That was the key to being able to master an instrument, to be able to do anything you do in one key in another key.

The more one studies the oral training system of jazz, the more one realizes how important this is. By playing phrases, or more rarely entire solos, in a variety of keys, one becomes capable of utilizing them in any situation that comes up, in the middle of any chord progression. And, since modern jazz playing is highly chromatic, practicing such phrases forces one to get familiar with all the nooks and crannies of one's instrument, all the fingering possibilities that one might encounter. Improvising on the blues requires an especially idiomatic use of chromaticism, and it is well worth the effort to try playing the blues in all keys.[2]

Heath played for me on his saxophone some specific examples of things he and Coltrane used to practice. They exchanged ideas about ways of connecting chords, trying different things they'd heard or read about or invented. Infrequently, they played in unison. Once they had practiced a phrase or pattern in all twelve keys, they focused in on one hard key to see if they could use the phrase in the context of a solo. Heath recounts:

"The first thing we worked on was the diatonic scale patterns, triads or sevenths":

"Trane added the neighbor to the fifth":

Sometimes they'd make patterns to end on the 7th of the dominant chord:

"We played just the seventh chords themselves like Parker":

"We'd play the same things with different rhythms":

"Trane was into the dominant seventh chord and he'd practice it in steps":

G7

"Trane liked four-note patterns; we did them all around the keys":

They also worked on patterns to play over ii–V–I progressions:

They played phrases from Parker's recorded solos and tried them in different keys, moving up or down diatonically:

"Then there was the one that Trane played that became a cliché with him, and everybody else played it." They'd practice this in each key diatonically:

There was another group of exercises that they practiced around the circle of fifths. They ran examples such as the following until they'd gone through all twelve keys:

As for music theory, Heath recalls that even back then, they were familiar with mode names such as Dorian and Mixolydian. They did not have a systematic approach to chord–scale relationships (such as the charts one finds today in Jamey Aebersold's publications that list which scales can be played with each chord type),[3] but they figured them out by ear. They became aware of melodic ways to use flatted ninths, sharp ninths, and thirteenths by hearing the ways that the masters used these "color tones," as they called them. Heath provided this example that Gillespie might have played:

Example of "color tones," as demonstrated by Jimmy Heath

They heard Tadd Dameron use a "sus chord" (a chord with a suspended fourth) as the first chord of his chart of "Lady Bird" for Dizzy's band.[4] Such influences found their way into the improvising of Coltrane and Heath as well as in their writing.

Benny Golson recalls that they all started writing at that time:

Jimmy Heath was writing, John wrote a thing, Ray Bryant—we all tried our hand at it. Not all of us, but many of us. I remember John did a thing for Jimmy's big band called "Nothing Beats a Trial but a Failure." We tried it and played it [at rehearsal], and it wasn't perfect, but it wasn't bad. He collected the music and we were walking home, as we always did, and he got to the corner and he took the whole arrangement and threw it in the gutter. It disappeared down below the ground in the grates. I said, "Why did you do that?!" He said, "Well, sometimes you win 'em, sometimes you lose 'em." I said, "All that work!"—copying the parts—and suddenly he threw it down the gutter. The title "Nothing Beats a Trial but a Failure" is an expression, a maxim or whatever. And he said, "Well, it was a failure."[5]

Coltrane wrote a more successful arrangement for Heath on "Lover Man." He used a countermelody that, Heath told me, "is so beautiful I still play it." Heath played it behind Lee Morgan on a gig years later. The lead was played possibly by a solo trumpet (Heath doesn't recall), and the counterline was probably played by the sax section, very softly. Here is how Heath reconstructed it for me:

Beginning of "Lover Man," showing Coltrane's countermelody, as demonstrated by Jimmy Heath.

"Lover Man (Oh, Where Can You Be?)" by Jimmy Davis, Roger "Ram" Ramirez and Jimmy Sherman.

Copyright © 1941, 1942 by MCA MUSIC PUBLISHING, A Division of UNIVERSAL STUDIOS, INC. Copyright Renewed. International Copyright Secured. All Rights Reserved.

Heath points out that it "connects perfectly." He says Coltrane liked to use this pattern starting on the eleventh of the chord, down to the fifth, up to the ninth (which becomes the sixth of the next chord in this case). It is in fact strikingly suggestive of Coltrane's "Naima" of 1959 and McCoy Tyner's "Aisha" of 1961, written and named for their respective spouses of the time. Heath recalls, "When I asked John to write more, he said he had no time for that—he used his time for practicing."

Like everyone else in the Heath group, Coltrane also freelanced and took other gigs around town during this period. One ongoing engagement, which included several people from Heath's band, is recalled by pianist James Forman. Forman met Coltrane through trumpeter Johnny Lynch but says he was a local legend even back then. "I heard a lot about him before I ever heard him play." At the Elate Club, every Saturday night at midnight from the fall of 1947 through around July of 1948, one could hear the Johnny Lynch quintet with Coltrane, Forman, Stanley Gaines (son of Charlie Gaines; later replaced by someone else) on bass, and Specs Wright.[6] Forman explains that blue laws required places that served liquor to close at midnight on Saturdays, and to stay closed through Sunday. But private clubs like the Elate could stay open later, as long as they didn't sell liquor.

They were reading music in Lynch's quintet. "Trane wrote some original things; he always wrote. But Lynch wrote most of everything. We also had arrangements of things like Ravel's *Pavane*. We had a jazz arrangement on that, and it was so gorgeous. We would rehearse right at my house, or Lynch's house. It was a lot of fun in those days," Forman says. Coltrane played alto but would also play tenor on occasion, and even clarinet.[7]

Golson remembers John playing clarinet at another gig: "That was over in the projects where Bill Cosby later was born. There was no particular leader, but Ray Bryant was the piano player, his brother Tom on bass. It was a small group, only two men out front, John and me—might have been a trumpet player, but I doubt it. We'd all gotten clarinets around the same time [Heath too, says Golson], but John, he practiced all the time, and he pulled it out that night and played 'Body and Soul.' It was great. He never pursued it, but he had a really good working knowledge of it. It sounded great."

A lot of things fell into place when Coltrane began to specialize in the tenor saxophone:

[W]hen I bought a tenor to go with Eddie Vinson's band [he may have borrowed Golson's before or owned a low-quality instrument], a wider area of listening opened up for me. . . . On alto, Bird had been my whole influence, but on tenor I found there was no one man whose ideas were so dominant as Charlie's were on alto. Therefore, I drew from all the men I heard during this period. I have listened to about all the good tenor men, beginning with Lester [Young], and believe me, I've picked up something from them all, including several who have never recorded.

The reason I liked Lester so was that I could feel that line, that simplicity. My phrasing was very much in Lester's vein at this time. ("Coltrane on Coltrane")

Heath recalls that they frequently saw "Pres" Young perform. A *Philadelphia Tribune* columnist caught Pres at Emerson's and saw Coltrane and Percy Heath in the audience: "I saw Percy Heath and his beard, Marty—Martin, Johnnie Coltraine and Joan Smithers."[8] Heath confides that they learned about alternative fingerings from Young, on the middle C, on D, and on A. "We'd watch his fingers!"

Young (1909–59) was idolized by the boppers and not only his music was imitated. He was the ultimate hipster with his lilting high voice and heavy use of coded slang, his flat-top (pork pie) hat style, and his sunglasses. The 1948 *Philadelphia Afro-American* reported that "Lester Young had all the bop kicks [fans] down at Emerson's. Brother, when he hits town, out come all the thick frame b-bop glasses."[9]

Coltrane's circle also held in high esteem local tenorist Jimmy Oliver, known as a hard-swinging protégé of Lester Young.[10] In fact, when the five-foot-tall tenor player performed at a "Battle of the Tenor Saxophones" alongside Lester Young at Philadelphia's Town Hall on Sunday, January 19, 1947, at 3:00 P.M., "Cool, little Jimmy Oliver, who has been nicknamed 'Bad Man', [played] the Lester Young style so faithfully, with a dash of what Jimmy knows Philly swing fans love [honking and blues style], that he created more of a stir among the listeners than Lester himself."[11] While in residence at the Zanzibar Cafe around 1946–47 for about six months, Oliver also played against the other leading tenor giants of the day, Coleman Hawkins, Ben Webster, Dexter

Gordon, Illinois Jacquet, Arnett Cobb, Georgie Auld, and Charlie Ventura. Philadelphia columnist Jimmie Brown noted, "And anyone attending these sessions . . . will lend affirmation to the fact that Oliver was playing like a demon and permitted none of the aforementioned to rest on their laurels."[12] Coltrane got to know and hang out with Oliver a bit. One of Oliver's few recorded solos—ironically, filling in for the ailing Coltrane—is on Gillespie's "She's Gone Again" from 1950, and his meaty tone, especially on swooping high notes, is just the kind of sound Coltrane developed by 1951.

Around 1948, Brown continued, Oliver ran "one of the swingingest combos to ever play or come out of Philly. It consisted of such talented musicians as, to me the greatest drummer, "Philly" Joe Jones, Williams [sic] "Reds" Garland (piano), and Steve Davis (bass). With this combo I yet believe, with the addition of one Johnny Coles (trumpet), there wouldn't have been any height too great to attain as far as the Jazz world is concerned."[13] Significantly, Oliver's colleagues would later become Coltrane's bandmates—Garland and Jones in the Miles Davis group, Davis in Coltrane's own. Drummer Joe Jones (1923–85) was advertised as early as 1946 around Philadelphia.[14] Once he became known nationally he was dubbed "Philly" Joe in order to distinguish him from the prominent swing era drummer Jo Jones, best known for his work with Count Basie.

John's interests soon went beyond Lester Young and Jimmy Oliver:

> I found out about Coleman Hawkins after I learned of Lester. There were a lot of things that Hawkins was doing that I knew I'd have to learn somewhere along the line. I felt the same way about Ben Webster. There were many things that people like Hawk [Hawkins], Ben and [altoist] Tab Smith were doing in the '40s that I didn't understand but that I felt emotionally. The first time I heard Hawk, I was fascinated by his arpeggios and the way he played. I got a copy of his "Body and Soul" [his most famous recording, made in 1939] and listened real hard to what he was doing. And even though I dug Pres, as I grew musically, I appreciated Hawk more and more. ("Coltrane on Coltrane")

Coltrane gives us a lot of information here—for example, that he emulated Young's sense of phrasing and line, and later Hawkins's use of arpeggiated chords. Hawkins was a very different type of musician from Young, one who consciously explored theoretical ideas, particularly about harmonic progressions. He was at ease with the innovations of the boppers and performed and recorded with Gillespie, Max Roach, Thelonious Monk, Miles Davis, and others when they were still relative unknowns. He also recorded several unaccompanied saxophone solos, the first two of which are undated but presumed to be from 1945 and 1948, a remarkable feat in itself but even more so when one hears them and experiences the freedom of his approach. On the later one, "Picasso," Hawkins appears to be improvising without the use of a pre-established chord progression.[15]

Heath believes that Don Byas may have had an impact on Coltrane as well; they had seen him perform at that first concert by Parker and Gillespie in 1945. Heath recalls that Byas used diminished patterns—later a favorite with Coltrane—early on, but I can't find a clear example. Byas was an amazing saxophonist, but Coltrane never mentioned him, and his potential impact on jazz history was reduced because he settled in Europe in 1946 and spent little time in America thereafter.[16]

Heath also points out that in order to work on tenor, one was expected to know the popular recorded tenor solos, especially Illinois Jacquet's on "Flying Home," a Lionel Hampton record from 1942, and some Arnett Cobb solos. Among the other tenor saxophonists Coltrane studied during the late 1940s were three who were his seniors by only a few years. "At that time," he said, "I was trying to play like Dexter Gordon [1923–90] and Wardell Gray [1921–55]. I liked what they were doing. I heard in them lots of the ideas of Lester Young, who was my first influence. So when I made the switch to tenor, I was trying to play like them." But he soon found he liked Sonny Stitt [1924–82] best of all. Stitt is often remembered as an alto saxophonist who sounded something like Parker, but in fact he was equally a tenorist and recorded on it from 1949 on. The Parker resemblance came partly from the mutual influence of Young. "Sonny's playing sounded like something I would like to do. He sounded like something between Dexter and Wardell, an outgrowth of both of them. All the time, I thought I had been looking for something and then I heard Sonny and said, 'Damn! There it is! That's it!'"[17] Upon hearing Coltrane's solo on "You're a Weaver of Dreams" (from a Cannonball Adderley session of February 3, 1959) Stan Getz said, "It sounds like Sonny Stitt, and it sounds like a Coltrane approach, and it made me realize how Coltrane got some stuff from Sonny Stitt; I never realized it before."[18] However, most listeners hear the Gordon influence stronger than Stitt's. Coltrane did say in 1960: "Of course, in the formative days, like years ago, it was Dexter Gordon that actually was a major . . ." (here the interviewer interrupted him).[19]

Jimmy Heath confirms that he and Coltrane "listened to Dexter together. That's why I know that Trane was inspired on tenor, when he first got it, by Dexter and Sonny Stitt." Stitt, Gordon, and Wardell Gray, like Coltrane, had absorbed the lessons not only of Young, but of Hawkins and Parker. They had already assimilated these lessons into consistent, identifiable styles, and so they in turn served as models for Coltrane, who strove for a style of his own, or, in jazz parlance, his own "sound." In African-American jazz circles this is the most valued goal.[20] When Coltrane switched to tenor, he was on the way to finding that sound.

8

Apprenticeship with Vinson
and Gillespie

Cleanhead Cleans Up: New Stars in His Band. Ann Arbor, Mich.—Eddie
(Mr. Cleanhead) Vinson introduced a band of completely new personnel
when he appeared here last week. Musicians now comprising the organization are: James Young, James Rhodes, Charles Rice, William Garland,
John Coltrane, John Coles and Louis Franks.

Philadelphia Afro-American, December 15, 1948

The instrumentation was Coles, trumpet; Vinson (called "Cleanhead" because
he had shaved his head ever since a botched hair-straightening attempt),[1] voice
and alto; Coltrane, tenor; Young, probably baritone sax (he was known as a
tenorist, but Vinson's group at this time always had one tenor and one baritone); Garland, piano; Rhodes, bass; Rice, drums.[2]

The *Tribune* presented a related story in January 1949: "Vinson Ork
Features Youngsters," it announced, "all of whom have yet to see their twenty
fourth birthday." Vinson made this decision "several months ago. . . . On
returning to New York after a recent road tour he disbanded the combination
he then had and started to build the present combination. . . . [He] made age
one of the requisites when he began interviewing prospective bandsmen. . . .
Many veterans questioned the wisdom of the new plan but Vinson argued that
'If you're going to play modern music, the kind youth appreciates and understands, then there is none better able to produce it than the generation that
creates it.'" Luckily for Coltrane, Vinson (1917–88) was a sophisticated musician who appreciated bebop. He was also a popular performer and recording
artist who could promise lots of work.

Drummer Charlie Rice remembers how and when it came about. Rice is "very sure" that it all started with Vinson's engagement at Emerson's, which must be the one from November 1 to 13, 1948. (Most publications have incorrectly stated—following Coltrane's lead—that he was with Vinson in 1947 and 1948.) Probably Vinson had given his current band notice that Emerson's would be their last gig. During those first two weeks of November and for a few days after the engagement, Vinson listened to musicians who sat in with his band and also heard musicians jamming at the black musicians' union hall, the Clef Club. He may have even held some relatively formal auditions at the union. Red Garland had already been hired and he recommended Rice and possibly Coltrane as well. Vinson said that he first heard Coltrane at the union hall.[3] Coltrane and Coles would have only returned around November 12 from an engagement in Detroit with Jimmy Heath's band.

Benny Golson heard that Coltrane was auditioning on alto at Emerson's— on the last day—when Vinson insisted on hearing him on tenor. A tenor player named Louis Judge hadn't done well. "I guess he was pouting," says Golson. "He didn't come back after the intermission. And they played a song that had this tenor solo in it, so Eddie told John, 'Pick up the tenor, play the tenor solo.' John was a little hesitant about it, and Eddie insisted, 'Pick up the horn!' He picked it up and he sounded like Dexter Gordon, of all people. And it sounded so good it was grooving—wherever Louis [Judge] was, he came running up to the bandstand and said, 'Give me my horn!' " Of course, Coltrane got the gig nonetheless.

Rice has vivid memories of the tour: "First we had a couple of rehearsals at our union down on Broad Street. Then we went right out, because we didn't rehearse that much." The first engagement that I know of is on November 20 in Charleston, West Virginia. Their itinerary in the chronology shows large jumps between gigs, sometimes several hundred miles, with a few days off now and then. They were mostly one-nighters. Rice continues, "I don't remember ever working any clubs where we were going to be there for a week. [It was] mostly ballrooms and those tobacco houses down south. [A tobacco house] was a great big place, like a warehouse [where bands played one night each week]. Because those people, they weren't about night clubs or dance halls. A few places we went were for music—some place in West Virginia was pretty good. But Beckley [West Virginia]—there were some bad people there. Man, they were fighting up on the bandstand, down on the floor, in the men's room. And Charleston, we had a lot of fun there because the people spoke so funny. It was terrible. You had to really stop and think what they were saying."

"I never really liked traveling," says Rice.

But back then it didn't bother me. Being young, you didn't mind going out and seeing different places. But that segregated thing was very heavy. You had to stay in people's houses, which I never liked. It's a funny thing, we went down south, and those people were strictly [into] blues. Eddie used to tell us, we can't start off playing any jazz, so we used to start out with the blues. And then we played other tunes, you know. It was a very, very good band. He wanted to really do the jazz thing, but you know, some things you can't make people accept. You go down south at those dances, they would stand outside [to hear you before they bought a ticket]. They were very critical if you didn't have a new recording out. And then we'd pay some blues and stuff, and they'd start coming in.

Vinson's recorded repertory up to this time consisted almost exclusively of twelve-measure blues pieces. But Vinson tried to put instrumental jazz into his program, if only as a warmup and coda to the show (Priestley, 20). Vinson premiered a bop arrangement of his hit "Empty Bed Blues" at Inkster, Michigan.[4] Rice recalls that the repertory also included "Four" and "Tune-Up," two Vinson originals that were later credited to Miles Davis; "Sippin' at Bells," which really was by Davis; and a "whole gang" of Charlie Parker tunes, including "Scrapple from the Apple" and maybe "Ornithology." Rice says he and the other band members already knew the bop tunes, which was one of the reasons Vinson hired them. "Back then, we used to learn all of the tunes. I worked a club in Philly called the Down Beat when I first met Red Garland, and we had a tenor player, Al Steele—good saxophone player—and [trumpeter] Red Rodney was working with us at the time. Al Steele used to write all these tunes out. As soon as he'd hear a figure [phrase] or anything, he'd bring it in and we'd learn it. We couldn't give them [the customers] a steady diet of it, but we used to do them."

While touring with Vinson, they would have a chance to meet local musicians, Rice recalls: "We'd all go together to clubs to sit in." And there was time for practicing: "Coltrane and Johnny Coles and Sax [Young] would be up in the room just going over music, reading through music books and stuff like that all the time. Most of the time, they'd be doing that."

Record producer Bob Porter says Vinson told him that Coltrane had very few solos in the band, but there was one number when he and Coltrane exchanged instruments. Thomas describes it: Vinson would play a blues line, "then they would exchange horns, each flipping his sax to the other and immediately duplicating what had just been played. . . . Sometimes they'd break off in mid-phrase, one taking up where the other left off" (39). If this is accurate, it must have been quite spectacular! Lee Lowenfish suggests, sensibly, that this would have been easier if both played alto for this number; Coltrane probably had brought his along.[5]

According to Vinson, Coltrane's personal habits caused only small problems (Thomas, 40–41). He was drinking and eating lots of sweets. In a small town in Georgia (possibly Birmingham, near Atlanta, on January 27, 1949)

Coltrane developed such a severe toothache that Vinson suggested he drink alcohol to stifle the pain. The next day Coltrane had to see a dentist and have two rear (possibly wisdom) teeth pulled, and he missed that night's engagement. But Vinson, a heavy drinker himself, appears to have had no hard feelings.

Rice recalls that the Vinson tour ended badly: "We went to New York to do a record date. It was on a holiday." He thinks it may have been the Jewish holiday of Passover, whose first seder (traditional celebration) was on April 13 that year. This would fit with the fact that their itinerary shows them to have been in Buffalo on April 2, but it would also mean that the tour was shorter than has been thought. But Rice suggests it could have Memorial Day or some other occasion. Anyway, he recalls: "Eddie Vinson, you know he drank something terrible. And the agent, which was Ben Bart or one of them, I think from the Gale Agency, was up there and we waited for Eddie. An hour later he came in. And he and the agent got in an argument. The agent said, 'I left my family and everything to be at this date!' In fact, they got into a fistfight. I decided right then that that was it for me. James Young was the guy who got everybody together. That Monday he called me and said, 'Charlie we're gonna leave.'" But Rice declined. "I told him I wasn't going. So when I didn't go, Red Garland wouldn't go."

Two more Philadelphia players came into the group: Rice was replaced by Willie Armstrong, and he believes the legendary pianist Hasaan Ibn Ali replaced Garland. Young and maybe the bassist stayed. Rice is not certain about Johnny Coles or Coltrane, but if they stayed, it wouldn't have been for long: "I'm glad I didn't go. They went to Florida and I heard everything blew up, just fell apart." My chronology doesn't show them going directly to Florida, but they could have gone in late April or May. In any case, James Young was back at the Cotton Club of Philadelphia by July 9, so Coltrane was probably back by then as well, at the latest.[6]

Just a few months after leaving Vinson, by September 16, 1949, Coltrane joined the big band he had idolized, that of Dizzy Gillespie. When Gillespie's family first moved from his hometown of Cheraw, South Carolina, in 1935, they had lived in Philadelphia for a while, and this band had a lot of connections with that city. Jimmy Heath says he had previously recommended James Forman, who had been playing piano with Gillespie since mid-1948. Forman, in turn, recommended Coltrane when the lead alto spot opened up. Coltrane later stated, "I entered Dizzy's band at the recommendation of his pianist" (Postif). Heath himself was hired around the beginning of October.[7] Heath's arranger, John Acea, became the band's pianist when Forman left in October or November. Beginning Friday, October 21, 1949, the Gillespie band played for a week at the Earle Theatre in Philadelphia, along with other acts. While they were at the Earle, drummer Teddy Stewart left the band in order to go on the road with Dinah Washington, who was also on the bill and with whom he had a relationship. Heath suggested that Gillespie get Specs Wright to replace him. "He had a good groove," says Heath, and he was a fine reader. So there was one more friend from home in the group.

Coltrane's childhood friend Franklin Brower wrote a short piece on John after seeing the show at the Earle Theatre:[8]

Dizzy's Saxist Realizes Dream

Coltrane Finally Ends Up at Earle

When he came here from North Carolina in 1943, John Coltrane had never heard of the Earle Theatre.

He soon found out, however, that it was the spot where all young Philadelphia musicians hoped some day to appear. Once you have showed there, he learned, you can consider yourself as having hit big time.

Realizes Long Desire

As a young saxophonist, Coltrane found the desire of appearing at the Earle contagious. But unlike many who have hoped in vain, he can now say he has realized that wish.

Now 23, Coltrane is a member of Dizzy Gillespie's Orchestra, which has just closed a week-long stay at the central-city movie house.

With Diz Two Months

The sax artist joined the high priest of bebop about two months ago. Prior to that he had been working his way up the entertainment ladder with combinations of various names and descriptions.

Coltrane, who lives at 1450 N. 12th St., when he isn't on the road, never owned a sax until he came here from High Point, N.C. He had, nonetheless, hoped to become a musician for many years and he purchased one soon after arriving here.

To the extent that he got his start in Philadelphia, Coltrane's career parallels that of Gillespie, who hails from the neighborhood of 13th and Catharine Sts.

PIANIST AT SPELMAN

ATLANTA—Erno Daniel, Hungarian pianist, opened the 1949-50 Artists Series at Spelman College.

Fig. 7. "Dizzy's Saxist Realizes Dream." (*Philadelphia Afro-American,* November 5, 1949, p. 8.)

It was indeed a dream to be with Gillespie. But at first there were two frustrations for Coltrane: One was that he was playing lead alto, which meant mostly reading and little improvisation, and no chance to use his now preferred tenor. The other is that Gillespie was trying hard to make his big band economically viable by featuring commercial material. Pat Harris, perhaps the only woman writing for *Down Beat* at the time, reviewed Gillespie's band at the Club Silhouette in Chicago. She noted, "To get his 'bop with a beat' and to make his band the danceable combination he wants, Dizzy Gillespie has sacrificed some of the spark traditionally accruing to the name and reputation of his music." She did allow that "on the whole the new Gillespie crew is an improvement over the sad unit he's been traveling around with recently. . . . For once, the saxes are in tune. . . . Paul Gonsalves, tenorist formerly with Count Basie, contributes some pretty horn from time to time, as does altoist Jimmy Heath. . . . Drummer Wright, described by Diz as more flexible than Teddy Stewart, though not quite as good a rhythm drummer, keeps the beat Diz wants and somehow the band manages to swing. On such tunes as J. J. Johnson's '191,' it achieved a really exciting punch and drive."[9]

Coltrane himself said, "This was the crazy period of Dizzy, the one where he wanted to find a new audience and played a sort of rhythm and blues in his own way, with [singer] Joe Carroll. It was a lot of fun, but I don't know if what we played was always sufficiently appreciated!" (Postif). Coltrane means by this last comment that even Gillespie's commercial material was musically sophisticated. As Gillespie himself wrote, "Dancers had to have those four solid beats and could care less about the esoteric aspects, the beautiful advanced harmonies and rhythms we played and our virtuosity, as long as they could dance."[10] And many challenging bop classics were in the book for performances, if not on recordings. Coltrane had the opportunity to play material that would certainly have an impact on his own writing: First, there were such modern charts as Gillespie's "A Night in Tunisia" and Monk's "'Round Midnight," both pieces that had unusual chords and employed the minor mode. (Thomas says Coltrane was featured on these and other titles (48), but Heath disagrees; at the most he may have had a very exposed lead alto part.) Coltrane's own compositions in later years reveal a preference for the minor. Furthermore, he retained some of Gillespie's repertory—with Miles Davis he did "'Round Midnight" and also "Two Bass Hit," and under his own name he recorded Tadd Dameron's "Good Bait," which was in Gillespie's book. And his "Liberia" from 1960 was a clear tribute to Gillespie's "Tunisia."

Second, Gillespie's material sometimes involved vamping on one or two chords, as happens in the A section of "Tunisia" and in some of the Latin numbers of the book, such as "Manteca." From late 1960 through about 1965, as we will see, much of Coltrane's repertory consisted of vamps on one or two chords. Third, Gillespie was one of the pioneers of the Latin jazz idiom. (This is connected with the last point, since many Latin pieces employ vamps.) We've already mentioned that Philadelphia had an active Latin musical scene. Latin music and its rhythms featured more prominently in Coltrane's music than most people realize. Its influence may be clearly heard on "Like Sonny," "Equinox," and even "Acknowledgement" from *A Love Supreme.* "Afro-Blue" by Cuban percussionist Mongo Santamaria was a regular part of Coltrane's repertory from 1963 on. So it is impossible to ignore the impact that Gillespie's repertory had on Coltrane, in its use of unusual progressions, in its use of one- or two-chord vamps, and in its emphasis on Latin rhythms. And, in introducing the fusion of Latin music and jazz, Gillespie also paved the way for Coltrane's later broadening of this to include other kinds of world music from India and Africa.

Gillespie served as a mentor to everyone who worked with him. As Heath recalled, "Dizzy was a teacher and a giver. He was the most accessible genius I've ever known. Whenever I'd run across him he'd sit me down at the piano and play some voicings and stuff. I could call him and get information whenever— he always would respond." He surely helped Coltrane as well.

Coltrane did a fine job as lead alto. Heath notes, "Trane was a great reader. He was like a sight reader. And he had already played clarinet also. And we used to run into some situations in shows, at the Apollo in particular with Dizzy's band, where they would have acts on the show, jugglers or comedians or whatever, and they would have some clarinet parts. And me never having played clarinet, at that time, Coltrane would take the clarinet parts and transpose them on alto. You know, he was an excellent musician in every sense of the word."[11] Lead trumpeter Willie Cook, who had been in the band since mid-1948, concurs: "He was a fine lead alto player: he had brought the section up to where it was a real good saxophone section. Him and little Bird [Heath] together on the altos. The intonation of the band at that time got very good."

Most of the saxophone solos were given to Paul Gonsalves, who had already worked with Count Basie and later become famous with Duke Ellington's orchestra. For a brief spell the other tenorist was Rudy Williams, but he was soon replaced by Jesse Powell, who was featured on several numbers. The altoists rarely soloed: Heath and Coltrane may have both played on "Cool Breeze," Heath thinks, but he is sure that Coltrane's feature was "Minor Walk" by Linton Garner (Erroll's brother). Significantly, "Minor Walk" was in Coltrane's favorite form, the minor blues (after the six-bar introduction). Gillespie had recorded it for RCA in 1947, and here is the theme:[12] (*See following page.*)

Piano

Beginning of condensed score of "Minor Walk," by Linton Garner, arranged by Walter "Gil" Fuller.
Copyright © 1949 (Renewed) by Consolidated Music Publishers, a Divison of Music Sales Corporation (ASCAP). International Copyright Secured. All Rights Reserved. Reprinted by Permission.

One night that stands out for Heath was a stop in Little Rock, Arkansas, where they attracted only a handful of people. The audience didn't want bebop, and Gillespie, in spite, called "Things to Come," a very fast number that the band hadn't played before. But Heath, Coltrane and others knew it because they had loved this piece from the records and played it in Heath's band. So they surprised Gillespie by playing it pretty well.

If one studies the lead alto parts of "Things to Come" and other numbers, one will have a sense of Coltrane's musical ability in 1949. He also continued to practice fanatically, as pianist James "Hen Gates" Forman recalls.[13] Forman recounts one incident while the band was in St. Louis: "Coltrane knocked on my room door [at the hotel] and asked me if I would loan him one of my piano books. I said, 'What do you want to do? You want to play piano now?' He said, 'No, I just want to see if I can find something out of these books.' He took my Hanon and Czerny piano exercise books, and some kind of way he was able to finger his horn to play these notes. I couldn't understand that. In fact, all of the musicians in the band were amazed. They couldn't believe that he would make a lot of the notes."

The sixty exercises of C. L. Hanon's *The Virtuoso Pianist* have been played by pianists all over the world for over a hundred years. The first thirty of the Hanon studies as written would not be difficult to play on the saxophone. They consist of sequences—the same pattern played up a scale step each time—designed to exercise certain fingers. The sequences are written in C major, and the fingerings and thumb crossings are carefully marked. On the saxophone the same benefits do not apply since the fingers are fixed in place—there are few fingering options, and of course no thumb crossing. But if Coltrane took each pattern into all twelve keys, this would indeed have become quite a workout. The first pattern is shown below:

C. L. Hanon's *The Virtuoso Pianist*, No. I (beginning)

Number 31 is more intriguing, since it involves taking wider and wider leaps from a fixed note. In later years Coltrane often worked such passages into his solos—as on "My Favorite Things"—and in fact his ease at jumping across registers, requiring the opening and closing of the octave key, is remarkable. So he must have practiced these leaps at some point, and Hanon may have been his source:

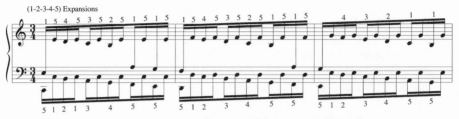

C. L. Hanon's *The Virtuoso Pianist,* No. 31 (beginning)

Again, he likely would have done this in every key. Similarly, number 49 involves leaps of a sixth in all registers; 56 involves scales played in broken octaves. Number 57 presents arpeggios played as 1, 5, 3, octave—another pattern that would involve a great deal of playing across the octave key on the saxophone. (They are written to be doubled in octaves, which of course cannot be done on the saxophone, so Coltrane could have just played the bottom note in each case.)

Numbers 39 through 43 of the Hanon book consist of major and minor scales and arpeggios, chromatic scales, and all the dominant and diminished arpeggios. Clearly, this is just the kind of thing Coltrane would want to practice—although he must have known the scales and arpeggios by this time from other books. Finally, numbers 44, 45, and 47 involve repeated notes, which are good exercises for tonguing on the saxophone, and 46 is a workout in trills. One of the distinctive and delicate features of Coltrane's later work is his use of trills.

Carl Czerny, a contemporary of Schubert and thus a generation older than Hanon, wrote many books of studies for the piano. Some of them, like the *One Hundred Progressive Studies,* focus so much on piano figuration that it's hard to see how Coltrane could have used them. However *The School of Velocity,* which may be the best known, has many scales, arpeggios, and patterns. Several, for example, are similar to Hanon's number 31 shown above, although Czerny is rarely as literal as Hanon in his repetitions and he attempts to create more of a melodic line. Turning figures such as those in the Czerny study below certainly figure in much of Coltrane's music. For example, his piece "Like Sonny," recorded in 1959 and 1960, is entirely built from such a figure:

Carl Czerny, *The School of Velocity,* **excerpt**

Looking at the Hanon and Czerny books, we begin to get a sense of how Coltrane collected materials freely from all sources and began to develop a new kind of jazz style, new in part because it didn't rely exclusively on traditional jazz materials.

Cook and bassist Al McKibbon both believe that Coltrane brought his tenor with him on tour. If he couldn't use it on the bandstand, he could at least keep in practice and play it at jam sessions. Cook recalls, "He was a fiery Lester Young type tenor player at that time. Not too much honking. He was very fluent on his horn. He could execute very well, and his ideas were very good."

He managed to record some solos on tenor as well. Until recently, it has been believed that Coltrane made his first commercial recordings as a member of Gillespie's band. Phil Schaap, who helped uncover the navy material, has also come upon a significant new find from the Gillespie period. Tenorist "Big Nick" Nicholas told Schaap that Coltrane had recorded with singer and pianist Billy Valentine. Schaap tracked down this lead and found a recording session, complete with extra takes and false starts (takes that end abruptly after a few seconds)—the tenor saxophone soloist is unmistakably Coltrane! Further research for a Mercury Records discography has placed this session on November 7, 1949, in Los Angeles while the Gillespie band was presumably performing there. (Schaap says it was March 1, 1950, in New York, but I don't have enough of the band's itinerary to settle this.) The other personnel are Coltrane's band mates guitarist John Collins and drummer "Specs" Wright—along with bassist Ray Brown, a former Gillespie-ite who settled in Los Angeles.

Valentine (ca. 1927–ca. 1992) was a smooth singer in the vein of Nat Cole or Charles Brown. He was featured with Johnny Moore's Three Blazers during this period, and was signed by Mercury Records to record under his own name. According to the black press, he "clicked with such discs as 'Smooth Sailing Baby,' 'Hard Loving Papa,' 'Ain't Gonna Cry No More,' 'I Want You to Love Me,' and 'Beer Drinkin' Baby.'"[14] The last three feature Coltrane solos. In his appearances here, Coltrane presents a warm, thoughtful sound on the tenor and has clearly gained a command of the chords since his first recordings in July 1946. He has a distinctive touch on the blues—one of the hallmarks of his style later as well.

Thanks to the careful listening of Norwegian researcher Jan Evensmo, who has recently made a study of tenor saxophone styles, we can probably add two more Coltrane solos to his recorded legacy. At the first Gillespie recording session on November 21, the only saxophone solos are by Gonsalves or Powell. At the second session on January 9, 1950, it has always been assumed that the same soloists were featured. But Evensmo pointed out to me that a third, distinct tenor saxophone voice is heard on "Ooh-La-La" and at the beginning of "Coast to Coast" (the longer solo at the end is definitely Powell's). This third person has some of Gonsalves' offbeat style but a lighter sound, and is rhythmically quite different from Gonsalves, even a bit awkward in places. In fact, he sounds something like Coltrane did in 1946, but on tenor! In "Ooh La La," tenor number three also plays a double-time run, something that Gonsalves did not do. Heath is adamant that Coltrane would not have soloed on tenor in the band; however, Willie Cook believes it is possible, since Coltrane did have his tenor around to practice. As late as 1954, on a live version of "Castle Rock," there are a few phrases in Coltrane's playing that suggest Gonsalves, so we may probably add him to the list of Coltrane's early influences, along with Hodges, Parker, Hawkins, Young, Jimmy Oliver, Wardell Gray, Gordon, Stitt, and others.

Somewhere along the line, Gillespie evidently noticed what a fine tenorist Coltrane had become; when his big band went out of business, he started a small group with Coltrane as the sole tenor. Gillespie was forced to break up the big group due to financial difficulties—that was a very difficult time to support a big band, and even Count Basie had a small group during 1950. Willie Cook remembers when the band broke up—June 20, 1950. "I remember that date," he explains, "because it was significant for me. That band was a special one of mine. We were in Pennsylvania—I was living in Pittsburgh at the time—and we broke up in some little town near Pittsburgh [probably Sewickley]. After that gig Dizzy said that was going to be the last one, you know. [Gillespie's wife] Lorraine wanted him to have a small band. Dizzy liked her input and he took her advice on quite a few things. She'd been trying to get him to do that for a long time—it wasn't just a spur of the moment thing." Gillespie wrote that Lorraine had said, "It's either me or the band"![15] Cook recalled, "He told everybody that that was gonna be the end. He told us about a week before time, you know." Cook's memory that this happened near Pittsburgh makes sense, since it was there, in Sewickley, that Heath distinctly recalls Gillespie marveling at Coltrane's work on "Minor Walk": "Trane jumped on it and stopped Dizzy from clowning and he looked around and said 'Blow!'"

Perhaps Gillespie took some time off, as Coltrane freelanced in Philadelphia for the month of August. At the end of August, Gillespie went on the road with Coltrane on tenor, Heath on alto, Milt Jackson on vibraphone, Percy Heath on bass, Specs Wright on drums, and one Fred Strong on conga drums. With the conga drum and no piano (sometimes Jackson played chords behind the others), this was a quite unusual instrumentation. This group toured far and wide for the rest of 1950, until personal problems began to tear it apart.

9

Obscurity: 1951–55

While they were on tour with Gillespie, Coltrane's and Heath's addictions began to interfere with their careers. It had started early in the year with the big band: Gillespie didn't realize that Heath, Coltrane, and six other band members had been snorting heroin. Coltrane may have already used hypodermic needles back in Philadelphia. They found when they traveled outside New York that the heroin was more expensive and weaker. In Harlem three dollars would get a big capsule of heroin; in Dayton, Ohio, that bought a tiny capsule that was weak and cut (diluted) and wouldn't make anybody high. They were hooked and were sick and nervous, and it was here in Dayton that the situation became more serious. Specs Wright brought in a girl named Dee Dee, recalls Heath, who came in with a set of "works" (needles and supplies), and she helped them all with shooting up, mainlining. That way they got high instantly. For Coltrane this may have already been familiar, but for Heath and some of the others it was new. "We all took off that day—that was a regretful moment in my life," states Heath with evident emotion. "It opened me up to seven years of horror." Coltrane was also to experience that horror.

Things got worse during the tour with the small group. In Los Angeles in late October 1950, Coltrane fell unconscious in his hotel room, and Heath revived him. After this scare, Coltrane quit heroin for a while, but he found himself drinking as a substitute. The problems came to a head at the very end of 1950 while they were at the Silhouette Club in Chicago. Heath recalls, "Trane had eased up [on heroin] at that time and was drinking. Specs and I went down to the basement during intermission, and Dizzy caught Specs with the needle in his hand." He fired them both with one week's notice; their next and last gig was in Canada (Toronto or possibly Montreal). There, "Dizzy threatened to fire Coltrane because Coltrane was drinking, and we were supposed to go on the stage, and Trane was in the bathroom asleep or something. And he fired Trane, but I think Trane asked him or begged to go back. I was arrogant—I said, 'I ain't gonna beg.'"

Heath went back to Philadelphia and was not replaced. Meanwhile, Coltrane remained with Gillespie for an extended stay at Birdland in Manhattan, where they worked with drummer Art Blakey, replacing Wright, and house pianist Billy Taylor. Taylor explains that drug use

> really bothered Dizzy because he was always aware of the audience; he wanted to present his music in a way that was consistent. Because he was always a bandleader—big band, small band, it didn't make any difference. He was a leader, and he wanted his music to be representative of what he was playing, and he was playing his tail off. If for any reason you weren't cutting it, he really didn't take kindly to that . . . [During breaks] we'd go sit at the table or go outside or get some coffee—that kind of stuff. Coltrane's habit got in the way, and so I didn't hang out with him as much as I might have had he not had other things to do. He was a very soft spoken and nice guy. It was frustrating for me because he was one of the first people that I met that I said, "Gee I wish there was something I could say or something I could do to convince him not to do this." And I didn't know him that well and I didn't want to impose—it wouldn't do any good. I said some things, but nothing that would change his mind at that point. And then years later, when he'd really recovered from all that, he didn't remember any of that and I never brought it up, because we had a really nice relationship later. I had such admiration for him—to have gotten over it and to just go straight ahead, you know.

Coltrane got to do some playing around Manhattan during his weeks at Birdland. Tenorist "Big Nick" Nicholas remembers Coltrane jamming with him on Gillespie's nights off at Birdland, and at the Paradise in Harlem. Coltrane told August Blume, "Miles [Davis] used to do these dance jobs in the Audubon [Ballroom] in New York uptown, way up on Broadway. I think on one of the jobs he had [tenorist] Sonny Rollins, and Bud [Powell], and [drummer] Art Blakey, forgot the bassman, and myself—on this dance job. That's the only time I worked with Bud. He was playing good. Whew!" Altoist Jackie McLean told Fujioka he played too, perhaps sitting in. The only known date is Sunday afternoon, March 11, 1951.[1] These were highly significant associations. Powell electrified listeners with his interpretation of the bebop style, and all later pianists listened, too. The dramatic drumming of Blakey placed him among the young leaders on his instrument, and Coltrane was to work and record with him several times in the 1950s. Rollins and Coltrane became close friends and ran neck and neck in the polls during the late 1950s. And this is the third time Davis has figured in our story—the first was when he heard Coltrane's navy recordings in 1946, the second was when he met Coltrane while with Parker in 1948.

Coltrane's early tenor style with Gillespie's small group is fortunately well documented. From the end of 1950 there are three tracks recorded privately at a club, and through the poor fidelity Coltrane can be heard soloing. On "Emanon," he sounds a bit like Paul Gonsalves. In much better sound, five twenty-minute radio broadcasts survive of the Gillespie group at Birdland from January through March of 1951, and Coltrane gets one or two solos during each broadcast.[2] Coltrane's sound is vibrant, his use of the upper register intense. His rhythms are basically constructed out of an eighth-note pulse. On a Billy Taylor original entitled "Good Groove" Coltrane navigates the chord progression using little patterns of the sort that would obsess him eight years later. His solos incorporate unusual scales, especially on minor pieces such as "A Night in Tunisia." On the version of "Tunisia" from January 6, Coltrane takes the unaccompanied two-measure break that is a famous feature of this piece, over an implied D minor chord.[3] By playing both B-natural and B-flat, Coltrane creates an interesting mixture of D melodic and harmonic minor, and he uses a dissonant A-flat as a passing tone to the G that begins the third measure, when the rhythm section reenters. (Carl Woideck notes that the A-flat might also be heard as a blue note.)

Beginning of Coltrane's solo on "A Night in Tunisia," January 6, 1951.
Music by John "Dizzy" Gillespie and Frank Paparelli.
Copyright © 1944 by MCA MUSIC PUBLISHING, a Division of UNIVERSAL STUDIOS, INC.
Copyright Renewed. International Copyright Secured. All Rights Reserved.

There is also a bright and aggressive solo on "Congo Blues" from the same broadcast, in which Coltrane quotes Lester Young's honking lick at the start of his second chorus (Priestley, 24).

Gillespie also took the group into a studio in Detroit on March 1, 1951, for a session on his own Dee Gee Records. Blakey had been replaced by Kansas Fields, Kenny Burrell was added on guitar, and there was no pianist, so Milt Jackson played piano chords where needed. Coltrane's energetic solo on the blues "We Love to Boogie" was the only work of his available to the general public until he joined Miles Davis late in 1955. (His work on the Billy Valentine session was unattributed, and the Gillespie broadcasts survived only among the few individuals who had home-recording equipment in those days.) Coltrane's two blues choruses (the band plays during the first four bars of his first chorus) are hot and sensuous and feature the same scalar exoticism as "Tunisia" did.

By early April, Coltrane was back in Philadelphia, freelancing and playing in a group called the Dizzy Gillespie Alumni, led by his friend Jimmy Heath. His stint with Gillespie had been musically invaluable, but it had not led to his being "discovered." Perhaps this was partly a result of his occasional unreliability when he was drunk or on heroin—he'd gone back on the drug. Besides, notes David Wild, it's possible that he had to go back and finish at the Granoff school before his veteran's tuition benefits ran out. In any case, for the next four years, he worked as a sideman in jazz and rhythm-and-blues bands. Some, like that of Earl Bostic, were famous, but none offered him exposure or much chance to improvise. As he told Postif, "You see, I stayed in obscurity for a long time, because I just played what the others expected from me, without trying to add anything original. I saw so many guys get themselves fired from a band because they tried to be innovative that I got a little discouraged from trying anything different!" Or, as he told Ira Gitler, "I just took gigs. You didn't have to play anything [original]. The less you played, the better it was. . . . Anytime you play your horn, it helps you. If you get down [put yourself into it], you can help yourself even in a rock 'n roll band. But I didn't help myself."[4] Coltrane primarily played tenor but still played alto on occasion where written ensemble passages required it. (He had done this for Gillespie after Heath left.)

Coltrane continued to study and practice relentlessly. He still saw Dennis Sandole for lessons on a regular basis and got together with fellow musicians to exchange ideas. A new influence was the legendary pianist Hasaan Ibn Ali. Born in Philadelphia in 1931, Hasaan, as he was called, toured with the R&B band of Joe Morris as a teenager, may have joined Vinson around the time Coltrane left, and then freelanced around home, where he became known as an original composer and theorist. He was interested in the properties of fourths, in chord progressions that moved by thirds or seconds instead of by fifths, in playing a variety of scales and arpeggios against each chord—all of which figured prominently in Coltrane's music later on. Saxophonist Odean Pope (born 1938) spent quite a bit of time at Hassan's house when he was a youth from around 1954, and he recalls Coltrane being there often. Pope says that he and Coltrane would work on Hasaan's compositions and delve into theoretical matters, sometimes spending several sessions poring over one problem. Pope recalls Hasaan using a voicing of B-flat, E and A (the seventh, third, and thirteenth) for a C-dominant seventh chord, before it became common in the 1960s. Coltrane and Pope would also get together on their own to explore such matters and to read through classical duets.[5]

In January 1952, Coltrane recorded with the Gay Crosse group in Philadelphia and perhaps in Nashville as well. Crosse, said Coltrane, "had a little band. He used to be with Louis Jordan. He had a little band that was patterned after Louis' band. He sang and played something like Louis" (Blume). Jordan, a leading R&B artist who primarily played alto and sang, generally led a small band that included a tenor saxophonist. Crosse is mentioned in the music news from his home town of Cleveland as early as November 1945, when he attracted notice in a music and dance revue entitled "Jumping the Blues."[6] Phil Schaap interviewed a drummer named Wes Landers who had played with Crosse around the early part of 1949. Landers said that Crosse would hold the sax as he directed the band but did not actually play it. He also claimed that Joe Alexander, a tenor player with the group (who later recorded with Tadd Dameron and as a leader), was an influence on Coltrane.

The Crosse titles were issued on small labels, and several remain unknown even to dedicated collectors. Of the titles that have been issued on CD, two, "Gotta Stop Lovin' You" and "I Got A Feelin'," have tenor saxophone solos. The latter is a squawky-sounding solo that I cannot associate with Coltrane, contrary to Priestley (70). The one on "Gotta Stop" is in a meaty Lester Young style that could possibly be Coltrane doing his best to fit in. Perhaps the most likely candidate to be a Coltrane item would be the serene lead alto playing on "Bitter Sweet," a Hale Smith composition.[7] Smith recalls his first meeting with Crosse: "Crosse was an arranger. This piece was originally named after my girlfriend, who is now my wife, Juanita, and I was in the studio making a demo of this, and Gay walked in. . . . It was written for a trumpet solo, and the trumpet player was a brilliant player named Howard Roberts—who [later] had the Howard Roberts chorale and conducted a number of Broadway shows. Gay took a liking to the piece and asked if I would do an arrangement of it for his little group." This was in the late 1940s. "Gay hired me to write four arrangements a week, and he paid ten dollars each arrangement." He describes Crosse as an "average" tenor saxophonist, not in Jordan's league, basically a commercial artist, who died fairly young, perhaps before he was fifty. Smith says Crosse played some of Jordan's charts.

Crosse rarely toured outside Cleveland, but Smith remembers the occasion with Coltrane because Crosse returned with a contract showing that he'd recorded Smith's tune. Crosse told him the recording company had suggested the name "Bitter Sweet" so as to avoid confusion with an old Spanish folksong "Juanita." "I never did care for the title," Smith says. "I never did think the performance was very good," he adds—the trumpet part is supposed to have a lot more punch.[8] Smith doesn't know why Coltrane played. He recalls that one Baron Lee (I presume not the 1930s bandleader, who was not known as an instrumentalist) was the regular altoist. Perhaps he was unavailable, or, Smith wonders, maybe Coltrane played tenor in place of Crosse. Smith believes that "Coltrane was never a real member of the group. Crosse went out on tour. . . .

When he came back he said 'I hired a kid out there to fill in and he's on the record and his name is John Coltrane.'" If some of the titles were indeed made in Nashville, then Coltrane may have been with the group for a short tour. Saxophonist James Moody reinforced that suggestion by recalling that he heard Coltrane on alto with Crosse in Cleveland.[9]

Starting in April 1952, Coltrane and his friend Specs Wright toured with alto saxophonist Earl Bostic (1913–65).[10] Coltrane stayed with Bostic until early December.[11] Coltrane and Benny Golson, both in Harlem with separate bands around 1950, had heard Bostic sitting in at Minton's. Bostic had extensive experience as a swing soloist but was popular at this time for a flamboyant style on ballads and R&B numbers. Although Bostic was not a modern jazz improviser, saxophonists held him in awe because of his fabulous technical mastery. Golson, who worked with Bostic for several years in the mid-1950s, recalls:

He could play! Best technician I ever heard in my life! Charlie Parker couldn't touch him—I'm not talking about style, I'm talking about technique on the horn. There was nothing he couldn't do. He was amazing. He was from another planet. Bird would step back and listen to him [if they shared a bandstand]. Bird knew what he was doing, the technique and how difficult it was. Bostic had the circular breathing together [breathing in through the nose while you're exhaling so there is no pause], he could transpose at sight, he played the clarinet and he could play in any key. I asked him, "How did you get like that?" He said, "Growing up in Oklahoma, I knew I was going to New York, so I approached it like a job. I would start [practicing] at 8 o'clock, take a lunch break from 12 to 1, and play to 5, every day except Sunday." And John Coltrane did the same thing, more or less!

Coltrane said, "I enjoyed it—they had some true music. He's a very gifted musician. He showed me a lot of things on my horn. He has fabulous technical facilities on his instrument and knows many a trick."[12] In particular, it is likely that Bostic shared with Coltrane his knowledge of the high range of the saxophone—something, remember, that Coltrane and Heath had studied from books—and his technique of circular breathing. George Goldsmith, who played drums in one of Bostic's last bands in the early 1960s, reports that Bostic even taught him how to do circular breathing, believing that it would help the drummer to phrase like a wind instrument. So it would be reasonable to assume that Coltrane would have learned about circular breathing from Bostic.

During this period, Coltrane was seeing a woman named Elaine Gross. It was a serious enough relationship that one of the local newspaper columnists referred to her as Elaine "Coltrane,"[13] though they were not married. She was a friend of Heath's girlfriend Connie, and they used to double-date and hang out.

Heath believes that Elaine was also an addict. Coltrane probably meant Elaine when he later told August Blume, off the tape, that his woman in the early 1950s was a junkie and caused a lot of trouble for him. But Coltrane continued to try and live an honorable life, despite his habit. Probably sometime in March 1952, he had purchased a house on North Thirty-third Street, in the Strawberry Mansion neighborhood of Philadelphia. Up to this time, he and Mary, his mother Alice, Mary's mother Bettie, and even his friend James Kinzer were still living in the two apartments on North Twelfth Street. But now Coltrane took advantage of one of his benefits as a veteran, a G.I. loan, in order to provide better for his family and friend. The building on North Twelfth was taken down and that whole neighborhood rebuilt around this time, so it may be that they had to move anyway. The Veterans Administration stood behind G.I. loans, guaranteeing the bank or other lender against loss up to 60 percent of a home loan with a maximum of seventy-five hundred dollars. The interest rate was to be no higher than 5 1/4 percent per year.[14] The total cost of the house was $5,416, with 10 percent down, so the loan would have been sufficient. His mother helped with the down payment with her savings from domestic work.[15]

But before they could move in, his Aunt Bettie, Mary's mother, had a stroke and was hospitalized. Mary recalls that Bettie stayed in the hospital for several months and passed away on June 2, 1952, while John was on the road with Bostic. Both John and Jimmy Heath came to the funeral and burial at the family gravesite in High Point. Shortly afterward, when Coltrane had some breathing space between gigs with Bostic, he, Mary, Alice, and Kinzer moved into the house on Thirty-third Street. (Kinzer went off on his own after about two years.) They were the third black family on the block. John lived there whenever he was in town. He'd also take advantage of his newfound space by holding jam sessions and rehearsals there using his mother's upright piano— John Glenn, a fellow saxophonist, helped move it from Twelfth Street.

During 1953 it seems that Coltrane freelanced around home. He worked with a band led by Specs Wright and probably appeared in a variety of situations. With Wright, the paper reported, "Specs' Special arrangement by piano man Coletrain titled 'Sambo Blues' is fine."[16] This tune has never been found, but it indicates that Coltrane was still writing and contributing to the groups he played with. In these years, as Coltrane said, he took whatever came his way, and he did what the job required. In Bostic's band, for example, he had occasionally to sing backup vocals with the other wind players (as one can see in the photo in Fujioka, 20). Some bands required other kinds of showmanship, such as "walking the bar," which literally meant walking on top of the bar while playing a wild saxophone solo. Bassist Reggie Workman, who later worked with him, remembers Coltrane walking the bar somewhere in Philadelphia—it may have been the Point Bar near the Blue Note, with some kind of put-together band. Golson once entered the Point Bar when Coltrane was on the bar, and Coltrane was so embarrassed that he said "Oh, no!" and walked right out of the club.[17] For all of Coltrane's good-naturedness—and he never seems to have complained about this kind of thing—he did seem to look back on these experiences with mixed feelings.[18] Steve Davis recalled one occasion that Coltrane actually declined to walk the bar (Thomas, 66).

According to columnist Jimmie Brown, in 1953 musical styles were changing and audiences were going to have to get used to less extravagant performance styles: "Gone are the days (with a few exceptions such as Big Jay McNeely) when tenormen wipe up the bandstand with their vines [clothing], disrobe while blowing, and stand on their heads while making music and mayhem. . . . Some maintain that the performers are cheating the customers when they simply stand and play their instruments as opposed to the disrobers who run up and down the bars upsetting the drinks."[19] But for the moment, Coltrane still had to put on a show.

It was probably sometime between 1953 and 1955 that he worked with another show band, Daisy Mae and the Hep Cats.[20] Daisy Mae Diggs had recorded as early as 1949 but only used the Hep Cats name on her recordings from 1955. Pianist Bill Evans, later a colleague in the Davis group, says that Coltrane described the Hep Cats as "the kind of band you'd find in Las Vegas lounges ten years later. Daisy Mae would shimmy out front in a sparkling dress while her husband the guitar player was boogieing behind her. John said the guitarist had discovered the lost chord, because it sounded as if he'd found the one chord that fitted everything—a chromatic crunch" (Thomas, 66). Vance Wilson remembers Coltrane playing with this group. When Wilson was with the Chris Powell band at Wildwood, on the tip of New Jersey, Coltrane was out there with Daisy Mae at Club Esquire. They'd meet in the afternoons and "have a couple of beers or whatever."[21]

Coltrane also worked at some point with Bullmoose Jackson, an R&B vocalist and tenor saxophonist (Simpkins, 44; Thomas, 66). Bullmoose, whose real name was Benjamin Clarence Jackson, was born April 22, 1920, in Cleveland. He joined Lucky Millinder in 1944 and began to lead his own groups after his vocal on "I Love You, Yes I Do" became a big hit in 1948. If Coltrane did work with him, it would have been an occasional gig in Philadelphia, nothing long-term. Coltrane's good friend Golson toured with Jackson frequently between July 1951 and March 1953 and says Coltrane was not there during that period.[22] Jackson played in Philadelphia quite a bit, so Coltrane could have worked with him in August 1949, August 1950, June 1951, or after 1953. Golson remembers that Jackson had an excellent band that included many of Coltrane's other friends, among them at various times Johnny Coles, bassist Jymie Merritt, and Philly Joe Jones; Tadd Dameron played piano and arranged the music during Golson's tenure.

By March 1954, or perhaps earlier, Coltrane joined the band of his original role model on the alto, Johnny Hodges. Hodges was an essential voice in the Ellington orchestra, except for the period from March 9, 1951, when he debuted his own septet at the Blue Note in Chicago, through August 1955. During a Hodges date in Philadelphia in April 1954, Coltrane attracted the attention of his hometown boosters: "Glad to have seen my old friend COL-TRANE in the group," wrote one. "He is getting greater with his tenor sax all the time."[23] During the first part of the Hodges stint, the band was enlarged to about ten or twelve musicians.[24] It included Coltrane's hometown colleagues Richie Powell (Bud's brother) on piano, the younger Jimmy Johnson on drums, and Benny Golson. Golson writes that "Johnny wanted to enlarge the group to play some one-nighters with Billy Eckstine, Ruth Brown and the Clovers, so John told him to call me. As we did the tour, every night I marveled at the things I heard [Coltrane] play. To save money (we weren't making very much) we became roommates and stayed at a Y.M.C.A. (pension-hotel for men) in whatever town we played, even sleeping in the same bed at times."[25] Golson further told me: "That tour must have lasted three or four weeks, something like that. It was not a jazz gig. . . . I remember we played one place in Ohio . . . and there was a fellow that was singing that Eckstine added to the show who had a harp behind him, and he joined us. I can't remember who he was or what the tune was, but he joined the tour and had this woman harpist with him. He had a spot—we played the background music behind him. But the harp was sitting out front as he was singing—looked good, I guess. He had a thing on the charts that was playing on the jukeboxes." This is interesting, because Coltrane later had a fascination with the harp.

After that tour the group became a septet. The LP that Hodges recorded in the summer of 1954 featured no Coltrane solos.[26] Fortunately a high-quality private tape of the band playing an engagement around June of that year has been preserved. In that more informal setting, Coltrane is featured in a short solo on "Thru for the Night" (listed as "Sideways" on the LP issue, Enigma 1052), where his relationship to Hawkins is evident in his edgy sound and double-timing arpeggios.[27] He is also featured on two blistering thirty-two-bar choruses of Ellington's "In a Mellotone," and throughout "Don't Blame Me" and Hodges's hit number, "Castle Rock." He can even be heard practicing briefly, repeating a pattern a couple of times, after "In a Mellotone."

On "Don't Blame Me," a pretty ballad, Coltrane sounds substantially different from his 1951 recordings. He plays faster and with a lighter tone, and many distinctive formulas may be heard, formulas that would later be recognized as his trademarks. (Thomas, 65, says that in concert Coltrane was also featured on "Smoke Gets in Your Eyes.") By way of contrast, "Castle Rock" is a gutbucket piece that requires Coltrane to perform in the raunchy style he was used to from his work with R&B bands. It is a fascinating document of this important aspect of his formative years. Most of the solo consists of honking low notes, wailing high notes, and a variety of glissandos. There is one run that sounds like Paul Gonsalves. While it's clear that Coltrane is fitting in with a certain expected style here, he also manages to put his own stamp on it. His approach is quite different, and more visceral, than the popular recording Hodges had made of this piece featuring Al Sears.

Coltrane was unqualified in his praise for "Rabbit," as Hodges was sometimes known: "I really enjoyed that job. I liked every tune in the book. Nothing was superficial. It all had meaning, and it all swung. And the confidence with which Rabbit plays; I wish I could play with the confidence that he does. But besides enjoying my stay with Johnny musically, I also enjoyed it because I was getting first hand information about things that happened way before my time" ("Coltrane on Coltrane"). In November 1961, when asked who his favorite musician was, "There was hardly a pause for thought. 'Johnny Hodges, the world's greatest saxophone player,' he said."[28]

But Coltrane's drug habit got in the way again, and he was let go (Thomas, 66). It is said that this happened in Los Angeles, and there Coltrane met Eric Dolphy, who loaned him money to get back East. If true, this was a highly significant meeting, for Dolphy was to become one of the musicians Coltrane loved most.[29]

He must have left Hodges near the beginning of September 1954. We may read in the *Philadelphia Tribune* for September 18 that "Mop Dudley and his Collates are still serving musical platters at Pitts' Musicalounge, 13th and Poplar Sts. Featured on tenor sax is John Coltrane, whose horn has been spotlighted in some of the country's leading bands. Two personable lassies, Dot Cornish and Ronny Douglass, are featured respectively on bass and piano. Leaderman Dudley is, of course, playing his characteristically tasteful, and soulful trumpet. The musical offerings of the group are very diversified, ranging from the lush, beautiful show tunes to house-rocking rhythms."[30]

So Coltrane was back to freelancing around town. Bassist Steve Davis recalled an engagement with Big Maybelle—who by this time had made a name and was not with Joe Webb—in Cleveland (Thomas, 66–67). Trumpeter Ted Curson (born in Philadelphia in 1935) recalls that on the last night of 1954 Coltrane was without a job: "I always admired his playing and he used to write out little things for me, the blues changes and stuff. But he never had a job, and one New Year's Eve—New Year's Eve, people work when they never worked the whole year!—well, he had no job. So I took him on my job [in Vineland, New Jersey], and he played 'Nancy with the Laughing Face,' I'll never forget that. I never heard anything so great, so intense, with so much feeling" (Priestley, 29).

It's even possible that Coltrane worked as the leader of a small group that alternated sets with his early idol and acquaintance Charlie Parker at the Downbeat Club. The club's owner, Jack Fields, recalled "I used Coltrane as a single. . . . When he would come into the club, I used him with Bird, which was incongruous, but it worked."³¹

During this period, Coltrane also played in several contexts with Bill Carney, a singer, percussionist, and impresario active in Philadelphia since the late 1940s. In 1954, "Mister C," as he is known, put together a trio called the Hi-Tones with the marvelous organist Shirley Scott (later it was Trudy Pitts, who became Carney's wife), drummer Al "Tootie" Heath (the youngest of the brothers, born in 1935), and Coltrane. Coltrane felt that this was a serious jazz group, telling Gitler, "We were too musical for certain rooms." Scott recalls: "It was a great experience. Coltrane was phenomenal even then. We played in and around Philadelphia on and off for at least a year, including New Jersey, and to Buffalo a couple of times. We played bebop (including 'Half Nelson' and 'Groovin' High'), straight-ahead music." Scott wrote some originals, and she thinks Coltrane may have written one or two. She also remembers that he liked to play on "Time Was," a standard song that he was to record in May 1957. "We used to play it in the key of A-flat [just like the LP]. We did rehearse a lot, and we had a lot of arrangements, most of them John's." That is, Coltrane would have his versions of other people's tunes. This was not a full-time job; Scott recalls that Coltrane was in and out of town on gigs.

There were some other significant gigs during this period. Periodically in the early 1950s, Miles Davis would play in Philadelphia at Club 421 and elsewhere with a pickup band including James Forman on piano. Sometimes, Forman relates, Sonny Rollins would play saxophone, and sometimes Coltrane. The infrequent association between Coltrane and Davis was soon to become critical.

In September 1955, Coltrane was working at Spider Kelly's in Philadelphia with organist Jimmy Smith. Smith, born in 1925 and later to become a hit-maker, had been attracting local attention since he played as a regular member of a trio called the Sonotones as early as 1952. Coltrane told Blume, "It was Jimmy Smith for about a couple of weeks before I went with Miles—the organist. Wow! I'd wake up in the middle of the night, man, hearing that organ. Yeah, those chords screaming at me."

Smith was reportedly interested in keeping Coltrane. But at the end of September, two things happened that would turn Coltrane's life around. Miles Davis hired him. And he married the Muslim woman who would help him out of his self-destructive pattern. Many young blacks were turning to Islam in an attempt to find a church that was not white dominated. Some of them felt that Christianity had never really accepted them as equals, even though they believed in Christ as fervently as any white person—more so than most. Perhaps in Islam they could find God and also feel more accepted among others of their faith. Gillespie wrote that many blacks found that as Muslims they could actually escape the stigma of being "colored": some establishments would accept them as Muslims but not as blacks.[32] Among the beboppers, Art Blakey, Idrees Sulieman, Yusef Lateef, Ahmad Jamal, and many others had become Muslims during the late 1940s and early 1950s. Most followed the traditional Arab (and Asian) practice of Islam; a smaller group were members of the Nation of Islam, which developed its own tenets under the leadership of Elijah Muhammad.

Islam was a particularly strong influence in Philadelphia. One of the local tenor stars, Lynn Hope, wore a turban when he performed and spoke of traveling to Mecca; his pianist sister and drummer brother were also Muslim. James "Sax" Young was another convert. Coltrane told Blume he was aware of "the Muslim thing" when he first came to Philadelphia in 1943. Later, Lateef encouraged him to pursue it. Lateef left Gillespie's band around the time John came in—there may have been a little overlap. Lateef suggested John read the Koran, the poet Kahlil Gibran, and Krishnamurti; Bill Barron gave him a book on Indian yoga (Thomas, 47), perhaps *Autobiography of a Yogi* by Paramahansa Yogananda (1893–1952), which first appeared in 1946.

Aisha Davis (who would marry McCoy Tyner in 1959) and her sisters were traditional Muslim. Her older sister Rosemary, known as Khadijah, was a jazz singer; she was married to bassist Steve Davis (unrelated of course), and she sang with Calvin Massey's group, performing mostly on weekends. Massey and Steve Davis were both friends of Coltrane, and Aisha remembers going with her sister from their mother's house on Van Pelt, near Twenty-first Street, to John's house on Thirty-third Street for jam sessions on Saturdays. Sometimes the sessions would be held at the home of Khadijah and Steve Davis. Gillespie, Sonny Rollins, and others would come to these sessions—even Charlie Parker was there once, Aisha recalls. At one of the sessions at Khadijah's house in June 1954 (Thomas, 68), John met the singer's good friend Naima, and soon a relationship blossomed.

Naima had been born Juanita Austin in 1926, probably January 2, in a small town in North Carolina.[33] This background was no doubt an instant bond between them; like Coltrane's family, the Austins were all Philadelphians now. Naima, or Nita—short for Juanita—as John called her, was the single mother of a daughter, Antonia, born in late 1949 or early 1950. Her Muslim name was Syeeda (or Saeeda, as she now spells it). She lived with her mother at 1816 North Seventh Street, according to a postcard Coltrane wrote to "Neet" in June 1955 (Simpkins, 258).

In Naima, Coltrane found a person he trusted, who would support him in his career and in his efforts to shake his addictions. By joining with her he was in a way reuniting himself with North Carolina, resolving that painful and unexpressed gap in his life, at least for a while. Coltrane was to write "Nita," "Naima," and probably "Wise One" for her, and "Syeeda's Song Flute" for her daughter.[34] When Naima joined John in Baltimore during his first week with

Miles Davis, they decided it was time to make the commitment, and they were married there by a minister C. Franklin on Monday, October 3, 1955, with the whole band as best men.[35] For a while Nita and Saeeda lived in the house on Thirty-third Street along with Mary and Alice. John joined them when he was not traveling with Davis.

Davis (May 26, 1926–September 29, 1991) had been through his own struggle with heroin, but he had quit around the beginning of 1954. His appearance with a rhythm section at the second Newport Jazz Festival in July 1955 woke everybody up to his brilliance and led to a new contract with Columbia Records and much publicity. All eyes were now on Davis, and all ears were on his new tenor saxophonist. With a recording contract, a position with a nationally known jazz group, and a new love, things were indeed looking up for Coltrane.

10

The Turning Point: Miles and Monk

The period from the time Coltrane joined Miles Davis in late September 1955 through the end of 1957 was critical. This was his shot at the big time, and the beginning of his fame—and notoriety—as a soloist. But his drug problem was holding him back, and he finally had to make the commitment once and for all to try and beat it.

Davis had been working with Sonny Rollins, but Rollins had decided to take a year off from performing to rid himself of his own heroin habit. In early September, Davis had tried out John Gilmore, an innovative tenorist known for his work with Sun Ra, at a Philadelphia club, but he wasn't quite what Davis wanted. "And then," said Davis, "Philly Joe brought up Coltrane." They brought Coltrane to New York for several days of rehearsals—probably in early September—but he and Davis didn't quite click, musically or personally. Coltrane returned to Philadelphia to work with Jimmy Smith.[1] But Davis already had gigs lined up as result of his success at Newport that July, and he and Philly Joe persuaded Coltrane to join. Davis said, "We practically had to beg him to come join the band," but he thinks Coltrane was playing hard to get (*Miles*, 195). (John got Odean Pope to take over with Smith at Spider Kelly's.)[2] Coltrane joined the band at the Club Las Vegas in Baltimore, for a gig beginning Tuesday, September 27, 1955; Naima came down on the weekend.[3] Soon, Davis recalled, "As a group, on and off stage, we hit it off together. . . . And faster than I could have imagined, the music that we were playing together was just unbelievable." He hadn't been sure about Coltrane, "But after we started playing together for a while, I knew that this guy was a bad motherfucker who was just the voice I needed on tenor to set off my voice. . . . The group I had with Coltrane made me and him a legend."[4]

That's not to say that there was no controversy. Coltrane was only a few months younger than Davis, but whereas Davis had been recording since 1945 and had been featured with all the jazz greats, Coltrane was unknown to the public. So to the world at large, Davis was an established artist who had discovered this young talent Coltrane. Partly for this reason, that he was seemingly some young kid without strong credentials, Coltrane was an easy target for critics.

For example, Nat Hentoff, reviewing the first LP released by the group, delighted that Davis was in "wonderfully cohesive form," but criticized Coltrane for sounding too much like his influences, Gordon, Stitt, and perhaps Rollins, showing a "general lack of individuality."[5] An English critic named Edgar Jackson was guarded in his praise. Writing that Davis "can be a most exciting player at almost any tempo," he continues: "One can say much the same about John Coltrane—except that he will try to say too much at once, thereby tending to befog his meaning and lessen his impact."[6] But Coltrane already had supporters as well. Bob Dawbarn, reviewing the Prestige LP *Relaxin'*, wrote that "Coltrane and Garland are two of the most underrated musicians in jazz and Coltrane in particular plays magnificently throughout. I particularly like his lyrical solos on '[You're My] Everything' and aggressive swooping on '[I Could Write a] Book.'"[7]

Sy Johnson, composer and pianist, remembers that when the Davis quintet first came to Los Angeles to play at Jazz City early in 1956, "Nobody knew what to expect. It literally blew everybody out of the water. It destroyed West Coast jazz overnight. I had to convince people to listen to Coltrane. They would say, 'When that tenor player plays I just tune him out and listen to the bass player.' . . . One problem was that everybody [was sure] the tenor player was going to be Sonny Rollins." Johnson recalls that one night at Jazz City, Stan Getz sat in—a great musician whom Coltrane respected. He says that Davis had to order Coltrane not to leave the bandstand when Getz came on; Coltrane didn't want to get into a cutting session against the great Getz. But Getz was a little out of practice—having had recent drug problems—"and he had a tough time playing with that rhythm section, so Trane just mopped him up." People were impressed "to see Trane rise to the occasion and cut Stan," and this may have changed a few minds in favor of Coltrane.

"I got to know the entire band during those weeks," recalls Johnson. "Coltrane was very strung out [on drugs] but was quite willing to talk about his musical problems. He couldn't get the horn to work the way he wanted to—he was aware that he was not doing what he wanted to. Nevertheless, there were a few of us who got an immediate positive reaction to Trane. He wasn't the greatest tenor player I ever heard, but what he was doing was good and interesting and worked well with the band." Johnson also says Coltrane was glad to meet somebody who appreciated him.[8]

At first Coltrane was apparently unsure what Davis wanted. Davis admitted in his autobiography that even at the first rehearsals, in September 1955, he had been hard on Coltrane: "Trane liked to ask all these motherfucking questions back then about what he should or shouldn't play. Man, fuck that shit; to me he was a professional musician and I have always wanted whoever played with me to find their own place in the music. So my silence and evil looks probably turned him off."[9] Coltrane explained how that felt from his point of view: "Miles is a strange guy: he doesn't talk much and he rarely discusses music. You always have the impression that he's in a bad mood, and that what concerns others doesn't interest him or move him. It's very difficult, under these conditions, to know exactly what to do, and maybe that's the reason I just ended up doing what I wanted. . . . Miles's reactions are completely unpredictable: he'll play with us for a few measures, then—you never know when—he'll leave us on our own. And if you ask him something about music, you never know how he's going to take it. You always have to listen carefully to stay in the same mood as he!" (Postif).

In 1961, when a French critic asked Coltrane if he had played so far out because Davis told him to—thinking that "the public liked novelty"— "Coltrane stifled a silent laugh: 'Miles? Tell me something? That's a good one! No, Miles never told me anything of the sort. I always played exactly how I wanted.'"[10]

Coltrane, always his own worst critic, had mixed feelings about his performance in the group. He was delighted to be with the group, saying in "Coltrane on Coltrane," "I always felt I wanted to play with Miles. He really put me to work." He was challenged in a positive way, but he wasn't quite pleased with himself: "I began trying to add to what I was playing because of Miles's group. Being there, I just couldn't be satisfied any longer with what I was doing. The standards were so high, and I felt that I wasn't really contributing like I should."[11] And he also seemed regretful of time lost: "All the things I started to do in 1955, when I went with him, were some of the things I felt I should have done in '47–'48" ("Coltrane on Coltrane").

Later, in a little-known 1961 interview with Kitty Grime published in the English magazine *Jazz News,* he was downright self-critical: "When I first joined Miles in 1955 I had a lot to learn. I felt I was lacking in general musicianship. I had all kinds of technical problems—for example, I didn't have the right mouthpiece—and I hadn't the necessary harmonic understanding. I am quite ashamed of those early records I made with Miles. Why he picked me, I don't know. Maybe he saw something in my playing that he hoped would grow. I had this desire, which I think we all have, to be as original as I could, and as honest as I could be. But there were so many musical conclusions I hadn't arrived at, that I felt inadequate. All this was naturally frustrating in those days, and it came through in the music."[12]

At this time, Davis was finishing out a commitment with Prestige Records and beginning what was to be a career-building relationship with Columbia

Records. Producer George Avakian says, "It was my brother who told me, 'Don't wait any more, Miles is ripe.' . . . So I went ahead and did it. I didn't want to wait until his Prestige contract expired, because who knows what would happen after that?" Avakian began a long and complicated negotiation with Prestige, who insisted that Davis finish out his contractual commitment with them by recording several more albums. Coltrane's first recording session with Davis, on October 27, 1955, was actually for Columbia but was not issued for a year and a half.

Even though they were recorded during the same period, the Prestige and Columbia recordings differ from each other considerably. Prestige was a low-budget informal operation (reportedly musicians were often paid in cash), and the owner, Bob Weinstock, encouraged musicians to record one take of each number and to get through as much material as possible at each session. Weinstock explains that, for one thing, noted engineer Rudy Van Gelder did not need to make takes just to get proper balances. And Weinstock did not believe in saving alternate takes if they were second best: "It wasn't fair to the musicians. . . . We didn't do everything in one take, by any means. But if they said, 'Let's do another one,' Rudy would say, 'One minute!' and he'd erase the take." He'd reuse the same tape. They kept very few alternates, only when it was clear that both takes had value or, conversely, that neither was perfect. Weinstock says it was not a matter of saving tape. "It was a matter of ethics to me. I didn't want bad takes around. Also Miles would leave it up to me. If I thought a take was okay he was satisfied. He didn't listen [back to the take]. He'd say, 'Next!'"

Weinstock wanted spontaneity, and he felt that the more you fussed with a record, the more you lost the freshness. This also meant that original compositions were fine, but not if they were complicated numbers that required rehearsals or retakes. "They could bring in all the music they liked. . . . We'd try it. And if it didn't go, I'd say, OK, forget it." And Weinstock would suggest a standard or a blues instead. Prestige would serve as the publisher of any originals. This saved money for the label (over paying another publisher), and if other artists recorded their songs they paid royalties to Prestige (a penny per recording sold). This gave the musicians a source of additional income. There may have been drug problems, Weinstock allows, but if so, the musicians kept this to themselves and were fully professional and reliable.

Prestige casually introduced a policy that was actually an innovation in the whole concept of making records. Sometimes they would issue a performance intact, even with Davis snapping his fingers, counting off or with the players making comments at the ends or beginnings of numbers. They had done this already—before Davis's voice was reduced to its famous whisper after an operation—on "Bluing" from 1951 and on some issues of his first take of "The Man I Love" from 1954. This way, instead of aiming for a polished gem, one could let the audience in on the process of recording. It appears to be Coltrane who says, "Can I have the beer opener?" after "Woody 'n You." The most famous moment begins "If I Were a Bell," when Davis, apparently in response to Van Gelder's request for the title of the next piece, quipped "I'll play it and tell you what it is later."[13] Weinstock recalls, "This started because of Rudy Van Gelder. I used to always edit with him, and we'd hear that and he'd say, 'Why don't you leave it in? It's historic hearing these guys say a few words.' You're supposed to be quiet for about twenty seconds after each take, in order to get a clean edit, but if someone talked we decided to leave it in." In the 1960s the Beatles and others would include studio chatter on their recordings, but at this time it was rare.[14]

Recording for Columbia was more formal. Each number was recorded for as many takes as needed to get it right, and usually all the tape was saved. Complicated arrangements were a plus—they added to the polish of the finished product. And splicing was fine if the saxophone solo on one take was good and the trumpet solo on the other was preferred, or even in the middle of a solo. For example "Ah-Leu-Cha" from the first session on October 27, 1955 has a splice right in the middle of the trumpet solo. Producer George Avakian explains: "If something was wrong, and it could be improved upon, it should be, and Miles agreed with that. . . . I wanted to get the best possible results of the artist, and if it was necessary to improve upon a peformance by correcting fluffs or making splices in order to produce the best possible results, then that was the way to go." Far from looking at editing as a distortion of true jazz, Davis delighted in the new possibilities of tape, and he tended to trust his producer's instincts. On the later sessions, as the band became more experienced, less splicing was necessary, and by *Kind of Blue* in 1959 there was virtually none.

The first Columbia album was named *'Round about Midnight,* a title that Dizzy Gillespie and others—but not the composer—had sometimes used for Thelonious Monk's "'Round Midnight." It was released on March 4, 1957, after the Prestige contract expired. (Prestige continued to release its material over the next few years.) For many the Columbia LP had a stronger impact, in sound quality as well as performance, than the Prestige ones, for all their virtues. Ira Gitler recalls, "I could hear something good on the Prestige records, but Coltrane sounded a bit tentative. But when I heard him in person I was knocked out. Coltrane sounds so much better on the Columbia album." (At the time listeners were unaware that the Columbia LP had been recorded over such a long time span.)

"'Round Midnight" was recorded on September 10, 1956, in a smoky, evocative arrangement that became a jukebox hit in black neighborhoods in its 45 RPM release. (The quintet recorded the same arrangement for Prestige on October 26, but that version remains less well known.) The arrangement is said to be by Gil Evans. Producer George Avakian is quite sure that Evans wasn't there. The composer and conductor Leonard Bernstein was there, because the main purpose of the session was to record a version of "Sweet Sue" for Bernstein's *What Is Jazz?* album. However, Avakian concedes, "It may be true that Gil had something to do with the arrangement of ''Round Midnight,' because Miles did not record that for me right away, although that's the first piece I wanted from him. [Davis had played it at Newport in 1955.] Now it may be—I don't remember any discussion like this—that Miles wanted to figure out a very strong interpretation of ''Round Midnight' and finally he got Gil to write something out for him. But he never mentioned that." Avakian doesn't recall seeing any sheet music for that piece, and there is only one known take (after a short false start), so it must have been well rehearsed.

In any case, the arrangement draws heavily on precedents set by Dizzy Gillespie, who was not only a mentor to Coltrane but the early idol of Davis. The Columbia recording uses the added beginning and ending that Gillespie introduced on records as early as February 1946. By 1948 Gillespie's big band was playing a chart that featured a shouting passage between choruses (or, on a live recording from July 1948, at the start, replacing the other introduction). Davis's own 1953 recording of "'Round Midnight" was also based on the Gillespie version.[15]

Davis's solo on the Columbia version is hushed and confidential, enhanced by his sizzling Harmon mute sound. After the break, Coltrane solos over a double-time feeling in the rhythm section—the chords go by just as slow as for Davis, but the drums and bass accent between the beats behind Coltrane to give more motion. Coltrane's solo is exotic, daring. It has a soulful sound and unusual ornaments. It is a mixture of balladic paraphrase—that is, using notes of Monk's theme—and technical passages.

At this time about half of Davis's repertory consisted of bebop material, including two other Monk items, "Straight No Chaser" and "Well You Needn't," Gillespie's "Woody 'n You"[16] and his coauthored "Two Bass Hit" and "Salt Peanuts," Parker's "Ah-Leu-Cha," "Tadd's Delight" by Dameron, Rollins's "Oleo" and "Airegin," Eddie Vinson's "Tune Up" and "Four" (both claimed by Davis as his own compositions), and Davis's own "Half Nelson" and "Budo," the latter coauthored with Bud Powell. The other half of Davis's repertory consisted primarily of show tunes. As an arranger, Davis acknowledged the influence of the highly stylized and tasteful approach of pianist Ahmad Jamal. From 1951 through 1955, Jamal was using the then standard instrumentation of guitar and bass—as featured by Nat Cole, Art Tatum, Oscar Peterson, and many others—and he had already recorded versions of "Billy Boy," "Ahmad's Blues," and "Just Squeeze Me."[17] These were all part of Davis's repertory at this time, although "Billy Boy" was only released in a version featuring Davis's rhythm section in 1958. As a soloist, Davis constantly challenged himself and, by example, his sidemen to create meaningful and original statements over these familiar chord progressions. His music partly relied on this contrast of asthetics, this dialogue (as musicologist Gary Tomlinson might say)[18] between the world of light and pretty and theatrical, and the guts and intensity of the blues and the black American experience.

But Coltrane was struggling to reconcile his two worlds, that of a succesful artist and of a self-abusing addict. Coltrane's heroin and alcohol habits were hampering his performance again, and he made several attempts to quit. Coltrane, Naima, and Saeeda had moved to Manhattan in June 1956, staying in hotels (Simpkins, 54) or at Paul Chambers's Brooklyn apartment (Thomas, 77). The Davis band was playing quite a bit at the Café Bohemia on 15 Barrow Street off Sheridan Square in Greenwich Village—they were there in June and for the month of September. Ira Gitler saw the group many times: "At the Bohemia a lot of times you wouldn't see Coltrane between sets. He would be in the basement practicing, and he was drinking a mixture of wine and beer. I guess he was trying to kick heroin. He just wasn't too communicative." So when Davis was invited back to the Bohemia for the last half of October, he used Sonny Rollins. Some authors have called this the first firing of Coltrane by Davis, but if so, it didn't last long. Coltrane must have shown some improvement, as he and Rollins were both onstage toward the end of the engagement, and Coltrane was back for Davis's Prestige recording session on October 26. Still, Davis gave Coltrane a warning before leaving for a tour of Europe as a single with the Birdland All-Stars from November 2–25. While Davis was away, Coltrane moved back to the house on Thirty-third street in Philadelphia (Simpkins, 55).

When Davis returned at the end of November, Coltrane went back on the road with him. But apparently the saxophonist's performance was still erratic. Davis said in his autobiography, "He'd be playing in clothes that looked like he had slept in them for days, all wrinkled up and dirty and shit. Then, he'd be standing up there when he wasn't nodding—picking his nose and sometimes eating it" (212). Alto saxophonist Jackie McLean, working with Art Blakey at the Cafe Bohemia opposite Davis in early April 1957, recalls that Coltrane was making progress in his valiant effort to quit drugs:

> He stopped using drugs right at the beginning of that job and he was going through cold turkey [without the help of any interim or substitute drugs] but he came to work every night being sick. Of course he was drinking quite a bit and trying to fight it off. . . . The next night when he came in, he was in miserable shape in the same clothes, same shirt, all creased up and dirty, same tie. . . . He came to work looking like that for four or five nights, then he got himself a shower, and some new clothes, he was feeling better and from that moment on, he played, really awesome.[19]

But apparently Coltrane's success didn't last. When the Bohemia gig ended on April 28, Davis fired him from the band. According to one story, Davis punched Coltrane backstage, and Monk happened to witness it.[20] Philly Joe Jones, also addicted, was reportedly let go at the same time. With the national exposure he was receiving now from the Columbia Records publicity office, Davis could not afford to have such problems in his group. "Here we were getting $1,250 a week [about $200 of that went to Coltrane] when Coltrane came back in to the band—and these guys are nodding out on stage."[21] But Davis did offer to take Coltrane back once he rid himself of his habit.[22] In the meantime, the newspaper ads proclaimed that "The New Miles Davis Quintet featuring Sonny Rollins" and Art Taylor on drums would perform at the Cafe Bohemia June 17 through 27.[23]

Coltrane was not sulking at having lost the engagement with Davis. On the contrary, he took this opportunity to get his career and his personal life together. He had begun rehearsing informally with Thelonious Monk. And he played as a leader in Philadelphia. Pianist McCoy Tyner remembers this engagement vividly. Tyner worked early on with Cal Massey, and believes he met Coltrane through Massey, perhaps as early as the summer of 1955: "Coltrane struck me as very quiet and serious. . . . He hadn't blossomed yet, but there was something about his sound and approach to improvising that was captivating. We kept in touch when John came back to town, especially during this period when Miles had let him go."[24] Through Massey again, they got to perform together during this period, probably in May 1957: "Cal, who wrote 'Fiesta' for Charlie Parker and songs for Carmen McRae as well, was a good composer and trumpeter and led a band I was working in at the time, with Albert Heath, [bassist] Jimmy Garrison and [saxophonist] Clarence Sharpe. [Sometimes Khadijah sang and Bobby Crowder played congas.] Cal and John used to practice together because John was in town on a sabbatical at the time. . . . While we were [at the Red Rooster], the club owner asked John if he wanted to come in the next week and play. John said he didn't have a band. He was at home at the time living with his mother, trying to work on a few things, so he asked Cal's rhythm section if we wouldn't mind working with him. Naturally, we said, that would be great! That was the first time I played with John. . . . We got pretty close. I used to go sit on his mother's porch and we would talk. He was like a big brother to me, it was more like family."[25]

Simpkins says that at the Red Rooster, Johnnie Splawn was added on trumpet (57), which is plausible since Splawn was a good friend of Coltrane and showed up at John's first recording session as a leader on May 31. Coltrane was apparently hoping to promote himself as a leader. The *Down Beat* issue of June 27 reported that he had formed his own group and had retained a manager named Tilly Mitchell. He had signed a contract of his own with Prestige Records which called for three LPs and some singles.

At the same time, Coltrane was trying definitively to quit heroin and alcohol. In fact, being dismissed by Davis turned out to be the shock he needed to clean up his act. Coltrane was plagued throughout his life by dental problems, partly because of his sweet tooth—sweet potato pie was his favorite, and Mary says going back to when he was a boy he always carried raisins in his pockets. He also took poor care of his teeth. We already learned of his toothache while with Eddie Vinson, and saxophonist Eddie Harris says in Thomas (55) that in 1951 in Chicago (or perhaps with Gillespie at the end of 1950) Coltrane had to get a cap for a badly chipped front tooth. Davis remembered that at one of their California stops Coltrane had a missing tooth and went to a dentist to get a replacement.[26] By 1959 Coltrane had to get teeth taken out and bridges put in. It may be that drugs and alcohol helped partly to cover up his frequent dental pain.

Coltrane's addiction to heroin was taking a heavy toll on his health and ability to play. When he couldn't get heroin, he was drinking to numb the pain of withdrawal. Coltrane knew that his addictions were keeping him from performing at his best. He acknowledged as much when asked by August Blume if working with Monk was the turning point in his career:

> *Coltrane:* Well—I don't know whether it was a turning point. About that time I made a decision, myself; that's when I stopped drinking and all that shit. I was able to play better right then, you know.
>
> *Blume:* Did you used to drink heavily?
>
> *Coltrane:* Yes. (pause) So by the time that he [Monk] started the group I'd stopped drinking, you know. Found I could—that helped me in all kinds of ways when I stopped drinking; I could play better and think better.

Coltrane's friends and family helped him to quit cold turkey.[27] John Glenn recalls that this was going on while John was performing with Tyner: "When he started at the Red Rooster on a Monday I'd take him home and we'd sit down and talk and have some food and and he would share tunes with me." Thomas writes that Coltrane stayed in his room the whole time (83), but Glenn says that was only during the day: "He was working nightly at the Red Rooster. And he sounded terrible—he sounded like a baby up there. He wasn't feeling right. I remember sitting in and he went for a walk. He left me up there." All this happened, it appears, during May 1957 in Philadelphia.

Coltrane won the battle against heroin during that period of between one and two weeks—he may have had a few more bouts with alcohol before beating it for good—and, rejuvenated, he began to work harder than ever on his music. Coltrane went to the Alvin Hotel near Fifty-second Street and Broadway in Manhattan on May 30 in anticipation of recording his first album as a leader for Prestige the next day (Simpkins, 65, 68)—to be followed, he hoped, by some engagements in New York. (Naima and Saeeda joined him there on August 10, and on August 23, the Coltrane family moved into its first New York apartment, on West 103rd Street and Amsterdam, near Central Park West.) The first LP was recorded at Van Gelder's home studio in Hackensack, New Jersey, on May 31. In June, according to Nellie Monk, Thelonious's widow and the namesake of his "Crepuscule with Nellie," Coltrane was working as a leader at the Coronet (later known as Blue Coronet) in Brooklyn.

This transformation was for Coltrane more than a decision to improve his health and keep his career on track. He once put it, rather glibly, that he had made up his mind to "get some fun out of life for a change."[28] But Coltrane, whose interests in Islam had led him to study other religions and philosophy, also felt that the experience had a spiritual aspect. He would later refer to this occurrence. "During the year 1957, I experienced, by the grace of God, a spiritual awakening which was to lead me to a richer, fuller, more productive life. At that time, in gratitude, I humbly asked to be given the means and privilege to make others happy through music. I feel this has been granted through His grace."[29] Similarly, he told Ralph Gleason, around the spring of 1961, "I went through a personal crisis, you know, and I came out of it. I felt so fortunate to have come through it successfully, that all I wanted to do, if I could, would be to play music that would make people happy."[30] His code was, "Live cleanly . . . Do right . . . You can improve as a player by improving as a person. It's a duty we owe to ourselves."[31]

Over the next several years, Coltrane, with Naima's help, went on special diets for his health and weight. He had to work at staying "clean" by watching his diet in this way, but he never did manage to curb a tendency to overeat. In turn, he never did quit smoking for good, because he found that when he didn't smoke, he ate more. By November 1962 he was smoking cigars, and eventually he turned to pipes.[32]

A practice regimen even more obsessive than before would help keep him focused on his music and away from a temptation that was hard to avoid because so many of his colleagues were still addicted. So practice he did, and Coltrane was more than ready when Thelonious Monk began to take an interest in him. The first document of the two together was their studio recording of "Monk's Mood" from April 16, 1957, while Coltrane was still with Davis, accompanied only by bassist Wilbur Ware. This first meeting produced a spare reading of this ballad, with great depth and sincerity. Soon, Monk and Coltrane began meeting for an occasional informal rehearsal, just for fun. Coltrane told Blume that he had initiated the contact: "I met him, you know, and I just started hanging around with him, I went down and I started going down to his house because I like that music. And we'd already recorded one song, 'Monk's Mood.'"

Blume: That was the one you came from Philly just to do.

Coltrane: Yeah, and I liked it so well I told him [before the recording] that I wanted to learn it, so he invited me around, you know, and that's when I started learning his tunes. We didn't know if we would ever work together."

As Coltrane told Postif: "I remember rehearsing at his place in the summer three or four months before the opening at the Five Spot."[33] Monk was an early riser, and Nellie recalls that Coltrane would come to the house in the morning, sometimes before breakfast. She says it was a nice feeling having Coltrane around, like family. Coltrane told Blume:

Well, I'd go by his house, you know, by his apartment and I'd get him out of bed maybe, or—[laughs]. And then he'd wake up and go to the piano and start playing, you know. He'd play anything, maybe just one of his tunes. He'd start playing it and he'd look at me I guess, and so when he'd look at me I'd get my horn and start trying to find what he's playing. And he'd continue to play over and over and over and over and I'd get this part, and next time he'd go over it I'd get another part. And he'd stop to show me some parts that were pretty difficult, and if I had a lot of trouble, well, he'd get his portfolio out and show me the music. He's got music, he's got all of them written, and I'd read it and learn it. He'd rather a guy learn without reading, you know, because that way you feel it better. You feel it quicker when you memorize it, when you learn it by heart, by ear, you know. And so when I almost had the tune down, then he would leave me with it. He'd leave me to practice it alone, and he'd go out somewhere, maybe he'd go to the store or go back to bed or something. And I'd just stay there and run over the tune. [Finally] I had it pretty well, and then I'd call him and we'd play it down together. And sometimes we'd just get one tune a day.

Coltrane told the English writer Jack Cooke that sometimes "Monk tended quickly to run through the music, then take him on long walks around Manhattan, pointing out all kinds of things about the city [Monk] loved."[34] On occasion they'd go to the home of Baroness Nica de Koenigswarter (a legendary patron of jazz): "We'd stay there the whole night; Monk explained a phrase or two to me at the piano, we listened to records, and the Scotch was flowing" (Postif).

Coltrane's early influence, Coleman Hawkins, as well as his former colleague from Gillespie's small group, Art Blakey, were present at Coltrane's next recording date with Monk, June 25 and 26, 1957. A famous incident occurred: Before he starts to play on "Well You Needn't," Monk calls "Coltrane, Coltrane!" According to the trumpeter at the session, Ray Copeland, Monk had to call out because Coltrane was nodding off from heroin just as his solo turn came up (Thomas, 81–82). But producer Orrin Keepnews and Alonzo White (Monk's nephew), who were in the studio, recall that Monk called Coltrane because the players hadn't settled in advance who should play next.[35] Coltrane comes in instantly, right next to the microphone, so he was surely more ready than Copeland thought.

Coltrane discussed that recording with Blume:

> *Blume:* That kind of thing, in my way of thinking, that makes great music. Where you catch mistakes as well as you catch great moments, you know. And even Hawkins came in wrong on that thing too.
> *Coltrane:* Yeah, well I couldn't advise doing that too many times, too often. . . . That's very spontaneous, brother.
> *Blume:* I guess you were so wrapped up with what Monk was doing.
> *Coltrane:* Yeah, well . . . actually he would throw me, quite often he would actually throw me because I hadn't played with him long then and I was unfamiliar with the changes and stuff. But as time went by I got used to him. And he can be awfully tricky, you know. He makes you keep alert—he likes that, you know. He likes to keep the mental process vibrating, you know? You get to like that thing [after] you get to play with him a while. But at first, I was afraid.

In point of fact, Hawkins did not "come in wrong." Nor would he have been likely to—he had been hip to Monk from the start, using Monk in his regular group in 1944 and recording Monk's tunes in 1947. But the openings of Coltrane's and Hawkins's solos both sound a bit strange because of Ware's inventive bass playing. He breaks up the beat at those moments instead of creating a typical walking bass line.

Soon Monk asked Coltrane to join him at the Five Spot at 5 Cooper Square in Greenwich Village, in what turned out to be a significant career move for both of them. Monk was playing at the Five Spot with a trio featuring Frankie Dunlop on drums beginning on July 4, 1957. Nellie Monk recalls that Coltrane was making seventy-five dollars a week at the Coronet. Monk offered him one hundred dollars a week to join him on July 18.[36]

Coltrane was thrilled. He loved working with Davis, but he seemed to have a warmer feeling for Monk as a person: "Naturally, I was extremely happy when it was announced to me that I would be playing with Monk, during the summer of 1957. I had always wanted to play with him, and this occasion was unique! . . . Monk is exactly the opposite of Miles: he talks about music all the time, and he wants so much for you to understand that if, by chance, you ask him something, he'll spend hours if necessary to explain it to you" (Postif).

The Monk quartet stayed at the Five Spot for most of the remainder of 1957. The personnel changed a few times. At first Wilbur Ware was on bass. Ware was from Chicago, where Jimmy Heath had met him as far back as 1947. He was a marvelous musician but also a drug addict, and when he did not show up on the night of August 13, Ahmed Abdul-Malik was hired as his permanent replacement.[37] Frankie Dunlop continued on drums but ran into union problems. (Dunlop became Monk's regular drummer from 1961 through 1963, so they evidently had a good rapport.) Shadow Wilson took over, except from September 5 through 10 or 11, when he was replaced by Philly Joe Jones. Beginning December 16, the drummer was Kenny Dennis (born in Philadelphia in 1930), who recorded with Sonny Rollins and a few others.[38] There was also quite a bit of sitting in—at various times one could have caught French hornist Julius Watkins, saxophonist Sahib Shihab, and drummers Max Roach, Art Blakey, and Willie Jones.

Many listeners were overwhelmed by Monk's quartet. J. J. Johnson, the magnificent trombonist and composer, said in 1961, "Since Charlie Parker, the most electrifying sound that I've heard in contemporary jazz was Coltrane playing with Monk at the Five Spot a couple of years ago. It was incredible, like Diz and Bird"—both of whom he'd worked with.[39] Johnson saw them only once and recalls, "I had never heard that kind of performance—it's not possible to put it into words. I just heard something that I've never heard before and I haven't heard since."[40] François Postif heard the quartet several times. His reaction was equally ecstatic. He predicted that Coltrane's influence on his generation would be "as great as that of Charlie Parker." He reported that Bud Powell was so impressed that he attended four nights in a row.[41]

But Coltrane remembered that there was still controversy: "The critics, at that time, were all appalled by what we were playing, but you know, for a musician, it's difficult to understand their position: Really, the only thing that counted for me, was not so much *what* I played as that I was *able* to play, and with Monk no less! We played full steam all night and that was really fantastic!" (Postif).

About Coltrane LeRoi Jones noted, "Opening night he was struggling with *all* the tunes" but he went through a transformation during the engagement.[42] Monk's compositions challenged Coltrane's knowledge of harmonic progressions, his spare and percussive accompaniment gave Coltrane a new-found freedom, and his motivically structured improvisations served as models from which Coltrane could learn. Significantly, Sonny Rollins had recorded with Monk during 1954 and also seemed to benefit greatly from the experience.

The only recordings of this quartet were made when Ware was still on bass, before August 13, 1957.[43] Coltrane's playing is dramatically different from that of the preceding months—incredibly more virtuosic, authoritative, and experimental. It is hard to believe that only a month or so had gone by since the session with Monk and Hawkins. Listen, for example, to "Trinkle Tinkle" by the Monk quartet. The theme itself suggests an approach to the solo—it is based on a dazzling twisted motive, which recurs again at the beginning of the bridge. The A sections each are missing two beats in the drum break at the end, but during the solos they avoid this potentially confusing device and stick to a straight thirty-two-bar AABA form. Immediately after the theme, Coltrane launches into a furious solo, filled with hundreds of notes and interspersed with honks from the lowest register and screams from the highest register of the instrument. Ira Gitler described Coltrane's rapid runs as "sheets of sound,"[44] a term that some have overapplied, because Coltrane soon moved on to other concerns. Of course, the "sheets" were not indeterminate groups of notes, but carefully practiced patterns.

Coltrane credited Monk with providing the proper setting for his musical improvement.

> I learned a lot with him. I learned little things, you know, I learned to watch little things. He's just a good musician, man—if you work with a guy who watches the finer points of things, it kind of makes you try to watch the finer points sometimes. Little things mean so much in music, like in everything else, you know? Like the way you build a house, starting with those little things. You get the little things together and then the whole structure will stand up. . . . Monk, he's always doing something back there [behind the soloist] that sounds so mysterious. And it's not mysterious at all when you know what he's doing. Just like simple truths. He might take a chord, a minor chord and leave the third out. Then he'll say, "This is a minor chord, man," but you don't have a minor third in there, so you don't know what it is. You say, "How do you know it's a minor chord?" "That's what it is, a minor chord with the third out." And when he plays the thing, it'll just be in the right place and voiced the right way to have that minor feel. But still it's not a minor because the third is not there. Little things like that, you know. (Blume)

And from "Coltrane on Coltrane": "Working with Monk brought me close to a musical architect of the highest order. I felt I learned from him in every way—through the senses, theoretically, technically. I would talk to Monk about musical problems and he would sit at the piano and show me the answers just by playing them." Coltrane started playing longer solos with Monk: "[Monk] also got me into the habit of playing long solos on his pieces, playing the same piece for a long time to find new conceptions of solos. It got so I would go as far as possible on one phrase until I ran out of ideas. The harmonies got to be an obsession for me."

Coltrane reveled in his newfound freedom: "He gave me complete freedom in my playing, and no one ever did that before." He told Postif: "Obviously, with Monk, I had enormous freedom: sometimes, Monk went to the bar to get a drink and left us alone, Wilbur Ware, Shadow Wilson, and me, on the stage of the Five Spot. And we improvised without any constraints for a quarter of an hour or twenty minutes, exploring our different instruments like madmen. . . . [Sometimes] Monk . . . after two pieces, would return to the dressing room and stay there looking through the window for two or three hours."

Blume was particularly interested in this aspect of the Monk group, and he quizzed Coltrane about it at some length:

> *Blume:* How did you used to feel when you were working down at the Five Spot and . . . in the middle of the tune Monk would get up from the piano and walk around to the side of it and do his little dance?
>
> *Coltrane:* (Laughs.) I felt kind of lonesome (both laugh). Yeah, I felt a little lonesome up there.
>
> *Blume:* When you're standing up there playing like that, how do you hear the changes? Do you think of the changes as you go along or does the bass player suggest them to you by what he's playing?
>
> *Coltrane:* Yeah, the bass player—I count on him, you know.
>
> *Blume:* What does he actually do? Like when Wilbur would be playing bass, would he play like the dominant note in each chord? I don't know how you phrase it.
>
> *Coltrane:* Well, at times. But a bass player like Wilbur Ware, he's so inventive, man, you know he doesn't always play the dominant notes.
>
> *Blume:* But whatever he plays, it sort of suggests notes that gives you an idea of which way the changes are going?
>
> *Coltrane:* Yeah, it may be—and it might not be. Because Wilbur, he plays the other way sometimes. He plays things that are foreign. If you didn't know the song, you wouldn't be able to find it. Because he's superimposing things. He's playing around, and under, and over—building tension, so when he comes back to it you feel everything sets in. But usually I know the tunes—I know the changes anyway. So we manage to come out at the end together anyway.
>
> *Blume:* Which always helps! (Both laugh.)
>
> *Coltrane:* Yeah, we manage to finish on time. A lot of fun playing that way though.
>
> *Blume:* I can imagine.
>
> *Coltrane:* A lot of fun. (Pause.) Like sometimes he would be playing altered changes and I would be playing altered changes. And he would be playing some other kind of altered changes from the [ones] I'd be playing and neither one of us would be playing the changes of the tune until we'd reach a certain spot, and we'd get there together. We're lucky (both laugh). And then Monk comes back in to save everybody. But

nobody knows where he is [in the form of the tune]! (Both laugh.) That's what impresses a lot of people anyway. They say, "How do you guys remember all that stuff?" We weren't really remembering much. Just the basic changes and then everybody (would) just try out anything they wanted to try on it.

Blume: Did [Monk] pull that on you after working on the job or had he done this before, previously, where he'd gotten up and left the piano and left you, sort of, holding the bag?

Coltrane: Well, he just started that on the job.

Blume: He just started that on the job? How did you feel when he first did it?

Coltrane: Well I started looking around for him the first time he did it. After that I got used to it, you know, and I just tried to hold up till he got back.

Blume: Why do you think he did it?

Coltrane: I don't know. He said he wanted to hear the band. (Blume laughs.) When he did that, he was in the audience out front, and he was listening to the band. Then he'd come back, he got something out of that thing.

Blume: I got the biggest kick out of the way he'd do this little shuffle dance on the side.

Coltrane: Yeah, I wanted to see that myself, you know.

Blume: (Laughs.) Did it ever occur to you to pull your horn away from your mouth and walk over and stand behind him and (leave Wilbur and Shadow there)? (Laughs.)

Coltrane: Yeah, I should have done that, man. I wanted to see it myself. It was so interesting. Everybody was talking about it. Every once in a while I'd open up one eye and peep at him. He was really enjoying it, he was getting a big kick then.

Indeed, everybody was getting a big kick out of Coltrane, and he was in demand: During the Five Spot engagement Coltrane was in the recording studios ten times—twice as a leader for Prestige, once for a special session as a leader for Blue Note, and the rest as a sideperson.

After the Five Spot engagement, Nellie doesn't recall much further contact between Coltrane and Monk, socially or otherwise, but they did play several times on double bills in the 1960s. Nellie says that in 1963 when they both brought their groups to San Francisco and San Jose, Coltrane sat in with Monk's group on at least one occasion!

But Coltrane was moving on. Monk was on a short hiatus from performing, and at the beginning of 1958, Miles Davis accepted, even welcomed, Coltrane back into his group. And this time Davis wanted to hold on to him.

11

Coltrane's Music: 1955–57

From the moment Coltrane began to work with Davis, he was in the public eye. He found that his every musical move was noticed and analyzed by critics and fans—not to mention potential promoters and producers. He had always been obsessed with music, but he had been able to progress at his own pace. Now he was under greater pressure to define himself, to express himself in a fashion that he—at least—would find satisfactory. He also had the opportunity to record some of his compositions, and it soon became clear that he was not only an individual improviser, but one of our most original writers of music.

While he was a member of the Davis quintet, Coltrane began to appear as a studio sideperson for many other artists. This was a way to pick up a little extra money. By 1958 union "scale" (negotiated minimum wage) was $13.75 per hour of recording for sidepersons and double that for the leader (who also received royalties on record sales), usually paid at the session or within two weeks of it. But there were many valuable musical experiences to be gained as well. One of the most notable occurred on May 24, 1956, when Sonny Rollins recorded an LP for Prestige with the rhythm section from the Davis group. Coltrane came along with them to the studio, saxophone in hand, and ended up on the recording. He and Rollins played "Tenor Madness," the only re-corded meeting of these two great musical minds and mutual admirers. This fast blues riff was evidently part of the jazz folklore because it had also been recorded by Kenny Clarke as "Royal Roost" or "Rue Chaptal" (on his date for RCA in 1946) and by Hank Mobley as "Sportin' Crowd" (on an Art Blakey LP, Blue Note 1508, in 1955) and its theme begins the same as the thirty-two-bar Gillespie tune "Oo Bop Sh' Bam." "Tenor Madness" features each saxophonist in an extended improvisation, then trading back and forth, providing a fas-cinating and exciting juxtaposition of these two masters at work. Rollins's hoarse, woodsy tone and highly motivic, rhythmically articulated style contrasts dramatically with Coltrane's light, gracefully poised sound and running formulaic style of this time. Rollins plays in a soulful, bluesy style with lots of blue notes and bent notes, whereas Coltrane tends to favor a lyrical approach without the use of blue notes. (Hentoff continued to be hard on Coltrane, pronouncing that he "appears to be pressing and lacks Sonny's compactness of impact.")[1]

Born in 1930, Rollins was younger than Coltrane, but he established a distinctive identity very early and was featured on recordings from 1948 onward with Bud Powell, Davis, Monk, and other major innovators. Coltrane, in contrast, was a late bloomer who was not seen as a major talent until he was about thirty years old. Coltrane always expressed the highest regard for Rollins: "Yeah, like some guys you know, you call great. Sonny, he's one. His talent is sure to last. It'll go on and on, and he'll reach that great status."[2]

This was only one of many valuable opportunities that came Coltrane's way as a sideperson. He also was able to unveil some of his original compositions, beginning at his first sideman date led by his quintet mate Paul Chambers—with Jones on drums too, and pianist Kenny Drew Sr.—in Los Angeles in March 1956. Here, he recorded "John Paul Jones," a rhythmically intricate blues theme that he apparently named for himself, Chambers, and Jones. It surfaced again at a Davis session for Prestige in May, under the title "Trane's Blues." In Coltrane's notebook he uses the original title (Simpkins, 276). Pianist Phineas Newborn recorded it in 1959 as his own "(Blues Theme) for Left Hand Only."

At another session as sideman for Paul Chambers, in September 1956, the quartet was expanded by the addition of trumpeter Donald Byrd and Kenny Burrell, the guitarist who had played with Coltrane at the end of his tenure with Gillespie. Horace Silver—one of Coltrane's favorite composers—played piano. Coltrane introduced two more originals, "Nita" and "Just for the Love." His striking originality as a writer of music was already apparent. "Nita," named after his wife, Juanita, is a thirty-bar construction in the form of A (eight bars)–A (eight bars)–B (fourteen bars). Not only is the length unusual, but it doesn't need to return to the A section at the end of the chorus. This piece also introduces the fast-moving ii–V–I sequences a third apart that fascinated Coltrane and eventually culminated in the composition "Giant Steps." Specifically, the chords in the first measures are B-flat major, then ii–V–I in D major, then ii–V–I in F major, then in A major. The roots outline a B-flat major seventh chord. (*See following page.*)

"Nita" by John Coltrane.

If it were strictly analogous to "Giant Steps," the key areas would outline an augmented chord, as in B-flat, D, and then F-sharp, not F. But the relationship is too close to discount. "Nita" also ends each chorus with six measures over a pedal point, a device that Coltrane used again on "Moment's Notice" and that assumed dramatic importance in his later repertory.

The other piece, "Just for the Love," is the trickiest chord sequence Coltrane ever wrote on a blues. It's unlike his other blues pieces for that reason—he usually liked a very down-home approach to the blues—and because it uses so many major seventh chords. In this latter respect it's very much like Charlie Parker, and after a few hearings it becomes clear that Parker was his inspiration here. John even incorporates in measures 3 and 4 a lick that brings Parker to mind.[3]

"Just For the Love" by John Coltrane.

It's a blues in F, but it begins a third away (like "Nita") on an A-flat major chord. However it does go to the B-flat IV chord on the fifth measure and to G minor and C in measures 9 and 10, which are enough to give us a sense of the blues progression.

Coltrane did not record between November 30, 1956, and March 22, 1957.[4] A session on April 20 included an interesting blues that has a vamp used as an introduction and ending to the theme. Entitled "Mary's Blues," it is credited to the late baritonist Pepper Adams. However, Coltrane said that he wrote a "Mary's Blues" for his cousin.[5] He may have meant "Cousin Mary," a blues recorded in 1959. But it is not uncommon for compositions to be credited to the wrong band member, so it may be that "Mary's Blues" is an unacknowledged Coltrane item.

Coltrane liked to compose at the piano, and he was often at his mother's upright. Coltrane described his writing process at the piano: "I sit there and run over chord progressions and sequences, and eventually, I usually get a song—or songs—out of each little musical problem." In other words, his composing grew out of theoretical concepts that occupied him at the time. "After I've worked it out on the piano," he continued, "I then develop the song further on tenor, trying to extend it harmonically."[6]

By 1957, Coltrane's reputation had grown to the point that Bob Weinstock offered him a contract for a series of recordings under his own name. (He had co-led a Prestige session with tenorist Paul Quinichette on May 17, but it was not issued until 1959.) The first, simply entitled *Coltrane,* was recorded on May 31, 1957, and released that September. It had the words, "the NEW tenor saxophone STAR" emblazoned on the cover (see photo section), indicating the level of fame that Coltrane had achieved since joining Davis, despite the negative vote cast by some critics and fans. Coltrane took this debut seriously: "About this time, I got the recording contract with Prestige, and I decided that if I was going to put anything on record, then it ought to be me."[7] He put together a sextet that he hoped to perform with, according to *Down Beat* of June 27. It included a friend, trumpeter Johnnie Splawn, making his only known recording. (Splawn had problems with his legs and had to use crutches, one reason his career never took off.) Coltrane brought out six interesting pieces, including two originals, "Straight Street" and "Chronic Blues." The former is, I suppose, named after his recent decision to go "straight" without drugs.[8] Again one notices the unusual lengths (an AABA form where all sections are twelve bars each and not blues related), and the original conception and chord progression. His pieces were not just new "heads" for old chords, themes written over the chords of popular standards such as "I've Got Rhythm," as was often the case with modern jazz compositions.

When Coltrane was with Johnny Hodges he used to query the bassist, Johnny Williams, about the possibilities of his instrument (Thomas, 65). This is provocative, because as a writer Coltrane was particularly attentive to the bass, often producing fully written bass parts instead of just chord symbols (until about 1961, when he started to leave things more open). As we will see, many of his compositions of the next several years are built around a bass ostinato, and Coltrane spoke to Postif about the importance of the bass in his music. As an example, here is the bass part of "Straight Street":

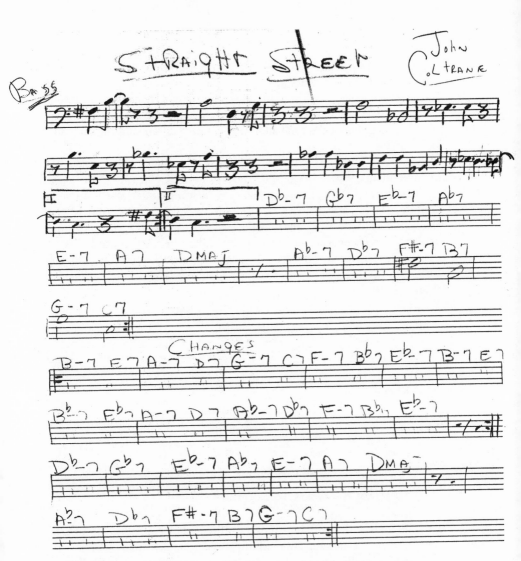

John Coltrane's handwritten bass part for his "Straight Street" (1957),
courtesy of Aisha Tyner.

Significantly, other jazz composers have found the bass part crucial to their music. Ellington's bass parts were often quite specific, not least on his critically acclaimed "Koko" and the 1937 recording of "Crescendo and Diminuendo in Blue." Ellington even worked with two basses from 1935 through 1938—unheard of at the time and unique until Coltrane did the same in his group in 1961.

"Chronic Blues" is a riff-based blues theme, interesting because of its minor modality. Several of Coltrane's most famous blues performances, such as "Equinox," were in the minor mode, as we'll see. *Coltrane* also featured two beautiful ballad performances, "Violets for Your Furs" and "While My Lady Sleeps." The latter was arranged by the leader over a pedal point, another step toward his preoccupation with pedal point in the 1960s. It was clearly a favorite song because it was the only song that Coltrane quoted repeatedly in his solos. He would use the opening of the theme while soloing at medium and fast tempos:

Beginning of "While My Lady Sleeps," by Bronislaw Kaper and Gus Kahn.
Copyright © 1941 (Renewed) EMI Feist Catalog, Inc. All Rights Reserved. Used by Permission.
WARNER BROS. PUBLICATIONS U.S. INC., Miami, FL 33014

The solo ends with a striking sound: Coltrane plays two notes at once, then another interval a half step lower. Multiphonics (literally "many sounds") is the technique of producing more than one note at a time from a wind instrument. These intervals or chords usually have a buzzy or squawky sound, but modern composers of chamber music have studied their effects, and jazz people have picked them up. Coltrane described the technique in 1961: "It's made by a combination of fingerings . . . the same way that guys used to make the things they call freak notes on the sax, you know. Like you make one note, then you make another fingering for the same note—it's the same principle. Only this time you listen for the note to split and you allow it to split, see? The other way, the idea was just to get another sound for the same note, and you can play it that way too. But also if you listen for a slight split in it, you can vary your lip— usually I loosen mine [to bring out both sounds]."[9]

Coltrane said that, surprisingly, "Monk was one of the first to show me how to make two or three notes at a time on tenor. . . . Monk just looked at my horn and 'felt' the mechanics of what had to be done to get this effect" ("Coltrane on Coltrane"). He added that he learned the specifics from John Glenn,[10] whom he met through Splawn and Clarence Sharpe. Glenn could get three or even four notes at once, and Coltrane asked Glenn to show him how. They used to get together at Coltrane's house in Philadelphia, probably in May 1957, just before the debut album. Glenn recalls, "Trane's student picked it up before he did. He had a student—I can't think of his name; he had a big band and he went to Africa and he died not too long ago. He got it just like that. And Trane was struggling with it." But by the time Glenn saw Coltrane later in Manhattan, he had perfected it: "He had developed it completely—he told me that he could do it chromatically all over the horn." Coltrane was to continue working on multiphonics, eventually integrating it into his improvising, but for now he worked it into rehearsed passages such as this ballad ending, where he could be sure to get it right.

The album *Coltrane* also included "Bakai," a striking number by Coltrane's friend Cal Massey—it reappeared on Massey's only album as a leader in 1961—and the standard "Time Was." The latter features a technically assured, fresh, and inventive improvisation, notable for the singing sound, rhythmic drive, and unique melodic lines. Each AABA chorus of "Time Was" begins with a brief, memorable melody. Chorus 2, the first improvised chorus after the theme statement, begins with an ascending elaboration of F, the starting note of the written theme. Chorus 3 starts with a relaxed descending arpeggio, while chorus 4 heightens the tension with a chromatic descent followed by eighth-note arpeggios. At the start of chorus 5, Coltrane plays an ascending arpeggio that is the perfect complement to the melody that began chorus 3.

At this point in Coltrane's career, he relied heavily on a personal collection of formulas, or licks as musicians call them. Jazz players—indeed, all improvisational artists—draw upon their personal repertory of formulas with little variation at certain points of the phrase and over certain chord progressions.[11] It is analogous to the way we speak: We have an idea of what we want to say, but we must improvise the exact wording by drawing, instantly, on our own repertory of words and favorite phrases—verbal licks. As we have seen, Coltrane was drawing ideas from a particularly wide pool—Bird and Pres to be sure, but also Hanon and Czerny, and scales from world music.

Some of the formulas Coltrane preferred at this time are shown below. (*See following page.*)

Some of Coltrane's favorite formulas from 1956 and 1957.

Descending formula utilizing the characteristic ornament of modern jazz (two instances)

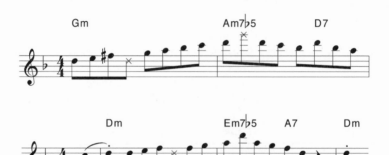

Two versions of a favorite formula in the minor mode, vaguely resembling "Anitra's Dance" by Grieg

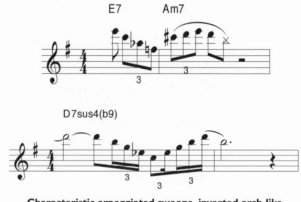

Characteristic arpeggiated swoops, inverted arch-like

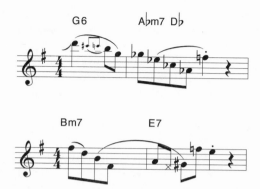

A variation of the above involving a leap back up at the end, a frequent Coltrane device

Typical motivic passage

On "Time Was," Coltrane uses the ones labeled (*b*) and (*c*), among others. He also employs motivic development—developing an idea by varying it before moving on—to connect the bridge and the last A section of chorus 3, and to create two matching four-bar phrases for the bridge of chorus 5. Three times, over an F minor seventh chord in the bridge, Coltrane plays a descending scale from B-flat, filling in the whole steps from B-flat to A-flat and F to E-flat. Around this time, when his gigs took him to Detroit, he'd been spending time with pianist Barry Harris. Harris was already known among musicians for his brilliant ability to codify the language of Charlie Parker and Bud Powell. He constructed "[dominant] seventh scales" or "bebop scales" and "sixth diminished scales" that helped musicians to understand where to put passing tones—which whole steps to fill in—in order to play idiomatically correctly. Coltrane's descending scale patterns may reflect what he gleaned from Harris.[12]

By the 1960s Coltrane was deeply involved in motivic improvisation and with building a sense of structure throughout each solo. Sonny Rollins was noted for his structural logic, and Coltrane surely would have been interested in that aspect of his colleague's art, although their approaches were quite different.[13]

Rhythmically, Coltrane's playing on "Time Was" is straightforward; his playing is dominated, as was most 1950s jazz, by smoothly flowing eighth notes. Soon, he would start to experiment dramatically with fractured and irregular rhythms; by the end of 1960, he was working with eighth notes again, but in a very different way. Harmonically, Coltrane's melodic lines typically enriched the chord progressions by suggesting upper extensions and substitute chords. For example, a simple ii–V^7–I progression might be interpreted as if it were iiø–V^{b5}–I, that is, adding upper extensions; or, substituting for the V^7, he might interpret it as ii–bII^7–I. These alternate progressions would be clearly implied in his improvised melody line, even if the rhythm section accompanists continued to play a basic ii–V^7–I progression.[14] All of the soloists of the 1950s did this to some degree; Coltrane used these substitutions more frequently than most of his peers and with greater daring—that is, implying changes more remote from the original. He credited Davis with moving him along in this direction, saying, "Miles has shown me possibilities in choosing substitutions within a chord and also new progressions."[15]

Coltrane was very serious about his art. Cannonball Adderley recalled, "Where sometimes Miles would take on some humor in his playing—or lots of times I might feel lighter than usual—John was heavily involved with being just serious and musical, all the time."[16] He almost never indulged in musical humor or in quoting entire phrases that would be familiar to listeners, and in this respect he was the opposite of Rollins, who is the musical quoter nonpareil. One of the few melodies that Coltrane did quote was the beginning of "While My Lady Sleeps," as we noted. A quote brings in a reference to the world outside one's solo. The effect varies; a quote may be funny, or it may suggest a homage to another artist, or it may simply establish a kind of common background with the audience and fellow musicians.[17] Coltrane's music, more and more, seems to have been about here and now, about being involved with what he and his group were playing at that moment. Quotations had no place in that world.

The serious tone of the minor mode may be one reason that Coltrane liked to use it (and later the Dorian). "Serious" is a generalization and does not apply to all minor melodies in all cultures; but it does seem fair to say that in Coltrane's music, minor tends to be serious.[18] On the blues he relies heavily on the flat seventh and third, which gives his blues playing a minor quality as compared with the major-sounding blues solos of, say, Parker and Lester Young. Significantly, Coltrane liked to write blues themes in the minor. A minor blues, he told Leonard Feather in 1959, "is always good." He said in 1965, "I have a natural feeling for the minor."[19]

Apparently, it was also during this period that Coltrane became interested in the possibilities of sequences of fourths, something that was to figure prominently in his melodies of the 1960s. "Big" Nick Nicholas, a Lester Young–inspired tenorist whom Coltrane knew and respected, remarked that Coltrane was "particularly interested in the violin parts of the first and third movements" of Bela Bartok's *Concerto for Orchestra* (Thomas, 105) and would sometimes play along with a recording of it. During the first fifty measures of the first movement, the strings explore the sound of stacking up fourths, as in (ascending) E, A, D, C, F, B-flat. The third movement begins with fourths moving chromatically, as in F up to B-flat, then B-natural up to E. Coltrane wrote that around the time he was with Monk "I started playing fourth chords" ("Coltrane on Coltrane"). However, it is hard to interpret his statement that he could create a bigger sound with "more volume" on fourths than on arpeggiated ninth chords. Perhaps this has to do with his practicing of multiphonics, which typically involves trying to bring out the overtone a fifth above (and thus related to the fourth below) each note.

Coltrane was always working on his sound. No doubt many of the hours that Coltrane spent practicing, throughout his life, were not devoted to finger exercises but were spent quietly experimenting with reeds and mouthpieces. Tom Dowd, Coltrane's recording engineer at Atlantic Records, remembers Coltrane's warmup routine: "John usually showed up about an hour before the session. Much in the manner of classical musicians practicing before a recital, he would stand in a corner, face the wall, play, stop, change reeds, and start again. After a while he would settle on the mouthpiece and reed that felt most comfortable to him, and then he would start to work on the 'runs' that he wanted to use during the session. I would watch him play the same passage over and over again, changing his breathing, his fingering, and experimenting with the most minute changes in his phrasing. Once in a while he would go back to a mouthpiece he had abandoned earlier."[20]

On the saxophone finding your own sound depends largely on finding your personal combination of mouthpiece and reed. Many types and hardnesses of reeds and dozens of mouthpieces are available. Each saxophone also resonates a certain way, and the shape of one's air cavities and sinuses will also help determine the sound one gets—this last, obviously, is not under the player's control. Some players, such as Charlie Parker, had a reputation for being able to get the sound they wanted even on borrowed mouthpieces and instruments. Coltrane was not easily satisfied—he searched hard for the perfect sound. Fellow saxophonist Wayne Shorter says that Dexter Gordon recalled giving Coltrane a mouthpiece to help him project. Shorter believes Jimmy Oliver gave him one too, and that Coltrane sounded so good on it that Oliver wanted it back. By all accounts, Coltrane eventually had a large collection of mouthpieces. Even when he found a mouthpiece he liked, he would sometimes have a specialist adjust it (by fine sanding and other methods) to get closer to what he heard inside his head.

Most photographs show Coltrane playing on a metal mouthpiece, usually an Otto Link model. (Occasionally in the early 1960s, he can be seen using a black, hard-rubber model.) One might think that the metal mouthpiece created the edge in Coltrane's sound, but it's not that simple. Metal mouthpieces generally are very resonant and reinforce the upper partials, but do not by themselves determine the resulting tone. Lester Young, for example, used a metal mouthpiece on his famous recordings with Count Basie during the 1930s, and his ethereal sound was worlds apart from Coltrane's.

Coltrane experimented with different ligatures—the strap that holds the reed onto the mouthpiece. He also tried putting a piece of rubber on top of the mouthpiece, where the teeth hit. (Today one can buy such a strip at an instrument shop.) Reportedly, Coltrane was so fanatic about having a perfect connection with the instrument that he had his upper teeth filed into a slight curve so as to match the curve of the top of the mouthpiece.[21] Coltrane talked with Postif about his setup: "I was in the habit of using extremely hard reeds, number nine, because I wanted to have a big, solid sound. And while playing with Monk I tried using number four. I very soon realized that the number nine limited my possibilities and reduced my stamina: with the four I had a volubility that made me give up the nine!" I don't know of any reed make whose numbering goes up to nine, but some mouthpieces do. Coltrane told Valerie Wilmer in 1961 that he used a hard reed, and that "my good ones usually last two weeks."[22]

Coltrane articulated even his most rapid passages with great precision. This is accomplished through the use of the tongue on the reed. The fingers must be very accurate as well, so that the closing of the keys is coordinated with the tongueing. Coltrane told fellow saxophonist George Braith around 1966 that he also obtained clarity through "a definitive way of closing the keys" without relying as much on the tongue (Simpkins, 235).

Except for early photos with Gillespie where he appears to be playing a King "Super 20" tenor, Coltrane was partial to Selmer saxophones—as are most professionals—and different Selmer models vary in sound quality and in ease of fingering. David Demsey and Carl Woideck, both saxophonists and educators, agree that in photos of the late 1950s Coltrane appears to be using the model known as a "balanced action," which was introduced in the mid-1930s and then revised around 1947. During 1960 Coltrane seems to have taken up the Mark VI model that Selmer had introduced in 1954.[23] Shorter recalls that in the 1960s Coltrane had a brand-new Selmer that he tried out at a club in Manhattan. But he couldn't get the sound he wanted, so he drove all the way back to Huntington, Long Island—where he was living then—to get the old one.[24] Coltrane was very dependent on having the right equipment.

On Coltrane's solos with the Gillespie small group in 1951, he exhibited a rich tone, a medium-fast vibrato, and pronounced use of portamento. Over the years, his vibrato slowed down considerably. By 1955, Coltrane utilized a very slow and relatively narrow vibrato, lending a poignant delicacy to his sound. At faster tempos, Coltrane's tone became more raspy and intense. Despite enormous changes in repertory, Coltrane always sounded aggressive and virtuosic on fast numbers, serene, lyrical and sensitive on slow pieces. Compare, for example, "In a Mellotone" with Hodges from 1954 with "Don't Blame Me" of the same date; from 1957, "Time Was" with "While My Lady Sleeps"; from 1960, "Liberia" with "Central Park West"; from 1965, "Vigil" with "Welcome"; and, finally, from 1966, "Leo" with "Peace on Earth."

Coltrane's respectful approach to ballad melodies reflects a tradition before bop; the Parker way was to improvise double-time lines and fills in a ballad. Johnny Hodges was famous for his sensuous ballad paraphrases, with his own distinctive set of ornaments applied similarly each time. It is extremely likely that Coltrane learned much about ballad playing from Hodges, although he certainly learned as well from recordings of Lester Young. Young had a similar way of pacing himself on a ballad. A graphic illustration of Young's dichotomy of style as of September 1949 may be heard by comparing his frenetic solo in "Lester Leaps In," full of overblown low notes and guttural effects, with his pure, singing rendition of "Embraceable You" from the same concert.[25]

Just a few months after *Coltrane,* the Blue Note label got special permission from Prestige to produce the second album under John's leadership. According to Orrin Keepnews and Michael Cuscuna, Coltrane had agreed to do this album before signing with Prestige.[26] *Blue Train* was recorded during his stint at the Five Spot, on September 15, 1957, and released that December. It quickly gained status as the best display of Coltrane's talents as a player and composer to date—all but one of the five tunes were his, and Blue Note paid for rehearsals.

The title piece is a haunting blues, basically a riff. The barrage of notes in his extended solo helps to create the urgency of a man spilling out his innermost feelings. (The first take, issued in 1997, has a much shorter, but still effective solo.) "Locomotion" is another blues riff, this time in AABA form—twelve-bar blues, blues again, eight-bar bridge, and blues again. Lester Young had used this structure in 1947 on "D. B. Blues," which Coltrane probably knew. Coltrane was to reprise this structure on "Traneing In."

On "Moment's Notice," Coltrane is preoccupied with placing changing harmonies under a repeated note in the melody. That's interesting, because

Dizzy Gillespie had done something like it on "Con Alma," which had been in his repertory since 1954, when he recorded it with Latin percussionists.[27] This exercise of finding different chords to harmonize the same note forces one to find some unusual chord connections, and I would suggest that sequences like these led partly to the unusual chord sequence of "Giant Steps." In "Con Alma" the first two chords under each note are a major third apart, paving the way for Coltrane's exploration of roots moving by thirds in "Giant Steps." Here are the chords to "Moment's Notice" as written out by Coltrane:

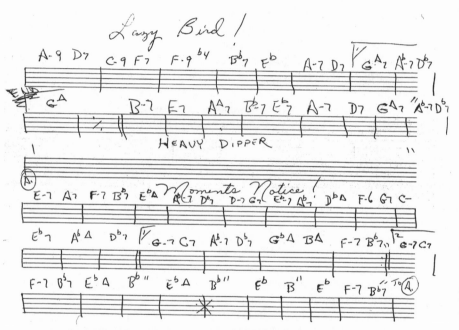

The chords to "Moment's Notice" and "Lazy Bird" as written out by their composer John Coltrane, courtesy Aisha Tyner.
Both pieces Copyright © 1957, Renewed 1985 JOWCOL MUSIC. International Copyright Secured. All Rights Reserved. Used by Permission.

On the same page we have the chords to Coltrane's "Lazy Bird," with the composer's cryptic comment "Heavy Dipper" under the bridge. The title of this piece is evidently a play on "Lady Bird" by Tadd Dameron, the much admired composer with whom Coltrane had in fact recorded in November 1956. This leads one to look for connections, but Dameron's piece is a sixteen-bar form without repeats and Coltrane's is a thirty-two-bar AABA. I suggest the following relationship: Take Dameron's sixteen-bar chord progression, transposed from C to Coltrane's key of G, but make each chord last half as long, so the whole progression takes eight measures. Now you basically have the A section of "Lazy Bird"—it becomes exact if you make the substitutions shown in parentheses:

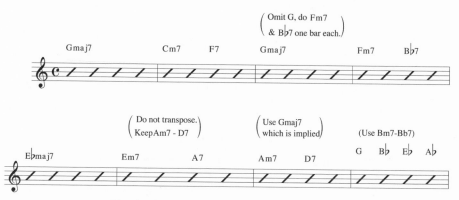

Chords of "Lady Bird" changed into "Lazy Bird"

For the bridge, Coltrane used a variation of the bridge of the standard tune "Lover Man," which he had arranged for Jimmy Heath's band nine years earlier.

The Bridge of "Lover Man (Oh, Where Can You Be?)"
By Jimmy Davis, Roger "Ram" Ramirez and Jimmy Sherman.
Copyright © 1941, 1942 by MCA MUSIC PUBLISHING, A Division of UNIVERSAL STUDIOS, INC.
Copyright Renewed. International Copyright Secured.

"Lazy Bird" by John Coltrane (1957).

The coda may be seen as a very extended version of Dameron's original "turn-around" (which brings the piece back to the beginning). Coltrane's fresh and bubbling solo here is particularly full of what Barry Harris calls "[dominant] seventh scales."

On *Blue Train* Coltrane impresses as a player and as a writer. When Davis took Coltrane back into his group at the end of the Five Spot engagement, he was getting a powerhouse of a saxophonist who played with charisma and authority. And he was getting a powerhouse of a person, with a renewed vision of what he could accomplish in life.

12

Back with Miles Davis

Coltrane stayed with Davis for the next fifteen months, but there was tension. John soon realized that he had enough of a following at this point to work under his own name if he wanted to. Besides, he was dreaming up a highly original group concept based on his own material, which he had to put on hold as long as he was with Davis. He ended up leaving once, but was coerced back by Davis—who clearly realized what he had in Coltrane. Finally, in April 1960, Coltrane left for good.

For the balance of 1957, Davis had at first carried on with Rollins in place of Coltrane. Philly Joe had evidently returned on drums, because an ad for the Philadelphia Jazz Festival for the weekend of October 19, 1957, lists the Miles Davis Quintet with "Reds" (as he was still known at home) Garland, Chambers, and Jones. The saxophonist is not listed because Rollins had gone off to form his own group, something he had wanted to do for a while. Around this time, Davis acquired a sparkling alto saxophonist, Julian "Cannonball" Adderley. Adderley (1928–75) was only two years younger than Coltrane, but had remained a local legend in Florida until he decided to move to New York in 1955. On occasion Tommy Flanagan replaced Garland.

Probably in January 1958, Coltrane rejoined the Miles Davis group.[1] The *Philadelphia Tribune* recognized its own with an article subtitled: "Philly Jazz Artist Wailing throughout the Entire Universe." Included in their listing are "Williams [Reds] Garland, piano—Johnny Coltrane, tenor sax—and Philly Joe Jones, drums, all with Miles Davis."[2] In late April, Bill Evans, who became one of the most influential of all jazz pianists, replaced Garland, and about a month later, Jimmy Cobb replaced Jones.

It was a very different Coltrane who returned to the Davis band. Among the most apparent traits of Coltrane's music since his time with Monk is the sheer speed, the blinding flurries of notes that Ira Gitler dubbed "sheets of sound." What Gitler was hearing was Coltrane's way of superimposing or stacking up chords. John explained his musical aims of this period in the important article, "Coltrane on Coltrane," published in 1960:

> About this time, I was trying for a sweeping sound. I started experimenting because I was striving for more individual development. I even tried long, rapid lines that Ira Gitler termed "sheets of sound" at that time. But actually, I was beginning to apply the three-on-one chord approach, and at that time the tendency was to play the entire scale of each chord. Therefore, they were usually played fast and sometimes sounded like glisses [glissandos]. I found there were a certain number of chord progressions to play in a given time, and sometimes what I played didn't work out in eighth notes, sixteenth notes, or triplets. I had to put the notes in uneven groups like fives and sevens in order to get them all in. I thought in groups of notes, not of one note at a time. I tried to place these groups on the accents and emphasize the strong beats—maybe on 2 here and on 4 over at the end. I would set up the line and drop groups of notes—a long line with accents dropped as I moved along. Sometimes what I was doing clashed harmonically with the piano—especially if the pianist wasn't familiar with what I was doing—so a lot of times I just strolled with bass and drums.

Notice the emphasis that Coltrane places on harmony. He explains the sheets of sound as well as the complex rhythmic groupings from the point of view of harmony. Both aspects of his music unavoidably resulted from the rapid superimposition of several scales over each chord.[3] This suggests an emphasis on harmony rather than rhythm: "I want to be more flexible where rhythm is concerned. I feel I have to study rhythm some more. I haven't experimented too much with time; most of my experimenting has been in a harmonic form. I put time and rhythm to one side, in the past." Elsewhere he said that at that time he would like to play several choruses "based only on the harmonies: that will be a great joy for me, but no doubt not for the listeners. I have to master the chords completely before concentrating on rhythmic problems."[4] Yet, clearly, Coltrane was not disregarding rhythm. He speaks of placing the groups of notes on the accents and emphasizing the strong beats. By "dropping" groups of notes I believe he simply means placing them on the important beats and accents. Notice that he refers to two and four as the strong beats, since they are emphasized in jazz.

Critical as ever of his own progress, Coltrane talked with Gitler about the "sheets of sound": "Now it is not a thing of beauty, and the only way it would be justified is if it becomes that. If I can't work it through, I will drop it."[5] By 1959, Coltrane used the sheets of sound more sparingly, attempting to integrate them into his solos by leading into and out of such passages more gradually. "If I

Were a Bell," live with the Davis sextet (September 9, 1958), represents the peak of Coltrane's "sheets-of-sound" phase. Almost the entire solo is constructed in sixteenth notes, executed with astonishing clarity at a fast tempo. Coltrane also explores the lowest register of his instrument, purposely producing an aggressive honking sound, and extends the upper register as well, reaching up to an altissimo a during the second chorus.

Here are some of the patterns that Coltrane used at this time. A favorite was based on the diminished scale, also known as the eight-note or octatonic scale.

Some of Coltrane's favorite formulas from 1958

This diminished-scale pattern was one of Coltrane's favorites

This one combines elements of three diminished scales

A stepwise descent was often followed by unexpected leaps upward

(All of the following from David Baker, *The Jazz Style of John Coltrane*.) Characteristic elaborations of one chord (**C**) by rapid arpeggiation and additional passing chords:

On "Little Melonae," from a quartet date during this same period (March 26, 1958), Coltrane mines an exploratory vein, with a particularly striking moment in which he seizes onto a downward run, partly scalar and partly chromatic, and develops it. This scalar idea was to return in his last period: a more diatonic version is, for instance, prominent in "Venus," which we will analyze later. It also became a favorite of Joe Henderson, a leading tenorist since the 1960s.

Excerpt from Coltrane's solo on "Little Melonae" (March 26, 1958)

Coltrane's style of this period is well illustrated by the live recording he made with Monk at the Five Spot, which appears to be from a one-night stand during a night off from Davis. He had told Postif in 1961, "We didn't officially make a recording live at the Five Spot, and that's a great pity, but I console myself with those that my wife made on our tape recorder. She arrived with me and recorded all night. I listen to that, on occasion, and I feel a little nostalgic!"[6]

Both Coltrane and Monk are marvelous on this live recording. Coltrane is especially uninhibited when Monk drops out behind his solos, leaving him alone with the bass and drums. For example, he double-times throughout most of his "Trinkle Tinkle" solo, and after Monk drops out he loosens up some more, getting into some high hollering. On "In Walked Bud," Coltrane plays for a long time without Monk, while Roy Haynes takes a very active role, playing figures involving the snare and bass drum. This recording is the earliest documentation of the rapport between Haynes and Coltrane; in the 1960s Haynes became Coltrane's drummer of choice whenever Elvin Jones was unavailable. On "I Mean You" Coltrane builds furiously until he is beyond double-time, into his sheets of sound, honking, shouting, playing in fast flurries, at one point working his way up on the saxophone, then stopping, then trying it again, going higher. It's an example of Coltrane working, "practicing" on the bandstand.

Of course he was practicing at home as well, and writing music for his own recordings and for an occasional date as a leader during breaks between Davis's gigs. Coltrane would perform with pickup groups, mostly in New York and Philadelphia. A list of songs in his handwriting may represent his repertory around this time (Simpkins, 276):

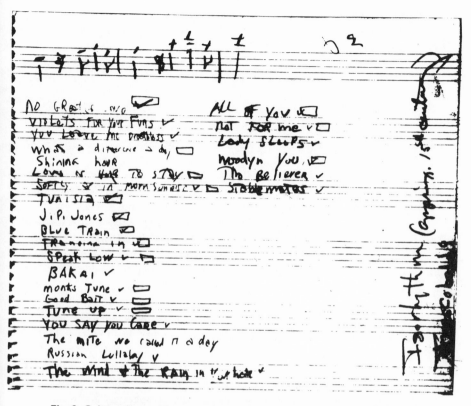

Fig. 8. Coltrane's song list, reproduced by permission of C. O. Simpkins, M.D. (from Simpkins, 276). Original courtesy of Saeeda and Naima Coltrane. The bit of music at the top is unidentified. On the side are notes from his studies of classical music history: "Frescobaldi," "Isorhythm (approx. 15th century)."

Writing was so important to Coltrane that when Blume asked him whom he admired most, he singled out musicians who were strong writers as well as players: "I'll name some that I like, you know. I might be leaving out quite a few. There might be quite a few I'm leaving out. Horace Silver for one . . . and all the great soloists, you know, like Miles, and Sonny Rollins and guys like that. When I mention a guy like Monk, to me, he's a soloist and he writes so many things, you know. There are few like him, really. Charlie Parker was like that. He could play and he could write—quite a few things, you know. Dizzy, he writes quite a bit too."

Blume: What about Benny Golson?
Coltrane: Benny Golson, he's another.

Blume: What about Quincy Jones?

Coltrane: Quincy. Gigi Gryce too. There's a guy playing, he's in the army right now, he plays tenor. His name is Wayne Shorter. I think he's going to contribute quite a bit too, 'cause he has this double talent. He can play, and he's got enough stuff that he can play a whole lot and then sit down and write a lot too.

While in the army, Wayne Shorter (born in Newark, New Jersey, in 1933) had performed a bit with Horace Silver. Shorter recalls:

I was playing somewhere with Horace Silver in New York [he thinks on a Sunday afternoon at the Village Vanguard] and here comes Coltrane's wife in the kitchen and she said, "Somebody wants to meet you." And . . . there's John Coltrane sitting there in the audience. And we shook hands and he said, "You're playing those strange funny things all over the horn like me. It's not the same way but like I'm trying—like I'm doing. That's some interesting stuff." It seemed like he found that it was nice to be with someone, you know—I think he was really alone in that.[7]

Shorter continued the story elsewhere: "He really wanted me to come over, and we could just talk the craft and all that together. And that's what I did. It was very late. He said, 'Stay over night.' And even if I wanted to go home, they wouldn't let me. They said, 'Have some dinner' and all that. And we would spend afternoons talking [during] a couple of weeks." Shorter found that Coltrane's experimentation was not only on the saxophone: "He would talk about his desire to speak the English language backwards, and not really in a playful way. It was, like, to speak backwards, to get at something else. To break patterns, I guess. It was that innovative spirit that he had."

Then, Shorter recalls, they played music: "I would play the piano and sometimes he might ask me to play anything, just the first thing that came to my fingers and he would actually match it, like go for matching or complementing anything I played. Even though it would be a tone cluster. He was going for the feeling. And I noticed sitting on the piano, there was a harp book. And that's one book he used to use. He'd play something that became sheets of sound. Like a harpist. And [there was a] similarity between his book and the book that was given to me by someone who said Charlie Parker gave that book to them in Central Park. It's an old violin book, German violin book."[8] Shorter's response suggests that both books had fluid arpeggiated patterns that were not usually played on the saxophone. Coltrane said in 1961 about the harp, "I got interested in it around 1958 when I was interested in playing arpeggios instead of just straight lines." Soon he actually acquired a harp and learned to play it a bit: "It's just pure sound, it's not even like a piano where you've got to hit the keys to make the hammers hit the strings. A harpist friend of mine showed me some fingering but I don't have time to sit down and make much of it. Right now I don't see any chance of making jazz out of it."[9]

Not everyone appreciated Coltrane's "innovative spirit." Some critics were quite harsh. One compared his sound to the bark of a dog; his ribbons of notes were "epileptic fits of passion."[10] John Tynan called his playing "superficially stimulating, lonely, and rather pathetic self-seeking" (*Down Beat* August 6, 1959, p. 32). Later Tynan wrote, "Slashing at the canvas of his own creation, Coltrane erupted in a fantastic onrush of surrealism and disconnected musical thought best appreciated within the dark corridors of his personal psyche." Tynan added that Coltrane's solos suggested "overtones of neurotic compulsion and contempt for the audience" (*Down Beat,* April 14, 1960, p. 42). One who apparently never liked bop wrote that "[Charlie] Parker's playing is like an electric fan being switched on and off; Coltrane's playing is like an electric fan turned on and left on" (Mimi Clar, *Jazz Review,* April 1959, p. 24). Don Gold, reviewing the Davis sextet's appearance at the Newport Jazz Festival on July 3, 1958, wrote that the "group's solidarity is hampered by the angry young tenor of Coltrane. Backing himself into rhythmic corners on flurries of notes, Coltrane sounded like the personification of motion-without-progress in jazz."[11] The "angry" epithet continued to dog Coltrane, and it bothered him. When Ira Gitler gave him a chance to respond, Coltrane said: "If it is interpreted as angry, it is taken wrong. The only one I'm angry at is myself when I don't make what I'm trying to play."[12]

Yet there's something missing in Coltrane's explanation. I believe that he didn't consciously feel angry, and I understand that he didn't like being perceived that way, but he may have been taking the question too literally. He was breaking new ground emotionally in jazz. When Illinois Jacquet plays high up on his tenor, those sounds are part of a jubilant, swaggering expression. When Coltrane does so there is a seriousness that puts it in a different emotional territory. Certainly his music is, at the least, intense, urgent, and fiercely passionate. It may be angry at some level, and it may be the intense shouting of a man in pain, of a man who had something important to say, something he desperately needed to say. And for all the flak, there were many critics and fans who heard and liked what he had to say. Throughout his career his detractors were a minority, but a sizable and outspoken one.

When Ira Gitler wrote that first feature article on Coltrane in the fall of 1958, they met in the Park Central Hotel, where Coltrane was staying for some reason. Late in 1959 (on December 23, according to Thomas, 116), Coltrane moved his family into a house at 116-60 Mexico Street in the St. Albans section of Queens.

In 1959 John's cousin Mary moved to New York City. Mary stayed with the trombonist Charles Greenlee—also known by his Muslim name Harnifan Majid—who had been with Gillespie when Coltrane was there. They lived for a while in the huge brownstone house that trombonist Slide Hampton owned at 245 Carlton Avenue in Brooklyn.[13] Hampton's other tenants included at times trumpeter Freddie Hubbard, guitarist Wes Montgomery, bassist Larry Ridley—all friends from Indianapolis—saxophonist Eric Dolphy, and the painter known as Prophet, whose surrealistic work graced the covers of Dolphy's first two LPs as a leader in 1960. "It was wonderful," Mary recalls. Dolphy dedicated a piece to the house—"245." Coltrane would drop by at times, and he strengthened significant associations there. He had used Hubbard on his last Prestige recording session, December 26, 1958; later he would perform with Montgomery. And Dolphy, already a close friend and musical soulmate—they'd discuss music over the phone—became a regular member of his group. In the early 1960s Mary had a loft where she held jam sessions every Friday; cousin John was a frequent participant.

But let us return to 1959, when Coltrane was still contemplating a group of his own. Davis had gone out of his way to support Coltrane's independent career. Late in 1958, Davis's booking agent Jack Whittemore had begun engaging Coltrane as a leader, between Davis's gigs.[14] Davis's personal and business manager, Harold Lovett, also took on Coltrane. Lovett noted that the Prestige contract was expiring and he negotiated a deal at Atlantic Records for a seven thousand dollars per year guarantee (probably for one year, renewable at the company's option), with a Lincoln Continental car thrown in. And, unlike the Prestige agreement, Coltrane kept the rights to his originals at Atlantic, which he would publish under an abridgement of his name, "Jowcol."[15] (When Coltrane left, Prestige still had Coltrane material in the vaults that they continued to issue through the 1960s.) Besides the help that Davis gave John with these matters, Davis's fees had doubled since 1956—Coltrane was now making around $350 or $400 for each week-long gig. It was hard for Coltrane to leave the financial security that Davis offered for the uncertainty of striking out on his own.

But Coltrane saw his bandmates going off and becoming successful leaders in their own right. By November 1958, Bill Evans had already left to lead his own trio. He was replaced by Red Garland for a month or two, and Wynton Kelly came in around the beginning of 1959. Cannonball Adderley was to leave to form a group with his brother, cornetist Nat, in September 1959. He was not replaced, and from that point on Davis's group was again a quintet.

Adderley could see that Coltrane wanted to follow his lead, and he believed that the rising star of Sonny Rollins was on Coltrane's mind as well: "Coltrane had appeared on most of the commercially successful records with

Miles Davis, and his material was becoming more and more popular. People were beginning to say 'John Coltrane' with some degree of serious feeling about it. At that time, also, Sonny Rollins had broken through with a little thing of his own in vogue, and I guess John thought that the time was right for him to start fooling around with his own stuff" (Gardner, 68). Adderley's reasoning makes sense: Coltrane must have felt envious to see all the acclaim Rollins had garnered since he'd left Davis. In fact, back on November 29, 1957, Coltrane had played with the Monk quartet at a special concert away from the Five Spot, but while his name was simply listed, the ads proclaimed: "Introducing in Concert the Brilliant Sonny Rollins." What's more, the critics were rating Coltrane as Rollins's runner-up. In *Down Beat*'s critics poll, released August 22, 1957, Coltrane had come in just behind Rollins as the new tenor saxophone talent. Russ Wilson wrote in the *Oakland Tribune* that "John Coltrane ranks no worse than second to Sonny Rollins as the guiding light among tenor saxophonists" (June 4, 1959; quoted in Simpkins, 89).

According to Wayne Shorter, Coltrane had been looking for his replacement since the beginning of 1959. At Birdland, Shorter was with Maynard Ferguson's band, alternating sets with Davis, and he reports that Coltrane said he wished Shorter would take his gig. Shorter says he actually approached Davis, but Davis wanted to hold out until Coltrane was definitely leaving.[16]

Finally, during one of Davis's visits to the Blackhawk, a San Francisco nightclub, Coltrane told Russ Wilson that he was considering leaving: "'There's nothing definite yet,' he said . . . 'but I have been seriously thinking of it.' Coltrane has informed Miles of this, and should the parting come, it will be amicable. Davis understands Coltrane's viewpoint and will not stand in his way." Evidently Coltrane had another reason for wanting to take a break: His dental problems were getting worse. Wilson also noted that "he had to get an eight-tooth upper front bridge in Chicago a few weeks ago"—Coltrane must have told him so (quoted in Simpkins, 90). Archie Shepp, a saxophonist, composer, and educator, recalls that around that time, you could only see his incisors when he smiled—he says Coltrane eventually had two bridge transplants.[17] So he probably needed a break in any case in order to get used to his new teeth.

"Should Coltrane depart from the group," Wilson continued, "his replacement will probably be James 'Little Bird' Heath."[18] Coltrane felt certain that Heath, a close friend of Davis as well as himself, would be acceptable. In fact, Heath has a postcard that Coltrane sent him from the Blackhawk: "When I came home in '59, Coltrane wrote me a card and said he was leaving and welcomed me back to the scene and all and Miles called me. He said, well look, get on the plane and come out to L.A. to join his band. I got on the plane and went out there and we played at a place called Jazz Seville in Hollywood."[19]

This was in mid-July. Coltrane played the first few nights, then quit once Heath arrived to take over.

The Davis sextet with Heath and Adderley toured through August 2, when they appeared at the festival in French Lick, Indiana. After this there were a few days off and Heath's probation officer had asked to see him, so he rode back to Philadelphia with Adderley; Adderley continued to New York where he was starting to plan for his own band. When he heard what the probation officer had to say, Heath was deeply hurt and disappointed: as a condition of his probation until early 1960, Heath was told he had to stay within a fifty-mile radius of Philadelphia. Local work was fine, but touring with Davis was out of the question.[20] The next gig would have been the Playboy festival in Chicago on August 7. Davis performed there with Adderley and the rhythm section, and no tenor saxophone.

Meanwhile, it seems that Coltrane wasn't performing. In fact, Roy Haynes remembers calling Coltrane to play one night at the Five Spot—probably during this time—and Coltrane told him he couldn't play because of dental problems, but he recommended Wayne Shorter.[21] Coltrane probably spent the time working on his embouchure (the manner in which a wind player holds his or her teeth, tongue, and lips). He conquered his problems, and since his attempt to replace himself with Heath had came to a disastrous end, and since Adderley had already announced his plans to leave, Coltrane agreed to return to the Davis band for an indefinite period of time, probably beginning at Birdland on August 13. As it turned out, the commitment wasn't too onerous because Davis wasn't performing much during this time. On August 26, while the group was at Birdland, Davis was assaulted by a policeman outside the club during a break. Davis was preoccupied with the ensuing legal proceedings on and off for several months. In the meantime, he didn't perform as much as usual. Then, Davis spent part of November with Gil Evans planning and recording Evans's arrangement of Rodrigo's *Concerto de Aranjuez* for the eventual album *Sketches of Spain*. So Coltrane found opportunities to lead his own groups.

When Davis asked Coltrane to tour Europe with him from March 21 through April 10—sharing the bill with Stan Getz and Oscar Peterson—Coltrane agreed but also made it clear that this was the last time—and he meant it. On March 15, 1960, before they even left for the tour, the *Philadelphia Tribune* announced that "John Coltrane, star sax player, has left the Miles Davis Jazz group and gone out on his own. He'll head his own group."[22] *Down Beat* had a similar report on March 17 and added on April 14 (8) that Coltrane had "postponed the formation of his own group until after he returns from a short European tour with Miles Davis." It appears that Coltrane hadn't initially planned on going, and that Davis had to do some coaxing. Davis had had bookings on the West Coast that he canceled in order to make this tour, and he had invited vibraphonist Buddy Montgomery—brother of guitarist Wes—who had already played some West Coast dates with Davis. Montgomery was listed and profiled in the official program booklet for the tour, but he hated flying and at the last minute backed out. Davis asked Jimmy Heath, only to find his probation period was not yet over. Coltrane may have finally accepted the European tour because he realized it was a step toward booking his own group overseas in the future.[23] As it turned out, his first trip to Europe was a very mixed blessing.

At the very first concert of the tour, in Paris's Olympia Theater, Coltrane found himself in the midst of controversy again. Luckily, the concert was recorded professionally for broadcast, so we can hear what happened. He clearly had a following in France, because after each of his solos there is tumultuous ovation and whistling. But there is apparently a smaller contingent who dislike his playing, and during his solo on "Bye Bye Blackbird," toward the end of this long set, it comes to a head, with a number of ovations countered by loud booing. One critic compared it to the premiere of Stravinsky's *Le Sacre du Printemps* in 1913![24]

The band moved on to Stockholm the next day, without incident, but Coltrane had become notorious in France.[25] The May 1960 issue of *Jazz Hot* featured statements by four critics under the heading "For or against John Coltrane."[26] Aris Destombes began: "Let's be frank. I do not appreciate John Coltrane at all. . . . Certainly this jazzman knows music well, as people say; certainly his technique and his facility are impressive. But the avalanche of notes, the labyrinth of phrases where the swing is often lost, and the general musical performances of this all-around athlete of jazz don't at any moment interest, move, or touch me." Destoumbes concluded that Coltrane's style was probably still in transition and not yet mature. Gérard Brémond started off this way: "John Coltrane is the biggest shock that a musician has ever given me in person. . . . His improvisations consist of torrential accumulations of notes, sometimes strongly contrasting, which are expanded upon in a terribly painful manner with genuine cries of anguish." But he acknowledged that there must be something to it, concluding, "Never has jazz music been more intensely dramatic."

Pianist and producer Henri Renaud expressed his disappointment in the audience members, saying that although he personally prefers players of the Lester Young school, "Coltrane has found his own sound, his own rhythmic conception—as [altoist] Art Pepper said, 'He starts playing and just flows through the rhythm'—and a very personal use of chords. Besides, in the United States he is the idol of numerous musicians who see in him a true innovator." Composer Jeff Gilson came more aggressively to Coltrane's defense, saying that "the public has badly received John Coltrane," and that if one doesn't like the music, one should keep silent: "That would be just as effective and much more polite. . . . He seems to have made enormous progress since his first records with Miles. He has truly found himself"—quite the opposite of Destombes' opinion—"and he is now one of the strongest personalities in jazz. . . . Bravo Mister Coltrane."

What happened at the Olympia? It is too easy to put down his critics. I can imagine a fan of the Davis sound—smooth, sophisticated, finger-snapping hip—coming to that concert. Sandwiched between Davis and the hard-swinging Wynton Kelly (the solo order never varied), Coltrane takes the longest solos by far, and he is sweating, screaming, reaching to break through that aesthetic, that veneer of slick. On "Bye Bye Blackbird" he strains for some high notes and squeaks, and he gets into a whole passage in multiphonics. Also—unlike him, and probably as a comment to his French audience—he throws in "Mona Lisa, Mona Lisa, men adore you" from the hit song. To be fair, the whole thing *is* outrageous and "torrential" and full of "anguish." I happen to love it, but I can see that many would not.

Perhaps it's no accident that "Blackbird" was not played again during the tour, as far as we know. (However, most of the other concert sets were shorter, so maybe they just didn't get to it.) What's more important to realize is that Coltrane's style could not be constrained to fit the group's concept at that time, and that he had a score of innovative original compositions and arrangements of standards, designed specifically for his approach, that Davis was not per-forming. Significantly, Coltrane did come back to "Blackbird" with his own group, and he played it with resounding success at the Olympia on his Euro-pean tour in November 1962. In the context of his own group, he sounded great—in Davis's group, he sounded great or bizarre, depending on your preset.

When Coltrane finally left, Davis desperately tried to replace him, using many of the top tenor players over the next four years. Wayne Shorter had gone with Art Blakey and was no longer available. Coltrane reportedly recom-mended Joe Henderson, with whom he'd played in Detroit in 1958, but Henderson had just been drafted into the U.S. Army Band at Fort Benning, Georgia.[27] Davis used Sonny Stitt during 1960. Jimmy Heath replaced Stitt for a week at Chicago's Regal Theater in October, but his and Davis's paths never properly hooked up again. Davis also employed Hank Mobley—along with trombonist J. J. Johnson for a year or so—George Coleman, and Sam Rivers, and finally settled on Wayne Shorter in September 1964. Commentator Ralph Gleason recalled in 1972 that he once joked to Davis during his fusion years that "he really needed five tenor players, his music was so complicated. He shot those eyes at me and growled, 'I *had* five tenor players once.' I knew what he meant."[28]

13

Giant Steps and Kind of Blue

Coltrane may have been stifled at the very end of his tenure with Davis, but along the way he had found the experience terrifically valuable, as he always acknowledged. This was an exciting time for him, and he created lots of significant music during that second stint from 1958 through 1960. During the spring of 1959, he was involved in what have become two of the most famous jazz albums ever made, representing two very different approaches: Davis's *Kind of Blue* and his own *Giant Steps*.

The latter was the title piece of his first album as a leader for Atlantic, released early in 1960. (In January 1959 he had co-led an Atlantic date with vibraphonist Milt Jackson that features some marvelous blues playing. It was not issued until 1961.) This time, all seven compositions were his own, and he was the only wind player. His writing and playing throughout were remarkable, but it was the piece "Giant Steps" that knocked the jazz world on its ear.

"Giant Steps" represents the culmination of Coltrane's developing interest in third-related chord movement. Its origins in Coltrane's mind are of course not possible to trace, but a number of interesting connections may be made, some more direct than others. We already mentioned Coltrane's own "Nita" and Gillespie's "Con Alma." The latter is perhaps a more remote connection, because, as Brian Priestley reminded me, it moves from I to III to vi— essentially from I to vi, down a minor third—whereas "Giant Steps" moves I to bIII to bVI—down a major third from the beginning, and into a different key. Priestley, however, also points out that the turnaround of Dameron's "Lady Bird" used a third relation between the first two chords (the chords are C, E-flat, A-flat, D-flat, and back to C)—as we have seen, Coltrane knew this piece well. Priestley went on to note that Monk liked that turnaround as well: "You can just see Trane getting into Monk's music, or that particular turnaround anyway, and thinking 'I/bIII/bVI is fine but what if you treat bVI as the new I?' "[1]

There are more possible connections: Carl Woideck observes that on a 1957 Blue Note recording of "Tune Up"—the Vinson tune that Davis claimed and recorded with Coltrane—Sonny Rollins's group uses as a turnaround Em[7], F[7], B-flat major[7], A[7].[2] Among musicians it is generally believed that Coltrane may have been influenced by the bridge of "Have You Met Miss Jones," written by Rodgers and Hart in 1937. The bridge goes through the keys of B-flat, G-flat, and D, each a major third apart, as in Coltrane's piece. (The first eight bars of "Countdown" use this chord sequence, in the same keys as "Miss Jones.")[3] McCoy Tyner did mention hearing the 1953 recording that Tatum made of "Miss Jones" (recalled by Priestley in a letter to the author), but he was referring to later times when he was already in Coltrane's quartet. Pianist Steve Kuhn told me that when he played "Giant Steps" with Coltrane he mentioned the link with "Miss Jones," but he was unclear from Coltrane's reaction whether he already knew about this or not.[4] Still, the fact that Tatum recorded it is worth noting, as well as the fact that Tatum speeds through the sequence of the bridge during his closing cadenza. (Tatum also recorded it in 1956 with tenorist Ben Webster.) All harmonically oriented musicians—Charlie Parker, for one—studied Tatum closely, and Coltrane probably did too. Coltrane wrote that he hadn't listened much to Tatum as a youth, but was floored when he heard Tatum and his protégé Oscar Peterson jamming all night, sometime in the early 1950s ("Coltrane on Coltrane").

These historical precedents for third relations are interesting to consider. Probably more directly relevant to "Giant Steps" were Coltrane's theoretical interests. "Giant Steps" was, after all, more than a tune that used third relations—it was a thorough study, an etude, on those relationships. Classical musicians have been interested in third-related keys for centuries—C. P. E. Bach was fond of such modulations, and Beethoven was not shy about them either (as in his "Waldstein" sonata for piano, which begins in C major and then goes to E). But changing from one key to another is one thing—a series of chords moving in thirds, one right after the other, generates a much faster pace. One finds composers interested in this during the 1800s. In fact, an 1853 treatise by Karl Friedrich Weitzmann makes the point that from an augmented chord such as E-flat, G, B, one can create other chords by moving one voice a half-step.[5] For example, make the G an F-sharp and you have B major; make the E-flat a D and you have G major; make the B a B-flat and you have E-flat major; thus creating the three key areas of "Giant Steps." Even in jazz, such progressions occurred, although infrequently, before Coltrane. For example, Carl Woideck noticed that pianist Teddy Wilson used a related progression— A-flat, B[7], E, E-flat[7]—behind Benny Goodman's solo on the trio version of "China Boy" from 1936.[6]

Suspecting that Coltrane's teacher at the Granoff School, Dennis Sandole, may have been interested in third relations, David Demsey wrote to him and received the written response that "Coltrane and I had probed into third relationships; also . . . deceptive resolution, chromatic root movement, [equal] division of the octave," and other "extended harmonic devices."[7] So Sandole had started Coltrane along this road.

As was his nature, Coltrane made an exhaustive investigation into the possibilities of third relations, and he employed them on a number of pieces during 1959 and 1960, notably "Countdown,"[8] "Exotica," "Satellite" (a variation on "How High the Moon"), "26-2" (based on Parker's "Confirmation," this originally untitled item was probably named for being the second piece recorded on October 26), and his influential arrangements of "But Not for Me" and "Body and Soul." He had several harmonic formulas. Most often, he would insert two extra V–I cadences a major third apart—the tonics outlining an augmented chord—into the original. So, for example, if the idea was to go through ii–V–I in C major, instead of just playing D minor and G dominant leading to C major, he'd start on the D minor and insert, moving quickly, V–I in A-flat, then in E (a major third from A-flat), then finally in C (a major third from E). Where the original began with a major chord and then a ii–V–I cadence, he would have to modify his plan accordingly but still managed to insert his extra cadences.[9]

As a case in point, "Countdown" was fashioned out of the conventional series of ii–V–I progressions in "Tune Up." Coltrane replaces each of the ii–V–I progressions of the original with his substitute formula. This speeds up the rate of harmonic motion and delays the arrival of each tonic chord until the fourth measure of each phrase instead of the third measure.

a. The chords to the first four measures of "Tune up"

b. Coltrane's formula to replace the above chords (a similar example is in Simpkins 246).

If one continues to apply the formula to the second and third phrases of "Tune Up," one gets the progression of "Countdown."

In the version of "Countdown" that appears on *Giant Steps*, Coltrane plays at an extremely fast tempo, over three hundred beats a minute, and launches directly into a blistering improvisation, stating the theme only at the end. It is an incredible tour de force. The late Art Taylor, drummer on the date, told me that he and Coltrane had rehearsed this before going into the studio.[10]

Simpkins (246) mentions that Coltrane devised other substitution formulas. David Baker, jazz performer, educator, and theorist, suggests that Coltrane's interest in minor-third relations—properties of the diminished chord and scale—would have led him to the realization that chords whose roots belong to the same diminished chord can always be substituted for each other. This is an extension of the common tritone substitution, for the tritone is two minor thirds. For instance, instead of Dm–E-flat⁷/A-flat–B⁷/E and so on as given above, one could play Dm–F-sharp⁷/B–F⁷/B-flat and so on. Why? Because the E-flat and F-sharp (G-flat) are in the same diminished chord, as are A-flat and B (C-flat), as are B and F, E and B-flat. In this way, one can travel just about anywhere one wants to go from the initial chord.[11]

Some of Coltrane's third-related experiments are lost. For instance, on May 4, 1959, he recorded a piece entitled "Sweet Sioux." It was never issued, and the tape was destroyed in a fire at Atlantic Records in 1976. Pianist Tommy Flanagan remembers: "That was supposed to have been a song based on 'Cherokee' [using] the same kind of chordal progessions that he used on, say, 'Tune Up,' which he called 'Countdown.' Everything was based on those major-minor things in thirds." The piece was difficult, "so we never got through it! . . . It was supposed to have been part of a suite—'Giant Steps' was one of them, and 'Countdown' was one, and 'Sweet Sioux' I guess would have completed the piece. Like a little trilogy or something." He also said the suite was to have been called "Suite Sioux," compounding the puns on the name "Cherokee" and the old song "Sweet Sue." Flanagan believes Coltrane had applied these types of chord progressions on the blues too. And there is an unissued (and unheard) practice tape of Coltrane playing "All the Things You Are" using his chord substitution formula.

This formula is known among musicians as "'Giant Steps' changes," yet it does not appear in exactly this form in that piece. The sixteen-measure chord progression of "Giant Steps" begins with eight measures whose root movements are largely in thirds, and closes with eight measures of ii–v–I progressions, separated by thirds.

"Giant Steps" by John Coltrane (1959).
Copyright © 1974 JOWCOL MUSIC. International Copyright Secured. All Rights Reserved. Used by Permission.

Pianist and educator Andy LaVerne has pinpointed the relationship between "Giant Steps" and the substitution formula, a relationship that has previously been assumed and felt but not explained. In his article "Twelve Steps to Giant Steps,"[12] he demonstrates that Coltrane used an abridged version of his formula: "If we place an F minor chord and an F#7 before the first B major of the tune, we have a complete Coltrane ii–V–I substitution in E-flat." (Compare this with the examples above from "Tune-Up.") LaVerne continues, "Then all we need to do is replace the A minor chord at the beginning of bar 3 [he means bar 4] with a C# minor, and we have another complete Coltrane ii–V–I substitution, this time for B major." LaVerne also provides numerous musical illustrations to show how one can apply these insights.

What about the second half of "Giant Steps"? Demsey points out that the most direct source for the second eight bars is the late Nicolas Slonimsky's *Thesaurus of Scales and Melodic Patterns.* Published in 1947, this book seems to have circulated among jazz musicians by the mid-1950s, and by several reports including Tyner's, Coltrane spent time with it. Demsey, with the help of Robert Wason, has convincingly demonstrated that the second half of "Giant Steps" derives from this book. One of Slonimsky's "ditone progressions" (dividing the octave into three parts by major thirds, or ditones) on the top of page 40 is Coltrane's melody starting on C (Coltrane's starts on G). And right on page vi of the preface—the only part of the book with text, explaining how one could apply the music examples in the balance of the book—is basically the same melody (starting on E), this time with chords underneath that are practically the same as Coltrane's.[13] Slonimsky's purpose here was to show that one can make his abstract patterns more tonal by underpinning them with dominant-tonic chords.

As for the particular form that Coltrane's piece takes—the use of major thirds dividing the octave into three parts, the use of three tonal centers—I wouldn't underestimate Coltrane's interest in religion and mysticism. He had a kind of ecumenical, open-minded interest in all traditions. During the late 1950s he would draw the circle of fifths and then connect the twelve key centers with lines. One such drawing appears in Fujioka (67), and Yusef Lateef has published two others (from 1960).[14] Sometimes he'd place an equilateral triangle within the circle, creating a "magic triangle," and Marcello Piras has shown that if one does that, the points of the triangle connect key centers a major third apart.[15] Surely Coltrane was interested in the mystical as well as aural implications of third relations.

By several accounts, Coltrane had been working on "Giant Steps" progressions well before the recording dates. For instance, McCoy Tyner told Priestley (53) that "Giant Steps" as well as "Like Sonny," "Equinox," and other pieces were composed as early as May 1957, when Coltrane was home in Philadelphia: "I used to go over to his mother's house when he was working on those cycles, you know. And, actually, I knew those songs before they recorded them, but I was still in Philadelphia so he used Tommy Flanagan on the album." But it is not clear whether Tyner means "Giant Steps" itself, or the substitution formula.

Naima's cousin Carl Grubbs remembers Coltrane practicing the "Giant Steps" cycle a year later. Carl was born in 1944, he and his brother, Earl Jr. (who died in 1989), were from Philadelphia. Their father, Earl Grubbs Sr., and Naima's mother were siblings. Carl had had about six months of piano lessons, but, he recalls, 1958 was when he came alive musically: "That was the year that my parents bought my brother an alto and bought me a clarinet." At Easter they went to New York to visit Coltrane and for the first time heard him play. He had played the night before so he slept late. Carl recalls:

We got there around 11:00 A.M. or noon, and he was still asleep. But we knew when he woke up because he started practicing. I didn't realize it at the time, but he was working on these "Giant Steps" intervals. He must have practiced for about an hour or something before he came out and talked to everybody. That was the first time I found out what improvisation was—I had gotten the records, but I thought they were reading!

As years went on when he'd come to Philadelphia we'd go over to his house on Thirty-third Street and ask him questions and he would show us some things on the saxophone. Like we heard him gliss, and we'd ask him what was that? He called it a drop [off the end of a note], and he'd show us how to do that. He also got me back playing piano by showing us chords, and how he would voice these chords on piano. From playing "Giant Steps" on the piano I could really understand how he would double thirds and fifths to get it to really work.

Wayne Shorter is another witness to the creation of "Giant Steps." His "sighting" is from late 1958 or early 1959: "When I was [at Coltrane's place] there was a lot of cooking going on in that house, you know. And there weren't so many musicians there when I was there. Maybe like myself, Freddie Hubbard would come by. And Cedar Walton stayed a little while. . . . And Trane would sit and play those 'Giant Steps' changes all the time, before he even recorded it. You know, just over and over like that."[16]

Coltrane ended his March 1958 recording of "If There Is Someone Lovelier Than You" with a quick rehearsed coda of four major seventh chords moving down by major thirds.[17]

In February 1959 Coltrane superimposed a thirds progression over the chords of "Limehouse Blues." The very opening of his charging solo clearly suggests Cm^7–D-flat^7–G-flat–A^7–D–F^7; all this over a simple F^7 chord played by the rhythm section for four measures.[18] He does the same over the next chord and suggests his substitution formula at a few other points of his solo and while trading with Adderley at the end of the take.

It's no wonder that Coltrane spent so long preparing for "Giant Steps." With its quickly changing key centers and fast tempo, it requires the player to prepare as much material as possible in advance. Coltrane chose to construct his solo largely out of four-note patterns that could be easily transposed to fit each chord. One basic pattern, involving the first, second, third, and fifth degree of each key, appears many times. This use of "pentatonic patterns," as they are called (because the sixth of the scale, which is omitted, would make it a pentatonic scale), is widespread today, primarily through Coltrane's influence. There are books that illustrate how to apply these and other patterns to technique practice as well as to improvisation, and to slower-moving as well as fast-moving chord progressions.[19] Coltrane alternated these pentatonic patterns with other material, most of it also related to pentatonic scales. Another kind of four-note pattern, the simple arpeggio, appears often, particularly during the first eight measures of each chorus. Coltrane employed contrasting upward and downward motion to add variety, especially during the first four measures of each chorus. He frequently also used a connecting scale, which may be seen as a filling in of the pentatonic scale. In short, Coltrane relies heavily on formulas, especially ones derived from pentatonic scales, to negotiate the first eight measures of this chord progression, but his repertoire of formulas is so vast that he is able to keep the solo interesting.

Beginning of Coltrane's solo on "Giant Steps" (master take, May 5, 1959).
Copyright © 1974 JOWCOL MUSIC. International Copyright Secured. All Rights Reserved. Used
by Permission.

The last eight measures of the "Giant Steps" progression are easier than the first eight because each key area is prolonged for two entire measures by way of a ii–V–I progression. This allows the player to improvise more freely and to think more lyrically.[20]

The first recording session for the *Giant Steps* album was held on March 26, 1959, with Cedar Walton on piano, Paul Chambers on bass, and Lex Humphries on drums, but the results were not satisfactory (to Coltrane, I assume), and none of it was used on the album.[21] Parts of the session were issued in 1974, including the last take—number 8—of "Giant Steps," and the complete session reel was issued in 1995. Not only does this offer us the first recordings of "Giant Steps," "Naima," and "Like Sonny," but we are able to hear how the takes progressed, to get a sense of how Coltrane worked in the studio, and even in a few places to hear him instruct the band. Every member of the rhythm section has a very specific part to play.

Cedar Walton knew Coltrane well (according to Ted Panken), and the two of them had rehearsed together before the session. But adding the bass and drums created problems, especially with endings. After take 2 of "Giant Steps" Coltrane says that it was too slow. After take 3 he discusses the ending. The little fills that Walton played during the second half of the theme were developed in the studio. Before the penultimate take, we can hear Coltrane instruct Walton to play those.

The take 8 of "Giant Steps" that was issued in 1974 moves at a pace of 260 beats per minute, slower than the originally issued recording. At the slower tempo Coltrane sounds more relaxed and more lyrical. Still, he does not invite Cedar Walton to solo on this difficult piece. (Walton is concentrating hard just to accompany Coltrane correctly.) This earlier version of "Giant Steps" provides instructive examples of the ways that Coltrane manages to avoid the somewhat mechanical quality of playing patterns. For example, while he does utilize the same phrase for the first eight measures of several choruses, he varies it each time, only once presenting it in its basic form. These are true variations, not just simple repetitions or inversions of his basic formulas.

Excerpts from Coltrane's solo on "Giant Steps" ("alternate" take from the first session, March 26, 1959).

On May 5, Coltrane recorded the originally issued version of "Giant Steps."[22] Tommy Flanagan, the pianist on this date, told me he was unaware that Coltrane had already recorded with Walton. Flanagan and Coltrane never performed together in public, although the pianist feels they may have played at a jam session at Coltrane's place or somebody's loft. But they were acquainted, as Flanagan explains: "I had heard him with Monk before, and even before he was with Monk I'd heard him with Miles and I knew Paul [Chambers] of course from Detroit. Just from visiting [the Davis band] I got to know Trane, and I loved his playing. For my first record date, I called him—that date they called 'The Cats'" (Prestige Records, April 18, 1957). He said elsewhere: "I had a song on there that was difficult for me, I wrote a piece called 'Solacium.' But I knew that Trane wouldn't have any problem with it, so I didn't hesitate to bring that to the date. . . . You know from that point he called me 'Maestro' because of that tune, like he thought I could cover anything that he could write."[23]

Tommy Flanagan is indeed a superb musician (he won a Jazz Masters Fellowship from the National Endowment of the Arts at the end of 1995), and it is no discredit to him that he found it difficult to solo on this daunting piece. Apparently, Coltrane had the sense to play the chords for Flanagan on the piano before the recording session. But he did not mention the style, so Flanagan had assumed it was to be played at a slow or medium tempo. Flanagan recalls, "We were neighbors, so he was right around the corner from me. He came around and he played it for me [a week or two before]. There was no need to give me any music to it. I said, 'All right. No problem there.' I didn't know I'd have to play on it and what tempo he was talking about! Not that it was *that* challenging, but you have to be more prepared than just playing the blues or something." At the recording session, Flanagan did see sheet music, although for "Giant Steps," "I don't think there was any melody, just the chord sequence, which spells out the melody, practically." (He believes that Coltrane collected the music at the end of the date.) On the title track of the original album he actually sounds fine—just not as fleet as we know he can be. On the other takes from this date, first issued in 1995, Flanagan has problems. On one, he stops in the middle of his solo; on the other, he restricts himself to playing the chords.

I'm certain that the little winding run that Coltrane plays at the end of "Giant Steps" has a classical origin, but I cannot quite place it. It basically embellishes the notes of a major arpeggio, and appeared in solos by Dizzy Gillespie and Powell during the early 1950s.

Ending of "Giant Steps" (master take, May 5, 1959).
Copyright © 1974 JOWCOL MUSIC. International Copyright Secured. All Rights Reserved. Used by Permission.

Coltrane, with the help of producer Nesuhi Ertegun, programmed the album *Giant Steps* carefully. It included three tributes to family members: "Cousin Mary" is a blues with unusual chords. Coltrane's working title for this appears to have been "Old New Blues" (Simpkins, 87). "Syeeda's Song Flute"— his stepdaughter had a recorder, probably plastic, sometimes called a song flute—is a bouncy piece that seems to me very Monk-like. "Naima" is a serene, exotic tribute to his wife, over a carefully rehearsed bass pattern. (One can hear Coltrane and Chambers working on the bass part during the first, previously unissued session.) The gorgeous ending is quite similar to one Coltrane had used on "Slow Dance," by Alonzo Levister, back in August 1957. It is typical of Coltrane that his slow pieces do not sound like "ballads" at all—there is no touch of that "Oh baby, I miss you" feeling. "Naima" is more like a hymn. It became one of his best-known pieces and stayed in his repertoire even when he and Naima were no longer together. As late as 1963, Coltrane said, "I especially like to play certain of my themes that, for me, are very pretty, like 'Aisha' [actually written by Tyner for his wife, and not included in any of John's known concerts] or 'Syeeda's Song Flute,' but I want to compose another for my wife, even prettier. The one I consider my best composition is 'Naima' but I can't play it at every concert."24 In 1964, he recorded "Wise One," which according to Simpkins (173) was the new piece for Naima, a tribute to the good advice and wisdom she had imparted to him.

"Mr. P. C." is another dedication, to Paul Chambers, Coltrane's bassist of choice. John often recorded with one or another of his Davis bandmates, but the one constant whenever he recorded under his own name—that is, when he chose the players—was Chambers.25 In the notes to the album Coltrane called him "one of the greatest bass players in jazz. His playing is beyond what I could say about it." Even in November 1961, when he'd been leading his own group for a year and a half, he told Postif, "A bassist of the stature of Paul Chambers is difficult to find in New York, because he creates a fusion: he listens to the piano and the drums, and all his work consists of improvising in relation to those instruments. His melodic line is a sort of result of the melodic lines of the two other musicians." In the process, Chambers did more than just keep a solid walking line. He created some original effects. Listen, for example, to his triplets behind Coltrane's last chorus on "Blue Train"; to his fills and ostinatos on "My Funny Valentine" (live with Davis in September 1958); to his beautiful and distinctive work on "Invitation" (for Prestige in July 1958). "Mr. P.C." is in Coltrane's favorite form, a minor blues, and it has become a standard among musicians.

"Like Sonny," a tribute to Sonny Rollins, was recorded at the same sessions as the *Giant Steps* album. Along with "Fifth House" and other tracks, it was released in February 1961 on the album *Coltrane Jazz*. Coltrane continued to praise Rollins. He said in March 1960, "I think he's the outstanding tenor man today. That's usually my man, you know. He's great."[26] It is an indication of Coltrane's genius for composition that he was able to develop this entire piece from a little turning figure that Rollins liked to use. Joe Goldberg pointed out one place that Rollins may be heard playing this lick: his solo on "My Old Flame" from Kenny Dorham's *Jazz Contrasts* album, May 1957. Coltrane took this little phrase, and in his typical manner, used it as the sole motive for the theme, taking it through several different tonal centers. Again, the keys are a third apart, but in this case the approach is simpler. There are no cadences except at the end of each section of this ABA structure;[27] most of the time it sits on each chord for two measures apiece. "Like Sonny" is also significant as a reminder of Coltrane's interest in Latin and African rhythms, even this early on. On the original version from March 1959, the bass and piano play an ostinato part in 4/4 outlining the tonal centers, while the drummer (Lex Humphries) plays a 6/8 style African pattern, twice per measure. One can hear Coltrane working with them for several takes on the complicated rhythm, and on making the transition from that into a more standard jazz swing feeling during his solo. At one point, after "Rehearsal 1," he instructs Cedar Walton to play in unison with the bass.

But "Like Sonny" was constantly developing. In its next incarnation, in December 1959, you can hear that the rhythm has become a kind of bossa nova, at a time when few Americans were yet aware of that style. A third version was recorded for Roulette Records in September 1960, with Billy Higgins on drums. In this lovely incarnation it was called "Simple Like"—perhaps short for "Simple Like Sonny"?—and the rhythm has become more free. (On Trip 5001, it was issued as "Simple Life," which is suggestive because that is an expression I heard his cousin Mary use.)

Coltrane felt good about his first album for Atlantic. In an interview with Carl-Erik Lindgren in Stockholm, March 22, 1960, during his last tour with Davis, he gave *Blue Train* as his favorite among his own records, adding, "There's such a good band on there." But when he was asked about *Giant Steps,* the usually reticent composer said, "I think it was my best quartet [as opposed to a larger group] recording, so far, with the exception of maybe *Soultrane.* I put them both about the same." This also makes one want to go back and listen to *Soultrane,* an album with Garland, Chambers, and Art Taylor from February 1958. Coltrane plays beautifully on five tunes, none his own.

With his typical openness, Coltrane expressed reservations about his own work on the back cover of *Giant Steps*—something that is never done in liner notes. He said: "I'm worried that sometimes what I'm doing sounds just like academic exercises, and I'm trying more and more to make it sound prettier." Later, in the 1960 Stockholm interview, Lindgren asked him if he meant that he was "trying to get a more beautiful sound." He had misunderstood, as Coltrane explained: "Well, I hope to play, not necessarily a more beautiful sound—

though I would like, tone-wise, to be able to produce a more beautiful sound—
but now I'm primarily interested in trying to work what I have, what I know,
down into a more lyrical line. That's what I mean by beautiful—more lyrical, so
it'll be, you know, easily understood." Just a minute before, he had said more
about this in response to a question about his being tagged as "angry":

> *Coltrane:* . . . The reason I play so many sounds—maybe it sounds
> angry—is because I'm trying so many things at one time, you see. I
> haven't sorted them out. I have a whole bag of things that I'm trying to
> work through and get the one essential, you know. And I just . . .
>
> *Lindgren:* Would you say that you're trying to play everything you hear at
> one time or something like that?
>
> *Coltrane:* Now, there are some set things that I know—some harmonic
> devices that I know [such as third relations] that will take me out of the
> ordinary path, you see, if I use these. But I haven't played them enough,
> and I'm not familiar with them enough yet to take the one single line
> through them, so I play all of them—you know, trying to acclimate my
> ear, so I can hear.

In other words, it was difficult to construct a smoothly flowing melodic line
that would connect all of the harmonies he was hearing with a minimum of
extraneous notes.

At the same time that Coltrane was developing his "Giant Steps" chordal
concepts, Miles Davis was becoming interested in doing away with chord
progressions. In 1958 Davis, with his pianist Bill Evans and the unrelated Gil
Evans, had begun to experiment with the use of modes. Musicians are often
unclear about just what they mean by "mode." Harold Powers has pointed out
that *mode* is used to refer to "two quite different phenomena." In actual
practice, *mode* would apply to "open-ended heterogeneous networks of melodic types"—such as the short melodic ideas that a sitarist will use when
playing a particular north Indian raga, or the ones that a Baroque composer
will use in a piece that has G for the tonic and two flats in the signature, or
perhaps the typical melodies that jazz musicians use on a blues in B-flat. But,
Powers continues, theorists and many other musicians use "mode" to refer to
"closed systems of music-theoretical categories" that are good for categorizing
pieces—such as a particular pattern of whole-steps and half-steps that we call
"major" or "minor." Powers feels that we need both approaches, but that we
need to be aware of the discrepancies.[28] For example, two pieces may both use
C as a tonal center and have no key signature, yet may behave very differently
melodically. On the other hand, within a particular genre, such as classical
music of the late 1700s and early 1800s, there are certain melodic types (jazz
musicians would say "licks") that define a piece as being in C major—major is

defined not only by the key signature but also by the content of the piece. Random note movement on the white keys will not give a feeling of C major; certain melodic directions are part of the language.

Davis, Coltrane, the two Evanses, and jazz musicians in general use *mode* in the closed-system sense. They define modes, in a somewhat oversimplified manner, as types of scales. They think of "modal" playing, rather pragmatically, as a way of learning new scales to use in their improvisations—some musicians will even call them "modal scales." Major (also known as Ionian mode) and minor (also known as Aeolian mode), for example, are the two most common types of scales—or modes—in American popular music. Barry Kernfeld has pointed out that, in practice, when jazz musicians improvise over these "modal" pieces, they hardly restrict themselves to the mode, since they add blue notes and other embellishments at will. Analyzing the solos on the *Kind of Blue* album, he also points out that both Davis and Coltrane suggest chords and tonality in their melodic lines, which is not a strictly modal approach. He has suggested that we do away with the label *modal jazz* altogether—not a bad idea—and simply say that we are playing over one or two chords, or over simple "vamps" (repeated backgrounds of one or two chords).[29]

So we must take Davis's statements about modal jazz with the above caveats in mind. Davis began to focus on what could be done with scales during 1958: "When Gil wrote the arrangement of 'I Loves You Porgy' [recorded August 18, 1958], he only wrote a scale for me to play. No chords. . . . Bill Evans knows too what can be done with scales. All chords, after all, are relative to scales and certain chords make certain scales. [This is the closed-system approach—a scale or mode is just a series of available notes.] I wrote a tune recently [possibly "Milestones"?] that's more a scale than a [melodic] line."[30] Davis and Evans were looking at scales not found as often in pop music, such as Dorian and Phrygian.

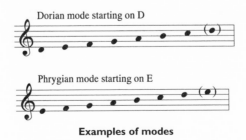

Examples of modes

These are only a couple out of the hundreds of scales in use throughout the world in folk and ethnic music. Miles said he and Gil were very interested in the music of Aram Khachaturian, a composer who drew on scales from his native Armenian and Russian background for his melodies. (His popular "Saber Dance" is an example, although this doesn't give a fair indication of the depth of much of his music.)

Another thing that was novel about this so-called modal jazz of Davis and Evans was the leisurely pace at which the modes (scales) changed. In most jazz pieces, the chords and their associated scales change about once a measure. But Davis's new music would stay on the same scale for as long as sixteen measures at a time. Finally, there was no set chord progression for the scale; one was encouraged to try any notes from the scale to get a variety of sounds. In a sense, one could say they were trying to use the scale freely, without being limited to the melodic types that may traditionally have been associated with its modal type. So "modal jazz" did identify a repertory of pieces that was different from other jazz of the time, but not simply because it used modes—virtually all music does. It was unique in the use of unusual scales, in staying on each one for many measures at a time, and in leaving the choice of chords open and free. Before Davis, only a few jazz players had experimented with modal jazz— primarily West Coast innovators such as Shorty Rogers, Jimmy Giuffre, and the lesser-known Duane Tatro, along with the visiting East Coaster Teddy Charles.[31]

The effect of modal jazz on Coltrane was profound. He explained what Miles was doing this way: "We found Miles in the midst of another stage of his musical development. There was one time in his past that he devoted to multichorded structures. He was interested in chords for their own sake. But now it seemed that he was moving in the opposite direction to the use of fewer and fewer chord changes in songs. He used tunes with free-flowing lines and chordal direction. This approach allowed the soloist the choice of playing chordally (vertically) or melodically (horizontally)" ("Coltrane on Coltrane"). It is interesting to see Coltrane using this distinction of vertical versus horizontal. That is a key concept in the teaching of composer George Russell. Coltrane was familiar with Russell's ideas and had recorded with him in September 1958.

Coltrane provided a quite specific discussion of his musical approach: "In fact, due to the direct and free-flowing lines of his [Davis's] music, I found it easy to apply the harmonic ideas that I had. I could stack up chords—say, on a C7, I sometimes superimposed an Eb7, up to an F#7, [resolving] down to an F. That way I could play three chords on one. But on the other hand, if I wanted to, I could play melodically. Miles' music gave me plenty of freedom. It's a beautiful approach" ("Coltrane on Coltrane").[32]

Illustration of "stacking up" chords as explained by Coltrane

This is another outgrowth of Coltrane's interest in third relations—in this case a series of minor thirds, whose roots outline a diminished chord. In practice, he was rarely so prosaic about it as in the example shown. He might use a scale or lick in each of the passing keys, rather than an arpeggio. German jazz scholar Gerhard Putschögl has found some examples in Coltrane's solo on "Double Clutching," an F blues from October 1958 (146). Sometimes the roots outlined an augmented chord, as in "Giant Steps": Putschögl found examples in "Double Clutching" as well (144–45). The effect of this "stacking" device is that we hear Coltrane getting further and further away from the tonal center of a passage, and then returning. It is a technique of enriching static harmonies that he continued to use in the 1960s, though his rhythmic approach then was much more direct. His procedure, though busy and daring, is also orderly and logical. His "sheets of sound" in 1958 were sometimes composed of all these harmonic ideas; at other times he simply played his diminished-scale patterns at incredible speed.

For the first *Kind of Blue* session on March 2, 1959, Davis had sketched some modal compositions.[33] He didn't rehearse them beforehand because he wanted to get the freshness of the first performances on tape—this had become his typical working method for recordings. He had some uncredited help from the two Evanses. For example, the brooding written introduction to "So What," which begins the album, appears to have been by Gil, and he presented it in a big-band orchestration with Davis at Carnegie Hall in 1961. "Blue in Green" is a Bill Evans piece.[34] Bill and Gil Evans may have made other suggestions as well. For instance, it seems significant that Bill's introduction to the gorgeous "Flamenco Sketches" comes from his "Peace Piece" recording session of the previous December. But the bulk of the work was by Davis.[35]

Modal jazz offered freedom, but it also posed a challenge—to make coherent and interesting music with a minimum of harmonic guidelines. It might sound simple to play on one scale, but it took great creativity. As Davis said to Nat Hentoff: "You don't have to worry about [chord] changes and you can do more with the [melodic] line. It becomes a challenge to see how melodically inventive you are."[36] During his spell replacing Coltrane with the group in July 1959, Jimmy Heath found it took some getting used to: "Well, what was hard for me was the unfamiliar territory and that it . . . stays in a mode and you don't resolve it at the end of a cadence like you do." Heath remembers playing the piece again as a substitute for Sonny Stitt in 1960, and by this time he was comfortable with it: "Miles knows what to do, and he used to always tell me about the way Sonny Stitt didn't play it the way he wanted it played. Sonny Stitt would play it like it was a D minor chord [emphasizing the notes D, F, and A], and Miles didn't want it to be like that. He wanted it to be all the white keys so that it could be C, F, it could be all kinds of other things happening." In other words, there was no set chord progression.

"So What" featured the simplest possible AABA structure: eight measures of the D Dorian scale, another eight of D Dorian, eight of E-flat Dorian, and eight again of D Dorian. Each soloist on "So What" chose a different solution to the challenge it posed. Alto saxophonist Cannonball Adderley implied diatonic progressions over the sustained modes. Bill Evans adopted a moody, chordal approach. Opening the improvisations, Davis brilliantly worked with short, tuneful motives in a solo so catchy that many people know it by heart. Davis begins his two-chorus improvisation with a simple elaboration of a d minor arpeggio, which reappears before the bridge of his second chorus and serves as a kind of motto for the solo. His A sections are comprised mostly of short, arpeggiated phrases. Both bridge sections contrast with the A sections by employing mostly stepwise motion in long ascending or descending lines. Davis communicates emotion through a rich array of expressive tone colors and articulations. He enters his second chorus with a leisurely, floating arpeggiation of the upper extensions of the D minor chord, then repeats it, softly, an octave lower. Pianist Bill Evans contributes to the beauty of this moment with his sensitive accompaniment, while Paul Chambers creates suspense with a pedal point during this first A section of the second chorus. (Chambers does the same thing at the start of Coltrane's second chorus.)

Coltrane spontaneously composed a tightly unified solo notable both for the abstract quality of its melodic motives, and for the way he develops each of them. His solo on "So What" begins with a plain, basic idea, consisting only of steps one, three, four, and five of the Dorian scale (concert D Dorian, E for the tenor). He develops this idea, varying its rhythm, extending it by adding more notes, for a full sixteen measures. (Here again, the accompaniment of Bill Evans heightens the drama.) After the bridge, he begins a similar procedure with a different idea. Taking a short, expressive motive, he adds notes to it with each repetition, until it climbs to a high e . Then, continuing into the second chorus, he takes the last three notes of the preceding variation, d , f′, and d, each preceded by a grace note, and they constitute a new motive. This time he extends the motive by adding notes to the *beginning* of it with each statement.[37]

John Coltrane's solo on "So What" from the Davis album *Kind of Blue* (March 2, 1959).

SO WHAT, by Miles Davis

After the recording session, the band added "So What" to its concert repertory. Reviews of the Davis band from June and July 1959 confirm that they were also performing "All Blues" in concert—one critic mentions "a blues that starts and ends in three-quarter time" while the other lists it by name.[38] These pieces were also in the band's book for Coltrane's final tour of Europe with Davis in 1960, and all of Coltrane's solos from this tour are worth study. For example, the version of "So What" from the Holland concert of April 9 provides a fascinating comparison with the studio version. Coltrane improvises ferociously for numerous choruses, developing his ideas at great length. Rather than modify his train of thought at the bridge, as he seems to have done on the studio version, he transposes each idea up a half-step and continues to work with it.

Excerpt from Coltrane's solo on "So What" (live, April 9, 1960), beginning at the fourth chorus, second A section.
SO WHAT, by Miles Davis
© 1959 Warner-Tamerlane Publishing Corp. and Estate of Miles Davis
All Rights Administered by Warner-Tamerlane Publishing Corp.
All Rights Reserved. Used by Permission.
WARNER BROS. PUBLICATIONS U.S., INC., Miami, FL 33014

Later in the solo, he introduces motives that end on sustained high notes, transposing them up a half-step for the bridge. He explores motives involving the extreme lower and upper registers of the saxophone, and superimposes a barrage of harmonic layers over the "monotonal" foundation. The style of this solo approaches that of Coltrane's solo on his own later version of "So What," his theme "Impressions." (Besides the two versions discussed above, there are a number of others from Europe, and an intense two choruses from a television show that Davis filmed on April 2, 1959.)

Improvisation is, after all, the discipline of composing in real time, in one take, without rewrites.[39] The goals and results are different from what one expects in written composition, even for Coltrane himself. He could hardly have improvised such erudite compositions as "Giant Steps" or "Lazy Bird." Coltrane's compositional process in "So What" spellbinds the listener. The process is very exposed, and one is able to follow Coltrane as he comes across an idea, works with it for a while, and then derives his next idea from it. Coltrane seems, as he suggested in "Coltrane on Coltrane," liberated by the slow harmonic movement. By spending so much time on each chord and mode he was able to grow in his ability to develop musical ideas while improvising. It also allowed him to concentrate on rhythm, as he had said he wanted to. Coltrane's approach varied from piece to piece and from day to day, but on "So What" he seemed consistently to work on developing his ideas, whereas on "Giant Steps" he was obsessed with manipulating short patterns to negotiate a fast-moving chord progression.

So the spring of 1959 was a time of great significance for Coltrane. He was taking tonal harmony as far as it had ever been taken in jazz. In fact, he said in the notes to *Giant Steps,* again with his usual modesty: "I feel like I can't hear but so much in the ordinary chords we usually have going in the accompaniment. I just have to have more of a blueprint. It may be that sometimes I've been trying to force all those extra progressions into a structure where they don't fit, but this is all something I have to keep working on. I think too that my rhythmic approach has changed unconsciously during all this, and in time, it too should get as flexible as I'm trying to make my harmonic thinking."

But at the same time, Coltrane was working with Davis on simplifying the chords to the point that they were almost eliminated. He said, "[I]t was hard to make some things swing with the rhythm section playing these chords, and Miles advised me to abandon the idea" of this complicated blueprint.[40] Pete LaRoca, who played drums with Coltrane in 1960, remembers discussing the repertory with Coltrane outside Small's in Harlem: "We were sitting in his car, and I was saying to him I thought the band got a better groove on the things that were modal. . . . We got a heavy groove on 'Equinox' [a minor blues], things were relaxed, whereas we were kind of hustling and chasing ourselves on that stuff from *Giant Steps,* where it had all those chords."

Coltrane began to see that it was possible for him to have his cake and eat it too—he could play through his harmonic ideas on the saxophone, creating some of those "prettier" lines he strove for, while the rhythm section supported him with more open, modal backgrounds. He said in 1961: "Now I prefer the rhythm to be free. I had to get it beat into my skull [laughs], but I accept this principle now. At first I wasn't sure, because I was delving into sequences, and I felt that I should have the rhythm play the sequences right along with me, and we all go down this winding road. But after several tries and failures and failures at this, it seemed better to have them free to go—as free as possible. And then you superimpose whatever sequences you want to over them."[41]

He tried this in December 1959 on "Fifth House," another fascinating original from this period. The title has several meanings: it has astrological significance, and it tells us that the piece is based on Tadd Dameron's "Hot House," one of the tunes Coltrane played at his first, informal recording session in 1946. "Hot House," you'll recall, is itself based on "What Is This Thing Called Love?" and the fifth house is said to represent love. What a distance he'd traveled since 1946! In this impressive transformation, the A sections are played over a pedal point while the bridge is speeded up using his "Giant Steps" chord substitution formula. But during his solo he is clearly playing the "Giant Steps" over the pedal point as well—in fact, in his sketchbook reproduced in Simpkins (282) he writes out changes for the A section of "Fifth House." These changes are implied in his saxophone solo but not played by the rhythm section. He also writes out an "Interlude" that does not appear on the recording.[42]

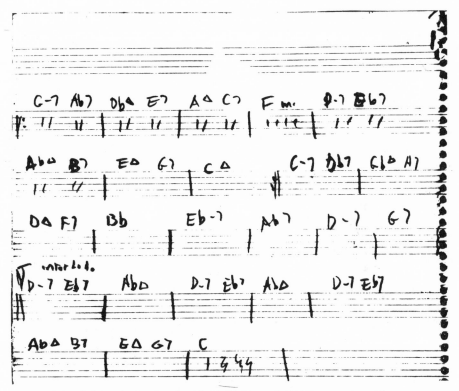

John Coltrane's sketches for his "Fifth House" (1959), reproduced from Simpkins 282, by permission of C. O. Simpkins, M.D. and Saeeda Coltrane.

The bass pedal vamp in C appears on page 277 in Simpkins. (At the piano solo the vamp ends and the bass walks through the usual changes of "What Is This Thing Called Love.")

On page 278, Coltrane writes out—in the tenor key of D—a different bass vamp (it kind of "turns around" the one he recorded) and an introduction based on some variant of an Eastern European scale. It resembles the scale Coltrane wrote out and labeled "Hungarian Gypsy" on another workbook page in Simpkins (113), but it could also be based on a similar scale that Coltrane devised, as he was taught to do with Dennis Sandole. (A version of the theme follows. A pedal point of G is suggested but not written.)

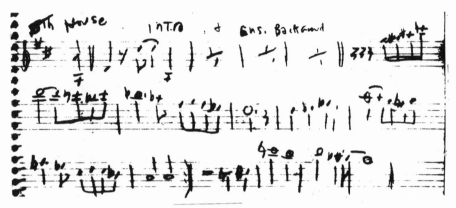

John Coltrane's sketches for his "Fifth House" (1959), reproduced from Simpkins 278 by permission of C.O. Simpkins, M.D. and Saeeda Coltrane.

Looking again at the melody of "Fifth House," we realize that it also is based on this scale. In the discarded introduction he was working out ideas that he was to use in the theme.

"Fifth House" by John Coltrane (1959).

So "Fifth House" brings together an amazing wealth of influences. Beginning with a standard song rewritten by Tadd Dameron, Coltrane retitles it with an astrological term. Then he reharmonizes it using his third-related chords formula. Then he eliminates the chords during the A sections and decides just to imply them in his saxophone playing while the rhythm section plays a pedal point vamp. Finally, he constructs a melody—he said himself that this was usually his last step—and instead of a diatonic-sounding theme like "Giant Steps," he creates a highly chromatic line that reflects his growing interest in world music, an interest that was to blossom once he organized his own quartet.

With all these incredible ideas bursting inside of him, it's no wonder that Coltrane was chafing at the bit to get out of Davis's band—which, wonderful though it was, specialized in a totally different repertoire from that which Coltrane had in mind. As soon as he got free, he dedicated himself in earnest to developing as a composer. But first, he had to build his ideal group around him.

14

"Today's Top Tenor" and His
"All-Star Band"

Coltrane's last concert with Miles Davis consisted of two sets in Stuttgart, Germany, on Sunday, April 10.[1] As soon as he got back home, he got busy with his own group. On Saturday night, April 16, "Today's Top Tenor" and his "All-Star Band" (I don't know who Coltrane used) was on a bill with the groups of vocalist Chris Connor—who got top billing—Dizzy Gillespie, Oscar Peterson, Jackie McLean "and others" at Manhattan's Town Hall. Although criticism continued to follow him, during the next few years his following grew rapidly and enthusiastically.

Joe Termini, who with his brother Iggy owned both the Jazz Gallery, just opened December 15, 1959, and the Five Spot, says he had encouraged Coltrane to start his own group. When Coltrane was with Davis, says Termini, "Everybody was talking about him. I said, 'John, make your own group, it's time.' He said, 'Well, I make three hundred fifty a week with Miles. I'm afraid.' I told him, 'I'll make sure that you make three-fifty a week—at that time that was big money—and I'll see that you get at least ten weeks a year between the Five Spot and the Jazz Gallery." (Davis's fee for a week at a club had increased to twenty-five hundred dollars and up—and much higher for concert halls—but over one thousand dollars of that went to Davis and his management.)

Termini was true to his word. On Tuesday, May 3,[2] Coltrane, "formerly with Miles Davis," opened with Mondays off at the Jazz Gallery at 80 St. Mark's Place (Eighth Street near First Avenue), for one dollar cover and $1.50 minimum. Apparently he had wanted to hire McCoy Tyner on piano, Art Davis on bass, and Elvin Jones on drums; but none of them were available. Tyner was touring with the Jazztet—a group co-led by trumpeter Art Farmer and Benny Golson—and he was not able to get free at the moment. The Jazztet debuted on

November 16, 1959, at the Five Spot, and had performed during the opening week of the Jazz Gallery, then played in Chicago and elsewhere. On May 3, the Jazztet began a two-week stay at the Village Vanguard. Art Davis was with Dizzy Gillespie. Jones had been touring and recording with veteran trumpeter Harry Edison at least through February, and then is said to have been arrested for drug possession and served time at Riker's Island in New York (Thomas, 124; Nisenson, 86).

So Coltrane opened with Steve Kuhn on piano, Steve Davis on bass, and Peter Sims "LaRoca" on drums, all fine players. Born in 1938, LaRoca took up the drums around age ten and had attended the High School of Music and Art in Manhattan. He continued playing through two years at the City College of New York, then worked with such established artists as Sonny Rollins and Jackie McLean.[3] LaRoca recalls that "Miles recommended me"—Davis had been in the audience and had heard LaRoca on occasion. During this period, around February through April, LaRoca worked frequently with trombonist Slide Hampton, owner of the musicians' boarding house in Brooklyn, so Coltrane and LaRoca may have met through Hampton as well.

We have already met Steve Davis as the brother-in-law of Aisha Tyner and friend of Naima. A Philadelphia native born in 1929, he was playing professionally around town as early as 1947.[4] He had been arrested for heroin possession the same weekend as Jimmy Heath in 1955 but was now back on the scene.

Coltrane seems to have been up in the air for a while about the piano chair. Bobby Timmons, who had made a splash with Art Blakey, was said to be in the running (Priestley, 41). But Timmons had just left Cannonball Adderley's group and gone back to Art Blakey, and *Down Beat* reported that Coltrane "emphatically denies the rumor that pianist Bobby Timmons will leave the Art Blakey Jazz Messengers to join his new group."[5] Meanwhile, Kuhn (born in 1938), a unique and lyrical two-handed improviser, had come to New York in the fall of 1959 and was soon working in the group of trumpeter Kenny Dorham, along with bassist Jimmy Garrison. He tells how he approached Coltrane about the gig:

> In early 1960, I heard Coltrane was leaving Miles's quintet . . . so I just took a shot in the dark. I'm basically kind of shy, but I called and I said, "You don't know who I am, but I'm working with the Kenny Dorham band at the moment and I would like it if we could get together some time. . . . He called Kenny and asked about me, and I guess he asked a few other people. And the next thing I know he called me and said "OK, let's meet." I was living at the Bryant Hotel, on Fifty-fourth and Eighth Avenue, which was kind of a dump.[6]

Coltrane rented a rehearsal room close by, at Fifty-fifth and Eighth, and met with Kuhn there. Kuhn continues:

I believe it was just a room with an upright piano, and we met one afternoon and he had his horn with him, and we played a little bit and talked, for maybe two or three hours. . . . And nothing was said more then, no commitment or anything. He just said thanks, and he called me maybe a week later and said he would like me to come to his house, which was in Queens. . . . We did the same sort of thing, except it was probably more like three or four hours. [Kuhn played on a spinet, in the living room.] Most of the music we were playing was from the *Giant Steps* record, and some other stuff he had written, and I was familiar with them. He drove me back into town at maybe six or seven o'clock . . . and still there was nothing. I figured this was two interviews and that was it.[7]

But, Kuhn recalls, "The next thing I knew, I guess it was a few days later, he called on the phone and he said, 'I'm starting at the Jazz Gallery . . . and would $135 a week be OK?' He could have paid me nothing!" Kuhn remembers that they rehearsed once, maybe twice. LaRoca was working in Pittsburgh with Slide Hampton and flew to New York on days off to rehearse. Kuhn was thrilled to be working with Coltrane: "He was and still is like a God to me. He was only ten years older than I was, but he could have been a hundred years older. He had really gotten himself together musically and it was a real education to be there with him on the bandstand. It was like electricity. The people in the audience were just going crazy—it was like a revival meeting. . . . It was almost hysteria in the audience. The energy he brought to the bandstand every night was incredible." The critics were raving too. Don Nelsen of the *New York Daily News* reported, "Run, do not walk or otherwise loiter on your way down to the Jazz Gallery. The reason is John Coltrane, a tenor saxophonist who has the future coming out of his horn." Variety declared, "Coltrane's driving, building choruses . . . might raise the dead . . . The saxman's tenor solo on 'Body and Soul' is a particularly brilliant exhibition and almost a history of jazz. The range of tonal effects covers both the Colemans, Ornette and Hawkins."[8]

The repertory included Coltrane's "Giant Steps," "Countdown" (called "Tune Up," its source, in Kuhn's music notebook), "Naima," "Straight Street," "Spiral" (from the *Giant Steps* album), "Cousin Mary," "Like Sonny," Cal Massey's "Bakai," and the standards "Little Old Lady" and "I Want to Talk about You." They also played Coltrane's new arrangements of "How High the Moon" (using "Giant Steps" chords, later recorded as "Satellite"), Parker's "Confirmation" (using "Giant Steps" chords, later recorded without a title and eventually issued as "26-2"), "Summertime," and "Body and Soul." "Liberia" was in the book but not played often, and both Kuhn and LaRoca agree that "Impressions" was already in the book. A page from Coltrane's workbook (reproduced in Simpkins, 279) shows a list of tunes that would probably date from this period; it includes the ballads "Mad about the Boy" (a poignant Noel Coward piece that he never recorded) and "I'll Wait and Pray," "My Shining

Hour" (the third-related chords for the break are near the bottom of page 281 of the workbook) and "The Night Has a Thousand Eyes," and the originals "Harmonique," "Equinox," "Some Other Blues," and "Fifth House." Most surprising, it lists "Temptation," an "exotic" number from 1933, with a bit of an arrangement on page 278. His ending begins with a third relation, E-flat to G-flat.

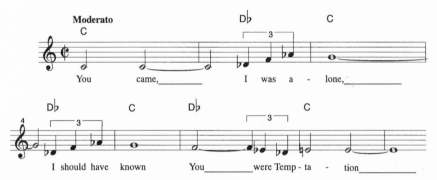

The beginning of "Temptation"
TEMPTATION, by Nacio Herb Brown and Arthur Freed
© 1933 (Renewed) Metro-Goldwyn-Mayer Inc.
All Rights controlled by EMI Robbins Catalog Inc.
All Rights Reserved. Used by Permission.
WARNER BROS. PUBLICATIONS U.S. INC., Miami, FL 33014

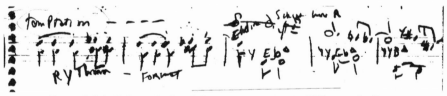

Beneath it is Coltrane's sketch for an arrangement of "Temptation"
Reproduced from Simpkins 278, by permission of C. O. Simpkins, M.D. and Saeeda Coltrane.

Although it doesn't quite work, one could see why Coltrane was interested in trying this, with its Spanish flamenco feel.

During 1959 and 1960, Coltrane also performed several of his own pieces that were never recorded. His friend Zita Carno, a classical pianist who had published an important article about him—the first to transcribe his solos—in

The historical marker erected in 1992 near Coltrane's birthplace in **Hamlet, North Carolina.** *Photograph courtesy of Steve Lindeman.*

The historical marker erected in 1996 in **High Point.** *Photograph by L. Porter.*

Coltrane's third grade class during the 1934–35 school year. Coltrane is standing at the top left with his hands in his pockets. His friend Franklin Brower is seated second from left in the front row. The teacher, seated on the right, is Mrs. Whitten. Rosetta Cousar Haywood is standing two to the left of the teacher, behind the second boy in the front row. *Photograph courtesy Willie Smith, with assistance from Rosetta Haywood and John Morton.*

1st picture (taken immediately after the last note of the session — as you see everyone was in much disorder, we were all spread out while cuttin', we had to get in a group for the pose ha.

dig Benny look of bewilderment —

Picture #2 completely at ease now (ha. we compose our selves for this weird shot — wild!)

To Goldie from Joe Theimer

The two photos from Coltrane's first recording date, a private jam session in Oahu with some navy colleagues, July 13, 1946. Beneath each photo are the handwritten comments of the drummer on the date, Joe Theimer (aka Timer). *Photographs and writing courtesy of Bill Goldstein.*

At a gig in the Showboat in Philadelphia around 1947, Coltrane standing on the right; young pianist Ray Bryant is next to him. Seated are, from the left, trumpeter Johnny Coles, James "Sax" Young (who was not on the gig but dropped by), and bassist James "Sugie" Rhodes. *Photograph courtesy of Ray Bryant.*

The historical marker in front of Coltrane's house, now the home of **Mary Alexander** and base of the **John W. Coltrane Cultural Society**, at **1511 N. 33rd Street, Philadelphia.** *Photograph by Lewis Porter.*

The cover of Coltrane's first album under his own name, Prestige 7105, recorded May 31, 1957. The photograph by Esmond Edwards must be from on or about that day.

Coltrane in an unposed moment around 1957. *Photograph by clarinetist Tony Scott, courtesy of Ray Passman.*

Pictured from left to right: John Coltrane, Earl D. Grubbs (brother of Carl), Earl Grubbs (father), and Carl Grubbs. This picture was taken in the living room of the apartment of John and Naima Coltrane, at 103rd and Broadway, Easter Sunday, 1958.

"In 1958 I had no idea what this day (pictured here) would represent to my life today. In looking back over the years since this picture was taken, I saw a whole new world open up to me. Not just in Jazz but in a way of living. It is a way of experiencing life that I never could imagine. I did not know what improvisation was, chords, and very little about scales. I just heard John Coltrane practicing 'Giant Steps' progressions. I had never heard a saxophone played like that before. The sound was amazing and I liked it very much. That was the beginning of my search to find out what he was doing. I think that this experience put me on the right path. Learning about Jazz is learning about being not just a creative person, but it also teaches you wisdom and understanding. No one can teach you how to be creative, but they can show you the path. I've been trying to follow that ever since." —Carl G. Grubbs. *Photograph courtesy of Carl Grubbs.*

Miles Davis and Coltrane on April 2, 1959 in a CBS TV studio preparing for a taping. Trombonist Frank Rehak was a member of the Gil Evans band, with which Davis also performed. *Photograph © Bill Spilka. Used by permission.*

Coltrane, Naima, and Saeeda around 1960. *Photograph courtesy of Saeeda Coltrane and the late Naima Coltrane.*

Coltrane and pianist Wynton Kelly in an unguarded moment, probably while on tour with Miles Davis in California in early 1960. *Photograph courtesy of Saeeda Coltrane and the late Naima Coltrane.*

Coltrane and fellow saxophonist Prince Lasha in San Francisco around 1960. *Photograph courtesy of Saeeda Coltrane and the late Naima Coltrane.*

Coltrane at the Village Gate, August 1961. *Photograph © Herb Snitzer. Used by permission. All rights reserved.*

The Village Gate, August 1961. Eric Dolphy is the bass clarinetist and Coltrane is playing the soprano saxophone. *Photograph © Herb Snitzer. Used by permission. All rights reserved.*

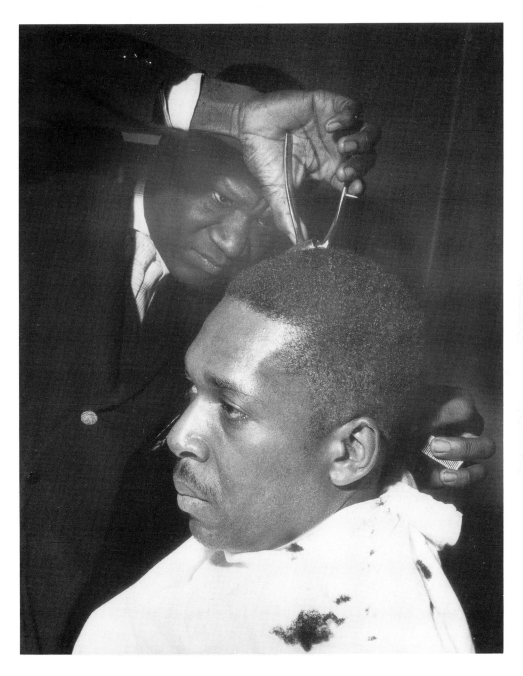

Coltrane gets a haircut backstage before his concert at London's Gaumont State Theater, Kilburn, November 11, 1961. *Photograph © Val Wilmer. Used by permission.*

CIVIC THEATRE
545 BARONNE ST.
New Orleans, La.
PROUDLY PRESENTS

JOHN

"MY FAVORITE THINGS"

★ COLTRANE ★

Admission $2.00

FRIDAY SHOWTIME 8:00 P.M.

MARCH 20, 1963

A poster for a gig that seems never to have happened. The photograph is by Valerie Wilmer, London, probably November 10, 1961. *Photograph © Val Wilmer. Poster courtesy Gordon Blewis.*

Coltrane being interviewed by the late Belgian writer Benoit Quersin in Paris, November 17, 1962. *Photograph by Michel Delorme. Used by permission.*

21st aug. 65

MOTOR HOTEL · CLEVELAND, OHIO 44115

Hello Randi,

I am fine & TRUST That you ARe well
& happy. Thanks FoR The interesting
LeTTeRs & PRints, etc. I Found. Them enjoyable.
You are STill in my opinion one oF These
RaRe souls — quite in Love with LiFe —
with much Love To Give — Bless you.

    with you.
     with Love —
      John

Randi W. Hultin
Bygdø Allē 2
Oslo 2 —
Norway

Air mail

A short letter that Coltrane wrote to Randi Hultin, Norwegian jazz journalist. *Courtesy Randi Hultin.*

Two photographs of the famous quartet with McCoy Tyner on piano, Jimmy Garrison on bass, Elvin Jones on Drums and unidentified audience members, at Boston's Jazz Workshop on March 1, 1964. *Photographs by the late Bernie Moss, courtesy of the Institute of Jazz Studies.*

John and Alice Coltrane during their tour of Japan in July 1966. *Photograph by Kuniharu Itoh, courtesy of Yasuhiro Fujioka.*

Coltrane's final resting place at Pinelawn Memorial Park in Farmingdale, Long Island, New York. *Photo by Lewis Porter.*

1959, had such superb skills that she could construct leadsheets to his pieces while he played: "I used to go equipped with music paper and a few well-sharpened pencils, and I would take them down during the performances, which amused Trane no end. He would come over to my table and look over my shoulder to make sure I'd gotten them right!" Apparently she did get them right—her changes for "Thing In D-Flat" agree with those in Kuhn's notebook, dictated by Coltrane himself. Only Carno has the melody. Coltrane told her that this piece was very loosely inspired by Gillespie's "Woody 'n You," which shares the D-flat key for the A sections and also uses a D-flat seventh chord on the bridge, though only for part of it. Coltrane's A section begins with a version of his "Giant Steps" sequence:

"Thing in D-flat," by John Coltrane (1960).
Copyright © 1997 JOWCOL MUSIC. Used by Permission. All Rights Reserved.

Carno's notebook preserved several other unknown Coltrane compositions—"Two Changes," which vamps over two chords; a B minor modal piece that she thinks he later named "1-2-3-4-5"; and "Something Chinese," and F minor vamp. She also has "Satellite" under its original title, "Moon Man," and a different version of "Fifth House" entitled "You Tell Me."[9]

Kuhn has very fond memories of his stay with Coltrane:

It was a great time for jazz, because Ornette Coleman had just come to town and Sonny Rollins had taken a sabbatical from performing, and they would all be coming into the club to hear John and talking between sets. It was just a great, great influx of musicians. . . . a lot of energy, a lot of ideas exchanged back and forth. It was a really special time, which I haven't seen again. I never met anybody so 100 percent dedicated to just dealing with music [as John]. . . . A lot of the guys I respected were involved with drugs, which he wasn't at the time. He was as straight as a pin. He had his problems prior to that, but he was clean as a whistle in those days. And he was just music, music, music, music. Because he had given up drugs, he had an addictive personality. So he got hung up on butterscotch Lifesavers. He would buy them by the case and he would just be popping them constantly. And instead of a cologne, he reeked of butterrum.

But Kuhn did not provide what Coltrane wanted from the piano.

It got to the point where I was going to give him my notice. Before I could do that, he gave me my notice. It was mutual. I was really not happy with my playing. I was looking for myself. I didn't really know what he wanted, and he would not tell me. He said he wanted to make a change, and I said it was probably for the best. I was heartbroken, but I was more upset with myself that I just wasn't doing what I felt I could do or what he needed or wanted. He said basically what he wanted was a springboard off of which he could play—he just wanted chords. The way I was playing for him was more than accompanying; I was sort of getting out there with him at times and maybe getting in his way.[10]

Kuhn further remarked, "But he couldn't tell me this. He said to me, 'I really have a lot of respect for what you do and I cannot tell you how to play.'—which I respect, but on the other hand, I wish he would have told me what he wanted at the beginning and I would have certainly tried to do it. But then again, I was a cocky kid in those days, and I might have rebelled a bit."[11]

Kuhn, who had also been the only white player in Dorham's group, got no sense of any racial problem from Coltrane: "It was a problem for a lot of his colleagues. . . . I know for a fact there were guys saying, 'Why are you hiring this white guy?'" Still, LaRoca reports that the band sounded great with Kuhn: "Steve and I had played together quite a bit. Steve's a marvelous musician. The band was happening then, and obviously it was also happening when McCoy came in." LaRoca believes that Coltrane was simply seeking something other than what Kuhn was providing. In June, *Coda* magazine announced that McCoy Tyner recently left the Jazztet; on the same page Coltrane revealed that "he will make a final change in the quartet"—not the final change, as it turned out.[12]

Around the end of the first month at the Jazz Gallery, Coltrane replaced

Steve Kuhn with Tyner, who would remain with him for the next five years. Both Tyner's parents were from Murfreesboro, North Carolina; his mother's family moved to Philadelphia, then his father's, and he was born there on December 11, 1938. Tyner also has relations in Ahoskie. As a teenager he used to go down there and work on tobacco farms; he told me he enjoyed being outdoors and loved the air down there.

Tyner's early musical idols were Bud Powell, who lived nearby for a while, and Monk, so much so that he was sometimes called "Bud Monk." He also listened to Bud's pianist brother, Richie. Tyner did some studying at the Granoff School, and already had a reputation as a teenager. Trumpeter Kenny Dorham wrote that in 1957, Tyner, not yet nineteen, was recommended "to Max Roach while Max was working at the Showboat. When Tyner walked on the bandstand after an introduction to Rollins, myself and [bassist] George Morrow, Max asked him if he knew 'Just One of Those Things,' and he said 'Yes.' He must have really meant 'Yes,' because when he finished playing, everyone was 'gassed.'"[13] That same year, as we noted, Tyner and Coltrane played together. After that, Tyner said, "Coltrane went back with Miles again, but we had sort of a verbal understanding that if he ever got his own group, I would play piano."[14] John indirectly confirmed this in 1961: "I've known [him] a long time: I noticed him when I was still in Philadelphia and promised myself to call him if I formed my own group one day."[15] When John did call, Tyner had a tough decision: "I don't think John wanted to ask me to leave the Jazztet because he was friendly with Benny Golson, but I believe Naima encouraged him. John left it up to me—he asked me what I wanted to do. It was a hard choice, even though I knew what I *wanted* to do. There were probably some bad feelings at first with the Jazztet, but I think they understood better later on. John's group was where I belonged."[16]

Over the next two years Tyner developed a particular type of voicing in fourths that was to characterize the sound of the quartet. (Fourth chords had already been used by a number of classical composers in an obviously different context, especially by Paul Hindemith.) Whereas triads have a certain earthy familiarity, fourth chords are abstract. Perhaps because they avoid the familar ring of popular songs, which are based on triads, fourth chords seem to add to the spiritual quality of Coltrane's music. Tyner also would create dramatic pedal points with his left hand in the lower register. Chick Corea and many others emulated Tyner's approach, and he has been a major influence on modern piano style, along with the widely acknowledged influence of Bill Evans.

Tyner knows that he was a critical part of the group's sound, and he credits his rhythmic approach as much as his harmonic techniques: "Personally," he said,

and without the least pretension on my part, I believe that Coltrane wouldn't have evolved in the same fashion if he hadn't had me as his pianist, and he was, besides, very aware of that. I can tell because when I had to be absent for family reasons, like when my wife was expecting a baby, he didn't replace me and played without a piano, because he knew that nobody would have been able to give him the rhythmic support that I gave him, and which he was used to. The fact that I, in my early years, had been greatly impressed and influenced by the intriguing playing of Thelonious may have helped to give John a similar terrain to that which he had encountered with Monk, when I joined his quartet. . . . The music of Monk is strange, fleeting, and presents the peculiarity of being at one time very shifting but also very grounded, with a very sure tempo. My playing, I believe, possessed also this metronomic rhythmic accuracy . . . because I have a good strong left hand. John knew that he could count on this rhythmic foundation, on this carpet, and that even when he threw himself into his wildest improvisation, he would always have behind him, unshakeable, the regular tempo of his pianist.[17]

So it was Tyner who finished out the Jazz Gallery stint, which ran for about ten weeks, into July. Then the group started to perform around the country. LaRoca went along for gigs that were within driving distance of New York. Aisha usually came along; less often Naima, who was more private, less gregarious, would be with them. At that time McCoy and Aisha lived in Springfield Gardens, Long Island, and John, Naima, and Saeeda were still on Mexico Street in Queens. LaRoca recalls that these drives were rather quiet, with little conversation. Usually, Coltrane would ask LaRoca to drive early in the trip, while he took a nap. When John was awake, Aisha recalls that he loved to sing—believe it or not—"O Sole Mio."

Beginning of "O Sole Mio" (Edoardo di Capua, 1899)

When the band went out to California at the very end of August 1960, LaRoca stayed home and was replaced by Los Angeles resident Billy Higgins, probably in order to save the expense of transporting a drummer and all his equipment. Higgins recalls how his short membership in the quartet began: "Coltrane asked me would I join him in California, so I just joined him there. He knew me from when I was working with Ornette [Coleman] in New York— we were supposed to get together before and never got together."[18]

Higgins and LaRoca are both wonderful musicians, but Coltrane still had

Elvin Jones on his mind. Aisha Tyner remembers Coltrane talking about Jones and saying that he was waiting for him to join the group. When Jones became available around the end of September, he contacted Coltrane. Coltrane flew Jones out to the next performance in Denver even though Higgins had already been hired. But Higgins understood and took it gracefully: "Both of us made the gig, me and Elvin made the gig. We just played. He would play some, sometimes we'd play together [on two drum sets], I would play some—you know, we'd switch off. I couldn't work in New York anyhow [due to a cabaret card problem]. He was supposed to work with Elvin before. That was just like a marriage, you know." LaRoca was also understanding. He didn't know at the time he joined that Coltrane wanted Jones, but "I knew it before I left. John might have said so; I'm not 100 percent certain." He doesn't remember being upset about that, but just feeling, "I was fortunate enough to get some time with [Coltrane.]"[19]

Born September 9, 1927, in Pontiac, Michigan, Jones was the youngest brother of pianist Hank and trumpeter Thad Jones. He'd first recorded in 1948 with Detroit saxophonist Billy Mitchell, moved to New York in 1955, and was soon recording there with Miles Davis, J. J. Johnson, Sonny Rollins, and others. Jones told François Postif that he first played with Coltrane at one of John's gigs as a leader or with Davis in Philadelphia, probably in 1958 or 1959. He had been hired to replace Philly Joe Jones, who at that time was forbidden to perform in his hometown due to his drug-related arrest record. Elvin recounted with some amusement that the police were waiting at the club and Coltrane had to explain to them that this was a different Jones.[20]

Jones shared Coltrane's amazing physical stamina. Equally important, he shared the saxophonist's powerful interest in complex rhythms. "I especially like his ability to mix and juggle rhythms," Coltrane said of Jones. "He's always aware of everything else that's happening. I guess you could say he has the ability to be in three places at the same time."[21] Jones implied the basic rhythm in a highly elliptical manner, yet he always swung furiously. He seemed to anticipate the rhythms of Coltrane's and Tyner's improvisations, sometimes playing their rhythms right along with them. Bassist Steve Davis said, "That first night Elvin was in the band [in Denver], he was playing so strong and so loud you could hear him outside and down the block. Trane wanted it that way. He wanted a drummer who could really kick, and Elvin was one of the strongest, wildest drummers in the world. After the gig, Trane put his arm around Elvin, took him to a barbecue around the corner, and bought him some ribs. Trane and Elvin were tight from then on" (Thomas, 130).

Unlike Tyner, Jones was not reliable, and Coltrane did have to replace him on occasion. When he had advance notice of Jones's absence he'd try to get Roy Haynes, a major figure in jazz drumming whom he'd played with at his reunion night with Monk in 1958. The longest absence occurred when Jones was incarcerated in Lexington, Kentucky from May through early August 1963, the delayed result of his having been busted in Boston for drug possession on returning from their European tour in early December 1962 (Thomas, 153 and 164). But sometimes Jones just didn't show up, and Coltrane had to find somebody local at short notice. One night, probably in August 1961, two drummers, George Goldsmith and Freddie Waits, went to the Minor Key in Detroit to hear the Coltrane quartet, and Jones didn't appear. Goldsmith recalls that Coltrane appeared irritated, but wouldn't say anything negative about Elvin. Coltrane had heard Goldsmith at a jam session at the home of a mutual friend, saxophonist Joe Brazil, so Goldsmith played up to the last set. "I was scared to death," Goldsmith recalls. "But when Elvin came in, he played so much Freddie Waits and I just grabbed each other and hugged each other and cried. Coltrane got to the mike and said to the audience, 'See, he's a genius, what can I say? He's just a genius.' Elvin burned the house down. He destroyed me." (But he also inspired Goldsmith, who afterward got to meet Jones.) Jones's remarkable music making, and his personal warmth, always put him back in Coltrane's good graces.

In one week of October 1960, the new quartet with Tyner, Jones, and Steve Davis recorded all the material that would eventually become the albums *My Favorite Things* (issued in March 1961), *Coltrane Plays the Blues* (not conceived as a blues album but compiled and issued in 1962), and *Coltrane's Sound* (issued in 1964). These recordings have the freshness of discovery. They're full of lightness and grace, buoyant, and yet at the same time fiery, passionate, and deep. And it's not only Coltrane who makes this happen. It's the joy of Tyner and Jones working with him, finding themselves and creating musical excitement.

These recordings also added to Coltrane's stature as a composer, as a writer of music. It became clear that he was one of the great writers for small groups, along with, say, Monk, and later Wayne Shorter, and a few others. Coltrane's approach to composition, and especially his approach to arranging the tunes of others, influenced the whole sound of the jazz small group. Coltrane discussed composing as if it were a chore he was forced into: "I just have to write the tunes myself. And I don't really want to take the time away from my horn. Writing has always been a secondary thing for me, but I find that lately I am spending more and more time at it, because I can't find the proper tunes." Bassist Donald Rafael Garrett, who worked with him briefly, observed, "He is a meticulous musician. He will often play a tune seven or eight different ways before he decides on just how he wants to play it."[22]

My Favorite Things was the first album issued from these October 1960 sessions, and it had a powerful impact. The title cut, and John's unique approach to the soprano saxophone, had much to do with this. Coltrane said his first experience with the soprano occurred by accident when a fellow musician left one in his car on the way back from Washington, D.C. (perhaps on November 2, 1958): "I opened the case and found a soprano sax. I started fooling around with it and was fascinated." He returned the instrument to his friend, who he elsewhere identified as ". . . a writer named Chip Bayen," and decided to get one of his own.[23] The earliest report of Coltrane playing soprano comes from Gary Goldstein, a bassist and physics professor, whose account seems to date from the Sutherland Hotel in Chicago between January 21 and February 2, 1959:

> Coltrane played the soprano on one tune. It was one of their regular medium tempo things . . . Trane was *experimenting* with the soprano— that was the impression I got. I liked what I heard, although he wasn't getting the soprano to stay in tune very well. But he was doing a lot of arpeggios then. And it seemed to fit in with his approach to the tenor at that time—streams of notes, breathlessly strung together. I felt that his ideas were being pushed out of the soprano faster than his technique could handle.[24]

During this gig, or on the way there, Coltrane had visited Tony Rulli (his contact at the Selmer company in Elkhart, Indiana, about sixty miles east of Chicago) to pick out a soprano (Thomas, 108). He used a Selmer metal mouthpiece as well.

Miles Davis said he bought a soprano for Coltrane from an antique dealer in Paris on March 21, 1960.[25] John practiced on it privately throughout his final tour with Davis, drummer Jimmy Cobb recalls (Thomas, 109). Near the beginning of the Jazz Gallery stay, Coltrane began performing regularly on soprano—the May 15 review mentions his "tremendous" work on soprano, and LaRoca remembers performing "My Favorite Things" sometime before he left at the end of August. In 1965 Coltrane said that he still performed on "the first one I bought," the one from the Selmer factory.[26] He evidently kept the antique that Davis gave him as a spare.

For years he'd been pushing the upper limits of his tenor, as if yearning for an extended range, and a buzzing, more exotic, tone. He had heard the brilliant Steve Lacy, who specialized in the soprano, and had even asked him what key it was in: "He . . . was surprised to learn that it was the same key as the tenor," Lacy recalled.[27] The fact that both were in B-flat would make it easier to switch between the two. Coltrane knew the classic works of Sidney Bechet and of Johnny Hodges, once a Bechet protégé. He loved Hodges so much, he said, that "I ask myself if, today, I only play the soprano saxophone to stay in the lineage of Johnny Hodges—unconsciously, of course" (Postif). The soprano was so little used in modern jazz that many purchasers probably had not previously seen the straight instrument featured in the cover photo.

The Rodgers and Hammerstein waltz "My Favorite Things" is best known today as sung by Julie Andrews and a crew of children in the movie of 1966, *The Sound of Music,* but in 1960 the show was a Broadway hit with Mary Martin in the leading role. Coltrane transformed this pretty little song into a grand symphonic statement by making several seemingly small, but telling, changes. People often make the mistake of assuming that Coltrane wanted to dress this song up because he must have thought it was silly. Quite the opposite; Coltrane was under no pressure to record such a song. In fact, he told Postif, "Lots of people imagine wrongly that 'My Favorite Things' is one of my compositions; I would have loved to have written it, but it's by Rodgers and Hammerstein." He treated the song respectfully. For one thing, he retains the original key center of E even though that becomes the key of G-flat, relatively uncomfortable for the B-flat soprano. (Of course John often practiced and performed in hard keys.) The song's structure as written is AAA'B. All of the A sections use the "rain-drops on roses" tune and emphasize happy things. The B part is the first mention of negative experiences—"when the dog bites"—but its point is that the good things help us to overcome the bad. It's a perfectly sensible, valuable message, not silly at all—it's just that it uses examples that a child would understand, because in the script, the song is addressed to children.

The recording begins with a four-bar introduction, played twice. Then the rhythm section begins vamping in 3/4. (One might call it 6/8, but Coltrane himself called it three.) Coltrane plays the first two A parts in minor at the beginning of his version, then an interlude in major. This serves as a substitute for the third A, which in the original goes to major for eight measures.[28] Then Coltrane plays two more minor As, which are not in the original, but which give a sense of a complete form. Only at the very end of the performance does he play the B part. The B as written ends in G major, so that all the E major and minor before gets "resolved." But Coltrane stays in E minor at the end, leaving it more brooding, thoughtful. It's like one gigantic chorus.

In the meantime, he stretches out the sense of time. As he told Postif, "This piece is built, during several measures, on two chords, but we have prolonged the two chords in order to set the scene and make it last. In fact, we have extended the two chords for the whole piece." In this way, he extends the list of good things that help one overcome the bad, and he dramatizes this opposition by lengthening the time span of minor versus major. After the theme, each solo follows a plan: the soloist, Coltrane or Tyner, plays over the E minor vamp as long as he wants, relying primarily on the Dorian mode rather than pure minor, and then moves on cue to the E major vamp. The cue is a return to the theme. You can hear Tyner return to the theme in the middle of his solo, which is his cue to the others, and then the vamp becomes major. Coltrane does the same during his solo. And during most live versions of this piece each soloist, including Dolphy where he's present, does the same. (The only exception is that on some TV and radio broadcasts they cut short some of the solos due to time limitations. Coltrane said, "We were playing it at one time with minor, then major, then minor modes, but it was *really* getting too long."[29] For example, Dolphy plays in minor for a while at the end of his flute solo on some of the European concerts from November 1961.) When the B section finally enters at the end, we feel that we have been through an entire world of music. (Coltrane also said to Postif, "We did the same thing with another piece: 'Ev'ry Time We Say Goodbye.'" Actually, on "Ev'ry Time," which follows the waltz on the LP, he replaces some of the chords with a vamp, but he follows the original song length, rather than leaving it open-ended as he does here.)

As we've noted, Coltrane tended to carefully work out the parts for the rhythm section, especially the bass. Now he had found a way, with the help of Elvin Jones, to retain his sense of organization and yet offer spontaneity. The repetitive patterns of the piano and bass on the simplified modal structure creates a feeling of organized stasis, while the extremely active soprano and drums create the opposite effect, of change and a sense of searching. It is a creative tension Coltrane would use over and over again.[30] On the original "My Favorite Things," Tyner and Jones are both more subdued than they would be on later versions, although they are still perfectly effective. In fact, McCoy remarked that he didn't like the song at first.[31] Coltrane's own playing is gorgeous; during his short solo in the major, right near the beginning, he plays some melodies that are unforgettable, that flow in perfectly balanced phrases.

Excerpt from Coltrane's solo near the beginning of "My Favorite Things" (1960).
Lyrics by Oscar Hammerstein II. Music by Richard Rodgers.
Copyright © 1959 by Richard Rodgers and Oscar Hammerstein II. Copyright Renewed.
WILLIAMSON MUSIC owner of publication and allied rights throughout the world.
International Copyright Secured. All Rights Reserved.

During his long solo later on, he produces swirling lines during the minor (really Dorian), then returns to the theme for the change to major. His playing in major is quite different—bouncy, songful, rhythmic, and full of little alternating motives like the one we compared to the Hanon piano book in chapter 8. There is quite a bit of strain in the high register, and some intonation problems—these problems disappeared as his mastery of the soprano grew—but nobody seems to mind. Even Coltrane, the harshest critic of all, said,

" 'Favorite Things' is my favorite piece of all those I have recorded. I don't think I would like to do it over in any way, whereas all the other discs I've made could have been improved in some details. This waltz is fantastic: when you play it slowly, it has an element of gospel that's not at all displeasing; when you play it quickly, it possesses other undeniable qualities. It's very interesting to discover a terrain that renews itself according to the impulse that you give it. That's, moreover, the reason we don't always play this song in the same tempo" (Postif).

Coltrane also recorded the blues "Equinox" (Aisha Tyner recalls that Naima named this) during that first spate of studio sessions with his newly formed quartet. Coltrane was a serious blues player, and his blues pieces reflect a desire to get back to a primal mood, and away from the emotionally lighter, harmonically more complex blues of the boppers. The twelve-bar minor theme of "Equinox" consists essentially of the first four scale degrees of D-flat minor. (It would be simpler to write the piece in C-sharp minor, with four sharps, but like most jazz musicians Coltrane prefered flat keys. However, he also hated the notes F-flat and C-flat that are required in D-flat minor, since it has seven flats. So his sketches in Simpkins use five flats in the key signature, and he writes in all the E and B naturals in the melody [277, 283]. I have honored his wishes in my transcription.) As in traditional vocal blues, the first two four-bar phrases are based on one melody. The last phrase provides the greatest harmonic activity of the theme by beginning on a flat VI chord (the e-flat of the melody is the raised eleventh), essentially a chromatic upper neighbor chord, before moving to the expected V chord in measure ten (the e-flat being reinterpreted as the fifth of this chord). This phrase is reminiscent of "All Blues" from the *Kind of Blue* album.

Six bars of a Latin rhythm introduce the piece, as shown in Coltrane's sketches in Simpkins (283; a different introduction is sketched on 277.) Then the rhythm section plays eight measures of an ostinato, which continues under the theme. The relentless underpinning of the piano and bass, contrasting with the leisurely, uncrowded melody, creates an ominous, primeval atmosphere. As in "My Favorite Things," the piano and bass provide the repeated foundation, while the drums and saxophone are free to fly. Elvin Jones takes advantage of this solid base to provide rolls and cymbal crashes that contribute to the drama and intensity of the theme and solo sections. He plays with mallets and has his snares turned off, so as to achieve a softer, darker, and more legato effect. The bassist, Steve Davis, is allowed little variation from his pattern throughout the piece. The piano part, played by Tyner, begins in octaves with the bass. Maintaining the same Latinesque rhythm, Tyner spreads out into chords under measures 5 and 6 of the theme, providing a counterline—E, E-flat, D—against Coltrane's melody. Throughout the improvised choruses, Tyner plays a chordal version of the original ostinato. Although Tyner is tied to this rhythm, he creates great variety through his chord voicings, providing a new voicing for each chorus and building the sequence of voicings so that they beautifully support the increasing tension of Coltrane's improvisation.

Over this background, Coltrane invents an astounding improvisation that builds and builds, then winds down again before Tyner solos. He starts simply, poignantly, building to faster and faster notes with each chorus, and to higher and higher notes. Each of his eight choruses (after the two theme choruses) has its own characteristic motive—furthermore, there is a logical development of motives from one chorus to the next. In a way, he's building on tradition: many jazz artists liked to increase the intensity at the start of each succeeding chorus of a blues. King Oliver did that on both versions of "Dippermouth Blues" back in 1923, Lester Young on "Pres Returns" (1956), and Miles Davis effectively built up his solo that way on the master take of "Bag's Groove" (1954). In another sense, Coltrane is sounding like a preacher, building to a higher and higher pitch (literally) as he exhorts his audience. This preaching aspect of his music becomes more and more powerful during the 1960s.

This solo provides a good illustration of how concise Coltrane's improvising became in the 1960s. His detractors were so busy noticing how many notes he played that they failed to grasp how sensibly he was using all these notes. Coltrane develops his solo on "Equinox" out of just a few motives, beginning with a repeated-note idea. This leads to an idea of alternating between two notes, in choruses 4, 5, 6, and 8. He plays ascending or descending triplets in many places, for example in the last five measures of chorus 4, and he combines this with the alternating-note idea in choruses 5 and 8. Much of the motivic material derives from the theme itself. For example, the theme basically consists of sustained notes, and the repeated note and alternating notes that Coltrane uses in his solo are methods of sustaining, or prolonging, one note. The repeated note itself makes up the third phrase of the theme, and most of the theme is based on the alternation between a higher and lower note, usually E and D-flat.

The "Equinox" solo is dramatically charged. For instance, chorus 7 is a little more restless, less intense than the ones before it. Then Coltrane produces in chorus 8 the emotional climax of the solo. His attacks on the upper register are more regular, more insistent, than before—the first held b′, reiterated in alternating eighth-note triplets, then the high d″-flat, reiterated in a wild blaze of sextuplets. Here, Coltrane intensifies his tone quality; by holding down lower keys while fingering the sextuplets in measures 5 and 6, he adds a raspy overtone to his sound. When he finally reaches up for a high e″ in measures 8 and 9, the sense of strain in his sound highlights the fact that this is the highest note of the solo, the goal toward which all of those myriad d″-flats were yearning. This e″ has a particularly intense sound because it is a high f-sharp on the tenor saxophone, the first note of the altissimo register.

Coltrane's solo on "Equinox" (1960). The first page contains ms. 1–6 of each chorus. Be sure to read across to the same line on the next page where each chorus is concluded, then back to the first page for the beginning of the next chorus. Notes with circles above them are played with alternate fingerings (generally holding down extra keys).

Coltrane's playing on Equinox, measures 1-6 of each chorus

Equinox, measures 7-12 of each chorus

After this, chorus 9 seems to be one long sigh of relief. It consists almost entirely of repeated middle d-flats, on the beat, and recalls the first improvised chorus. The opening idea of chorus 10 is that rarity in Coltrane, a melodic quotation. It closely resembles the song "Nightingale" by Xavier Cugat. (Perhaps measure 8 of chorus 6 was a quotation also. It suggests one of the themes from the song "Blues in the Night," which Coltrane surely knew.) It is also the only long, lyrical line in the piece. The balanced ascending and descending triplets of measures 9 and 10 create a sense of repose and finality, and Coltrane concludes his magnificent improvisation and sets the stage for Tyner.

Every piece recorded for Atlantic has its story, and its distinctive musical flavor. We already mentioned some of the items that use his "Giant Steps" approach to chords. One of them, "Central Park West," is vaguely reminiscent of "Peace," by Horace Silver, whom Coltrane said he admired. Both have the unusual length of ten bars, and both use third-related key centers (B-flat and D-flat in Silver's case). "Liberia" is clearly a tribute to Gillespie and his "A Night in Tunisia." Coltrane transformed Gillespie's ballad feature "I Can't Get Started" into his "Untitled Original," also known as "Exotica," with some use of third relations. "Mr. Syms" is not named for drummer Peter Sims LaRoca but for Coltrane's barber in Philadelphia. It presents an unusual harmonic approach to the blues, and we have here, courtesy of Steve Kuhn, Coltrane's own handwritten score of the piece. Note the piano voicings, fully written out, and the carefully planned bass part. Also notice Coltrane's spelling, "Sims," which either he or the producer later changed.

Coltrane's handwritten leadsheet for his "Mr. Syms" (1960), courtesy of Steve Kuhn.

"Blues to You," without piano, is a fascinating illustration of the way Coltrane uses dissonance. In the third and fourth measures of a chorus, he tends to play a half step higher than the chords suggest. He tends to play a half step lower than the chords during the last four measures of a chorus. (This vaguely suggests the way Charlie Parker leads into the bridge on his second chorus of "Koko.") He also suggests third motions during those endings, which he did as far back as the end of the first chorus on "Slowtrane" in 1957.

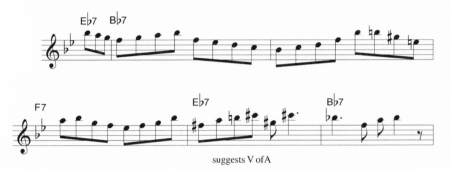

suggests V of A

**Excerpt of Coltrane's solo on "Blues To You" (1960), end of chorus 6.
Chords are implied by the bass line.**

The way Coltrane uses this kind of dissonance, it becomes a type of bluesiness, another way that his approach to the blues was distinctive and nontraditional, yet powerful and basic in emotional impact. This may be heard on "Chasin' the Trane" (named in part after Parker's "Chasin' the Bird") and his other blues from this period as well.

That week of October 1960 was a great one for Coltrane. But he didn't enter a recording studio as a leader again until May 23, 1961, when he started to record for Impulse. (In March he guested with Davis, on the album *Someday My Prince Will Come*. That was the last time they played together, except for one undated night that Davis sat in with Coltrane's quartet at Birdland.)[32] He had signed with Impulse in April 1961. According to Bob Thiele, who came to Impulse after Creed Taylor left toward the end of 1961, Coltrane's Impulse contract was the best deal any jazz musician had received, except for Davis. It was a one-year contract with two-year options, paying a ten-thousand-dollar advance against royalties the first year and rising to twenty thousand dollars for the second and third years, as long as Coltrane recorded a minimum of two LPs per year (Thomas, 143). Coltrane was given complete artistic control, even over the packaging of the LPs. The contract was renewed in April 1964, raising his yearly advance to twenty-five thousand dollars. Coltrane was financially successful, and he stayed with Impulse from then on.

Again there was an overlap of contracts, and Coltrane went back to Atlantic to record his last album for them on May 25, just two days after his first Impulse session. For fans at the time there was a confusing variety of new Coltrane material coming onto the market each year. For example, during 1961 Atlantic issued *Bags and Trane* (with Milt Jackson) and *Coltrane Jazz,* both recorded in 1959, and *My Favorite Things* from 1960; Impulse issued *Africa/ Brass* from 1961; and Prestige issued *Settin' the Pace,* material from March 1958. This pattern continued for the next few years. But, confusing though it must have been—especially for European listeners wondering what to expect in concert—overall the attention helped Coltrane's career.

Down Beat honored Coltrane as "Jazzman of the Year" in its review of the year 1961. In both its International Critics Poll and Readers Poll that year he won for best tenor saxophonist and for miscellaneous instrument (soprano saxophone); the critics also voted his the new star combo. Barbara Gardner wrote, "It was John Coltrane's year. . . . His influence on other musicians continued to grow; many young tenorists continued slavishly to imitate him. . . . In 1961, John Coltrane came into his own."[33] In England's *Melody Maker* he was the second highest rated tenorist in the Reader's Poll and third in the Critics' Poll, and *Blue Train* was selected in June 1961 as that publication's jazz LP of the month. (It had only just come out in Britain.) Established musicians continued to express their approval. J. J. Johnson, who had been thrilled by Coltrane's playing with Monk in 1957, loved the new quartet as well. "That was exciting," he told me. "That was mind-blowing, as a matter of fact! Exciting is an understatement. They raised the roof!"

All this praise didn't go to Coltrane's head—not in the least. He told a French writer during his tour of Europe in November 1961, during which he was coupled with the group of his mentor Dizzy Gillespie:

In fact, I don't accord these polls more importance than they deserve, inasmuch as they are capable of giving you a rating. But, on the other hand, it makes me aware of being surrounded by a certain number of people who have confidence in me, and that I must not disappoint them, in any way, in order to show my gratitude. But if this [success] happened to me without [achieving] what I personally wanted, I wouldn't sacrifice my personal search for the satisfaction of my fans. Honestly, it's not possible to be fooled. And then, besides, I wouldn't be able to. I worked too hard to pursue my evolution, on the technical level, to stop along the way under the pretext that it would please a considerable number of people. There are still many things I want to do; all that remains for me to desire is to continue to find people who like my music in the course of its evolution. That way I'll be able to pursue my research on the sensual level.

I repeat to you, I believe that it would not be honest for me to stop because I've found a big enough audience to get me a good place in the polls. However, I was very happy to see that I am able to touch an extended public, because I have always had to resolve the problem of communication with my listeners. In this regard, it's unnecessary, I suppose, to tell you how much I admire Dizzy Gillespie. I have to prove to them that they had reason to have confidence in me, and really, that's all that I want to succeed in doing.[34]

He seems to be afraid that he will feel pressured commercially to do certain things, but he is resolved to follow his own path. In an unpublished segment of a taped interview with the late Ralph Gleason, he did refer to this in a good-humored way, saying that he was always looking for another "My Favorite Things."[35]

Postif couldn't help but notice the change in the audience when Coltrane returned to the Olympia Theater that November 18, 1961, this time with his own group playing his music the way he wanted it. Coltrane went to grab a bite between shows, Postif recalls.

The concert was going to start, and we were surrounded by two or three hundred fans asking for Coltrane to come out of the shop. The grocer, a very admirable man who had seen this kind of thing before, suggested booting these fans on their backsides and putting on the latch. We finally took our leave, John and me, just in time, thanks to the composure of the shopkeeper who I wish to thank here publicly. But I report this little story simply to point out that a musician who was hissed during his tour with Miles Davis in [1960] was able to find himself [a year and a half] later with several hundred fans waiting to get his autograph. When I spoke with him of the preceding tour, he told me: "But there were also boos at this concert; I heard them clearly. That doesn't make me happy, of course, but at least it shows that one is being discussed."[36]

This time much of the controversy had to do with John's addition of Eric Dolphy to the group around the beginning of 1961. Dolphy (1928–64), who played alto saxophone, flute, and bass clarinet, was a performer with exceptional technical agility, and a clear, singing, yet distinctive tone quality on each of his instruments. As we mentioned in chapter 9, John and Eric met in 1954. Since then, Dolphy had earned a reputation by playing with drummer-bandleader Chico Hamilton and then with Charles Mingus.

Dolphy's approach was quite different from Coltrane's. Where Coltrane, even in his extensions of the tonality, went for an earnest, bluesy sound, and would develop a melodic kernel at some length, Dolphy went for a highly dissonant, sprightly sound—he liked to emulate the sounds of birds on his flute[37]—and would play more by stream of consciousness. His melodic lines often change direction and leap unpredictably. His note choices are difficult to explain from the point of view of functional tonality—for example, he would arpeggiate a minor chord over a major one and vice versa. But he was well aware of music theory and, as he maintained, he had a consistent way of approaching chords.

Sometimes he was a little too consistent. Fresh and startling as his melodic lines were, he would sometimes repeat the same phrase several times during a given solo. Rhythmically, he stayed surprisingly close to the prevailing eighth-note standard of modern jazz. But Dolphy was a thrilling and unique player and composer whose influence is as strong as ever. The unbridled freedom of Dolphy's harmonic approach made a strong impact on Coltrane and stimulated the tenorist to search for his own avenues of exploration. John told Barbara Gardner: "I listen to other groups, records, the men I work with, trying to find what I'm looking for. I learn a lot from the fellows in the group. Eric Dolphy is a hell of a musician, and he plays a lot of horn. When he is up there searching and experimenting, I learn a lot from him, but I just haven't found exactly what I want yet."[38]

Coltrane's only regret was that all his arrangements were written for a quartet. It would have been better, he said, to wait until he had added a fifth voice to write charts: "I was broken-hearted to have to do it this way, but I had to make a quick decision about the European tour, and I thought that we would have more variety with a fifth voice. I recently made an album for Impulse with the quintet [*Live at the Village Vanguard*] and you will see that it's more balanced than what you have heard in concert" (Postif).

But the American critics were about to have their say. In September 1961 the Coltrane quintet with Dolphy had appeared at the Renaissance Club in Hollywood. The November 23 issue of *Down Beat* contained a scathing review from John Tynan, who called their music "musical nonsense currently being peddled in the name of jazz" and "a horrifying demonstration of what appears to be a growing anti-jazz trend."[39] Coltrane later told Frank Kofsky that this kind of criticism had really hurt: "Oh, that was terrible. I couldn't believe it, you know, it just seemed so preposterous. It was so ridiculous, man, that's what bugs me. It was absolutely ridiculous, because they made it appear that we didn't even know the first thing about music—the first thing! And there we were really trying to push things off."[40]

At the invitation of the editor of *Down Beat*, Don DeMicheal, Coltrane and Dolphy responded with an article. Coltrane said, "Quite possibly a lot of things about the band need to be done. But everything has to be done in its own time. . . . There may be a lot of things missing from the music that are coming, if we stay together that long."[41] Coltrane generally responded to criticism with this kind of admirable composure, and he always took the time to explain himself. Consider, for example, his patient response to a rather unhappy critic in London. As in the case of the Olympia Theater in Paris in 1960, the first stop on his tour in 1961 proved to be the most daunting, but this time it was England. The English critics were merciless—partly for this reason, Coltrane never performed there again. (England would have been a stop on his fall 1966 European tour, but that tour never materialized.) Yet he seemed more concerned than upset in an interview for London's *Melody Maker:*

> *Dawbarn:* I found your quintet's music completely bewildering. Can you explain what it is you are trying to do? Surely you and Eric Dolphy are not following the normal chord sequences?
> *Coltrane:* I can't speak for Eric—I don't know exactly what his theory is. I am playing on the regular changes, though sometimes I extend them. I do follow the progressions. The sequences I build have a definite relationship to the chords. Can you give me a particular example of something that puzzled you?⁴²

In a letter to England's *Melody Maker,* a reader said "I came to the conclusion that, for this particular concert, he was playing 'joke' music," to which the editor appended, "Scores of other readers have been equally puzzled." Jack Cooke has pointed out that the Atlantic and Impulse LPs with Elvin Jones were not available in England yet, that the soprano was still unfamiliar, and that Coltrane's choice of "My Favorite Things" as a more accessible number "went for very little."⁴³ While most of the English critics and even musicians hated the London performance, another writer, Kitty Grime, had a more balanced response:

> I was very shaken up by it, you know, because we'd not heard anything quite like that. I was astonished by it; I can't say I liked it exactly, because it was so different. It made an incredibly strong impression. Well, I thought this was going to change the way people play tunes and things. And there was constant repetition, and there seemed to be no chords to it except one, which just went on and on—a bit different from bebop, which I'd been raised on, and I was accustomed to following tricky sequences. . . . We'd not heard those long, long pieces."⁴⁴

Maybe the criticism hurt Coltrane, Grime says:

> He didn't strike me as a hard sort of person. Of course, I didn't know much about him then. I didn't know about his history of being a recovered addict—that wasn't known at all here at the time. He was just thought to be, from what we'd heard of his playing [on records], a sort of

wild person, and then of course [it was a surprise] to find out he was this very serious person.

Grime interviewed both Coltrane and Elvin Jones at their hotel: "I got on very well with Elvin and in fact we hung out quite a bit. . . . I knew his brother Thad quite well, because he'd been over with [Count] Basie." She found Jones very articulate, and pointed out, "He didn't have so much pressure on him" because he was a sideman.

In Coltrane's interview with Grime, he responded at length to the recurring charge that he played angry music:

> I've been told my playing is "angry." Well, you know musicians have many moods, angry, happy, sad—and since those early days perhaps more sides of my musical nature have been revealed on records. I don't really know what a listener feels when he hears music. The musician may feel one way and the listener may get something else from the music. Some musicians have to speak their anger in their playing. The beauty of jazz is that you're free to do just what you feel. But while their playing might express anger, I wouldn't know whether they're angry as people or not. If a man can play well, I get an elation from his music, even if he's playing angry and hard. An aggressive frame of mind can create pretty stern music. But this may well be a very rewarding experience for the listener. You can get a feeling of expectancy and fulfillment in a solo, and an artist of ability may lead you down paths in music where many things can happen. I'd hate to think of an audience missing out on music, because they think it's nothing but anger.

Coltrane discussed, as he had with the French press, his concern with communicating to the audience:

> Jazz is a companionable thing, and I like playing in smaller places, so that I can see what people feel. I would like my music to be part of the surroundings, part of the gaiety of a club atmosphere. I realize I'm in the entertainment business, and I'd like to be [the] sort of guy who can set audiences at ease. If you go about music without a smile, people think you're not happy. I don't make a habit of wishing for what I don't have, but I often wish I had a lighter nature. Dizzy has that beautiful gift—I can't say "Be happy, people"—it's something I can't command. But you have to be true to your own nature. May I say, though, that when I go to hear a man, as long as he conducts himself properly, and moves me with his music, I am satisfied. If he should happen to smile, I consider it something added to what I have received already, if not, I don't worry because I know it is not wholly essential to the music.[45]

But Coltrane's press got even worse early in 1962, when Impulse released an album of Coltrane's quintet entitled *Live at the Village Vanguard*. The *Down Beat* issue of April 26, 1962—the next issue after Coltrane and Dolphy had offered their response to the critics—featured two reviews in order to provide a range of opinion; both focused on the long blues solo that was called "Chasin' the Trane." Pete Welding described it as "a torrential and anguished outpouring, delivered with unmistakable power, conviction, and near-demoniac ferocity." He said it was "a remarkable human document," but it lacked the detachment of true art: "But the very intensity of the feelings that prompt it militate against its effectiveness as a musical experience." This recording was even too much for Ira Gitler, who had been an important booster of Coltrane in the 1950s. Gitler was harsh, writing, "Coltrane may be searching for new avenues of expression, but if it is going to take this form of yawps, squawks, and countless repetitive runs, then it should be confined to the woodshed."

Bob Thiele, Coltrane's producer at Impulse, decided it was time to showcase the more accessible side of Coltrane's art. In September 1962 he paired Coltrane with Duke Ellington in a quartet setting; in November he recorded a session of romantic ballads by Coltrane's regular quartet, which were coupled with some earlier recordings to fill out an entire album of ballads; and in March 1963, Thiele added the gorgeous voice of Johnny Hartman to the quartet for yet another album of ballads. All of these were done in complete cooperation with Coltrane, who was thrilled to work with Ellington and had admired Hartman's singing since about 1950.[46]

Coltrane made a revealing statement to Frank Kofsky in 1966 about the ballads: "I chose them; it seemed to be something that was laying around in my mind—from my youth or somewhere—and I just had to do them." He also went on at some length about technical problems he was having at that time, saying that he had unintentionally ruined his best mouthpiece and found it difficult to play "that certain fast thing that I was reaching for" on other mouthpieces, and that it therefore seemed like a good time to change gears and do the albums of slower material.[47]

For his part, Thiele said his idea was not to make Coltrane commercial, but to prove to the critics that Coltrane had roots and a wonderful ability in traditional standards.[48] His tactic did succeed in winning over a lot of people to Coltrane's music—Ellington's endorsement was worth its weight in gold, and even the most hardened cynic could hardly resist the beautiful, elegant sounds on these three albums.

Thiele also said that Coltrane learned a valuable lesson from Ellington, who, having recorded prolifically since 1924, had more experience than anybody. Coltrane tended to make more takes than necessary, hoping to get a perfect one, tiring everyone out and spending a lot of studio money in the process. But when Thiele asked Ellington if another take was needed, he said

"Don't ask him [Coltrane] to do another. He'll just end up imitating himself." Coltrane sounded almost, but not quite, convinced: "I would have liked to have worked over all those numbers again, but then I guess the performance wouldn't have had the same spontaneity. And they mightn't have been any better!" Thiele says Coltrane tried to use fewer takes on his quartet sessions after that.[49]

It remained for Coltrane to settle the personnel of his group, something which he continued to work on through early 1962. He continued to experiment with the idea of adding people to the group, and his top choice was guitarist Wes Montgomery. He performed with Montgomery at a San Francisco club in September 1961. Then, on September 22, they drove up to Monterey to perform that night at the festival as a sextet. The French critic Louis-Victor Mialy was living in San Francisco at the time, and he ended up driving Coltrane, Dolphy, and Montgomery. Once they arrived in Monterey and starting looking at hotels, Mialy remembers that the conversation suddenly became animated:

> *Montgomery:* Eric, you're a pain in the ass, you haven't stopped knocking my guitar with your feet!
> *Dolphy:* OK, Daddy, I'll be careful.
> *Coltrane:* Our rooms are reserved at the Travel Lodge, where all the musicians are staying. That's much too noisy, so let's try to find a quieter room, maybe in Carmel—do you agree, Lou?
> *Mialy:* That's fine with me! Let's continue to look; but there's no point in getting upset, we have plenty of time.
> *Dolphy:* It doesn't matter to me, it's all the same to me, as long as we're able to find some women.
> *Montgomery:* You dirty old man, that's all you ever think about.
> *Dolphy:* Only when I come to California; it's the sun that makes me do that!
> *Coltrane:* I'd love to stay a few days in Carmel to celebrate my birthday in quiet; I'll be thirty-five years old tomorrow morning!
> *Montgomery:* Let's celebrate that in style; they have some great restaurants in Carmel: escargots, coq au vin . . .
> *Coltrane:* OK! I really want to; but no snails for me.[50]

This lively group performed an hour-long set that night but never jelled as a regular lineup, reportedly because Montgomery didn't like playing such long numbers. In England that November, Coltrane suggested to Valerie Wilmer that his group might have sounded better and gotten a better reception if Montgomery had been included: "I very much wanted to have Wes here in England. He's really something else because he can make everything sound that much fuller."[51] As late as June 1962, John was still talking about hiring Montgomery (Thomas, 152–53). But it is hard to imagine the guitarist's lyrical mainstream style fitting in with Coltrane's ceaseless explorations.

Dolphy remained with the group until around the beginning of April 1962, and Coltrane didn't replace him, saying, "That was perfect. He's the only soloist who gives me complete satisfaction. . . . He's the kind of musician I'd like to have again. I don't consider it important to find a trumpeter who could play in this fashion, but in fact, I don't see anyone at the moment who truly pleases me. I like all the young trumpeters of today but I don't see anyone who I would want to have in my group. Until I find him, I prefer to play in a quartet."[52]

By this time John had also resolved the question of the bass chair. Steve Davis left early in 1961 after a gig in Philadelphia (Thomas 135), where he remained in obscurity.[53] Reggie Workman replaced him and stayed until the end of 1961. Born in Philadelphia in 1937, Workman had worked with Tyner there and was working with Dolphy in Manhattan. He is a highly creative musician, so in every way he was a natural choice for the group. At first Workman had a tendency to go along with Jones's rhythmic excursions, but Coltrane in his terse way let him know that he preferred for the bass to remain independent of the drums: "One day John called me aside and said, 'You know, Reggie, ain't but four of us in this band. And if you're doing the same things [as Elvin]—the band becomes a trio!'" Workman saw the wisdom in this and took Coltrane's advice.[54]

During 1961, Coltrane often paired Workman with a second bassist, most often Art Davis, sometimes reportedly Donald Garrett. Davis, born in Harrisburg, Pennsylvania, in 1934, is a prodigious talent who had been "rated top bass and tuba-man for two years" in high school. He had led his own quintet which by 1956 had been featured on radio, TV, "and at major colleges and clubs throughout the Pennsylvania area." He had already worked in the Harrisburg Symphony and was offered scholarships to three of the leading music conservatories—the Eastman, Juilliard, and Manhattan schools. He chose to study at the latter two and began to work around New York by 1958.[55] Coltrane used to practice with Davis in 1959, until the bassist went with Gillespie from late 1959 through early 1961. Coltrane told Valerie Wilmer that Davis had been his first choice: "I actually wanted Art to join me as a regular bassist, but he was all tied up with Dizzy and so I had to get in Steve Davis and when he left Art still couldn't make it, so I got Reggie [Workman]."

Garrett, a Chicago resident, explained to Barbara Gardner how the two-bass concept came up: "We have been friends since 1955, and whenever he is in town, he comes over to my house, and we go over ideas. I had this tape where I was playing with another bass player. We were doing some things rhythmically, and Coltrane became excited about the sound. We got the same kind of sound you get from the East Indian water drum. One bass remains in the lower register and is the stabilizing, pulsating thing, while the other bass is free to improvise, like the right hand would be on the drum. So Coltrane liked the idea."

Coltrane elaborated, "I'd heard some Indian records and liked the effect of the water drum and I thought another bass would add that certain rhythmic sound. We were playing a lot of stuff with a sort of suspended rhythm, with one bass playing a series of notes around one point, and it seemed that another bass could fill in the spaces in the straight 4/4 line. . . . Once I was in town and I said to Art to come on down because I liked him so much and I figured that he and Reggie could exchange sets. But instead of that they started playing some together and I got something from it." According to Eric Dolphy, Wilbur Ware joined in one night to make it three basses![56]

Coltrane described the effect in a taped interview:

The other bass is used in a percussive sense, you know, sort of like—makes it sound like a tuned drum in a bass. It's like a drum but melodious, you know, little melodic thing going, and it fills in some of the spaces that are left open, you know. In some of these songs that we play with a droning bass, something with a droning bass line, the other bass playing in between fills it in, and if they get the right counterplay and interplay going, it makes it sound like one thing moving along, you know. You get a more solid pulse from it. I've used Art Davis. Art Davis is very good because he can play against whatever Reggie's playing underneath. He plays high in the high register—he's pretty good at it. On some of the songs it's very effective.[57]

Davis had been with Gillespie from the fall of 1959 until early 1961, then worked with Lena Horne in London, and was back in New York by late May. Coltrane hoped to add him as a regular member, but Davis had other gigs in New York which limited his freedom to travel, so he mostly joined when John was appearing in town.[58]

Eventually Coltrane decided one bassist was sufficient: "For some of my interpretations, I sought the possibility of more rhythmic variety than usual, and I believed I could get that with two bassists. But at the present, I don't intend to continue in this direction and to renew that experience. Undoubtedly, I'm going to try to obtain the same effect with one bassist, or possibly—why not?—no bassist at all. One can indeed imagine a trio in which the rhythmic continuity will only be suggested by the tapping of our feet. But if I keep a bassist, I want him to be able to play without constraint, that is, not to stay a prisoner of a rigid rhythmic line."[59]

In keeping with this attitude, during 1960 Coltrane had been offering more and more freedom to his colleagues, instead of, for example, writing out bass patterns. Of Workman, Coltrane said in the notes to *Live at the Village Vanguard* that he "has a rich imagination and he has a good sense of going it alone. That's important in this band. Most times, the other musicians set their own parts. Reggie, for example, is very adept at creating his own bass line." Still, by the end of 1961, Coltrane expressed some dissatisfaction: "I'm not especially pleased with my current bassist, Reggie Workman. He's not mature yet" (Postif). Workman was plagued by personal problems at the time—his father was ill, and he was being pursued by the draft board—and he left the group.[60]

Coltrane told Postif what he was looking for in a bassist: "I am accustomed to Elvin's playing now. The way he plays, a bassist has to be a force of nature, because he plays with such force that if you don't respond with the same authority, you're practically smothered. With Elvin, it's necessary to have a flexible bassist, because he's often ahead of the tempo: it's necessary at the same time to follow him and to precede him [in order to keep the tempo stable]. It's very difficult, and I don't know at the moment an available bassist who is able to do that. Possibly Wilbur Ware, but he's so available [so unemployed] that nobody knows what's become of him!"

Late in 1961, Coltrane called his favorite bassist Art Davis again, but again he was unable to join. Davis explains, "The third time John asked me to be in his group was when I was hired at NBC-TV [as a staff musician] in the breaking of racial barriers. I just got the gig and John called me to join for the third time . . . John said he understood very clearly and this was an earth shattering endeavor that would ease the hiring of other African Americans. John then hired Jimmy Garrison." This must have been decided by early December, if not before the European tour, because on December 16 the change was announced in a British publication called *Disc*.[61]

Garrison (1934–76) had played with Coltrane at the Village Vanguard in November 1961, sometimes with Workman, and sometimes as the sole bassist. Born in Miami, he was raised in Philadelphia and had been on the gig with Coltrane and Tyner in 1957. He'd been working around New York since 1958, most recently with the Ornette Coleman group, which Coltrane loved. Garrison joined Coltrane at the end of 1961—possibly beginning with the Carnegie Hall concert on December 30. He provided the bedrock of time and melody for the group, even in its wildest moments. His lines were straightforward patterns, without a lot of notes—he drove the rhythm section without cluttering its texture. The power of his sound, which cut through the group, was essential to his rhythmic power. When called upon, as on the title cut of the Impulse album *Impressions,* he could produce a walking bass line with tremendous drive. At other times, he was flexible enough to play short melodic phrases that broke up the beat, or to strum chords. Even his walking lines were often varied with such creative devices, but because of the clarity of his thinking the beat remained evident. When it was time for a bass solo, Garrison's bandmates would usually drop out, leaving him to play a rhythmically free rhapsody, often working over diatonic material with great depth of sound and feeling.

Garrison said in 1967, "I found that I could play more than one string at a time and have it make sense. Also, a lot of bass players play, for example, from the tonic to the seventh; I found there was so much after that seventh—flat 9ths and raised 9ths and 13ths. And I found I could use them. . . . Elvin plays in such a way that you can play four if you want or not play four if you don't want to, so there was nothing that said you had to play a timekeeping four beats. But I did find that it usually was better for the quartet as a whole if I played four—with an occasional something else if I felt it."[62]

This version of the quartet—Coltrane, Tyner, Garrison, and Jones—remained basically intact from April 1962 through the fall of 1965. During that period, they collaborated in music that drew on a wide range of influences. Each of them—not Coltrane alone—deserves credit for some of the most moving and exciting group creations ever recorded.

15

"So Much More to Do"

For some years Coltrane had been exposed to the music of other cultures—India, parts of Africa, Latin America—through Dennis Sandole, Dizzy Gillespie, Yusef Lateef, and others. He must have also learned from Ahmed Abdul-Malik, Monk's bassist, and John had him play the droning Indian tamboura (wrongly listed as the Middle Eastern oud, for which he was better known) at the Village Vanguard in November 1961. Coltrane was among the first to play what is now called "world music." Coltrane was also excited about new approaches from within the jazz community, especially by Ornette Coleman—the so-called avant-garde. Once he formed his own group, these studies began to bear fruit. As usual, he was concerned with expressing these influences in written forms that he could explore with his group. "I've really got to work and study more approaches to writing," he told Nat Hentoff. "I've got to keep probing. There's so much more to do."[1]

Coltrane commented to Kitty Grime in November 1961 about the rhythmic changes that had occurred in jazz:

> Change is inevitable in our music—things change. A big break with the dancing tradition of jazz came in the forties with Diz and Bird. You got broken rhythms, complicated harmonic devices. There is so much beauty still in this music.
>
> Then, almost ten years later, Miles, who'd been with them at the beginning, swung over to the other side again. You can dance to most of Miles' most popular things—like "Green Dolphin Street." Now, in the music of people like Cecil Taylor and Ornette you have a swing back to broken rhythms again. It's a fact that everything in life is action and reaction. Things evolve, not necessarily consciously. But there are certain elements

that are inherent in jazz, and you must be watching for them. If those elements are there, you'll get it.[2]

On November 28, 1959, in one of his appearances as a leader while with Davis, Coltrane had led a quartet at Town Hall, Manhattan, on the same bill as Coleman's and Taylor's groups (as well as Monk's group, a Count Basie quartet with Elvin Jones on drums, and the Jazztet with McCoy Tyner on piano). Of Cecil Taylor's piano style—John had recorded an album of standard jazz tunes in October 1958 with Taylor—he told Postif, "It's much too complicated!" During 1961, they may have had happier experiences when Taylor sat in with Coltrane's quintet with Dolphy—"He and Dolphy can hear me," said Taylor.[3] But Coltrane was unreserved in his praise for Coleman, who was born in 1930 and had come to New York in 1959 after recording in Los Angeles. He raved to Benoit Quersin,

> I love him. I'm following his lead. He's done a lot to open my eyes to what can be done. . . . I feel indebted to him, myself. Because, actually, when he came along, I was so far in this thing ["Giant Steps" chords], I didn't know where I was going to go next. And I don't know if I would have thought about just abandoning the chord system or not. I probably wouldn't have thought of that at all. And he came along doing it, and I heard it, I said, "Well, that must be the answer." . . . Since I have a piano, we have to consider it, and that accounts for the modes that we play, but . . . after a while, that's going to get a little monotonous to do it on every song, so there probably will be some songs in the future that we're going to play, just as Ornette does, with no accompaniment from the piano at all— except on maybe the melody, but as far as the solo, no accompaniment.[4]

Coleman was incredibly controversial at that time, more so even than Coltrane, and in Coleman's case the controversy has never totally subsided. Mainly at issue was his contention that the use of prearranged chord progressions (changes) stifled jazz improvisation. To his credit, Coleman has always had a charming, matter-of-fact way of responding to all the catcalls. He wrote: "Using changes already laid out gives you a place to start and lets the audience know what you're doing. I mean if they can whistle the song in your solo. But that means you're not playing all your own music, or all the music you're playing's not yours. Playing popular tunes or tunes based on popular tunes has got to hold you back." Elsewhere he said: "For me, if I am just going to use the changes themselves, I might as well write out what I am going to play [during the improvised section]."[5]

A composer of wit and originality, Coleman might or might not provide chord progressions for his themes. In either case, he expected the improvisor to use the theme and the basic tonality as inspiration. Coleman had not rejected musical structure, contrary to the claims of his critics. He simply preferred to create a logical structure during his improvisation instead of relying on the given structure of a chord sequence and chorus length. And in fact, most of the time he swung hard over a walking bass. Coleman's accompanists followed him as they saw fit. The bassist—usually Charlie Haden, but also Scott LaFaro and Jimmy Garrison—provided a complementary melodic line but didn't always match Coleman's harmonic directions, so that at times there could be two tonalities suggested at once.[6]

On June 28 and July 8, 1960, Coltrane got together with Coleman's associates and recorded three of Coleman's tunes, one by Coleman's trumpeter Don Cherry, and one by Monk. He also made his first studio appearance on soprano, but the session was not released until 1966. It is revealing that, perhaps feeling he was not yet ready for free improvisation, Coltrane chose for his session some of Coleman's earliest compositions that do have prearranged chord progressions. And he certainly didn't play like Coleman—Coltrane's own musical personality was too well established to incorporate Coleman's saxophone style. It was Coleman's concepts and his liberated, poetic spirit that influenced Coltrane. And of course, during the next few years Coltrane's music did venture farther and farther from tradition. By 1965, Coltrane improvised without prearranged chord progressions and ventured far out of the mode in which a given theme was grounded.

Coltrane talked quite a bit about music with Coleman. "In the early '60s he was studying with me," explains Coleman. "He was interested in non-chordal playing, and I had cut my teeth on that stuff. He later sent me a letter which included thirty dollars for each lesson, and thanked me."[7] Martin Williams spotted Coltrane—"quiet, constantly listening"—at a rehearsal of Coleman's quartet in late 1961 when Jimmy Garrison was on bass.[8] John told Postif that as of November 1961, "I only played with him once in my life. I went to hear him in a club and he asked me to join him. We played two pieces—exactly twelve minutes—but I think this was definitely the most intense moment of my life!" They performed again in February 1964, when Coleman played trumpet—a new instrument for him—with John's group at the Half Note. In January 1965, Coleman recounts, "He called me up and asked if I would join his band. I was very interested in trying to get the things I was playing in the public's eye, but I was having too much trouble with the business, so I hadn't been out in clubs for a long time. I thought I'd better go out and see what's going on. When I went to the [Village] Vanguard, Max Gordon called me over and said, 'Somebody just cancelled—could you bring in a band?' And that's the only thing that stopped me from joining Coltrane."[9]

Sonny Rollins was thinking about Coleman's approach too, and Coltrane was very interested in what Rollins was doing. Rollins had retired from performing for about two years, and Coltrane expressed his admiration: "Progress in jazz can be made consciously—think of Sonny Rollins—he was back in November and we'll see something! Sonny 'retired' before, and when he came back, he'd added quite a bit. I admire his tremendous powers of concentration. You have to do a lot of work consciously, then you can leave the rest to your subconscious later on."[10] Jack Cooke reports that while in England, John was "worried" about Rollins making his debut that week in New York at the Jazz Gallery. "He didn't know what Sonny had got up his sleeve but his wife [Naima] was flying to England with a tape that evening."[11] That tape remains a mystery, but Rollins's recordings show that he was using a rich tone, a free attitude toward going in and out of the key, and occasional multiphonics and other effects. By 1962 Rollins, like Coltrane in 1960, was actually recording with Coleman's musicians—in fact, he toured with Don Cherry, Billy Higgins, and later the pianist Paul Bley, who was an important early colleague of Coleman's. With them he would change the key or tempo of a piece in the middle of his solo. Unlike Coleman, Rollins did all his experimenting on standard song forms—his contribution was to show how free one could be within these strictures. His 1960s recordings for RCA were an inspiration to many musicians, including this writer.

Of the composer, bandleader, and bassist Charles Mingus (1922–79), Coltrane was respectful, but for some reason less enthusiastic. In 1961 he remarked, "I wouldn't at all like, at this time, to make a record with Charlie Mingus, simply because I'm not familiar with his music, and I'm not sure I understand his theories. I'm not saying that if we worked together it would necessarily be a failure—no, the result might possibly astonish both of us—but I must say that the idea doesn't enthuse me, for the moment at least" (Postif). A year later, he said he would be "interested" in playing with Mingus, but added, "Our encounter would surely be touchy because Mingus works outside the usual forms and structures, and I don't think I'm going as far as he—no, really I don't think so."[12] The two never did play together.

Coltrane was open to other influences and was generous in acknowledging his sources. When Leonard Feather said in 1964 that all the young saxophonists were copying him, the comment was "modestly shrugged off": "I don't think people are necessarily copying me. In any art, there may be certain things in the air at certain times. Another musician may come along with a concept independently."[13] Similarly, Coltrane told Frank Kofsky in 1966 that he couldn't take sole credit for his music: "It's like a big reservoir, that we all dip out of."[14] He had broad listening habits and was able to identify the players and even the composers of the recordings played for him on his 1959 "Blindfold Test" in *Down Beat*. As an example of how influences go around, he told Kofsky, "I listened to John Gilmore kind of closely before I made 'Chasin' the Trane,' too. So some of those things on there are really direct influences of listening to this cat, you see. But then I don't know who he'd been listening to, so . . ."[15] Gilmore (1931–95) was best known for his work with bandleader Sun Ra, where he played everything from high-register squeals and honks to hard-driving solos over changes. Coltrane was also well aware of Ra's innovative music—with Davis in March 1956 he'd shared a bill with Ra in Chicago. Ra's large group recorded free group improvisations as early as 1960. Coltrane said of Sun Ra, "I've heard him and I know that he's doing some of the things that I've wanted to do."[16]

Apart from the influence of particular musicians, and of this "reservoir" of ideas within jazz, Coltrane was getting more and more interested in the larger pool of ideas to be found in folk music from Black America and from other countries. He recorded the English folk song "Greensleeves." An example of a Black American song he adapted is "The Drinking Gourd," renamed "Song of the Underground Railroad" after it was recorded at the "Africa" sessions. Another is "Spiritual," but in this case the original title was not given. It was first recorded in the Village Vanguard sessions of November 1961, although in the liner notes to that LP Coltrane said, "It's a piece we'd been working with for some time because I wanted to make sure before we recorded it that we would be able to get the original emotional essence of the spiritual. . . . I like the way it worked out." Simpkins notes that Coltrane may have drawn his inspiration from a book in his personal library, a collection of spirituals edited by James Weldon Johnson (137). On page 140 of *The Book of American Negro Spirituals,* originally published in 1925, one finds the song that Coltrane called "Spiritual," in the same key of C minor and with the same first and second strain. It is a melody for "Nobody Knows de Trouble I See" that Johnson calls "a rare version," since it is not the one most people know:[17]

a. Beginning of "Nobody Knows De Trouble I See," "rare version."

b. "Spiritual," by John Coltrane (1961).

Outside of America, the music of India was a particular interest of Coltrane. We mentioned his use of a repetitive bass part on "My Favorite Things" in October 1960; to many this suggests the music of India, but Coltrane said, "Since, I've been listening more and more to Indian music, and I've been trying to use some of their methods in some of the things we're doing, but at that time it was more or less subconscious."[18] Early in 1961 he began listening closely to North Indian music, especially the recordings of sitar virtuoso Ravi Shankar. Shankar, born in 1920, had been to America with a dance troupe as a youth, but became known as a soloist beginning with his return here in 1956. Coltrane told Postif that he would love to record with Shankar: "I collect the records he's made, and his music moves me. I'm certain that if I recorded with him I'd increase my possibilities tenfold, because I'm familiar with what he does and I understand and appreciate his work. I also hope to meet him when I return to the United States." The plans for the meeting had been confirmed that same day: "Coltrane was bothered by his shirt collar—one of the buttons had popped off. While he changed, he showed me on the table a letter he had just received. A New York impresario told him that he had set up at his request a meeting with Ravi Shankar . . . Trane . . . was happy and flattered by this appointment."[19] They met that December, at the beginning of one of Shankar's tours, and they stayed in touch.[20] Coltrane even named his second son Ravi in 1965.

The impact of North Indian music is reflected in Coltrane's work over a single sustained drone, in his interest in exotic scales, and perhaps in the way he likes to repeat and develop short motives in his improvisations, which brings to mind the Indian style of sitar improvisation. (But then, John Gilmore did that too. There's that reservoir of ideas again.) The influence is explicit in "India"— a chant in G that never moves from the G pedal point. Composer and jazz scholar Bill Bauer has found the probable source of the tune—a recorded Vedic chant (that is, with a text coming from the Vedas, religious books of the 1500s) that appears to have been issued on a Folkways LP at that time. The singer's melody is nearly identical with Coltrane's. In this instance Coltrane was following the lead of Miles Davis and Gil Evans. They based "Saeta" from the album *Sketches of Spain* directly on a field recording of the same name (complete with the marching band at the beginning and end) that had been recently issued on an LP. "The Pan Piper" was based on the first track of the same LP.[21] Nisenson also points out that "Mr. Knight," a blues from a year earlier, resembles "India" (124–25). But he is wrong to suggest that "India" is the same as that blues— the relationship is basically in the opening vamp. Maybe this is an example of something that had stayed in Coltrane's "subconscious."

Carl Grubbs, Naima's cousin, offers some more information on Coltrane's studies of India. When he visited Coltrane's place in Queens, he noticed a page of Indian scales that had been copied out of a book. Grubbs made his own hand copy.

Indian scales from Coltrane's notebook, hand copied by and courtesy of Carl Grubbs. (I penned in the penultimate D-flat because it appeared on another of Grubbs's copies.)

Two more pages of scales, in Coltrane's own hand, are reproduced in Simpkins (113). Over each scale, Coltrane has written a source: "Algerian," "Chinese," "Japanese," and so on. There are also three ragas from India, the third, at the top of the second page, being the type that differs slightly when ascending and descending.[22]

Coltrane's interest in scales and modes from India and elsewhere, was, as he explained, really part of a broader mission, to discover the universalities in music:

> I like Ravi Shankar very much. When I hear his music, I want to copy it—not note for note of course, but in his spirit. What brings me closest to Ravi is the modal aspect of his art. Currently, at the particular stage I find myself in, I seem to be going through a modal phase. . . . There's a lot of modal music that is played every day throughout the world. It's particularly evident in Africa, but if you look at Spain or Scotland, India or China, you'll discover this again in each case. If you want to look beyond the differences in style, you will confirm that there is a common base. That's very important. Certainly, the popular music of England is not that of South America, but take away their purely ethnic characteristics—that is, their folkloric aspect—and you'll discover the presence of the same pentatonic sonority, of comparable modal structures. It's this universal aspect of music that interests me and attracts me; that's what I'm aiming for.[23]

It wasn't only the sound of world music that attracted him; Coltrane was interested in all kinds of religion, and in all kinds of mysticism. He knew that in some folk cultures music was held to have mystical powers, and he hoped to get in touch with some of those capacities. He told Nat Hentoff, "I've already been looking into those approaches to music—as in India—in which particular sounds and scales are intended to produce specific emotional meanings."[24] As he explained: "I would like to bring to people something like happiness. I would like to discover a method so that if I want it to rain, it will start right away to rain. If one of my friends is ill, I'd like to play a certain song and he will be cured; when he'd be broke, I'd bring out a different song and immediately he'd receive all the money he needed. But what are these pieces and what is the road to travel to attain a knowledge of them, that I don't know. The true powers of music are still unknown. To be able to control them must be, I believe, the goal of every musician. I'm passionate about understanding these forces. I would like to provoke reactions in the listeners to my music, to create a real atmosphere. It's in that direction that I want to commit myself and to go as far as possible."[25]

On May 25, 1961, he recorded the album *Olé* with his quintet plus guest

Freddie Hubbard on trumpet. (Ostensibly because Dolphy was under contract to Prestige Records at the time, the original issue identified him as "George Lane.") From the opening title track, "Olé," it is evident that the group has changed considerably in the seven months since "My Favorite Things." The basic idea of a repeated bass and piano vamp is still there, with Jones and Coltrane thrashing freely around it, but everybody is looser now. Tyner has begun reaching into the lower register of the piano, the two basses create a churning undercurrent, and there is a sense of endless time and energy. The improvisation sections now take place over one vamp—there is no second part and no need to cue one. Coltrane's interests had led him to Spanish music— thus the title—which may be another legacy of *Sketches of Spain*. Like "India" and Davis's "Saeta," "Olé" was based on a genuine folk source, a song known as "Venga Vallejo" or as "El Vito."[26]

Coltrane also studied recordings of African music by Nigerian drummer Michael Babatunde Olatunji. Olatunji and Coltrane played opposite each other, alternating with a third band, Art Blakey's Messengers, at New York's Village Gate during the last week of August 1961. John wrote "Tunji" for him in 1962. Coltrane seems to have applied some of the concepts he heard in the music of Olatunji and in folkloric African recordings to his own music. First of all was the use of ostinatos, with each instrument having its own rhythm that adds into the whole. African structural concepts may have influenced him too— West African drumming groups will repeat one section until the leader gives a cue to go on to the next, much as Coltrane does in "My Favorite Things."

In June 1958, Coltrane had recorded flugelhornist Wilbur Harden's composition "Oomba," which had three different sections, each based on one mode and one bass ostinato. (The sessions with Harden also featured "Dial Africa," "Gold Coast," and "Tanganyika Strut," in more conventional forms but illustrating the fascination with the motherland.) In May 1961, Coltrane began consciously utilizing African elements in his recordings. "Dahomey Dance," a blues from the album *Olé*, is said by Simpkins to have been inspired by a field recording of two African singers (128). This is likely, and a Folkways album could have been the source, but I haven't yet been able to track down the exact recording. Meanwhile, Coltrane's first recording for Impulse, begun on May 23 just before *Olé*, was *Africa/Brass*, with the largest ensemble he ever used. Coltrane told Ralph Gleason on May 2 that he had spoken with Gil Evans, but for unknown reasons Evans was not involved with the date; the liner notes credit Eric Dolphy for the arrangements.[27] However, the notes also acknowledge that McCoy Tyner played a major role. In order to set the record straight, Tyner explains that "at the time, John was trying to encourage me to arrange music. He approached me and said the session was a good opportunity, so I wrote the arrangement for 'Greensleeves.' . . . For the other compositions, Eric came to me and said, 'What are you doing on the piano?' And then he copied my voicings for the arrangement. Originally, I didn't get any credit for that. Plus my name was misspelled McCoy Turner. Eric got the credit for the arrangement on 'Greensleeves.'"[28] Coltrane supported Tyner's claim years ago with the statement, "We've taken what McCoy was to have played at the piano and arranged it for orchestra."[29] On the most recent release, the credit has been corrected to read ". . . arranged by John Coltrane and McCoy Tyner and orchestrated and arranged by Eric Dolphy."

Dom Cerulli, in the notes to *Africa/Brass*, described the way Coltrane prepared for these sessions: "He listened to many African records for rhythmic inspiration. One had a bass line like a chant, and the group used it, working it into different tunes. In Los Angeles, John hit on using African rhythms instead of [swing style] 4/4, and the work began to take shape." Coltrane told it just a bit differently to Ralph Gleason, reminding Gleason that he had gotten away from basing his compositions on complicated chord sequences. He wanted to concentrate more on melody, and the rhythm was often his starting point: "I have an African record at home and they're singing these rhythms, some of their native rhythms, so I took part of it and gave it to the bass. And Elvin plays a part and McCoy managed to find something to play, some kind of chords. I didn't tell him *what* chords, I said, 'I'm through with it.' And so he's on his own, and I'm going on my own, see? . . . Still no melody, though. [laughs] I had to make the melody as I went along. But at least I'm trying to think of a melody; I'm not referring to the chords to get the melody."[30]

Later in 1961 he told Kitty Grime that he was looking for different rhythmic approaches: "Mingus says, 'the beat[31] must go,' and I admit I don't love the beat, in the strict sense. At this phase I feel I need the beat somewhere, but I don't really care about the straight 4/4 at all—though this is just a personal feeling. In a rhythm section I like propulsion and a feeling of buoyancy, which fits under and around the horn, and has a lift to it. A sense of the pulse, rather than the beat, can take you out of a stodgy approach. And, of course, you can swing on other time signatures than 4/4. But what happens depends on the musicians I have playing with me."[32]

Coltrane elaborated on his concept of time on an unpublished tape:

It is necessary to have a firm beat going, but it's not necessary to have everyone playing 4/4, I mean rigidly. Between the three man or the two man [pianoless] rhythm section, there should be enough interplay to give you at every point of the song the same solidarity that you get in 4/4, but it will be implied sometimes instead of actually played. Now this thing, it can be done and sometimes it is done but it has to be the right combination of individuals playing. They have to really feel this way, and they have to have very good sounds. They have to be able to produce good quality sound on the instrument so when they do play, what they play will sustain and thus create this level [of sameness] underneath, although it will be broken actually as it's played.[33]

So Coltrane looked for ways to thicken the rhythmic texture of his music even as he simplified its harmonic motion by keeping to a repeated pedal point. He said in 1964, "I feel that since we have used fewer chordal progressions, we need more rhythm, and I want to experiment."[34] The growing rhythmic complexity of his music, his adaptation of African rhythms, and his encouragement of Elvin Jones's polyrhythms, led by late 1965 to the elimination of strict time-keeping in his groups. In doing so, Coltrane helped create a new rhythmic basis for jazz. He also helped spawn a trend toward including ethnic instruments and tunes from around the world in jazz groups, and in so doing he helped to make jazz an even more international music. Groups from all over—especially Scandinavia—realized that they could create a more personal and unique jazz sound by drawing upon their local folk melodies. And when Coltrane joined the movement among black Americans to look to the music of mother Africa for inspiration, he gave it a tremendous lift.

Reggie Workman says that during his year with the group they rehearsed very little. However, since they spent so many nights on the bandstand, and two or three sets per night, there was time to try things out on the stand. If there was a particular bass rhythm, as on "One and Four" (also known as "Mr. Day"), "He would write something like that out and say, 'Do this through the changes,' or he'd sit down at the piano and say, 'We might try this progression next time,' and we'd have to remember that or write it down." Coltrane told Postif in November 1961: "I have some problems with this quartet, but I think they will quickly resolve themselves. We rehearse very little, only for recording sessions, and that's not enough. As a general rule, I prefer to record pieces that I'm used to playing in public, because I already know the reactions of the listeners and, besides, it all reaches a peak in the studio recording."

Eventually, Coltrane moved away from recording music they'd played in public; in fact, the recording sometimes was the world premiere performance. He took a tip from Miles Davis by not rehearsing new music or even showing the music to his group before the recording session in order to preserve the spontaneity. If anything, he'd show them a chord chart without the melody, since only he had to play the melody anyway. And he might have committed that melody to memory, or sometimes wrote little dots on a page as a mnemonic aid, so he didn't even write it down for himself. On a modal piece, he'd just set the vamp without using any notation. Jimmy Garrison once noted, "Often there was *no* written music. He'd just announce what key we'd be playing in, or that we'd be playing in twelve tones [free improvisation, mostly after 1965] and we'd take it from there."[35] (For this reason, music in Coltrane's hand after 1961 is scarce.) A sample of his spoken directions to Tyner are included at the start of his "Dearly Beloved" (not Jerome Kern's song of the same name), from August 1965:

> Then you go into there [another vamp or section sketched on paper or previously discussed at the piano]. But I think it'd be better to keep it pressing so we, you know, keep a thing happening all through, you know. [Maintain the energy and continuity between sections.] But you can go through it the way you feel it, let it happen. Ready?[36]

Back in 1962, he told two French writers, "I hope that all that I've done up to now is just the beginning. Two and a half years ago, I formed my own group. . . . We had worked out several projects and I sincerely believe that the things that we completed after that were really the things that we had in mind at that time. But the point where we now find ourselves is the end of the first phase. The time may have come for another approach—I really think that it has come. We are ready."[37]

16

More on Coltrane's Music of 1961–65

Coltrane's style was always changing. He moved more and more into developing a self-reliant sound world, a world that by the 1960s had less and less in common with the music that he started with—the music of Lester Young and Charlie Parker. For one thing, Coltrane was never partial to quoting. What's more, he developed a vocabulary of licks that are in many cases not traceable to his predecessors. One way that Coltrane developed this unique sound world is by bringing into his music—and through his influence, into all of jazz and beyond—an eclectic collection of method books, exercises, and scales from around the world. The eclecticism gave his style originality—the more widespread one's sources, the less one sounds like any one of them. Eclecticism, it seems to me, is one hallmark of genius. Another part of Coltrane's genius lay in anchoring these diverse sources in the power of the blues, particularly the minor blues.

It's well known that Coltrane utilized many books and studies—he began this in earnest after the navy, for example, in his studies with Sandole. In itself that is unremarkable. In fact, one of the clearest differences between the beboppers and the previous generations is that, while the older players knew the scales and chords, Parker, Gillespie, Monk, and their circle were interested in theory for its own sake. What's unusual about Coltrane is that he seems to have built his style out of many of these resources, instead of leaving them at home strictly for practice and technique development. It would be as if pianists who studied Hanon's sequential exercises in their youth went on to invent or write music based on Hanon. That generally doesn't happen. Yet in Coltrane's case it did—quite literally.

Coltrane's sound world with his quartet was built around little fourth-based motives such as the chant from *A Love Supreme*, rather than the arpeggios of major chords that are such a critical part of most jazz—and of Western music generally. This gives his music a serious, rather abstract sound, and, as noted earlier, it probably contributes to the spiritual element in his music. The way he builds his solos by developing short ideas at length, repeating them in different registers and building up to higher and higher notes, makes him a preacher on the saxophone. He does this most clearly on a slow out-of-tempo piece such as "Psalm," as we'll see. But as German jazz educator Gerhard Putschögl has pointed out, Coltrane builds his solos the same way even when working with the rhythm section at a medium or fast tempo.[1] And because those fourths are a basis of the blues, his music is simultaneously drenched in blues feeling. That mixture of intense blues and spiritual fervor gives his music astounding power.

Jazz historian Dan Morgenstern recalls a typical evening at the Half Note around 1964 or 1965, "The intensity that was generated was absolutely un-believable. I can still *feel* it, and it was unlike any other feeling within the music we call jazz. . . . It carried you away. If you let yourself be carried by it, it was an absolutely ecstatic feeling. And I think that kind of ecstasy was something that Coltrane was looking for in his music."[2]

The rhythmic intensity of the music was one aspect of that ecstatic experience. During the 1960s when Coltrane played at a medium or fast tempo, his line seemed to be conceived as a continuous pulse of eighth notes, with notes left out here and there. We can see that he conceives of the music this way, and not as a series of short independent phrases, by examining constructions in the example below. A sizable rest (say a quarter note value or more) does not necessarily denote a phrase ending. It is often a part of the phrase. There is an additive procedure at work here, where short units add up to longer phrases. Coltrane had left "sheets of sound" behind around 1960.

Excerpt of Coltrane's playing showing "additive" rhythms, from "Impres-sions" (1961), beginning of chorus 14.

His approach to the soprano differed in that he played much more flor-
idly, filling in long, rippling legato lines where an eighth-note run might have
served on the tenor. He was very conscious of the differences between the two
saxophones, and each had its own reserved repertory. Just as "My Favorite
Things" was a soprano feature, "Impressions" became his tenor theme song.
This is based on the same AABA structure and D Dorian mode (E-flat for the
bridge) as "So What," but there has been confusion about the origin of the
melody, which is totally different from "So What." As Priestley (67) has correctly pointed out, the A melody is from Morton Gould's "Pavanne" (*sic;* this
word is usually spelled with one *n*), a movement of his second "American
Symphonette" from 1938. Gould's charming music was very popular, and
deservedly so. The "Pavanne" was arranged for swing bands, and Coltrane may
well have known Jimmy Lunceford's recording from 1940, which is a rather
faithful arrangement of the original. He very likely knew Ahmad Jamal's trio
versions from 1955 and 1960, the latter issued right around the time Coltrane
founded his quartet. The "Pavanne" has two themes: the first was a sprightly
tune that many jazz musicians knew—Wardell Gray and others quoted it. The
second theme is played only twice (in keys a minor third apart, by the way), and
it is identical with Coltrane's "Impressions."

The B section of "Impressions" is taken, believe it or not, from yet another
"Pavane," Maurice Ravel's famous and touching "Pavane pour une Infante
Défunte," originally written for piano in 1899 and arranged by Ravel for
orchestra in 1910.[3] Again, Coltrane has taken part of the second theme, which
in 1939 had been made into a popular song, "The Lamp Is Low," that Coltrane
probably knew as well. James Forman told me that he and Coltrane played an
arrangement of Ravel's piece in 1947 or 1948 (see chapter 7).

What are some of the building blocks of Coltrane's style of the 1960s? His
lovely ballad performances drew upon a repertory of unique ornamental figures. Coltrane's paraphrasing of a ballad melody did not vary much from one
performance to another of the same piece, even in the specific locations and
types of ornaments added. This suggests that he tended to conceive of a definitive paraphrase of a given melody, and he proceeded to hear the melody a
similar way each time he played it. The paraphrase version became a distinct
gestalt, ornaments and all. For instance, hear his 1962 performance of "You
Don't Know What Love Is." Notice the very close agreement between the first
theme statement and the last one, both in free time. The treatments of the
third, fourth, and sixth measures are almost identical. A few types of ornaments are discussed below.

1. This figure, with its graceful leap of a fifth or more, is Coltrane's most
personal ornament. He generally places it at the beginnings of phrases. It often
serves to break up a potentially boring whole note.

Octave leaps, a special case of the above, appear at decisive moments, such as chorus beginnings.

2. Coltrane casually tosses off elaborate turns like this.

We also notice in "You Don't Know What Love Is" some of the devices Coltrane employed to embellish a melody that are not, strictly speaking, ornaments. These appeared at all tempos, not only ballad performances.

3. Breaking up long notes into repeated notes.

Rhythmic variations on repeated notes add interest to the long notes of the melody without drastically altering the melodic line. This time-honored device was a trademark of Louis Armstrong, as well as Lester Young, one of Coltrane's early idols.

4. Breaking up long notes into alternating notes.

The melody note alternates rapidly with a lower note, usually a third or fifth below, but sometimes a fourth or other intervals. The second example, from "Equinox," shows how an entire phrase could be built out of this simple principle.

5. Scalar (gapped or continuous) ascents into high notes. Sometimes Coltrane uses exotic scales in these runs.

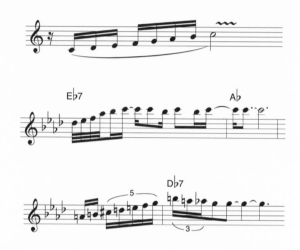

6. Arpeggiated descents from high melody notes.

These are sequential, with a four- or five-note pattern repeated in each octave descending. They continued to figure prominently in Coltrane's last works, in free rhythm.

7. One of Coltrane's favorite formulas involved a dissonant ascent beginning with honks in the lowest register of his instrument.

V   IV   I   V

a. "Take The Coltrane" (1962), last four measures of a blues chorus in F

**b. A similar ascending phrase from "Impressions" (1961), end of chorus 15,
over D Dorian**

By winding and twisting upon itself, this ascent could be stretched out to as
long as four measures. A careful study of Coltrane's dissonant lines reveals
certain formulaic elements, particularly rhythmic units.

"Impressions" (1961), from the bridge of chorus 15, in E-flat Dorian

8. Many of Coltrane's other melodic formulas are diatonic, not dissonant
like the ones above.

Diatonic formulas of Coltrane

Opening solo on "A Love Supreme" (1964)
Copyright © 1977 JOWCOL MUSIC. International Copyright Secured.
All Rights Reserved. Used by Permission.

Opening of "So What" (1959)
SO WHAT, by Miles Davis
© 1959 Warner-Tamerlane Publishing Corp. and Estate of Miles Davis
All Rights Administered by Warner-Tamerlane Publishing Corp.
All Rights Reserved. Used by Permission.
WARNER BROS. PUBLICATIONS U.S. INC., Miami, FL 33014

Common on the blues (from "Take the Coltrane," 1962)

The contrast between such diatonic formulas and the dissonant patterns became an increasingly prominent dialogue in Coltrane's work during the 1960s, especially from late 1964 on.

By November of 1961, Coltrane frequently ventured out of the home key altogether, playing in another key than his accompanists for a measure or more. At first, during late 1960 and early 1961, he briefly moved to a scale a half step away or a third away from that on which the piece was based. Musicians sometimes call this "sideslipping"—both Art Tatum and Charlie Parker had done this, especially on live recordings. By late 1961, when Coltrane was performing with Eric Dolphy—no doubt encouraged by Dolphy's example—he interpolated whole phrases that were outside the key. Coltrane's harmonic excursions are not usually analyzable as being in a particular contrasting key, one reason that *dissonance* is the appropriate word here and not *polytonality*. This is one reason his playing on modal pieces has so much variety. He transposed melodic patterns around the instrument, altered and adjusted patterns so that they led out of the key (as in *b*, where measure 5 leads off to the sharp side, almost F-sharp minor), and sometimes actually suggested a specific contrasting key (such as G major over G minor in example *a*).

Some dissonant patterns used by Coltrane

a. Over a G minor chord, on soprano, from "The Promise" (1963)
Copyright © 1977 JOWCOL MUSIC. International Copyright Secured.
All Rights Reserved. Used by Permission.

b. All over an F minor chord ("Afro Blue," 1963)

Many musicians believe that Coltrane's free playing was derived from playing "Giant Steps" patterns over the modal pieces. An early example was "Fifth House." But in that case he actually had a specific chord sequence in his mind while the band played a pedal point. Can one really find the "Giant Steps" technique in his playing over strictly modal pieces like "Impressions"? David Demsey believes so and provided me the following analysis of Coltrane's live 1961 recording of the piece, the title track of his *Impulse* album. Demsey writes:

> I've found numerous instances in the 1961 solo which relate to the "Giant Steps-Countdown" period. There are no direct lifts from "Giant Steps" or "Countdown," nor should there be, since "Impressions" is in a minor key and the thirds-based harmonic technique would not have the same sound in a minor key. That is, C major⁷–E-flat⁷–A-flat, etc. is a more distant and aurally distinctive key shift (one sharp to four flats) than is C minor–E-flat⁷–A-flat (three flats to four flats).
>
> There are, however, two elements of the "Impressions" solo that relate most directly to the vocabulary used in the "Countdown" solo (I use "Countdown" here for reasons described later, although "Giant Steps" could perhaps be involved in this once I've looked at it more closely): (1) A number of brief segments that undoubtedly imply key shifts by minor and major third and/or root movement from a tonic center up a minor third to a dominant sound. (2) Numerous four-note groups that come directly from the vocabulary used in "Countdown."
>
> *1. Thirds-Related Key Shifts Implied in "Impressions."*   There are at least fifteen phrases within this solo that imply thirds-related harmonic mo-

tion. Most of these phrases imply the same chord progression: D minor–
E-flat[7]–A-flat major–F-sharp[7]–B major–A[7]–D minor. Is it a coincidence
that "Countdown" begins similarly, E minor–F[7]–B-flat major? This segment moves through three key centers separated by minor thirds (A-flat–
B–D). It occurs in: chorus 4, second A section; chorus 7, first A section;
chorus 11, bridge into last A section; chorus 15, first A section; chorus 19,
bridge (!) and last A section; chorus 22, second A section; chorus 28,
bridge (nebulous in this segment); chorus 31, first A section.

From Coltrane's solo on "Impressions" (1961), chorus 4, second A section.
Copyright © 1974 JOWCOL MUSIC. International Copyright Secured. All Rights Reserved. Used by Permission.

The second A section of chorus 31 also has an interesting progression
different from all of these, one that implies a complete major thirds cycle:
the final three measures of this section imply A[7]–D major–F[7]–(B-flat
major omitted)–D-flat[7]–G-flat major.

From Coltrane's solo on "Impressions" (1961), chorus 31, second A.

Perhaps more important than the actual chord progressions used in the above examples is the familiar thirds *sound* which is evoked. As is true in "Giant Steps" and "Countdown," this sound is created by the use of cross-relations in the voice leading. An example: In a thirds shift from the key of C to the key of A-flat via E-flat[7], the third of C (E-natural) moves to the root of the E-flat[7]; the root of C moves to the seventh of E-flat (D-flat) etc. This type of chromatic voice-leading does not occur under "normal" fourth-related situations.

2. Melodic Patterns Related to Coltrane's "Countdown" Solo Found in "Impressions."   It is commonly known that Coltrane relied upon a relatively small number of four-note melodic patterns in creating his "Countdown" solo. In fact, these patterns make up nearly 90 percent of the material used in the solo. These patterns also appear in numerous instances during "Impressions," appearing almost exclusively as a vehicle for playing "outside" of the modal key center. There are two in particular which Coltrane often uses as a "doorway" out of the home key to another key center. One is marked 4b on the examples.

There are also two audible interval patterns that outline thirds. These occur in chorus 16, second A section, where major thirds are outlined by successive downbeats, as circled; and in chorus 22, second A section, where minor thirds are outlined in a similar melodic outline.

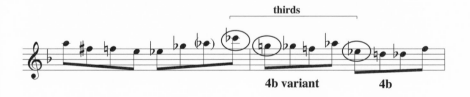

From Coltrane's solo on "Impressions" (1961), excerpts from choruses 16 and 22.
Copyright © 1974 JOWCOL MUSIC. International Copyright Secured. All Rights Reserved. Used by Permission.

Gerhard Putschögl has found fleeting traces of thirds patterns as late as the recording of "Brazilia" in May 1965 (234–36), and we will show them in "Venus," one of his last works. These analyses reinforce one's sense that Coltrane's playing, for all its abandon, is tightly organized. Elvin Jones explained, "I was closer to Coltrane than to anyone else, so I can speak with more authority on him than on others. He was perfectly aware of what he was doing and had almost supernatural control over what he was doing. Even though it gave an impression of freedom, it was basically a well thought out and highly disciplined piece of work."[4]

For example, here is a thirty-two-measure AABA chorus from that 1961 "Impressions" that is based almost entirely on the motive labeled a. In this chorus he stays almost obsessively in the Dorian mode, concentrating on the development of a rhythmic motive. The home key is further emphasized by the reiteration of scale steps 1 and 5 in accented positions. For example, we hear D or A on the first beat of measures 5, 6, 9, 11, 15, 25, 27, 30, 31, and 32, and E-flat begins three of the eight measures of the bridge in E-flat Dorian. At the beginning of the chorus in the example he tries several ideas, until he hits upon motive a at the upbeat to measure 7. The upbeat to measure 8 leads into a string of eighth notes, a kind of "turnaround" pattern to connect this phrase with the next. Motive a accents beats 1 and 3, and Coltrane plays with this idea for the next four measures (9 through 12), first in single quarter notes, then in two-note units based on triplets, ending with eighth notes again. During measures 13 through 16, Coltrane returns to the idea of pairing motive a with a string of eighth notes, to form two-measure units in which the stop-and-go of the first measure contrasts with the flow of the second, whose momentum then carries over into the next two-measure unit. The variations during the succeeding bridge and A sections are clear. The pause before the last measure of the bridge and the quarter note triplets within it serve as a kind of built-in ritard, separating it from the preceding music and emphasizing its function as a turnaround into the last A section. Coltrane neatly concludes the investigation of motive a by creating variations of it alone for measures 27 through 30, reserving a final eighth-note release for measure 31.

Chorus 5 from Coltrane's solo on "Impressions" (1961).
Copyright © 1974 JOWCOL MUSIC. International Copyright Secured. All Rights Reserved. Used by Permission.

We are witnesses to a brilliant mind at work, coming across motivic ideas, developing them, and moving on to explore related ideas in a similar fashion. Only the rhythm of the motive remains relatively intact. Characteristically, Coltrane completely altered the shape and direction of his motives in the course of developing them. For example, the original descending shape of motive a, shown above measure 7 in the example, becomes an ascending line at the beginning of the bridge, then moves unpredictably up and down within the span of about an octave. A higher ascent sets off the beginning of the last eight-measure section by making the shape a straight line. Coltrane creates a rhythmic momentum needed at this point to separate this section from the preceding bridge.

Looking beyond the shapes of short motives, we find a similarly logical underlying pattern among entire phrases. For example, the disjunct melodic motion of measures 6, 7, and 8 conceals a descending line. This can be clearly seen by reading the pitches on beats 1 and 3 of each measure—a′ (f is really the main note here, as reinforced by what follows), f, e, d, c#, and d, forming a simple cadential melody line. A very similar pattern appears in measures 12, 13, and 14, this time spelling g, f, f, e, c#, and d. For all its apparent motion, the entire bridge revolves around the middle e-flat, and the last eight measures keep returning to the d.

Another motivic process may be heard on "Take the Coltrane," a blues by Ellington from their joint session. On the blues, Coltrane would often take the diatonic arpeggios and rhythmicize them. The simple alternation of these arpeggios fascinates the listener because of the unpredictability of the sequence. This is another example of how he plays the blues without using the old-fashioned "bluesy" licks, and yet with powerful down-home soul.

Excerpt from Coltrane's solo on "Take the Coltrane" (1962)

One of Coltrane's favorite developmental techniques was to transpose (with necessary alterations) a motive into the various registers of the saxophone. He especially liked to alternate high- and low-register statements in a kind of dialogue with himself. During his last two years he expanded this effect, often jumping up and down across a two-octave span, as in his solo near the beginning of "Ascension" (Edition II) and, as we shall see, in "Venus."

For all his brilliance and power, one can try to understand where the criticism came from. His lines are not "tunes" in the usual sense—there is no long hummable phrase that comes out of Coltrane's playing, and people who were looking for that had to be frustrated. But if one could go along with him and get involved in his concentrated and focused discipline of improvisation, and get involved with the powerful energy and passion of the whole group at each moment, it is, as Morgenstern said, like no other experience in jazz.

In performance, he liked to improvise for a half hour or more at a stretch, almost certainly setting a new record for jazz, as his detractors angrily noted. But there was good reason for this seemingly inordinate length. He was concerned with following his compositional ideas to their end, and he preferred not to try to curtail, edit, or predetermine this process. As he explained to one interviewer: "When some evenings, in beginning to play, we feel inspired and we foresee the possibility of realizing good things, it seems illogical and unreasonable to us to shorten our solos. . . . My ideas have to develop themselves naturally in a long solo."[5] In playing extended solos, Coltrane was aware that he risked running out of ideas: "If I feel that I'm just playing notes . . . maybe I don't feel the rhythm or I'm not in the best shape that I should be in when this happens. When I become aware of it in the middle of a solo, I'll try to build things to the point where this inspiration is happening again, where things are spontaneous and not contrived. If it reaches that point again, I feel it can continue—it's alive again. But if it doesn't happen, I'll just quit, bow out."[6] He acknowledged that he sometimes played too long: "If I'm going to take an hour to say something I can say in ten minutes, maybe I'd better say it in ten minutes!"[7]

He provided a more specific description of the structure of a long solo to Postif:

> Let me explain the mechanics of these solos that go on and on: we have a certain number of given landmarks, which indicate to us what should happen next. Obviously, it's not a question of always placing these landmarks in the same place, but simply moving them around or even leaving them out sometimes. That's what creates the suspense: my musicians never know when I'm going to give them the cues! If we have to keep it short, I arrive immediately at a certain spot near the end of the piece: when I know that we can take our time, I may sometimes come back to one of the landmarks. This method of operating permits us to never lose touch with the moment in our pieces, and to never be caught by surprise.
>
> Here's how I play: I take off from a point and I go as far as possible. But, hopefully, I'll never lose my way. I say hopefully, because what especially interests me is to discover the ways that I never suspected were possible. My phrasing isn't a simple prolongation of my musical ideas, and I'm happy that my technique permits me to go very far in this domain, but I must add that it's always in a very conscious manner. I localize—that is to say that I think always in a given area. It infrequently happens that I think of the totality of a solo, and very briefly: I always return to the little

fraction of the solo that I'm involved in playing. Chords have become for me a kind of obsession, which gives me the impression of approaching music by the wrong end of a telescope.

Coltrane was writing more and more, because he found that as his approach to improvisation changed, and as his quartet evolved, he needed appropriate material.

Choice of material is entirely individual. I've played some jazz forms so long and so much that I feel the need for other forms, and perhaps for no form. When I started the group, I used to plan routines like mad, now I don't have to plan so much, as I learn and get freer. Sometimes we start from nothing, no 'in' plan, no intro, or solo routines. I know how it's going to end—but sometimes not what might happen in between! I try to accept songs as they are, with a different approach for everything. I make suggestions to the group, as to what I feel, and we use this as a starting point.

I like extended jazz works and written compositions, if they're well done. I'm studying and learning about longer constructions. If I become strong enough I might try something on those lines. I don't study the music of any particular period, but harmony and form from a natural standpoint. I try to look at it all. I want to understand music, so that I can do things in an objective way. So far, I've only written from the piano, with melodies that come out of the chords. I'd like to be able to write away from the piano. It is very useful, though, as you have a whole band under your hands with a piano, and it's the best thing for working on chord forms.[8]

Soon he was to produce some of the most significant extended works of his era.

17

A Love Supreme

In an interview in Paris on November 1, 1963, Coltrane said he needed to get away from playing the same tunes over and over. One of the few new pieces that he'd recorded so far that year was not an original—it was his arrangement of "Vilia" from the popular operetta of 1905, *The Merry Widow,* by Franz Lehar. Coltrane planned to begin writing new material during the next month: "I'm working on approaches to the problem of writing for a group. I've gotten enough solved to do a few things which I think might be up to the standard of what we have done so far. . . . I'm going to let the nature of the songs determine just what I play. . . . It might be modal, it might be chord progressions, or it might be just playing in tonal areas."[1] By this last phrase he meant something like what Ornette Coleman does, taking a certain note as the tonal center—maybe C—and playing freely around it, not restricting himself to C major or minor or any particular mode on C.

He had earlier expressed interest in writing music that was atonal—without a tonal center at all—and in the serial or twelve-tone system of Arnold Schoenberg that facilitated this approach. He had discussed twelve-tone music with jazz composer George Russell and used that system in 1961 to write the theme of "Miles's Mode" (also known as "Red Planet"), but used a mode for the solos. Asked if it would be possible to adhere to the twelve-tone method while improvising, he had replied "Damn the rules, it's the feeling that counts [during improvisation]. You play all twelve notes in your solo anyway."[2] When the subject of atonality came up again in the 1963 interview, he replied that he didn't want to commit himself to one approach: "I don't know. Probably so. But I don't know whether I can call it that because I don't know just what it will be. I think the thing that I'm going to do will be nearer a modal thing than atonal. But I'm not sure. It's probably going to be shades of each, it's gonna overlap—you know? It's not going to always be something where you could say this is it, because it's not going to always be the same thing. In other words, I think that every piece of music demands a certain type of interpretation, just by the nature of the song itself. And that's what I'm going to allow myself to be governed by, just what I feel the song calls for."

When he got back to New York, he did record a new piece, the haunting "Alabama," and in 1964 he introduced "Crescent," "Song of Praise," "Wise One" (this is probably the piece he meant when he said in late 1963, "I want to compose another for my wife, even prettier [than "Naima"]),[3] "The Drum Thing," "Bessie's Blues," and his first and most famous suite, *A Love Supreme.* Coltrane had come to see his music as an extension of his religious beliefs; he was leaning more and more toward a kind of universal religion: "My goal is to live the truly religious life and express it in my music. If you live it, when you play there's no problem because the music is just part of the whole thing. To be a musician is really something. It goes very, very deep. My music is the spiritual expression of what I am—my faith, my knowledge, my being. . . . When you begin to see the possibilities of music, you desire to do something really good for people, to help humanity free itself from its hangups. I think music can make the world better and, if I'm qualified, I want to do it. I'd like to point out to people the divine in a musical language that transcends words. I want to speak to their souls."[4]

Coltrane reached the souls of many listeners with *A Love Supreme.* Recorded December 9, 1964, and issued the following month, it became Coltrane's best-known and best-selling album. Typically, his Impulse albums sold well enough by jazz standards—about 30,000 each. But this one sold roughly half a million copies by 1970, and more than that since. Many bought it because of its spirituality, not necessarily because they were jazz fans. Today, a church in San Francisco even builds its services around this album and reveres Coltrane as a saint. Although that is surely not what Coltrane had in mind, he obviously meant the album to be an important statement: he wrote the liner notes and a poem and selected a drawing of himself for the inside of the foldout album and a photo of himself for the cover.[5] The photo, reproduced on both the front and the back covers, shows him serious and preoccupied, looking away from the camera.[6]

The music has a carefully worked out plan. The four sections of *A Love Supreme,* "Acknowledgement," "Resolution," "Pursuance," and "Psalm," suggest a kind of pilgrim's progress, in which the pilgrim acknowledges the divine, resolves to pursue it, searches, and, eventually, celebrates what has been attained in song. The four parts of the suite form an archlike dramatic succession. Part 1 functions as a prelude; the tension increases in part 2 and peaks in part 3, the fastest section. A long unaccompanied bass solo introduces the last part, a relatively calm postlude. On the *Impulse* LP the suite runs about thirty-three minutes. A live performance from a festival at Antibes, France, in July

1965 that has been issued on CD runs forty-eight minutes. The live version is different enough from the authorized studio version that it becomes clear that Coltrane only wrote a simple sketch for each part, relying on his group to fill it out, as he said he liked to do. The French version runs longer mostly because of a much longer saxophone solo in part 3, and it adds a frenzied drum solo for the bass solo before the postlude. I know of no other performances of *A Love Supreme*. Perhaps Coltrane considered it too special for standard concert fare. He read the poem at St. Gregory's church in Brooklyn, April 24, 1966; what music he played after is uncertain; but it was likely at least part of the suite. It is said he played "Acknowledgement" at his last concert.

The framing prelude and postlude differ from the middle parts not only in mood but also in form. The middle two sections have a chord progression and chorus structure (twenty-four bars in part 2, twelve-bar blues in part 3). Parts 1 and 4 are more relaxed and even more exploratory and open-ended, with no recurrent underlying chord progression. Instead, the improvisation moves within the boundaries of a pentatonic scale, accompanied by a bass ostinato in part 1 and by a freely responsive accompaniment in part 4.

Much of the melodic and harmonic material of the suite is derived from this pentatonic scale. The basic collection is shown below in the key of F. The note G, while not strictly part of the scale, appears frequently during the improvisations as an upper neighbor to F. The notes D-flat and D-natural both occur; D-flat is more common and appears as part of arpeggios, while D-natural sometimes is used during scalar passages as a passing tone between C and E-flat. D-natural is rare enough that it makes a distinctly audible impression when it does turn up.

or *D♭*

The basic scale employed in *A Love Supreme*

Coltrane divides the scale into two nonoverlapping (disjunct) fourths. The scale and its resultant cell, which I have labeled cell *a*, figure prominently in all four parts of the suite, helping to unify them. Coltrane uses the cell most explicitly and literally in the outer sections, one and four. During the long saxophone solo that opens the suite, he derives his motivic material from the cell, working with it at length. But here he prefers to rotate the scale so as to begin on C, creating two conjunct fourths sharing the note F. In his solo he uses cell *a* in isolation as well as this scale composed of two conjunct cells.

The derivation of cell a

The basic scale and cell *a* appear in all parts of the suite, in their original forms, in rotated forms, and transposed. Part 2 descends a whole step to E-flat. On both recordings, the ending ostinato of part 1 suddenly moves down to E-flat, which prepares for part 2. In this part, "Resolution," the cell is less explicitly present than elsewhere in the suite. Coltrane said the twenty-four-measure theme "is composed of three groups of eight measures," each with a slightly different ending.[7] It descends an octave from high e-flat″ to e-flat′. One might hear a connection with the basic cell in that the structurally important notes e-flat′, g-flat′, and a-flat′ outline a fourth and spell out the notes of the cell transposed to E-flat. The pentatonic scale is completed by the less important notes, b-flat′ and d-flat′.[8] This passage also outlines two disjunct fourths, e-flat″ to b-flat′ and a-flat′ to e-flat′. The seventh measure is comprised of notes from the pentatonic scale in E-flat. But this theme also stands apart from the rest of the suite in its suggestion of harmonic minor, especially in measure 6. (It is also, as Bill Kirchner notes, a bit reminiscent of Coltrane's old favorite, "While My Lady Sleeps.") The improvisation derives from the theme and relies similarly on much chromaticism and dissonance. Pentatonism is only implied, except for a brief passage built upon variants of cell *a*.

a. The basic scale

b. The theme of "Resolution," structural notes circled (1964).

"Pursuance," the third part, opens with a drum solo in free meter, after which Coltrane and the bassist and pianist enter playing a fast twelve-measure theme in B-flat minor, "It's simply . . . minor blues," he said.[9] The pentatonic theme is again based on cell *a*, particularly appropriate because it is frequently found in blues performances, which also make much use of pentatonic scales.

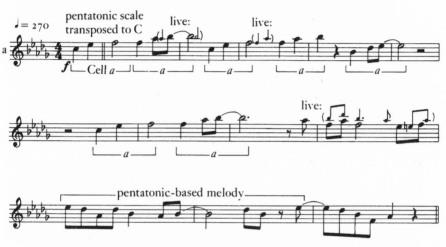

a. The theme of "Pursuance" and the derivation of its scale (1964); live version also noted (1965).

Copyright © 1977 JOWCOL MUSIC. International Copyright Secured. All Rights Reserved. Used by Permission.

b. The scale starting on C

It is fascinating to realize that the same notes are used but the collection is rotated so that it begins on C and ends on the tonic B-flat. This creates the identical arrangement of conjunct fourths that we found in part 1. Coltrane could conceivably have transposed the scale to the key of B-flat but instead uses the same scale in a different tonal framework, so that the first note, C, now functions as the second degree instead of the fifth. It is functionally a different pentatonic scale, but by retaining the same pitches Coltrane establishes a strong connection between this part and the first. After the second part, which seemed to have relatively little in common with the first, this strategically located reminder of the opening secures the unity of the suite while also showing the listener new characteristics inherent in the opening materials. Coltrane may not have consciously planned it, but it is still effective.

Of course, "Pursuance" employs B-flat as its tonal center, and one expects to hear the basic scale simply transposed, that is, B-flat–D-flat–E-flat as the bottom fourth, and F–A-flat–B-flat above it, disjunct. The D-flat is the only note not in the conjunct arrangement that starts on C. In fact, Coltrane's last two improvised choruses, the fifteenth and sixteenth, suggest this scale in their use of the D-flat. But the C scale is used literally during much of the solo. As the solo develops, it also becomes increasingly dissonant. Chorus 10 varies cell *a*, starting it on D-flat. The succeeding choruses involve chromatic runs, until those last two choruses stabilize the tonality before the recapitulation of the theme.

The final section, "Psalm," is based on a scale that also begins on C, but in this case it is an actual transposition of the original F scale; that is, [C–E-flat–F] [G–A-flat–B-flat]. The G is the note that makes this scale new, and there is much outlining of the triad C–E-flat–G in this section, unlike the others, which are more exclusively fourth-based. This creates a strong sense of finality and repose for the concluding solo.

The overall tonal plan suggests several levels of significance. The tonal centers of the four sections, F, E-flat, B-flat, and C, are all notes in the original F scale. (Only A-flat is missing.) The progression between centers is symmetrical: from F to E-flat is a whole step, E-flat to B-flat a fifth, and B-flat to C a whole step. The inner two movements, E-flat and B-flat, are in a relation of I–V, as are the outer two, F and C. Furthermore, the scales employed are interrelated, as we've seen, in ways that transcend the differences in tonal centers.

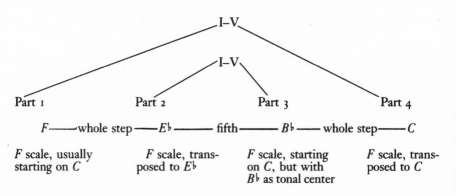

The tonal plan of *A Love Supreme*

Let us turn now to the details of scalar and cellular structure in part 1. At the outset of the suite, Coltrane plays a sort of fanfare built of fourths that includes an interval sequence that he takes up immediately thereafter.

The beginning of *A Love Supreme*

This fanfare is in E and does not outline a complete pentatonic scale but is clearly related to it by virtue of the disjunct fourths, B to E and F-sharp to B, suggesting a gapped scale, E–F-sharp–(G-sharp)–B–(C-sharp). (Tyner provides the G-sharp, as opposed to G-natural.) The E music serves as a leading-tone to F.

After this opening flourish, the music settles down on an ostinato in F. This clearly expresses cell *a*—its notes are F, A-flat, and B-flat. There is no written theme, or, as Coltrane said, "the first part is not composed of a fixed number of measures."[10]

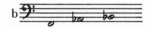

a. The bass ostinato from "Acknowledgement"
b. Cell a

The pianist plays chords built of superimposed fourths, using notes from within the pentatonic scale. The drum part, in a style jazz musicians call "Afro-Latin," might be thought of as a one-man interpretation of polyrhythmic percussion teams heard in Caribbean music.

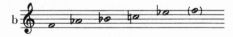

a. The piano chords from "Acknowledgement"
b. The scale from which they are derived

Before Coltrane's solo begins:

cymbal (suspended)
clave sound on snare drum rim
large tom-tom
closing hi-hat cymbals

When Coltrane's solo begins the cymbal part changes to:

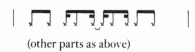

(other parts as above)

c. Drum part from "Acknowledgement"

Of course, Jones and Tyner are very free with this basic outline.

Over this modal vamp, Coltrane's solo is a tightly argued exploration of a few motives, most notably a rhythmicized version of cell *a*. Coltrane uses three techniques to get the most out of his restricted selection of materials. First, he intensifies the rhythm of cell *a*, playing it in smaller and smaller note values and with increasing frequency. Secondly, he utilizes the range of his instrument, building up to the altissimo register for climaxes. Coltrane performs up to a high written c''' for the tenor saxophone—that is, a fifth above the normal top f''.

Third, Coltrane transposes the motive outside the scale. As he ventures farther and farther from F minor, dissonance occurs between his melody and the accompaniment. Often, the bassist and pianist respond by following him in a kind of improvised modulation. The concert version contains some particularly extended passages of dissonance. During much of this version, the bassist, Garrison, forgoes the ostinato pattern, at first using the same rhythm but different notes, and eventually moving into broken rhythm patterns. He plays notes outside the F scale, and uses double stops, mostly fourths. But the music always returns to F, and the listener tends to hear this all over an F background even when F is not sounded. It is really transposition over a pedal point. Even Coltrane's transpositions are usually constrained by patterns, such as sequences a fifth apart, so as to retain the connection with the home key.

The solo keeps building up to higher and higher notes, then descending, then building up again. For instance, in the opening measures of the solo, Coltrane's line steadily ascends until it reaches a high g'' in measure 15; then it quickly descends to top-line f'. This section is based almost entirely on cell *a* and the basic scale that was rotated to begin on C. Coltrane begins immediately by outlining the two conjunct fourths that comprise the scale, C to F and F to

B-flat. The G and C are just upper neighbors, but their inclusion provokes comparison with the opening flourish, which contained the same interval sequence. In this passage he repeatedly attacks the conjunct fourths with increasing vehemence and added ornamentation. The complete scale appears in several places, and the section ends with a strong statement of the tonic note.

Measures 1–17 of Coltrane's solo on "Acknowledgement"

The next part of the solo has the same overall shape as the first but differs in detail. It ascends higher than the first (a-flat″ instead of g″) and begins to depart from the home key. Beginning in measure 33, the scale starting on C is methodically transposed to several levels. Breaking it down smaller, we might say that cell *a* appears in conjunct pairs, beginning on several pitches. First, we hear the original version of the scale comprised of conjunct fourths on C and F (measures 33 to 36). Notice that Coltrane carries the line through to the next conjunct cell, on B-flat, at the end of measure 35, setting up the dissonant passage to follow. We next hear the scale beginning on B-flat, but the E-flat fourth is stated first (measures 36 to 38). This continues the B-flat fourth stated in measure 35 and confirms that Coltrane conceives of the scale as two cells, since he treats them separately. Measures 39 to 42 present the scale on D and its fourth on G. Finally, in measures 43 and 44, the levels are recapitulated, with a rapid succession of the B-flat version, D version (without the top half on G), and back to C. Then the peak of the section is reached, the high a-flat″, followed by a very rapid descent, again ending on the tonic.

Measures 33–48 of Coltrane's "Acknowledgement" solo showing use of Cell a. (The first few instances of a are bracketed. Transposed versions of a are circled.)

Coltrane continues with an area of relative calm before the storm. It is more strictly pentatonic than the second section and ascends and descends twice. After that he ascends to the highest note of the solo, an intense and climactic c‴, while frequently going out of the home key. Bridging this section and the last is a reflective passage containing the first prominent use of D-natural as a passing tone in the melody. Here the D suggests a new modal coloration; in the earlier passage it was just part of a sequence of transpositions.

The last section gradually releases the tension. It is based entirely on the rhythm and shape of the bass ostinato. Coltrane transposes it to every one of the twelve keys and utilizes the middle and low registers. Although Coltrane does not follow a regular key scheme, there are many fifth relations—the first statement in G is followed by one in D, A-flat is followed by D-flat, E-flat by A-flat by D-flat, B-natural by E-natural and back to B-natural. These fifth relations derive from the relations of the two fourths within the basic scale, and each pair of fifth-related statements represents a variation of that scale.

His insistent repetition of the rhythmic figure is puzzling at first; during the last six measures, he plays it on the ascending pattern of D, E, F-sharp, G, A-flat, and finally plays in unison with the bass in F. This reconfirms that Coltrane hears cell *a* as his basic unit of composition, isolatable from the scale built upon it. At this point, Coltrane and another voice—probably himself overdubbed—chant the words "a love supreme" in unison with the bass ostinato and we realize that this was the goal toward which Coltrane directed his solo. He brilliantly executed a reverse development, saving the exposition—or perhaps "revelation" would be a better word in this case—for the end. He's telling us that God is everywhere—in every register, in every key—and he's showing us that you have to discover religious belief. You can't just hit someone on the head by chanting right at the outset—the listener has to experience the process and then the listener is ready to hear the chant. As we listen to the music, its meaning unfolds for us. We realize that there is a method behind the unusual sound and structure of the piece—Coltrane's music is not abstract, but is dictated in part by the messages he wishes to convey.

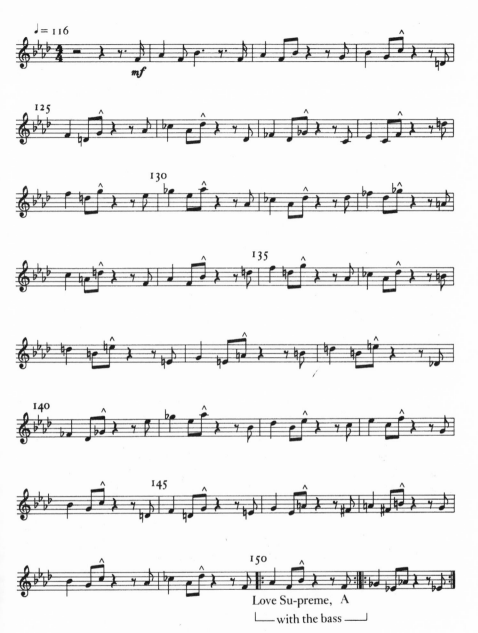

Love Su-preme, A

⌐—— with the bass ——⌐

Measures 121 to the end of Coltrane's "Acknowledgement" solo.
Copyright © 1973 JOWCOL MUSIC. International Copyright Secured. All Rights Reserved. Used by Permission.

On the French version of "Acknowledgement," Coltrane begins with the scale in its '"root position" on F, unlike the studio version; he improvises on the notes F, A-flat, B-flat, and C. He quickly proceeds to obsessive repetitions, variations, and building into the altissimo register. For a while he treats cell *a* alone, transposing it down by successive whole steps, then takes the scale starting on C and repeats the procedure. He takes up the bass ostinato and transposes it only into a few close keys, such as B-flat and C, before joining the bass in the key of F. The vocal chant is omitted in this version.

We saw that a spiritual message partially accounted for the structural plan of Part One. Spiritual meaning is even more important in the closing part of the suite, "Psalm." At first hearing, this part is even more nontraditional than the first. Not only is there no recurrent chord progression, there is not even a steady beat. Jones provides cymbal splashes and rolls on a timpani. Tyner drones on open fifths in the left hand, C–G–C, while providing some tension by superimposing quartal harmonies in the right hand, such as D–G–C, and F–B-flat–E-flat. Coltrane provided a cryptic clue to the structure of "Psalm" in his liner notes in the record jacket. He wrote, "The last part is a musical narration of the theme, 'A Love Supreme,' which is written in the context." But what does he mean by that? Remember, *A Love Supreme* is not only the title of the LP, but of a poem by Coltrane that appears in the liner notes. A comparison of the poem with Coltrane's improvisation reveals that his saxophone solo is a wordless "recitation," if you will, of the words of the poem, beginning with the title, "A Love Supreme."[11]

Lines 1–16 of the poem "A Love Supreme" as played on the saxophone by Coltrane as "Psalm."

What's even more amazing, his playing beautifully expresses the meaning of the words—serene on the word "beautiful," shouting out "He always will be." You can just see him shaking his raised finger. Each section of several lines has an arched shape—an ascending phrase, a recitation on one tone, and a descending phrase. The recitation tones ascend as the piece builds in intensity. This is just the way black American preachers work—but remember, he was Methodist and may not have grown up with this kind of preaching. Somehow he picked it up. Ethnomusicologist Jeff Titon describes the procedure of black American preachers for intonational chant.[12] The chant is divided into sections according to what Titon calls "pitch apices," for which we may use the more familiar term *recitation tones*. The first section uses a recitation tone a perfect fifth above the tonal center. Succeeding sections have progressively higher recitation tones—minor seventh, and, at points requiring special emphasis, the octave. The final section is the most intense and uses a mixture of all the preceding recitation tones. Coltrane adheres to this general outline—the first sixteen lines of the poem do emphasize the note G, the fifth above C—but of course he is very free within this basic approach. After those lines it's not clear that there is particular recitation pitch for a while, and he never does chant on the minor seventh, the B-flat. During the middle of the poem he sometimes goes up above the octave and chants on a high g″, for example beginning at "I have seen ungodly."

I have seen un-god-ly; none can be greater, none can compare with [Thee] God.

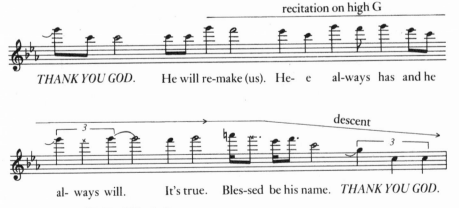

al- ways will.   It's true.   Bles-sed be his name.   *THANK YOU GOD.*

Lines 57–62 of "Psalm"

You can follow his solo along with the poem, and you will find that he plays right to the final "Amen" and then finishes. There are no extra notes up to that point. You will have to make just a few adjustments in the poem, however: Near the beginning, where it reads, "Help us to resolve our fears and weaknesses," he skips the next line, goes on to "In you all things are possible," and then plays "Thank you God." Where he says "Thoughts—deeds—vibrations, etc. They all go back to God," the "etc." and "They" don't quite fit—when I read it I leave out "They." Toward the end, he leaves out "I have seen God." On the next line, he stretches out the word "to" in "none can compare to God." When I read it I say "with Thee" instead of "to." Finally, when he says "He will remake us," you can't really hear the last word. Perhaps more to the point, his communication of the words is so clear that you can actually hear these fine points!

Coltrane's poem is punctuated with the frequently recurring words "Thank You God." These words are associated with a formula characterized by a minor third or fifth descending to the tonic, resembling formulas used by black preachers for such phrases as "Yes, He did" and "Oh, Lord." Coltrane uses this formula almost every time the words "Thank You God" appear. There are only two exceptions out of thirteen, lines 24 and 56. There, instead of descending, these two receive a version of the familiar cell *a,* ascending to the tonic from below. Apparently, the ascending motive occurs at moments of relaxation where the finality of the "Thank You God" motive would disrupt the flow. The larger scheme seems to be that, in either case, *God* always returns to the tonic.[13]

At the end, Coltrane descends to the fifth again, then descends to the tonic with a final "Thank You God." Significantly, the "Amen" is set to a variant of the cell *a,* backward and starting on D, that permeated the entire suite. Elvin Jones indicated to me that he was unaware that Coltrane was reciting the poem on his saxophone. This would be in accord with his practice since about 1961 of providing minimal information to the group in order to encourage spontaneity. Bob Thiele, the producer, confirms that the quartet first learned the music to *A Love Supreme* at the recording session.[14]

Even after the recording session, Coltrane didn't intend to publicize his "reading" of the poem. When asked, "Do you think the text and the poem that you wrote aid in understanding the music?" Coltrane replied:

Not necessarily. I simply wanted to express what I felt; I had to write it.
Question: Do you often write poems?
Coltrane: From time to time; I try. This is the longest that I ever wrote but certain pieces on the album *Crescent* are also poems, like "Wise One," "Lonnie's Lament," "The Drum Thing." I sometimes proceed in this manner because it's a good approach to musical composition. I am also

interested in languages, in architecture. I would like to arrive at the point where I am able to grasp the essence of a certain place and time, compose the work and play it on the spot naturally.[15]

He doesn't necessarily mean that the pieces from *Crescent* express the actual rhythms of a poem as does the "Psalm"; more likely, these poems were intended as inspiration. Nevertheless, it would be fascinating to see what he wrote.

If you listen closely to the stereo separation at the very end of "Psalm," you will hear that another saxophonist joins Coltrane. This has puzzled me for years—Bob Thiele and Archie Shepp told me they were unaware of it, and no writer had ever mentioned this. Rudy Van Gelder, after some thought, offered the following: He distinctly recalls that Coltrane overdubbed those notes himself. This would not be the only time Coltrane overdubbed—some of his saxophone playing with Johnny Hartman was added later, and on "Living Space" in June 1965 he overdubbed tenor and soprano on the theme. But the second saxophone here sounds like an alto, playing with a big vibrato. And he only plays an octave, but has trouble reaching the upper note—hardly typical of Coltrane. Still, Van Gelder's is certainly the best and most authoritative answer we will get.[16]

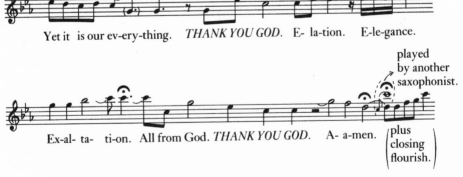

Lines 63 to the end of "Psalm" as played by Coltrane.

The concert version of "Psalm" differs from the studio version because it does not follow the poem. It's a freely structured improvisation in the key and mood of the studio version. Coltrane employs many of the same melodic formulas and follows the same kind of dramatic plan—the recitative, beginning softly, building several times to a fever pitch and subsiding again. But he makes no effort to conform to the poem's rhythms. His opening phrases are variations of a melody, as in the studio version, but each one begins on C' (as in C–B-flat–C, C–B-flat–C) before reciting on second-line G. Since the words aren't used, there is no recurring "Thank You God" formula.

The concert "Psalm" develops into a rapid barrage of notes. During a climactic moment, Coltrane alternates a repeated g'–f'–g' recitation with contrasting notes from the bottom of the instrument's range, such as the b-flat and a-flat a twelfth below. Shortly thereafter, he turns this upside down by repeating notes in the middle register and alternating them with higher and higher notes from the altissimo range. Eventually, he calms down and returns to a version of the opening phrase, reciting on G (omitting the c' he used earlier). He ends his improvisation with the same "Amen" as on the studio version.

There is a little more material relating to *A Love Supreme*. Coltrane wrote in his notes that Archie Shepp and Art Davis recorded "on a track that regrettably will not be released at this time." On December 10, 1964, the day after the suite was recorded, he went back into the studio and made a version of "Acknowledgement" with the addition of his two guests, but he decided not to use it. He told a radio interviewer he chose the quartet version because it had the "singing—not singing, chanting" on it. He also worked a little bit on "Resolution" with just the quartet but decided to keep the version from the previous day.[17] The studio recording, as issued, remains the definitive statement of the musical and spiritual aspirations of this quiet, unassuming man.

18

The Man: "A Quiet, Shy Guy"

There is absolute consensus about three things: First, Coltrane was a sweet, quiet man, a man of few words. In recordings his voice is deep and sonorous, smooth and warm. He's got a definite Southern accent and a slow, measured pace. Second, he had a dry sense of humor if you caught him in the right mood. Third, he practiced constantly and obsessively.

He was also obsessive about sweets. Ever since he was a child, he had a terrible sweet tooth, and in his thirties he started to develop weight problems, gaining twenty or thirty pounds and then trying to take them off. Coltrane was also an avid reader about all things religious and philosophical, and he was well informed about astrology and other subjects. (In Simpkins he comments on a book by Aaron Copland and a biography of Van Gogh [159–60]. A published photo shows him with Raymond Aron's 1955 critique of left-wing conformism, *The Opium of the Intellectuals*.)

Personality

John Coltrane was one of the nicest, warmest, kindest people I ever met in the business. He never got a big head. He was a lovely man. I was shocked when people said he was into drugs. I couldn't believe it. You wouldn't know, I swear. He was so nice. . . . He always had a smile on his face. (Bob Weinstock)

He was very quiet, very humble. (Ira Gitler)

John was a quiet, shy guy. He talked kind of slow. (David Young)

One of the nicest guys I ever knew in my life. I always felt very close to him, even if I hadn't seen him in a while. He had a reserved warmth. (Ray Bryant)

We used to room together on the road [during the first month that John was with Gillespie], trying to save money. He was a very reserved, beautiful person. He never talked a whole lot unless you engaged him in conversation. He always used to seem to be in another groove entirely. He was constantly thinking about music all the time. He wouldn't even go sightseeing—only once I got him to go to a museum with me. But he wasn't an oddball or anything like that. It was just that he was such a deep thinker. (James Forman)

Just to be with him was exciting, even without talking—he didn't talk a lot. He didn't talk for nothing. He didn't ask "Hey, Daddyo, how's your wife, how's your grandmother?" He didn't talk about the weather. But when a subject could come up and he was an expert in it or was interested, he would ask questions, and he would talk at length. Serious stuff, constructive stuff, enlightening things. (Louis-Victor Mialy)

John Coltrane is certainly the most modest and agreeable musician that I have ever had the pleasure of interviewing. His answers are direct, unemotional but also not evasive, and they are always presented objectively, as if there is nothing personal. (François Postif)[1]

I was terribly impressed with him as a person. I found him very quiet. . . . And he was very serious—he didn't do any more than answer the questions. But he answered them, I thought, very thoughtfully. He was nothing but thoughtful and honest. I asked very naive questions . . . but he was extremely patient. The contrast between his very sort of calm demeanor off the stand and then this extraordinary torrent of sound was very striking, I thought. (Kitty Grime)

An interview with Coltrane must be something like intruding into a human being's soul. His honest love and respect for his work and his unembarrassed humility in his current dilemma [to find new approaches] gush forth, almost unasked for. He seems to want to share his stalemate with the world in the faint hope that someone someplace might have a key to unlock for him the entire world of music. (Barbara Gardner)[2]

Coltrane was the most humble, wonderful person. I never in my life heard him put anybody down. (Charlie Rice)

I never heard him raise his voice, I never heard him say anything bad about another person. And I don't care who it was he was talking with, how inexperienced that person was musically, I never heard him discourage. All he did was encourage and make you feel that, "Hey, I can do this!" (George Goldsmith)

I saw a woman come into the club and with the hook of her umbrella try to grab him around the arm while he was playing with the quartet. I could have killed that woman! But after the set, when she came up to scold John for playing this loud, crazy music, he was so kind to her, so understanding. (Anthony Braxton)[3]

I was really sick [with pneumonia, probably in the early 1960s], and I could not afford to stay in the hospital. I did not have any money, so they told me to go home . . . although I could barely walk. Trane picked me up as I was getting out of the car. He carried me up to the seventh floor to my room. I told him, "I know I'm heavy, man," because he looked as though he was about my size. He said, "That's all right, that's all right." I did not feel him weaken in his strength; he was very strong. (Howard McGhee)[4]

Quiet, introspective. Sweet guy. (Al McKibbon)

Sense of Humor

He could joke, and he had nicknames for most of the guys. He used to call me "Bucket," because my head was a little bigger than normal. I called him "Coaltruck." (Ray Bryant)

He used to call Art Taylor "Brushmouth," because of his big moustache. (Steve Kuhn)

He had a sense of humor that people don't know anything about. Coltrane used to complain say, "Man, Jim, my feet hurt so bad, it hurts me to put on socks." You know, different things, like another thing, when he wouldn't spend time in a barber shop because it would take too long. And he would try to cut his own hair. And at that time they didn't have quite the right tools. And sometimes it would look kind of ridiculous. But he'd say, "Aw, Jim, I don't have time to go in that barbershop because all they're doing is talking and wasting time." (Jimmy Heath)[5]

We were doing a session [in February 1958] and we were hung for a tune and I said, "Trane, why don't you think up some old standard?" He said, "OK I got it. Ready, Rudy?" They always said, "Ready, Rudy?" [to Van Gelder]. And they played "Russian Lullaby" at a real fast tempo. At the end I asked, "Trane, what was the name of that tune?" And he said, "Rushin'

Lullaby." I cracked up. He had that type of sense of humor—riddles and cute things. (Bob Weinstock)

I remember one time that show came on about the talking horse, Mr. Ed. John looked at the TV and said, "Well, I'm not into talking horses today." (Mary Alexander)[6]

He laughed a lot—when people got in trouble, he'd really laugh at you. One time we were in class and we had a test and I was looking in the book—cheating a little—and I dropped the book. I got the book back up and he laughed and kept looking at me and I started looking at him and laughing. The teacher never found out who dropped the book. He was just that type of person, he would laugh—he wouldn't tell on you, but he really had a sense of humor. I never knew him to get into arguments or misunderstandings with anybody. (Rosetta Haywood)

Health Regimen

Coltrane lifted weights for a while in the late 1950s. On and off, especially when traveling, he also went on special health diets, because when he was in New York he'd sometimes gain weight. He told Postif, "When I worked at the Half Note [in 1960] I let my musicians play while I went to eat some spaghetti. With this regimen I gained a lot of weight."

John Coltrane is on a diet, and, what's more, a bit of a vegetarian. After the 6 o'clock concert, since he was hungry, we went to a grocery shop on Rue Caumartin (a very narrow street adjacent to the Olympia) that specializes in serving the stars between shows. John picked here and there some leaves of lettuce, some hazel nuts, and cracked an egg to eat at his seat. He also asked for fresh spinach to build his strength back up, but when they only had canned spinach, he declined. . . . I met him later, affable and relaxed, in his room at the Claridge Hotel, busy squeezing some oranges and eating some leaves of lettuce.[7]

More than one writer has recalled Coltrane ordering tomato juice in a bar, and Jack Cooke recalls Coltrane's breakfast of tomato juice and raw eggs as being "modestly unusual" in a British hotel in 1961. "The eggs were stacked in a pint glass still in their shells" because the employees couldn't understand what Coltrane wanted![8]

The waiter delivered "the usual" to Coltrane. . . . It was a big cup of hot water. (Ray Coleman)[9]

He tucked into a slightly bizarre dinner of two raw egg yolks, clear soup, milk, iced water and fresh peaches. (Mike Hennessey)[10]

He told me that he had adopted a vegetarian diet and wanted to eat some fruit before getting an early night. It was the first time I had ever met anyone who talked about health concerns, and a far cry from the popular image of the wild, drug-crazed jazz musician beloved of the press. It was an important part of my wider education, too. I would come to realize that it was precisely through having had the enormous privilege of meeting a man such as Coltrane that I began to discover a new way of looking at the world as well as the music. (Valerie Wilmer)[11]

Practicing

In high school he was always interested in his horn. He was always practicing on his horn. (Rosetta Haywood)

A practicer. He would practice that horn all the time. (Al McKibbon)

In New York I lived on West End Avenue, and he lived on 103rd Street. I used to get up and go around to his house, but I never hardly saw him because he was always practicing! It didn't matter how early I would go! There was a room he would use just to practice, and Naima would take his lunch in and stop him from playing to take his dinner. Naima used to sew, and sometimes I would too. I mean, he played every day, all day long. And then he would stop to get ready to go to work that night. And of course I'd be listening to what he was playing. Music was really his life. (Shirley Scott)

And he wasn't into women like me and Philly [Joe Jones]. He was just into playing, was all the way into music, and if a woman was standing right in front of him naked, he wouldn't have even seen her. That's how much concentration he had when he played. (Miles Davis)[12]

If his wife wasn't home, you couldn't get in if you rang the bell. He wouldn't stop practicing! (Benny Golson)

The first time I saw him [in 1963], he would leave the bandstand when he finished his solos and go into the men's room in the club and practice through McCoy Tyner's piano solos. (You couldn't hear it unless you went by the men's room.) Then he would come out, he would finish the piece, and with barely any hesitation go into the next piece, and do the same thing. At the end of the first set he went into the men's room and practiced through the entire intermission. He never stopped playing the tenor until the end of the second set, after about three hours! (Bob Blumenthal)

He was very quiet and very lonely to a certain extent. That horn was his partner. (David Young)

Coltrane regularly recorded himself while practicing, from the late 1950s through the 1960s. Often, I believe, he would reuse the same tape, recording over it each day. But there are at least a few surviving hours of practice tapes that remain unavailable. Mike Hennessey noted that for ninety minutes before his interview with Coltrane, "He stood at the table blowing [tenor and so-prano] into a portable tape recorder and then playing it back. Unhurriedly he changed reeds, adjusted mouthpieces, tore off characteristically intricate and extended runs." Coltrane said he was listening to the tape "just to see how the notes were coming out—whether they were coming through clear and in tune." He did not practice as often as he wished: "I think four hours' practice a day would be good for me. That little bit of practicing just then—well, I didn't play a thing I didn't know. But after four hours I would get through all that and then maybe I'd break into something new."[13]

Kitty Grime commented on Coltrane's relationship to his instrument: "He was doing that thing of eating sweets all the time. He constantly ate sort of fudge and things. And also he was constantly fingering the instrument. He had the instrument right with him [all during the interview]. I felt he was a very obsessive person, and he busied himself all the time, as if the minute he stopped busying himself something else might happen."

Astrology

Coltrane had the conjunction of Pluto, Mars, and Saturn [in his sign]— three negative planets that bring death. And he knew that. At the time [September 1961] I was studying astrology in San Francisco. Coltrane was ahead of me because he knew metaphysics and he was also involved with oriental astrology, which is different from the astrology we use in the west—so he knew about the sign of the snake, the dog, the horse. He had a great knowledge of many things. We didn't discuss religion at all, but you could see that he had knowledge of and respect for religions and for belief in God. (Louis-Victor Mialy)

Mialy: John, I know that you are passionate about astrology; what's your zodiac sign?

C: Libra! I'm interested in all the sciences—metaphysics, astrology, astronomy, mental physics. Wes is a Pisces and Eric is Gemini. And you, Lou?

Mialy: Cancer with the moon in Taurus.

C: What year?

M: 1930!

C: For the Orientals, that was the year of the serpents, that's very good for you! I also have my moon in conjunction with Mars in Taurus, in direct opposition with Saturn, the deadly planet, in Scorpion, the sign of death! Also I have my ascendant and my Venus in the sign of Virgo; three bad aspects of my birth chart. I won't live to be very old!

Dolphy: You haven't finished bullshitting, you two?! Let's get there quickly, I'm dying of thirst![14]

His personality was more Virgo than Libra—he was interested in details. People born under the sign of Virgo always ask, "Why, why"— they want to get into details. He had two personalities, kind of—one very insecure, and one extremely willing to go in certain directions. But he was never sure that it was the right direction. He was never satisfied about himself. You could see by his face, that he was anxious—not about his life, but about his art. He was also struck by beauty. For instance, he had a pair of binoculars and, back in San Francisco, during the intermission from his playing at the Jazz Workshop, we'd walk ten blocks to a field down by the freeway, and he'd start looking at the stars. He knew where the Milky Way was, and everything. (Louis-Victor Mialy)

Elsewhere, Mialy wrote of those intermissions:

Coltrane looked at the sky, the stars, scrutinizing the night for a long moment of infinity as if to discover the secrets of the universe, a universe that appeared to trouble him with its complexity, its power and its unknown dimensions . . . After a while, we climbed back up, slowly and always in silence, the slope to Broadway, I to recover my corner and continue to listen feverishly; Coltrane to anxiously reclaim his saxophones and his work of research, his mysterious quest. . . .[15]

Philosophy and Religion

Blume: Have you read anything about philosophy?

Coltrane: I'll tell you what I've read. You know these books that they put out, "This Made Simple," "That Made Simple"? Well, they got one called *Philosophy Made Simple.* Well I read that. That's the only thing

I've actually read all the way through. And I bought a few books, little things, something I picked up called *Language, Truth, Logic*.[16] Stuff like that I just picked up. Some I get into, man, and I don't get any further then the first few pages—then I start looking around, trying to find things.

Blume: What do you think you're looking for—you're interested in philosophy, I mean, what—?

Coltrane: I don't know . . . I don't think it's really that I'm looking for as an end, but it seems to be something in it that I kinda like. I guess I'm trying to decide if it would be a good idea to see what other people thought about it. . . . People who think better than I do. See what they think about living, just, you know, life.

Blume: Let me ask you this, what do you think about living and life up to this point?

Coltrane: I couldn't give you an answer to that, because I haven't pulled it together. I don't *think* I have. I couldn't say, you know.

Blume: Do you think there seems to be an overall plan to this thing and you think that your life is predetermined or that you're your own free agent and you make what you want with your life?

Coltrane: Well . . . it seems like I make, I believe when you say that you make almost what you want, in a way you do, but like *when*. That seems the part that we don't have much to do with.

Blume: Not much control over it.

Coltrane: Yeah, like . . . you kind of set your course, but when you arrive and things like that, you know. It doesn't always happen as you plan, you know . . . You can kind of set it.

Blume: Before you got interested in philosophy and started to think about philosophy what did you . . .

Coltrane: Well I'll tell you. It started with religion, I guess. And then the first questioning of religion. That brought on everything. You know, I got to the age when I started to wonder about things. . . . And after I'd say my late teens, I just started breaking away. I was growing up, so I questioned a lot of what I found in religion. I began to wonder. . . . About two or three years later, maybe twenty-two, twenty-three [the late 1940s in Philadelphia], this Moslem thing came up. I got introduced to that. And that kinda shook me. A lot of my friends, you know, they went Muslim you see. So I thought about that, anyway, it took me to something I'd never thought about—you know, another religion? So that started me to think. But I never did anything about it. I just thought about it. I was too busy doing other things, and I forgot it. I think I put it out of my mind for the next several years. I didn't bother to think about it. And recently, I started looking into, well maybe I can just see what people are thinking. 'Cause I realized that's what *I'm* trying to do. That's why I sort of turn to things like this, you know. I haven't devoted as much time to it as I want to; I haven't actually learned or covered as much ground of it as I'd like to. I'd like to cover more ground. I'd like to get my own thoughts together, composed the way I feel like it should be, you know. I was like, religion man, I was always—I was disappointed when I found how many religions there were and how—

Blume: You were disappointed?

Coltrane: Yeah.

Blume: In what way?

Coltrane: Not disappointed—I don't know what the hell. When I saw there were so many religions and kind of opposed somewhere to the next and so forth . . . it screwed up my head. And, I don't know. I was kinda confused . . . and I just couldn't believe that just one guy could be right. Because if he's right somebody else got to be wrong, you know . . .

Blume: Well, is there a kind of a chance of all the religions that there are, actually being tied in with one another? . . . And that people have actually changed the face of religion, so to speak, but the basic things involved are all pretty much the same?

Coltrane: Sure, I think the basic things will bring them all together man. If it was just . . . If there was anybody to say "well, let's get together."

Blume: In other words then you would like to see something like a universal type religion where instead of there being all these differences and one guy knocking the next because he has a different faith, that there is something basic to all of them and that they should all get together.

Coltrane: Yeah, it should be, I think. It should be that way. It's like when you see what these people say about good. Philosophers, when they start talking about good and bad man, they take those two words and go so far with them. It could be a complicated thing. But it's got to be simple, to really get some good out of it. To really realize something you got to make it simple. And religions, they've got it made if they can get together because when they say what they preach is good, it seems good to me.

Blume: Do you think that when you finish reading a certain number of books and have had time to absorb and think these things over that it will change you in any way or change your outlook on life in any way?

Coltrane: Well, I don't think it will change me, I think it will help me to understand, you know, like I'll be able to walk a little surer. Just take a little confusion away. I think I'll be the same.

Blume: Do you think very many musicians are more than confused, just like everybody might be, about this religious business? That they might be interested in this, in the same way that you might be interested in this, by trying to gain a little bit more understanding of just what's going on? . . .

Coltrane: Yeah, well. [pause] I think the majority of musicians are interested in truth, you know—they've got to be because a musical thing is a truth. If you play and make a statement, a musical statement, and it's a valid statement, that's a truth right there in itself, you know. If you play something phony you know that's phony. All musicians are striving to get as near perfection as they can get. That's truth there, you know. So in order to play those kind of things, to play truth, you've got to live with as much truth as you possibly can, you know. And as far as [being] religious; if a guy is religious, then I think he's searching for good, he wants to live a good life. He might call it religious or he might not call himself religious. Maybe he'd say "I just live a good life." But a religious man would call him a religious man—he lives a good life. So quite a few musicians think about it; I've talked with quite a few of them about it.

Blume: Are there any that stand out on your mind as having views that you feel are closer to the truth than other fellas might have? Are there any musicians that you respect because of their views in this matter?

Coltrane: Well . . . Not offhand, I can't think of any one, any one more than the others. I've talked to quite a few of them. They all seem to be searching, trying to find some way, most musicians I know. And some don't talk about it at all. They seem to be pretty well content. They've found just what they want. [Pause] I don't know—

Blume: It's a long deep subject to try to get into.

Coltrane: I get wound up in it, man, you know, and I get confused. Then I have to forget about it for a while.

Eventually Coltrane accepted the diversity of human belief as representing different ways of recognizing one God. The titles of Coltrane's last compositions suggest a mixture of religious influences—only "The Father and the Son and The Holy Ghost" is specifically Christian; others such as "Dear Lord" and *Meditations* are more general, while "Om" suggests Eastern beliefs. He is quoted on the back of *Meditations* saying, "I believe in all religions." He made a special study of India. Around 1966, John Glenn gave him *Light on the Path,* "a little book about the occult," inspired by Indian Buddhism, and Coltrane kept it with him. Alice Coltrane said that John continued to follow the writings of Paramahansa Yogananda, and enjoyed the writings of Gandhi. But he also was interested in what Sonny Rollins had to say about the Rosicrucians. And he found Einstein's profound mixture of science and mysticism especially inspiring.

I am [Christian] by birth—that is, my mother was and my father was, and so forth; and my early teachings were of the Christian faith. Now, as I look out upon the world—and this has always been a thing with me—I feel that all men know the truth, see? I've always felt that even though a man was not a Christian, he still had to know the truth some way. Or if he was a Christian, he could know the truth, or he could *not*. It's according to whether he knew the truth. And the truth itself doesn't have any name on it. Each man has to find this for himself, I think.[17]

On the afternoon of July 9, 1966, an opening press conference was held in Tokyo for the Coltrane quintet. To the question, "What would you like to be ten years from now?" Coltrane responded, "I would like to be a saint." Unfortunately we do not know the context or the tone of Coltrane's comment, but it can only be interpreted in one way; that he wanted to be a saintly, that is, a virtuous person. Clearly he did not mean that he wanted to die and be canonized!

Race and Politics

I don't know the criteria capable of differentiating a white musician from a black musician, and besides, I don't believe that it exists. If a man knows his instrument well, if he feels the type of thing that we play and if he loves our music, there's no longer any problem and he would therefore be able to play with us without difficulty. There are musicians who feel more easily than others the strength, the feeling of a band. These people who give the impression of understanding what's going on and who naturally blend their sensibility with the band's are very often young musicians coming to listen to their elders, from whom they hope to learn something. They are at first attracted by the music that they themselves feel profoundly; then, secondly, they begin to be influenced by it; and finally, when they have acquired a certain maturity, they integrate themselves into this band or in others of the same kind. It is entirely a problem of understanding and has nothing to do with questions of skin color. (John Coltrane)[18]

Coltrane was a man who weighed his words carefully, and who rarely made extreme statements on issues of race or politics. He was quiet, but not docile—he would not let himself be led into making a statement he did not fully believe. He was also reluctant to make a judgment on a topic that he had not carefully considered. For example, when Frank Kofsky asked if club owners treated jazz artists with contempt because they were black, Coltrane simply said, "I don't know." But when it came to the meaning of music and its power in the world, Coltrane had plenty to say.

Kofsky: Do you make a *conscious* attempt to express [the political and social issues of the day]?

Coltrane: Well, I tell you for myself, I make a conscious attempt, I think I can truthfully say that in music I make or I have tried to make a conscious attempt to change what I've found, in music. In other words, I've tried to say, "Well, *this* I feel, could be better, in my opinion, so I will try to do this to make it better." This is what I feel that we feel in any situation that we find in our lives; when there's something we think could be better, we must make an effort to try and make it better. So it's the same socially, musically, politically, and in any department of our lives. . . . I think music is an instrument. It can create the initial thought patterns that can change the thinking of the people. . . . [Jazz] is an expression of music; and this music is an expression of higher ideals, to me. So therefore, brotherhood is there; and I believe with brotherhood, there would be no poverty. And also, with brotherhood, there would be no war.[19]

During the last years of his life, Coltrane, in his thoughtful way, was becoming a spokesperson for the younger generation, white or black, who were concerned about civil rights, world peace, and spiritual awareness. And this new following brought with it an intense fervor, even a cultism, that was unfamiliar to jazz fans. At the same time, Coltrane's music began to change in ways that alienated some of his former audience. The passions around the man and his music were raised to a fever pitch.

19

Final Years: 1965–67

Coltrane never saw himself as a guru—he was too modest for that, and too self-critical. He always felt he could be better and could do better. He was always pushing himself, always searching for new things. In 1961 he had said, "I work a lot by feeling. I just have to feel it. If I don't, then I keep trying. . . . I haven't found it yet. I'm listening all the time, but I haven't found it. . . . I don't know what I'm looking for. Something that hasn't been played before. I don't know what it is. I know I'll have that feeling when I get it. I'll just keep searching."[1] In 1965 he was saying almost the same thing: "I don't know if you can ever be a complete musician. I'm not. But I don't think I'll know what's missing from my playing until I find it."[2] His search led him to make major changes in his life, and by the end of 1965 he found himself with a new band—and a new family.

The response to *A Love Supreme* was tremendous: it was voted album of the year by both *Down Beat* and *Jazz* in 1965, and *Down Beat* readers also named Coltrane "Jazzman of the Year," best tenor saxophonist, and elected him to the magazine's Hall of Fame. The only two tenorists already in the Hall of Fame were Lester Young and Coleman Hawkins, and no artist had ever won so many awards from *Down Beat* in one year. Coltrane had also became something of a father figure to the growing avant-garde. He helped to arrange a recording session at Impulse for Archie Shepp and recommended many other artists. He was always generous about letting these younger players sit in with his group at performances. When in March 1965, Coltrane appeared at a concert under the rubric "New Black Music," he seemed to validate the most daring music of the time.

On June 28, 1965, he gathered ten of these musicians together—he told a radio interviewer, with considerable understatement, that it was a "big band" date—for a studio session that produced one of his most awesome, and daunting, recordings, "Ascension." Besides his regular quartet and bassist Art Davis,

Coltrane added trumpeters Freddie Hubbard and Dewey Johnson, alto sax-ophonists Marion Brown and John Tchicai, and tenor saxophonists Pharoah Sanders and Archie Shepp. Perhaps inspired by Ornette Coleman's 1960 double-quartet record, *Free Jazz,* Coltrane created in "Ascension" a forty-minute piece that linked passages of hollering group improvisation with in-tense solos. All this begins with a five-note theme, somewhat like that of *A Love Supreme,* which he states at the beginning and which is taken up again at various points in the piece. Two complete versions of "Ascension" were re-corded; when the LP came out in 1966, the first take was used. Then Coltrane decided he liked the second take better, primarily because the two altoists didn't solo back-to-back. The album was rereleased with that take (even though the solo order didn't match that given in the liner notes). Both are now available on CD.

Bob Thiele recalls that Coltrane handed out lead sheets at the session.[3] It's uncertain just what he gave out; in the liner notes Shepp states, "The ensemble passages were based on chords, but these chords were optional. . . . In those descending chords there is a definite tonal center, like a B-flat minor. But there are different roads to that center." Alice Coltrane reconstructed some descend-ing chords for the published version, but it is not obvious how to relate these to the recording.[4] Marion Brown states, "Trane had obviously thought a lot about what he wanted to do, but he wrote most of it out in the studio . . . [H]e played this line and he said that everybody would play that line in the ensembles. Then he said he wanted crescendi and decrescendi after every solo."

Several commentators have noticed that "Ascension" seems to be loosely based on scales, which are more easily heard than chords in this dense ensem-ble. Ethnomusicologist David Such hears four scales: B-flat minor, D phrygian (which has two flats like B-flat major; at this point there is a distinct shift in modality and some band members play D, C, B-flat, A, suggesting this scale), G-flat lydian (all flats except for C and F naturals), and F phrygian (the same notes as G-flat lydian but starting on F).[5] During most of the ensemble pas-sages, Coltrane evidently signaled by his playing (and probably by nodding as well) when to change chords, with corresponding changes in scales. The other musicians then start with the indicated scale but quickly branch out from there. For the individual solos, the first scale—B-flat minor—is the general foundation. The resulting work is thrilling; Coltrane's solos are miraculous. He said "I particularly appreciate that session with seven winds." Shepp suggests in the liner notes that the whole work recalls Coltrane's favorite form, the minor blues, in B-flat minor.

Coltrane had been gradually moving away from playing over a steady beat; in his music there would soon be no walking bass, nor a beat you could snap your fingers to. Instead he aimed for a general churning pulse of fast or slow. He had taken one step along the road when, in 1962 and 1963, he made it a practice to perform a long unaccompanied cadenza at the end of the ballad "I Want to Talk About You." This gave him a chance to explore, for three minutes or more, what he could accomplish without a steady beat supporting him.

By September 1965, Farrell "Pharoah" Sanders had joined Coltrane's group. Sanders, born in 1940 in Little Rock, Arkansas, lived in Oakland, California, between 1959 and 1962. He played in blues and R&B groups while attending junior college. He met Coltrane there at the beginning of June 1959, while he was on tour with Davis, and they spent a day trying out mouthpieces together in pawnshops. Then Sanders spent a year or so in New York, where he worked with Sun Ra, and seems to have recorded with Ra and with the Latin Jazz Quintet. (Dolphy had been a guest on a 1960 album by this group.) He met Coltrane again when the quartet was playing at the Half Note in 1963. Sanders recalls, "I was outside. I couldn't go in because I was dirty and all, but John saw me and let me in. We exchanged . . . well, he gave me his number, and I tried to stay in touch with him. We started talking a lot."6 Things picked up for Sanders: In 1964 he recorded two albums as a leader, one for ESP and one for Impulse.

Sanders moved back to California, and when he went to hear Coltrane at the Jazz Workshop in San Francisco in September 1965, "He told me then that he was thinking about changing the group and changing the music, to get different sounds. He asked me to play with him."7 (Elsewhere he said that Coltrane simply told him where the next gig was.) Sanders had played on modal pieces and chord changes, but at this point he was into sheer sound— his harsh shrieks and wails of wavering pitch placed him in the same camp as Albert Ayler (1936–70), whom Coltrane admired. Sanders explained, "I stopped playing on changes a long time ago, long before I started playing with Coltrane. They limited me in expressing my feelings and rhythms. I don't live in chord changes. They're not expanded enough to hold everything that I live and that comes out in my music."8 Ayler had also played on changes in his first recording, but soon concentrated on a huge sound and wide vibrato and on a mastery of high-pitched sound effects. His playing was highly expressive, even expressionistic. Record producer Michael Cuscuna told me that Coltrane was interested in Sanders and Ayler because he thought their approach was the next frontier, "beyond notes." When Kofsky asked Coltrane whom he listened to besides Sanders, he replied, "Albert Ayler first. I've listened very closely to him. He's something else." At the Antibes festival in July 1965, Coltrane improvised for hours along with a live recording of Albert Ayler.9

Coltrane was now moving quickly—he sensed that he was onto something and opened his group up right away to a whole slew of young musicians and influences. He no longer wanted to swing, and from this point on Garrison never played a walking bass with him, but broke up the beat with short phrases and strumming. Jones slashed away at full force, and Tyner's fine work receded more and more into the background. Coltrane wanted to document his new music on tour, without waiting to get back to Van Gelder's studio, and at his own expense he recorded the group with Sanders at the Penthouse in Seattle on September 30. On a few numbers, Donald Garrett, Coltrane's friend from Chicago, was added on bass and bass clarinet. Like John, Garrett had become interested in spirituality and world music, and he brought along bamboo flutes and thumb pianos.

The next day, October 1, 1965, they recorded "Om" in a local studio. This time there was one more guest. Joe Brazil, a part-time but talented saxophonist whom Coltrane knew from Detroit, now living in the Seattle area, played flute. Nat Hentoff writes in the album's notes that one sense of "Om," in the Hindu religion, is a name for God. Coltrane is quoted in those notes saying, "'Om' means the first vibration—that sound, that spirit, which set everything else into being. It is The Word from which all men and everything else comes, including all possible sounds that man can make vocally. It is the first syllable, the primal word, the word of power."[10]

Some fans were taken aback by the group chanting (reputedly taken from the *Bhagavad-Gita*, a classic poem of Hinduism) at the beginning and end of this twenty-nine-minute piece. The final words were: "I, the oblation and I the flame into which it is offered. I am the sire of the world and this world's mother and grandsire. I am he who awards to each the fruit of his action. I make all things clean. I am Om—OM—OM—OM!" During the course of the performance, especially in the second half, everyone is shrieking on their instruments and somebody's voice (I think Garrett's) is heard as well. Coltrane was allowing an informality and spiritualism into his recordings and performances that some found amateurish; others found it freeing and revolutionary. He was to use voices briefly on some other recordings: On February 2, 1966, the group chanted "A-um-ma-ni-pad-me-hum," said to represent "the seven breaths of Man," at the start of "Reverend King." That was issued posthumously on the album *Cosmic Music*, on which Coltrane and Sanders also recite a short prayer: "May there be love and peace and perfection throughout all creation, oh God." (The tape of the prayer is undated but may have been recorded at the same 1966 session; it is used to lead into a 1968 track by Alice Coltrane and Sanders.)

Coltrane may have been tripping on LSD when he recorded "Om." It is certain that he did begin using LSD around this time.[11] It may be that Coltrane understimated the powers of this hallucinogen: one friend "remembers that Coltrane would get so disoriented from acid during some gigs that after intermisson he had to be guided back to the stage. And Miles Davis once told me that 'Coltrane died from taking too much LSD'" (Nisenson, 166). This ought not to be taken literally—physically, LSD is virtually harmless, although Davis had heart palpitations on one of the few times he tried the drug. But his exaggeration has a point—frequent use of LSD can cause flashbacks and some lack of control of one's mental functioning. And it may have been partly the reliance on LSD that caused Coltrane to allow his health to deteriorate so much that by the time he went to a hospital in the spring of 1967, he couldn't be helped. On the other hand, it is unreasonable to suggest that Coltrane played the way he did because of LSD, or for that matter because of his weakening health, as some have claimed. Clearly, Coltrane had a vision of what he could do with music. His own playing is perfectly coherent on all his late record-ings—in fact, incredibly so. At the most, he probably felt or hoped that LSD could help him in the direction he already wanted to go.

After Seattle, Coltrane went to Los Angeles; Brazil stayed home, but Frank Butler was added on drums, and for a recording there, Juno Lewis read his poem "Kulu Sé Mama" and played percussion. A *Down Beat* review of a return engagement in November commented that "the sound level when Jones and Butler got warmed up, was, to say the least, intense." Asked about the expanded group, Coltrane was characteristically low key: "This is purely experimental. I just wanted to see how it would work out. I may try it again later."[12]

As it turned out, Coltrane decided to try out two drummers on a regular basis, and beginning at the Village Gate in Manhattan in November 1965, he most often engaged Rashied Ali as the second player. Troubles ensued and soon meant the end of the quartet. Jones and Ali did not get along personally or musically. Jones, claiming that with Ali on stage he could no longer hear what was going on rhythmically, tried to outplay Ali, who reciprocated. For a while, dismayed audiences heard a barrage of drumming that threatened to drown out the rest of the group. Besides, both Jones and Tyner were unhappy with the group's moving away from a steady beat. As daring as they are, the one thing they both relied on was a steady and propulsive beat to work off. Despite their innovations, they were not "free jazz" players.

Tyner finally grew frustrated enough to leave at the end of 1965. In early 1966, he was working with clarinetist Tony Scott and rehearsing his own trio. He said he wanted to expand musically, and leading his own trio was "the next step" for him. After five-and-a-half years with Coltrane, "I felt I had put in enough time and that I had to be on my own to continue to grow." As a "secondary" reason—but I suspect, the primary provocation for choosing this particular time to leave—"What John is doing now is constructive for him, but not as compatible to me as before." He defended Coltrane's right "to do what he wants to do as a creative artist" but clearly spelled out that it was not for him.[13] In a different interview he was more bitter: "I didn't see myself making any kind of contribution to that music. At times I couldn't hear what anybody was doing! All I could hear was a lot of noise. I didn't have any feeling for the music, and when I don't have feelings, I don't play."[14] Later he specified that he felt Frank Butler and Jones had worked well together, but that Jones and Ali were a bad combination: "Elvin was in his corner, Rashied in the other. And I was in the middle of them!"[15] He told Len Lyons: "I felt if I was going to go any further musically, I would have to leave the group, and when John hired a second drummer, it became a physical necessity. I couldn't hear myself. John was understanding. In fact, I think he admired my courage."[16] By April 1966 the McCoy Tyner group—a quartet—was performing at Slug's on East Third Street in Manhattan.

Next, it was Jones's turn to leave. Jones gave the same reasons as Tyner, almost in the same words: "At times I couldn't hear what I was doing—matter of fact, I couldn't hear what anybody was doing. All I could hear was a lot of noise."[17] Jones left in January 1966 to accept an offer from Duke Ellington: "Duke dug Elvin, and Elvin dug Duke. The solution seemed obvious—and on January 26 Jones took off without notice from the Coltrane gig at San Francisco's Jazz Workshop and flew to Frankfurt, Germany, to join the Ellingtonians for the remainder of the tour, which had begun three days before." However, to his dismay Jones found that Ellington intended to keep his other drummer, putting Jones back in a two-drum team. (Ellington had been into using two bassists way before Coltrane, and now two drummers.) Jones played four concerts January 28 through 31, then left, stopping off in Paris and finally returning to New York, where he announced plans to freelance. "Though he said his parting with Coltrane was amicable, he has no plans to return to the saxophonist."[18] Coltrane had dreaded this moment, saying that he was most afraid of losing Elvin. He had had no premonition of Jones's departure. "He said he just felt he needed to do it," Coltrane explained.[19] Jones returned for a few gigs in March and April, then left for good. But he and Tyner always held John in the highest regard. Jones even defended Coltrane's late music, saying, "Well, of course it's far out, because this is a tremendous mind that's involved, you know. You wouldn't expect Einstein to be playing jacks, would you?"[20]

Before Jones and Tyner left, however, on November 23, the Coltrane sextet, with Jones and Ali and Sanders, made one remarkable album, *Meditations*. (This suite had been recorded by the quartet in September, but that version was released years later as "First Meditations" to avoid confusion.) The opening theme appears to be a rhythm played by the two winds, with a firestorm of complex drumming burning around them. It is a variation of "Bless This House O Lord We Pray," as composer Noel Da Costa points out: "He uses the intervals of this song, particularly the third, to produce a very moving composition."[21] Coltrane's title, "The Father and the Son and the Holy Ghost," suggests the religious ecstasy that the piece intends to convey, here taken to exquisitely painful limits. Released in 1966, this was the last new album issued while Coltrane was living. As before with Coltrane's controversial music, *Down Beat* assigned two reviewers for the December 1, 1966 issue: one gave it five stars, the other only one.

Rashied Ali took much criticism for breaking up the quartet. But this was unfounded—Coltrane was still very much in charge. As John explained ". . . I figured I could do *two* things: I could have a band that played like the way we used to play, and a band that was going in the direction that the one I have now is going in—I could combine these two, with these two concepts going. And it could have been done . . . I believe it would have worked, but Elvin and McCoy . . ." (his voice trailed off). Coltrane told Kofsky that Ali's full power "hasn't quite unfolded completely," but he defended Ali to the hilt, telling Nat Hentoff, "The way he plays allows the soloist maximum freedom. I can really choose just about any direction at just about any time in the confidence that it will be compatible with what he's doing. You see, he's laying down multi-directional rhythms all the time. To me, he's definitely one of the great drummers."[22] And in fact, Ali's playing with Coltrane is tasteful and coloristic, shimmering and suggestive—not at all the "noise" one might have been led to expect.

Ali, born Robert Patterson in 1935 in Philadelphia, told his story:

> I knew about 'Trane before, even before Miles Davis, because I have cousins, second cousins, my father's first cousins—Charlie Rice and Bernie Rice, who plays drums also. They both play drums, and they both played around with each other, Jimmy Heath and Charlie Rice and Coltrane and they all played together, so I've always heard of him, heard of him through that source. I have two brothers who also play drums [one, Muhammad Ali, is also a jazz recording artist] and we would put bands together with saxophone players, and we would sometimes just have two sets of drums and three saxophone players for the whole band. We were just doing a lot of drums and saxophones, a lot of saxophones and drums and stuff like that—double quartets—coming from Ornette type of thing, like two groups playing at the same time simultaneously. Stuff like that we were doing, stuff like that around Philly. This was in the late fifties and early sixties. . . . During the time [Coltrane] was working with Miles Davis, we used to go around to his house just trying to see if we could see him outside or sitting around. Anywhere. And a lot of times we would just hear him practicing out of his window, so we just sit around the steps and sit around and listen to him practice. Actually to meet him and to talk to him came years later, after I had really got into playing, I mean. I met him first at a club in Philadelphia.

Ali moved to New York in 1963 and worked with Sun Ra, Archie Shepp, Sanders, and other members of Coltrane's circle. He first got to sit in with Coltrane in 1965.

> I would go over there [to the Half Note] and I would just, like just sit around on the steps, and I asked to play and he said "Well, no, not today."

. . . One day I just came there and I don't know—fate, whatever—Elvin wasn't there yet, and it was time to play and everybody was walking around the stage to play. And I said, "Can I play?" And he looked at me for a long time and he said, "All right, c'mon." And I went up and I played for a whole set before Elvin came back, and then I got down. And the next day I was there again and I said, "Can I play?" He said, "Sure, c'mon." And I played again. And, then I went there one time and Elvin seen me coming, and he said, "C'mon up here and play for me." He had to run somewhere.

Coltrane invited Ali to play on the recording session in June, but he declined:

I'm gonna tell you, man, I had an ego bigger than this building at that point, playing with 'Trane, you know. Just sitting in with him just inflated my ego to the point when I was ridiculous. I was young, I was ridiculous, and I said, "Yeah, I would like to play. Who else is gonna play?" He said, "Elvin is gonna play." I said, "You gonna have two drummers like that?" He said, "Yeah." I say, "Well, I don't think I wanna play with two drummers." He said, "Oh, you don't?" I said, "No, I don't think so." So I blew the date "Ascension!"

Of course, during the time Ali was in the group, he became accustomed to working with other percussionists:

He was in a drummer thing. . . . There has been times I played with Trane, he had a battery of drummers. He had about three conga players, guys playing batas [drums of African ancestry that are used in Cuba], the guys playing shakers and everything. . . . And then sometimes he would have double traps [two drum sets] like in Chicago. I played double traps with a young drummer that was coming up there, named Jack De-Johnette, at that time."

(DeJohnette went on to become one of the leading drummers in jazz.) ". . . In fact, he loved drums so much, if we would have a second set of drums on the stage, sometimes he would come up there and play them."[23]

Garrison would leave as well, but not until the end of the summer of 1966. Tyner says that the idea of he, Garrison and Jones touring as a trio came up, but was dismissed.[24] Garrison worked at first in a trio with pianist Hampton Hawes and was replaced primarily by Dewey Johnson's brother Sonny Johnson. Sirone (Norris Jones) also played bass on occasion. Garrison did return to play on John's recording sessions of 1967. So for the moment, having brought in Ali on drums, Coltrane first had to replace Tyner, and he brought in Alice McLeod, an experienced jazz pianist. And therein lies a story, because by this time she and John were living together and had two baby boys.

As far back as 1958, there were stresses on the marriage of John and Naima. Sheila Coltrane was born around this time. Mary Alexander explains, "She was somebody who was blamed on John and he accepted it and helped take care of her. He accepted that. After [John and his family] went to New York, they would come back at Christmas time or something, Sheila would come over here [to the house on Thirty-third Street]. She and her mother lived in New Jersey. She'd [also] been out to the house where they lived in New York."[25] Surely this situation must have engendered tension. But Naima appears to have handled the situation with grace and understanding.

Naima had had two miscarriages (Thomas, 157) and she and John never had a child of their own. Coltrane was very close to Saeeda. But it may be that he yearned to be a father, and that the absence of new children made for a gap in his married life. Having lost his own father, maybe he had a psychological need to be one himself, to replace his own father as it were. His father having died young, this may have added to his fear of death based on his astrological chart, and this fear would have driven him to want children before he became old.

Another factor was that, as a nonmusician, Naima probably began to feel alienated as John became more and more of a world figure, and this is suggested by stories apparently told by Naima to Thomas (119). As Coltrane's career changed, his marriage changed and this must have exacerbated tensions leading to the divorce. He told Frank Kofsky, apparently referring to the period around 1962, "That was a funny period in my life, because I went through quite a few changes you know, like home life—everything, man . . ."[26] As Coltrane wrote at the end of 1964 in his liner notes to *A Love Supreme*, "a period of irresolution did prevail. I entered into a phase which was contradictory to the pledge [to God] and away from the esteemed path." This enigmatic passage seems to refer to his family troubles.

During his first Jazz Gallery stay, at the end of May 1960, John began a relationship with a white woman that was to continue, on and off, for the next three years. Thomas reproduces several excerpts from this unnamed woman's diary (137–39, 144–45, 152–53, 162–63) that are convincing because the dates tie in accurately with John's known movements. Finally, Naima says John moved out in the summer of 1963 (Thomas, 166)—I believe at the end of the summer, around Labor Day. Soon he was living with Alice McLeod. Mary had a difficult position being in the middle, trying not to hurt anyone. Each party— Naima and Saeeda; John and Alice—wanted Mary to be on their side. "I've had a lot of heartaches around that," she told me—"a lot of heartaches."

Alice McLeod was born in Detroit on August 27, 1937, the fifth of six children. Her mother, Anne Johnston, was from Athens, Alabama, and her father, Solon McLeod, was from elsewhere in that state.[27] Anne played piano and sang in a church choir. Alice began the piano at age seven, and her early idols were the legendary pianist and vibraphonist Terry Pollard, whom she met, and jazz harpist Dorothy Ashby. Alice had a half-brother Ernie Farrow, born in West Virginia in 1928. Farrow was an accomplished jazz bassist who recorded with Yusef Lateef and others, and he played with and encouraged the young Alice as she progressed. McLeod played at churches in Detroit, and studied classical music in Manhattan for a bit. She went to Europe in 1959; while in Paris she spent some time with Bud Powell—a major influence. She said he didn't formally teach her, and that she mostly hung out with him and his wife and son, but that he was a supportive mentor. He made constructive suggestions, said Alice, and "always pointed out something helpful—something you could do right there to bring that out." She also played with such major expatriates as Lucky Thompson and Oscar Pettiford.[28] She married the singer Kenny "Pancho" Hagood overseas, and they had a daughter Michelle in 1960. But that marriage broke up, and Alice returned to Detroit with her daughter.

Soon, probably in 1962, Alice McLeod was performing around Detroit in a cooperatively led group with Farrow and drummer George Goldsmith in the rhythm section, and with George Bohannon on trombone and the young Bennie Maupin (born in 1940) on reeds. Goldsmith says, "Alice was kind of a fixture around the city. She was a great piano player, she was playing a lot of bebop. And she could play vibes too." McLeod wrote a song for Michelle that was their theme song at the classy Twenty Grand Lounge, where they worked. According to bassist Vishnu Wood, then known as William Wood, this group was a "lounge act"—the members sang vocal harmonies, and Alice sometimes played an "organa" (apparently a small, portable organ). He remembers her as being "very, very shy."[29]

McLeod spent much of 1963 in the quartet of vibraphonist Terry Gibbs, who had a track record of playing with accomplished female pianists. In the mid-1950s he'd toured with Terry Pollard and later Pat Moran. Now it was Alice, who on the liner notes to her first recording session in January 1963 was called both Hagood (her married name) and McCord (an error for her birth name). That LP was *Terry Gibbs Plays Jewish Melodies in Jazztime,* an enjoyable meeting of a klezmer band—who play briefly at the beginnings and ends of some tracks—and Gibbs's hard-swinging jazz quartet. Alice's solos here are impressive—the melodic approach of Powell is evident, but she double-times most of the way and also gets into some polytonality during the straight-ahead swing portion of "Bei Mir Bist du Schön." She sounds inspired, deeply involved in what she's doing, and has plenty of technical panache.[30] Leonard Feather wrote: "Harmonically advanced and technically an accomplished musician, she ranks with Toshiko Akiyoshi among the most modern-oriented girl jazz pianists"—pardon the old-fashioned sexism![31] Wood, who played bass with the group for part of 1963—as did Farrow—remembers that McLeod often introduced chord subsitutions.

She had seen Coltrane perform in her native Detroit at one of his visits in 1962 or earlier in 1963, and they had a chance to meet when the Terry Gibbs Quartet shared the bill with Coltrane at New York's Birdland for the last two weeks of July 1963. She recalls,

> When we really actually met, it was really like two friends that had known each other many, many years, like meeting again. It was so beautiful. And so everything on my agenda stopped. He said, "You are concertizing with this group, but I would like you to get permission from your mother to travel with me wherever I'm going around the world." So I told him that if I got my mother's permission and blessings that I would leave that group and I would travel with him. So I called her and she gave her permission . . . I traveled quite a bit with the quartet [often with her daughter Michelle].[32]

During this period her own career was on hold, and she stopped performing.

Their first child was John W. Coltrane Jr., born on August 26, 1964; the second was Ravi John Coltrane, born August 6, 1965. Regardless of the fact that John and Naima had married in Baltimore, as New York residents they were subject to the laws of that state, which in those days allowed for divorce only in cases of adultery. Such a suit would have been very unpleasant for all parties, and Naima was apparently not inclined to initiate the process. However, in Mexico a divorce could quickly and easily be obtained that was valid in the United States. Naima must have signed a form permitting her to be represented by a lawyer so she would not have to be present. Coltrane and Alice went to Juarez, Mexico, across from El Paso, Texas, around August 1966 and John obtained in one day a divorce from Naima and a marriage to Alice.[33] Soon after, they moved into a comfortable house at RFD 6, Candlewood Path, in the Dix Hills section of Huntington, Long Island. Their third son, Oranyan Olabisi Coltrane, known as Oran, was born on March 19, 1967.

Alice seems to be a calm personality who created a kind of maternal, protective world for John. It strikes me as meaningful, and not accidental, that Alice was also the name of his mother and of her mother, his grandmother. Surely, at some level, conscious or not, this added to the appeal that she held for him. And with Alice he satisfied his desire for children. Equally important, she was a fine musician who could fully participate in his career.

With Coltrane from the end of 1965, Alice played in a free style. When she first joined the group, "He was very patient with me, because I hadn't played or even practiced in almost two years and I was blowin' some wrong chords. But he showed me how to build the sort of impact he wanted."[34] John encouraged her to use the whole range of the piano, not just the middle three or four octaves that serve for much modern jazz. Her piano soloing also suggested her own flowing harp music. Alice was "encouraged by John to study the harp," recalls Reggie Workman. "John used to take harp lessons with a musician in Chicago, and he bought one and was often dealing with one because he liked the way the arpeggios sounded with the harp. And Alice Coltrane's pianistic approach began to take on the characteristic of harp music at that time, and I think that was something that John realized in the way that they dealt together musically."[35] We have already mentioned that Coltrane liked to adapt harp music to the saxophone. Carl Grubbs and writer Joe Goldberg remember seeing a harp in Coltrane's place in Queens in the early 1960s, when he and Naima were still together. "It helps me with harmony," he told Goldberg.[36] He had tried to get Naima to take lessons on it (Thomas, 119). He was apparently a big fan of Harpo Marx's playing in films.

Coltrane was interested in other instruments as well, Alice recalled: At home he played flute and bagpipes. . . . Sometimes just, you know, he would like to go over the drums, listening for new rhythmical patterns." Coltrane knew Rufus Harley (born in North Carolina, his family moved to Philadelphia when he was an infant), a saxophonist who had taken up the bagpipes as a jazz instrument at the end of 1963. Coltrane also had an acoustic guitar, and, said Alice, "it was interesting, some of the sounds that came out." He said in Paris in 1961, "I bought it in Glasgow [around November 14, the night he performed there with Davis]. My neighbors in the hotel complained that I was making too much noise practicing my saxophones. It's a beautiful instrument." Coltrane told an English interviewer that he had bought the guitar "for company. I got lonesome and had read everything I had. . . . Maybe I'll stumble across something I wouldn't get on piano."[37]

John's close friend Eric Dolphy had died in Berlin on June 29, 1964, from complications of diabetes. Dolphy's mother had given John Eric's bass clarinet and flute, so John felt a special responsibility to work on these instruments. He played the bass clarinet on his tribute to another inspiration, "Reverend King," and he played the flute on "To Be" in 1967. He also was given an electronic Varitone attachment for his saxophone, which adds to the sound when played through an amplifier. Although he endorsed this device commercially, he never used it in performances or on records.

Coltrane continued to study music from around the world, Alice confirmed:

There were so many cultures of music that he listened to. I cannot say which one that he would state 'this is my favorite, this is my highest inspiration.' He listened to so much music. I mean music from Buddhist temples, like the bells from their temple worship. Japanese music he listened too, the shakuhachi and koto and some of their beautiful instruments. He listened to their spiritual music and music for worship. Again, music of Africa and the classical music of Brazil. He researched, he investigated all the musics of the world, because he knew that everyone had something. . . . Sometimes he would travel. And he would bring back [laughs] I mean a whole case of books, tapes, records. This is what he did, and sometimes he would have to ship things home, because they would be just replete with all kinds of music and tapes and so forth. Now Ravi Shankar did invite him to come to India. Of course that one never came to being, but I'm sure that would have been quite an interesting spiritual and musical experience.[38]

Coltrane also recognized the immense power of Stravinsky's modern classical music.

The quintet with Alice, Pharoah Sanders, Garrison, and Ali—and frequent guests—was the most controversial of all Coltrane's groups. For one thing, there was the free rhythm. Over a steady beat, one can be very adventuresome and still hold an audience; take away the beat, and you lose most of your listeners. Beyond that, there was the intense complex of emotions in Coltrane's music. Even Shankar, who attended a Coltrane performance at the Village Gate on November 10, when Tyner was still on piano, admired the music but found it unsettling: "The music was fantastic. I was much impressed, but one thing distressed me. There was a turbulence in the music that gave me a negative feeling at times, but I could not quite put my finger on the trouble. . . . Here was a creative person who had become a vegetarian, who was studying yoga and reading the *Bhagavad-Gita,* yet in whose music I still heard much turmoil. I could not understand it" (Thomas, 199–200).

The critics could be much harsher than Shankar. And audiences had trouble with the music. At a concert at Temple University, probably on Veteran's Day, 1966, in his own Philadelphia,

Coltrane drew a reverent, overflow crowd about equally divided between students (both black and white) and North Philadelphia bloods. . . . [T]he walkouts began 15 minutes or so into the evening's first tune, which lasted approximately an hour. . . . What was shocking about the exodus was that these were Coltrane addicts presumably undaunted by the turbulence and complexity of his music to that point, but grief-stricken by what they were hearing now. . . . To many of Coltrane's fans, including some who looked as though they wanted to leave but sat rigid with disbelief, this concert and others like it amounted to a breach of trust for which he still hasn't been completely forgiven.[39]

Coltrane must have been particularly dismayed to see himself losing touch with the more traditional part of the black audience. In fact, Simpkins relates a story (211), confirmed by saxophonists Byard Lancaster and Leo Johnson, that when the Coltrane group appeared at the Front Room in Newark, New Jersey, also late in 1966, the audience and manager became hostile and insisted that he play some of his old standards. Byard Lancaster clearly heard Coltrane respond that he was sorry, but he had to do something with his music and he could not go back. The gig was actually canceled after the first night. How humiliating it must have been for this international celebrity to be treated like some unknown having a bad audition! Yet Lancaster, who rode back in the same car, describes Coltrane as being quite calm and resolved. Alice recalls: "When he became avant garde, as they termed it, he lost many people, many followers. They didn't like it, they didn't approve of it, they didn't appreciate it. And there was no way he could go back, there was no road to return on. It was his commitment, it was his decision."[40]

John was always quick to censure himself, and facing this kind of resistance undermined his confidence in the direction he was taking. He said, "Everybody wants to hear what I've done. Nobody wants to hear what I'm doing. . . . I've had a strange career. I haven't yet quite found out how I want to play music. Most of what's happened these past few years has been questions. Someday we'll find the answers."[41] In August 1965 he told *Melody Maker,* "Whenever I make a change, I'm a little worried that it may puzzle people. And sometimes I deliberately delay things for this reason. But after a while I find that there is nothing else I can do but go ahead."[42] And he would ask people around him for their responses. John Glenn remembers that Coltrane asked him, "What do you think?"

At the other extreme, those who did appreciate the band were just as impassioned as those who did not. Touring Japan in July 1966 was a wonderful experience for the group. They were treated like royalty, Ali remembers: "When we came off the airplane, they had life-size posters of us like, you know, like in the sheath—how you carry a flag—they had life-size posters and bigger, cutout to shape of each one of us at the airport and then they took a red carpet and rolled a red carpet from the plane into the terminal for Coltrane. That's the way they did it in Japan."[43]

Daniel Berger gives a sensitive account of Coltrane's appearance at a benefit for St. Gregory's church in Brooklyn on April 24, 1966, an appearance that reunited him with Elvin Jones. Cal Massey, a friend of the church, had prevailed upon Coltrane and others to donate their services. There was an audience of about a hundred black people for the first of two shows: "Towards the end of the afternoon, Trane, his wife [Alice] and their little kid [probably John, Jr.] arrived on the scene, calmly, followed by Elvin [who was there to perform with saxophonist Roland Kirk as well] and Jimmy Garrison. He asked for silence and, instead of playing, he began to recite his poem 'A Love Supreme.' I don't know if he cried, I don't know if he smiled. I know that he was infinitely calm, that his voice came out timid, fearful. . . . He read his page without haste and looking in the air, staying in the same place. Nobody said anything. Then he began to play at the limit, yet again, of the possible and the perceptible. . . . He never played without giving all."[44]

Many persons responded to Coltrane's music with cultish devotion. Alice remembered the effect of their music: "Someone in the audience would stand up, their arms upreaching, and they would be like that for an hour or more. Their clothing would be soaked with perspiration, and when they finally sat down, they practically fell down. The music just took people out of the whole material world; it lifted them up."[45] Many people still speak of how their lives were changed by hearing Coltrane perform. Sometimes people would point out to him that he shared the same initials as Jesus Christ—an observation that greatly offended this deeply religious and profoundly humble man.

The barrage of sound presented by Coltrane's last works may, unfortunately, conceal from many listeners the magnificent power of Coltrane's playing. What seems to be chaotic is just the opposite. Coltrane managed to create long solos that flowed seamlessly from theme to improvisation—which is just what he said he wanted. And the improvisations were devoted relentlessly to the exploration of abstract motivic ideas.

The motives that Coltrane used are not so different from the ones he used before 1965, such as the little cell that runs through *A Love Supreme*. But because he's playing without a steady beat, it may be hard to recognize their similarity. Besides, Coltrane was no longer working with chord progressions. He wrote tonal melodies but specified no chords, instructing the soloists to play in any keys they wished. (In this tonal freedom, he certainly was preceded by Ornette Coleman.) Since there was no steady tempo, the distinction between ballads and other pieces becomes blurred. Still, most pieces suggested a basic pulse through a combination of the number and duration of the notes played by each instrument, that is, by the density of sound. Some pieces comprised many fast notes played by all the instruments. Others began with longer notes played by Coltrane, supported by spare colorations of the cymbals, and occasional piano chords. These latter, dubbed "rubato ballads" by Ekkehard Jost, differ from traditional ballads in that they often build gradually in pace and intensity until reaching a fever pitch, at which point they usually return to the balladic mood of the opening. So, while some pieces are clearly ballads because they retain the slow feeling most of the way through (such as "Reverend King" from February 1966), many are unclassifiable because they move quickly away from a ballad pace (such as "Venus").

Coltrane's sound was changing dramatically. He told Kofsky that he had had problems with his tone ever since he accidentally damaged his favorite mouthpiece around 1962. With his last group, he came upon a richer tone, with fuller vibrato, than he had ever used before. It may be heard to gorgeous effect on a slow work such as "Peace on Earth" (Japan, July 1966). He also extended his altissimo range up to a full octave above the f′ and didn't hesitate to produce squeals even higher than that. He increased his control of multiphonics so that he could better sustain a combination of them as a "chord," or, on the other hand, he could inject them into fast patterns. Sometimes he produced the effect of two lines weaving at once.

The new context of Coltrane's last music changed the meaning of his dissonance. Since he had abandoned the use of prearranged chord progressions and key centers, his dissonant formulas now suggested changing key centers instead of serving to enrich a tonal center already established. Since there was no other key center being maintained, "'polytonality'" was not the issue, except insofar as the bass and piano might momentarily suggest different keys in their support of Coltrane's improvisations. So it was not about polytonality but shifting or changing tonalities. Coltrane's changing-key approach also differed from the earlier music in that he could stay in each key area as long or as briefly as he wished. With no need to move back to a home key, he could move from one key to any other at will. In practice, he tended to create some tonal structure in his improvisations, by moving back and forth between keys, sometimes in a particular sequence.

On February 22, 1967, Coltrane recorded six duets with Rashied Ali that were issued posthumously. These duets are an ideal starting place for the listener who wants to understand Coltrane's last music—it's so easy to hear what he's doing. I would guess that he intended these pieces to comprise a suite. Each one begins with a theme, moves away from it, and returns to it at the end. Of the group, "Mars" has the most literal arch form in that some ideas leading up to the climax occur in reverse after the climax, on the way back to the theme. But all of the pieces encompass some kind of working up to a climax followed by a calming down, which leads to a recapitulation.

Coltrane does not necessarily derive his material from the theme of each piece. Instead, he creates several musical events, which are interrelated and stylistically consistent. The sequence of events is dramatically effective, but not necessarily in an obvious way, such as a continuous increase in activity. The events fall into several types. (Because it is meterless, this music must be transcribed in relative note values, without barlines.)

1. Very fast descending scales, repeated over and over. Similar passages appeared as early as 1958 in "Little Melonae," as we've seen.

Compare the above excerpt with the one in the next example, from "Jupiter," which employs two scales.

Coltrane is really attempting to create an orchestral effect with these scales. He wants to give the listener an impression that the top notes are the melody, and the scales are the accompaniment. We may rewrite the first example as long notes over a fast accompaniment.

I believe this accurately represents Coltrane's intention. He seemed intent on breaking loose from the monophonic restrictions of his instrument.[46]

2. Rapid and extreme changes in register. Another attempt to suggest two lines of activity at once.

One of the earliest examples I know of this occurs on his furious solo on a half-hour long "Impressions" from a concert in Stuttgart, November 4, 1963—never issued at this writing.

3. "Right-side up and upside-down"—creating variations of a motive by changing its shape, going up instead of down, using the same rhythm or the same number of notes in different ways. This is similar to the way classical composers will write out a motive and its inversions, retrogrades (backward version), and rotations (the same pitches in a different order), but in improvisation one cannot be this methodical. This instance is from "Mars" (1967).

One motive that Coltrane particularly liked to treat in this fashion was a lyrical two-note sliding figure, like a glissando.

All of the above types of musical events occur in certain of the duets. Of course, many of the events do not fit as neatly into such categories.

An important aspect of Coltrane's style at this time is the contrast between lyrical passages with long note values and textural passages composed of myriads of extremely short notes perceptible only as groups. (Ekkehard Jost has suggested that the term "sheets of sound" describes these latter passages better than anything in Coltrane's 1958 work.)[47] This opposition becomes a major structural principle in some of his late works. Sequences are another favorite device.

Let us look in detail at the duet entitled "Venus."[48] I want to point out some changes of texture and of structure, but it is difficult because not all aspects change at the same time—they overlap. I hear the following sequence of events: Theme statements; sequences in changing tonalities; increasing speed, addition of chromatic scales; implied chromatic ascent from g-flat to a′; explicit chromatic ascent from a′ to d-flat″; climax—chromatic ascent from d″ to d-flat‴ and beyond; retransition toward the theme, involving atonality; expanded recapitulation with some development.

At the outset there are seven brief theme statements labeled A, all different, some contracted or expanded. The first statement introduces several important characteristics. It is a single descending phrase based on the notes E and G of a C major arpeggio (with the seventh, B, added). (The complete solo follows this discussion.) There is never a pause on the tonic C, lending a restlessness to the phrase that pervades this whole opening and sets up further activity to come.

The eighth theme statement (end of line 7, p. 1) ends halfway, leading into changing-key music that is quite different than the theme. The key areas are sometimes ambiguous, and it might be best to simply identify where Coltrane is venturing to the flat side and where to the sharp side. Nonetheless, it seems clear that Coltrane prefers to move among third-related keys to avoid a sense of tonal modulation—for example, E-flat and C, B and E-flat, and, to a lesser extent, E-flat and G-flat, A-flat and C. He often connects these key areas by means of a repeated common tone—for example, E in the key of C is repeated, holding over into the key of B; G-sharp in the key of B is then repeated to become A-flat in the key of E-flat.

Coltrane builds his phrases out of motives (at B), which he moves sequentially through various keys. Then at C, he incorporates shorter note values and faster changes of direction but continues the use of sequences. There are several antecedent-consequent pairs, each sharing motivic characteristics (and thus continuing the sequence). We begin to realize that what, at first hearing, may have seemed to be an undisciplined proliferation of notes is actually an elaboration of various patterns, mostly sequential. Coltrane moves into longer and faster streams of notes, more abstruse and less clearly articulated. Still, patterns emerge. There are a series of note groups, each containing an implied polyphonic lower voice that moves conjunctly, and each coming to rest with a ritard on the last few notes. The lower voice at E, for instance, is e-d-c-b-a. Ken Schaphorst has pointed out to me that, beginning with the eighth-note triplets (at the top of p. 2), Coltrane's playing moves higher and higher, suggesting a central note that he moves up one half step at a time. First there's a g leading to an a-flat at the top of each triplet. After the triplets end, an a-natural seems to be stressed. On the next line Coltrane moves up to work around a b-flat, and so on. The stressed pitches are identified with capital letters on page 2 of the "Venus" solo.

Although various keys are still implied, the changing-key interpretation becomes problematic as the solo progresses. Just after H (p. 2) we hear the first bit of a chromatic scale in the piece so far, an indication of the movement toward atonality. Each note group is constructed primarily out of arpeggios, and key areas are implied at first (a ii-V-I in C is implied just after the chromatic run at H), but soon it makes more sense to speak of arpeggiated ascents or descents than of tonal areas. Most of the note groups are constructed in waves of arpeggios, each successively lower or higher than the one before. Coltrane delves into the lowest register of the saxophone for honks on low A and A-flat (the lowest note on the tenor, in concert key) at the end of line 9 (p. 2) and elsewhere. He also purposely overblows when the octave key is depressed, so that in places he achieves a rough and expressive mixture of middle and high registers at once. The central tone is e′-flat for a long time (middle of p. 2), then moves up to e′-natural (end of line 8).

Coltrane briefly relaxes the tension with a tonal phrase in the key of A-flat (beginning of line 10). Tonal ambiguity reenters with an exploration of the tritone f to b for several seconds. There are some arpeggios in the key of B (middle of line 11, p. 2, starting with the high b), leading to some less tonal music.

A few seconds later (at J, top of p. 3), a chromatic descent is followed by a long chromatic ascent that gets caught on a repeated a′. The repeated a′ gives way to a b′-flat, b′-natural, and c″ as Coltrane begins a long chromatic climb. This time the central note is explicit. He intersperses the repeated high notes with loud notes from the bottom of the horn's range, setting up a subsidiary line. This lower line is not as one directional—Coltrane mixes the A-flat and A-natural scales. All of this sets up the climax of this passage, the arrival at d″-flat, highlighted by a majestic sweep two octaves down to d-flat and back up again (at the end of line 5). After a bit of that sliding motive mentioned before (line 7), Coltrane continues his chromatic ascent into the extremes of the altissimo register. In this passage the emotional tone becomes intensely violent, aggressive, even frenzied. Picking up where he left off, Coltrane begins on high e-flat concert, the top note available through normal fingerings, and continues upward. A four-note motive, underlined at K, reappears on the next two lines. After he attains each new pitch, he "falls off" with a rapid descent, then "climbs" back up to the next higher pitch. This contrasts with the disciplined alternation of repeated notes and low notes that began the ascent from a′ a few moments before. As in the previous passage, d-flat is the climactic note, although this time it is an octave higher. After a long descent in the key of A-flat (at L), Coltrane tries to reach even higher than the d-flat‴ but fails, producing high screams of indeterminate pitch.

The opening theme was so short and limited in range that an immediate return to it after this explosive climax would be very abrupt. He takes his time setting up the theme. At M, he employs clear antecedent-consequent phrasing, each pair sharing motivic material in sequential manner, as he did earlier; some of the pairs are underlined. His tone opens up and relaxes. The tonality changes less often; for example, B major is strongly implied for a while at M. But soon, the pace of tonal shifting quickens. An ascending series of triplets, changing key with each triplet (line 4, p. 4), is answered in like manner by a descending phrase. The notes come more rapidly, and the groupings grow longer and longer, breaking into the longest note-groups of the piece, and the most truly atonal. Coltrane mixes flats with sharps, inserts short chromatic runs, and avoids arpeggios with tonal implications, to create the only moments of real atonality in this piece. After having explored the other extreme, the return to the simple C major pedal point of the theme will seem more necessary, more conclusive than it would have otherwise.

Coltrane sets up the return by playing some notes in C major, followed by A-flat major, reemphasizing the importance of third relations in this piece (and of that particular third-relation) (line 10, p. 4). Then, the implied bass note drops to G, the A-flat is reinterpreted as the flatted ninth of the V chord in C, and we hear, over the implied dominant pedal in C, this flatted ninth, the flatted thirteenth, third, octave and seventh, resolving to the third of the tonic chord, the note E, which begins the reprise of the theme, A. Coltrane adds dimension and grandeur to the recapitulation through the orchestrally conceived descending scales described above as event type 1. He barely begins the e–d trill when it gives way to rapidly repeated scales.

Toward the end (line 4, p. 5), he brings out the thematically important notes g′ and e′, which he seems to hear as sustained notes over the scalar accompaniment. Finally, we hear the theme four times. The final time, Coltrane plays the original ending interval, e up to g, but varies the size of the interval, playing d–g, e-flat–g, then e–g, and more. These expanding cells recall the polyphonic lines that figured so prominently in the piece. The final trill reminds the listener of the trill in the theme that played such an important role.

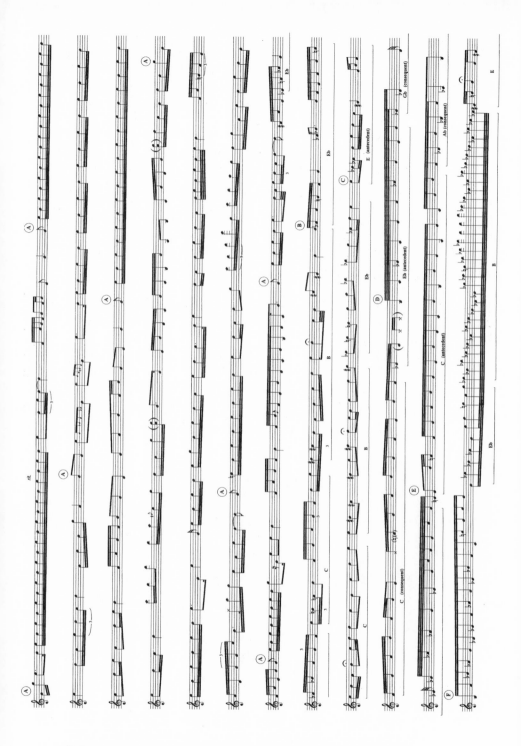

Coltrane's saxophone playing, complete, from his "Venus." Accidentals are valid through the end of each staff. On some high notes (ledger lines) one hears squeals and other overtones along with the pitches written.

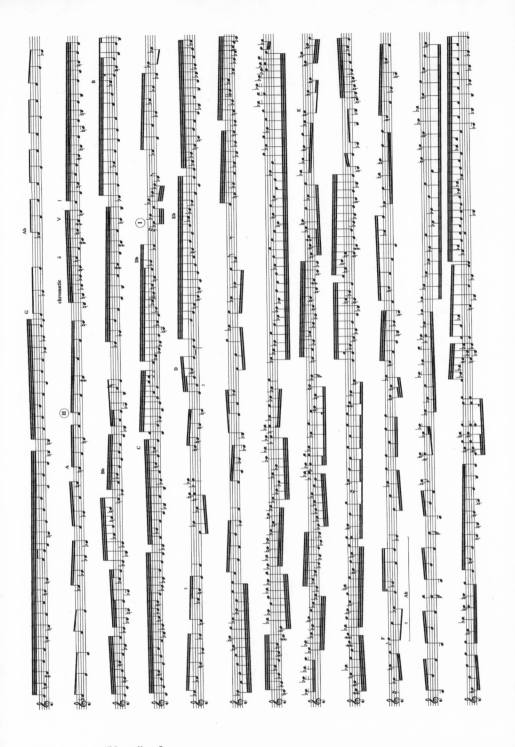

"Venus" p. 2

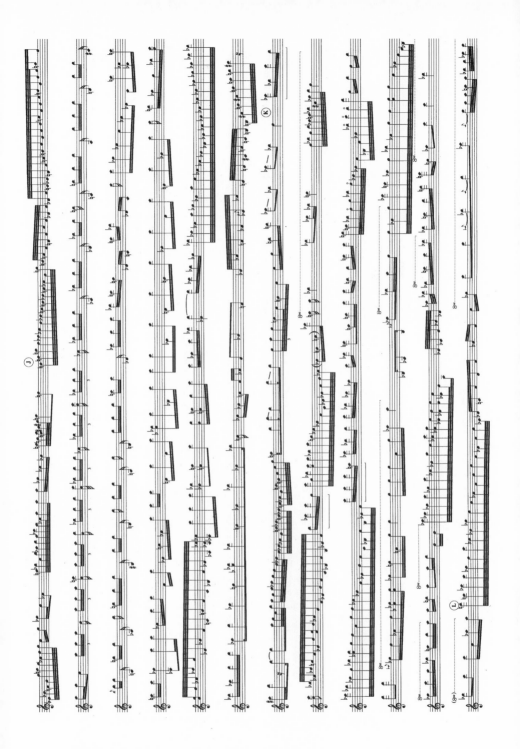

"Venus" p. 3

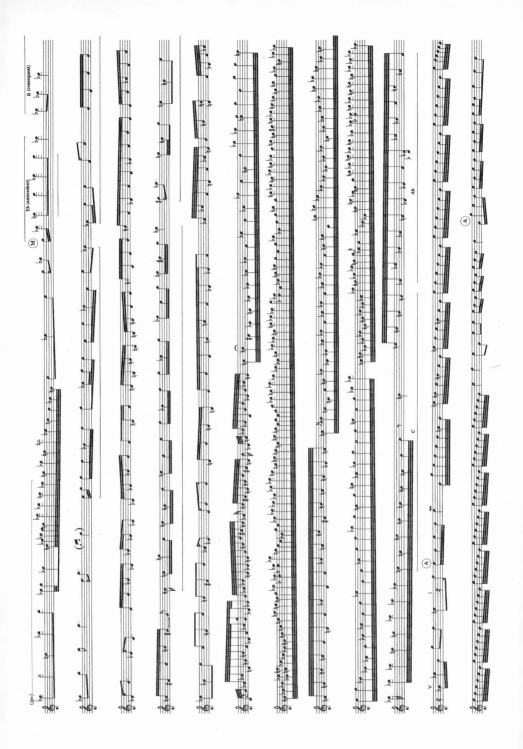

"Venus" p. 4

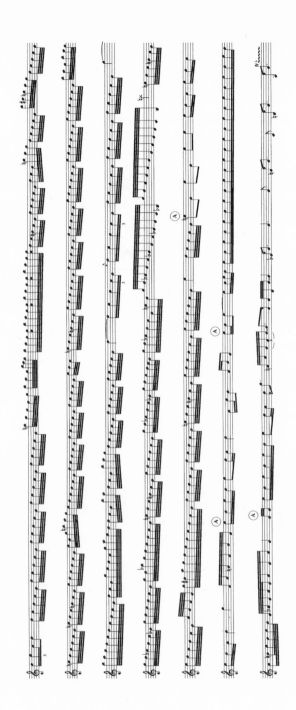

"Venus" p. 5

So, with a few brief and elegant gestures, Coltrane concludes "Venus." For someone who was accused of playing loud, noisy music during his last years, what impresses most is his incredible control of dynamics, from a whisper to a holler. Beyond that, "Venus" is a profound and deeply moving work. And Coltrane has succeeded, precisely *because* he gave up chord changes and the restriction of a steady beat, in creating a seamless musical construction, not divisible into choruses.

His playing is so astounding on "Venus," so full of life, that it is hard to imagine that he was already ill, although undiagnosed. But he was slowing down. He canceled his European tour in November 1966, which would have included his second visit ever to Britain and a television taping there,[49] and he began performing less often. In August 1966, when Kofsky asked him how he liked having Pharoah Sanders in his band as an additional tenor, he replied: "Well, it helps me. It helps me stay alive sometimes, because physically, man, the pace I've been leading has been so hard and I've gained so much weight, that sometimes it's been a little hard physically. I feel that I like to have somebody there in case I can't get that strength. I like to have that strength in the band, somewhere."[50]

On April 23, 1967, Coltrane appeared in a benefit concert for and at the new Olatunji Center of African Culture on East 125th Street. Billy Taylor was the m.c., and he recalls the two sets on that Sunday: "[John] called me and asked me to do that. Olatunji was right around the corner from the radio station [WLIB, where Taylor had a show]. I knew Olatunji's work and on the station we played him a lot. He was really trying to do something to awaken the community to his view of the African heritage, which was a lot deeper than many people had delved into it prior to him. So [the Olatunji Center] was really a very viable place in terms of bringing people together."

A question period was advertised—"Ask Mr. Coltrane questions about his music and sound," promised the flyer—but Taylor does not think they did it on the first set, and he had to leave to go on the air during the second set.

> There was such a crowd that after he played they had to empty the room and bring in the next group, so if there were questions it was after the second set. . . . His music was always so passionate at that period that I had to digest it. There was just so much going on. The volume in that room was much higher than I was accustomed to. But I enjoyed it. The difference between John Coltrane screaming and doing some of the kinds of things he was doing in that period—it took me years to realize that he had learned how to do that in rhythm-and-blues bands, and he was using that kind of a cry, that kind of utterance on the saxophone, in a totally different way, than many guys who came along after and said, "Oh, physically he's doing this to make that sound."

With Coltrane, it wasn't just an effect. It was an honest outgrowth of his whole history.

Rashied Ali recalls that "he was playing strong, but I noticed he was sitting down in a chair so I guess he was a little tired." Mary Alexander says, "At that time I had moved from the lower East Side and I was living on Sullivan Street over on the West Side, the Village. . . . Some Saturdays he would come over. . . . By that time he couldn't eat a lot of food and all that sort of thing, and I would always have something he might be able to eat." But nobody knew what was wrong with his health, and certainly nobody guessed that the Olatunji concert was to be his last performance.

Other concerts that had been announced for April, May, and June were canceled. In May, a press release for the Newport festival to be held at the end of June listed Coltrane, but he was soon removed from the advertisements.[51] But Coltrane continued to make plans. In April he had signed a new contract with Impulse raising his advance to forty thousand dollars a year. He had begun work on his own record label as well, with the cooperation of Impulse. This was a part of an initiative to take more control of his own business affairs, which had become a major concern among black musicians. As part of this effort, he was also planning some self-produced concerts jointly with Olatunji and Yusef Lateef, and they already had at least one date reserved, January 14, 1968 at Lincoln Center's Philharmonic Hall (now known as Avery Fisher Hall).[52]

Coltrane said, ". . . I intend to make a trip to Africa to gather whatever I can find, particularly the musical sources." Olatunji said he wanted to transfer Yoruba chants to the saxophone.[53]

And he was in New Jersey looking at real estate. Lateef recalls, "A couple of weeks before he died he was at my house in Teaneck, New Jersey. . . . He wanted me to introduce him to a real estate agent. He wanted to buy a house in Teaneck so it would be close to New York. He wanted to open a club where children could come and listen to the music."[54] Alice said it was to be a place for "music and meditation."[55] David Young, his high school friend, lived in nearby Englewood, where he ran a sign-painting business. He hadn't met Coltrane again but heard that Coltrane was thinking of buying a house right near him. "I heard it from the fellow that lived in the house. I couldn't wait." Coltrane had a particular property in mind and was thinking of moving his family there, while his mother would stay in the house on Long Island. In December 1966 he said, "I'm thinking of opening some kind of place where I could play whenever I felt like it and could invite other groups."[56] He may have envisioned this separately from the New Jersey location; he described it to Bob Thiele as a loft in Greenwich Village where rehearsals and performances would be open informally to the public for a nominal charge.[57] By the spring of 1967, he was considering performing less often or even taking a break altogether, while he concentrated on producing younger artists and possibly doing some teaching.[58]

But by May, Coltrane was complaining of intense pain in the area of his stomach. He went into a hospital and had a biopsy but did not have any treatment at that time. According to Alice, he rejected his physician's suggestion to operate—perhaps because the chances of success were slim—and spent days stretched out on a couch, listening back to his recent recording sessions. "Maybe I didn't know how bad he felt," Alice said, "because he wouldn't tell me. I used to leave him alone when I thought he wanted to be alone. I was busy with the kids and I didn't want to bother him, to get in his way or to bug him." She says he would make ominous statements about "if I ever play again" and "if I have to leave you." Mary Alexander remembers telling him that he wouldn't have the energy to run the performance space he was contemplating. "Don't worry, I'm going to live," he responded.[59]

Mary says Coltrane was in the hospital again about two weeks before he died. Coltrane met with Bob Thiele on Friday, July 14, to finish plans for releasing four pieces he'd recorded in February and March. He suggested the title *Expression*. It turned out to be his first posthumous album. By Sunday, July 16,[60] he could not even eat soup, and he went to nearby Huntington Hospital. Alice recalled that "he was such a strong man that he walked out the door himself. He was walking slow, but he made it. And then he went down so fast."[61] He died in the hospital of liver cancer at 4:00 A.M., Monday, July 17, 1967, two months before what would have been his forty-first birthday.

His death was a devastating shock to Alice, Naima, and Mary; to friends and family; to musicians and fans worldwide. Miles Davis said that Coltrane's death "fucked up everyone. Coltrane's death shocked everyone, took everyone by surprise. I knew he hadn't looked too good and had gained a lot of weight the last time I saw him. . . . But I didn't know he was that sick—or even sick at all. I think only a few people really knew that he was sick, if they really knew. I don't know if Harold Lovett—who was our lawyer at the time—even knew. Trane kept everything close to his vest."[62]

Daniel Berger thought that Coltrane had seemed different in recent years: "How not to interpret retroactively the madness of his improvisations as panic before death, as a great cry from the precipice, an immense shout before the gods, unknown and mysterious? Did Trane know he was condemned? He'd never said anything. Since 'Love Supreme,' his demeanor had changed. An even greater anxiety had come through. It had become more hidden, but at the same time more noticeable, more directly felt."[63]

Other people searched their memories for clues, and the rumors began. I've heard it said that Coltrane was bloated because of his liver disease—water retention is one possible side effect. But it may be that he simply ate too much.

He had a chronic weight problem, a concern he shared with other former addicts and alcoholics. He told Don DeMicheal of *Down Beat* that he was ashamed to be seen in public because he weighed two hundred and forty pounds (Thomas, 222). Audience members at a concert at the Massachusetts Institute of Technology in Cambridge in late 1966 remembered that he had to be led onstage by Alice—but more likely she was just holding his hand, or he could have been tripping on LSD. He certainly was not an invalid at any point, particularly not that early. Rashied Ali told Simpkins that photographs taken during the tour of Japan show Coltrane frequently holding his side (207, and photo section). But the photographs are not convincing—he just seems to be resting his hand on his potbelly. In any case, it is unlikely you'd *feel* pain in your liver.[64] The pain that Coltrane felt later, in May 1967, indicated that by that time the disease was affecting the operation of other internal organs; in addition, it may have spread to the large intestine. (In fact, the cancer often originates elsewhere and then spreads to the liver.) According to Ravi Coltrane, there was no autopsy—contrary to rumor—so we will never know the exact extent of the damage.

Liver cancer is medically known as hepatocellular carcinoma (hepatoma for short), a carcinoma (cancerous mass, or tumor) of the liver (hepato) cells. It's a relatively uncommon tumor in the United States, although very common in some other countries.[65] Liver cancer is extremely difficult to detect—it can be quite advanced before it is indicated by blood and urine tests. It is also very difficult to treat. At an early stage when only a small part of the liver is affected, the diseased section can be surgically removed. Once the damage has spread beyond the liver, most typically to the lungs and bone, there is nothing to be done.

Fifty to 80 percent of the people who develop liver cancer also have cirrhosis of the liver, a disease involving destruction of liver connective tissue, which occurs mostly in people who drink large quantities of alcohol. As Nisenson notes, many musicians have speculated that Coltrane hurt his liver during the years of alcohol and drugs—that even though he stopped, the damage was done and cirrhosis had begun its course (217). But Nisenson counters, "The etiology of liver cancer is still basically unknown, and there is no reason to believe that alcohol or drugs had anything to do with Coltrane's illness." That's basically true, if overstated. It is unusual for someone to develop cirrhosis years after abstaining, and especially to die of it, but not impossible. However, people who die of it are usually active drinkers at the time of death. It may have been that Coltrane had damage elsewhere that spread to the liver through the bloodstream. Sometimes what appears to be liver cancer—even when there is a known tumor—could have spread from the kidney, pancreas, adrenal gland, or lower intestine. Since he experienced pain in the lower abdomen, that may indicate that the lower intestine was diseased.[66]

There was cancer in his family—his grandmother had died of breast cancer, and his father of stomach cancer—but there is no known hereditary connection between those and liver cancer. Still, one can't help but wonder if Coltrane's premonitions of death had to do with a fear of cancer.

As for drugs, LSD is not dangerous to the liver. David Weiser, M.D., psychiatrist in Briarcliff Manor, New York, told me that neither heroin nor the contaminants that may go along with it are factors in liver cancer so far as is known. (Heroin on the street in those days was probably very impure.) If heroin is taken intravenously, there is a risk of hepatitis, and that can lead to a tumor or cancer. It's possible for people to have hepatitis and for it to be what's called subclinical, which means with minimal symptoms, so they could even feel like they had a cold and not know it was hepatitis.[67] Hepatitis infections are the most significant causes of liver cancer worldwide, and in patients who have hepatitis it is harder to detect the tumor.

So it could be that in the long run, the needle killed Coltrane. But the sad truth is, nothing could have been done about it. Coltrane's death was a tragedy in the classic literary sense—unpredictable, unstoppable, incurable, striking down a good man in his prime.

And he was the one who had risen above all the self-destructiveness in the jazz life, who had told Kofsky, "I feel I want to be a force for good."[68] He had really become that force—just as he wanted—by inspiring so many younger than he to lead a better life, and by setting an example for them. They had no idea that during his last year he was confused about his musical direction, was increasingly exhausted, and was finally in pain. For he was after all a man.

20

Epilogue

One thousand people mourned John Coltrane on July 21, 1967, at St. Peter's Church in Manhattan under Rev. John Gensel, known as the jazz pastor for his service to that community, with Rev. Dale Lind, who took over that role when Gensel retired in the early 1990s. Coltrane's old friend Calvin Massey read the poem "A Love Supreme." The quartets of Ornette Coleman and Albert Ayler performed one number each. After the ceremony the family drove out to Pinelawn Memorial Park in Farmingdale, on Long Island, where John Coltrane was interred.

Coltrane died without a will.[1] His estate, that is, finances and property under his name only (not jointly with Naima or Alice), was valued at $318,500. A large portion of that went to estate taxes; another large share went to his widow Alice; and small shares went to the three young boys. There was also a cash total of $185,424 (from trusts or possibly life insurance). Alice Coltrane received $108,825. The remainder of his life insurance was distributed to his mother, to Naima, his cousin Mary, and his "descendant" (as she is called on the document) Sheila Coltrane.[2]

In recent years, the Blair family has dwindled away. Coltrane's uncle John Blair had come up from Hamlet to attend the funeral with his wife Ethel, who was distressed at hearing jazz bands playing at the service. Georgetta Watkins says that wouldn't have been proper back in North Carolina, but she thought it was fine. John Blair suffered from an organic brain disorder toward the end of his life and passed away on December 13, 1995.

According to the printed funeral program, two more of his mother's siblings were still alive in 1967—Coltrane's Aunt Minnie, known as Minnie Fowler of Norfolk, Virginia, and his uncle William Wells Blair, residing in Orange, New Jersey. Both have since died. Coltrane's older cousin Viola lived until around 1990—she resided in South Philadelphia, and Mary helped care for her.

Mary moved back to Philadelphia in 1968. Later she married and divorced one David King. Her "real husband," as she likes to say, was a sweet man, a carpenter named William Alexander. They married in January 1977, and were together until his death on April 20, 1995. They might have waited a bit longer to marry, but John's mother Alice Gertrude Blair Coltrane, living in Atlantic City, was very ill, and she really wanted to see the wedding, so they married early for her sake. John's mother passed away in September 1977 of breast cancer—a genetic illness that had also killed her mother, the first Alice, back in 1939. She was buried in the Blair family plot in High Point, North Carolina. Mary has no children—although she has been very close to Saeeda's—and considers herself to be just about the last of the Blairs.

Saeeda, once divorced, has two boys and two girls. She remarried in November 1996 and had hoped for her mother to be there. Sadly, Naima died suddenly of a heart attack at 6:00 A.M. on October 1, 1996. Besides Saeeda and her family, Naima is survived by a son—a year or more after John moved out in 1963, she adopted a boy who had already been named Jamal Dennis. Born in 1963, Dennis is now a talented composer and bassist in the pop studio world who takes pride in his membership in the Coltrane family.

Alice's daughter Michelle, from her first marriage, is a musician too: "I started playing real young when I was in school. I started out, I think, with the viola and I played violin all the way up to high school. So I started playing when I was seven, I think. . . . I started to get interested in [singing] in my early twenties and I went to Japan for a little while. I did some work there. Original songs that I've written or I've done background work for commercials, things like that. I haven't really done my own album or anything like that but that's something that I look forward to maybe doing in the future."[3]

The three boys of John and Alice are musical as well. John Jr. played the bass until he was tragically killed in an automobile accident in 1982. Oran and Ravi, as well as a nephew of Alice, have played on John's saxophones.[4] Oran studied at the California Institute of the Arts beginning around 1990. He is an alto saxophonist of some accomplishment but has not recently played in public.

Ravi, on the other hand, has become a regular fixture on the New York jazz scene. He started on clarinet and began working on tenor saxophone in earnest when he went to the California Institute of the Arts in 1986. He was in a student band there that won a *Down Beat* award, and his piece "Dear Alice," a tribute to his mother, is on their CD. Since 1990, he has performed and recorded with such artists as Elvin Jones, Steve Coleman, Geri Allen, Jack DeJohnette, Joanne Brackeen, and Art Davis, and he sounds terrific—nice warm tone, great technical fluidity.

It must be difficult being the saxophonist son of one of the most famous saxophonists of all time, working with people such as Jones and Davis who were associated with his father, facing all those expectations and prejudgments. It must be more sensitive yet because he never knew his father—he was not yet two when John died. Yet Ravi handles this delicate situation with grace and intelligence, modesty and honesty. He has said that his mother "was always playing classical pieces on the piano in the house. . . . When I discovered jazz, I discovered it on my own. There was a point when it was the son listening to his father to figure out what his father was about. Later I was a musician listening to John Coltrane to find out what music is about."[5]

Ravi studied John's legacy just as musicians all over the world do; not because it was his father, but because there's no way to be a jazz musician since Coltrane without knowing his music. The challenge is to learn from Coltrane without imitating him. For instance, when English tenor saxophonists Ed Jones, Alan Skidmore, and Steve Williamson discussed Coltrane's influence, they all agreed with Williamson that many musicians copy Coltrane, and that "being a copyist is not a sincere way of following either your own music or Trane's." Aside from all the technical innovations, says Jones, "Trane was also about the search for a personal voice." "There seems to be danger," writes the moderator, Barry Witherden, "that if you study Coltrane too deeply . . . you will be overwhelmed."[6] Among the many who developed a distinctive voice out of the Coltrane legacy are Charles Lloyd, Ralph Moore, David Liebman, Joe Farrell, Steve Grossman, Pat LaBarbera, Michael Brecker (who has a large following of his own), Bob Berg, Jan Garbarek, and numerous other players of tenor and soprano saxophone. But his influence extends far beyond saxophonists—he affected the whole field of jazz improvisation, influenced the ensemble sound of jazz groups, and set forth an attitude about what jazz is and what it can be.

Musicians on all instruments have taken the so-called pentatonic patterns that he used on "Giant Steps" and applied them to all kinds of chord progressions. Over a rapid rate of harmonic change, musicians play one such pattern over each chord. Over a slow-moving piece harmonically, such as a blues or modal piece, they may play a sequence of four-note patterns that implies faster harmonic activity, enriching what might otherwise be moments of stasis—in this case they are learning from what Coltrane did in the two years following "Giant Steps." Pianist Chick Corea, the late trumpeter Woody Shaw, and saxophonists Greg Osby and Steve Coleman are only a few of the many musicians who developed Coltrane's pentatonics in an original direction.[7] The development of patterns has been simplified and systematized so that even musicians who have difficulty conceiving of dissonant melodies may learn to create them. In this way, Coltrane's innovation becomes part of the mainstream, a skill that anyone can learn.

As a writer for small group, Coltrane has been much imitated. Not only have such modal pieces as "Impressions" become staples of the jazz repertory, but, more significantly, the Coltrane type of modal piece—a simple, dramatic theme, usually in the Dorian mode, perhaps with open-ended cues—has thousands of offspring. These modal pieces, often dedicated to Coltrane, bear such titles as "Talkin' about J.C." (Larry Young), "Trane's Bag," "For John Coltrane," or, relating to Coltrane's mystical and astrological pursuits, titles such as "Pisces," "Karma" (Pharoah Sanders), "Bridge into the New Age" (Azar Lawrence), and the like. Some groups specialize in this kind of modal material, among them some of the groups that have been led by Coltrane's former colleagues, McCoy Tyner and Elvin Jones. (Recently, Tyner's repertory includes quite a few standard songs as well.)

Coltrane's influence was not confined to the jazz world:

> Some of the most influential composers of today's concert music—Philip Glass, Terry Riley, La Monte Young and others—have cited Coltrane as a key influence on them, especially their move toward Eastern modes, rhythmic cycles and improvisation. More than five years before the Beatles, Mr. Coltrane studied [the music of] Ravi Shankar and made the drones, the rhythms and the melodic purity of India's ragas a part of 20th-century Western music. The Byrds, the Allman Brothers, Eric Clapton, the Who and many other innovators of 60s rock have spoken of their admiration for and debt to Mr. Coltrane and his influence.[8]

Coltrane's fans also have included Carlos Santana, Bono of the Irish rock group U2 (who used Coltrane's image in one of their videos around 1993), and the late Jerry Garcia of the Grateful Dead.

Through his spiritual messages, his influence extended beyond the world of musicians into other arts. He inspired poems by Michael Harper, Amiri Baraka, and Al Young, as well as a number of paintings. (Even "primitivist" Ralph Fasanella told me he liked to paint to Coltrane's music.)[9]

Some people feel that Coltrane had a special relationship with God. Tyner has said that Coltrane's presence shows that "God still speaks to man" and sends us "messengers." Elvin Jones said "I believe that he was an angel."[10] This attitude was taken to its logical extreme by the One Mind Evolutionary Transitional Church of Christ in San Francisco, founded in 1971 by by Franzo Wayne King, who plays saxophone. The Sunday ritual at this small storefront is centered around the album and poem *A Love Supreme* and their meeting place is adorned with photographs of Coltrane. Everybody, including King, plays instruments (percussion at least) and sings to the opening ostinato of *A Love Supreme* and other Coltrane compositions. But this material is integrated into a traditional service in devotion to Jesus. They do not worship Coltrane per se;

they are devout Christians who see Coltrane as somebody who experienced redemption in his own lifetime. They spell John's middle name "Will-I-AM," after God's words from the burning bush. The church members also distribute free meals to the needy, give concerts, and host a weekly radio program of Coltrane's recordings.

At one time Alice Coltrane and King were colleagues, but in 1981 she initiated a 7.5 million dollar lawsuit against the church, charging that it was illegally using John's name "without family sanction and is misrepresenting us and infringing on copyright laws." The suit was unsuccessful. In January 1982, the church became part of the African Orthodox Church and Coltrane was officially accepted as a saint. The new name was St. John's African Orthodox Church, and in May 1984 King became a Bishop.[11]

Mrs. Coltrane has become a mystic, an advanced disciple of Swami Satchidananda, whose name suggests the achievement of spiritual "reality" in Hindu. Vishnu Wood said that he introduced her to the Swami when he visited the United States around 1969 because "she was having some personal problems that were pretty severe" and he felt the swami could help her.[12] Coltrane doesn't perform or record much anymore, although she can be most impressive when she does—I particularly like her organ playing in a trio with Reggie Workman and Roy Haynes on *Transfiguration*.[13] She performed during the first John Coltrane festivals in Los Angeles, which she began in 1987, but now she only helps direct the festival, usually two days of concerts held around his birthday each year. Her spiritual studies have taken first place in her life. She was known for a time as Turiya Aparna, and since she became a teacher herself she has been known as Turiyasangitananda. In 1975 she founded the Vedantic Center, a religious retreat, in Northern California. Since 1983 the center has been located in Agoura Hills, just west of Los Angeles.[14] She spends part of the year there and in her house in nearby Woodland Hills, and the rest of her time in India. In 1978 she authored a "spiritual autobiography" entitled *Monument Eternal*, and around 1987 she published *Endless Wisdom*, a book of verses that she says she received from the Lord in English and Sanskrit. In it she writes: "Over the years, I was divinely instructed to preserve a written record of the Lord's sacred communications. Those that appear in the form of this book have all been sanctioned by the Lord." She has produced a spiritual program for Channel 18 in Los Angeles and released two tapes of spiritual chants, *Turiya Sings* and *Divine Songs*.

She says that she has seen John and spoken with him on occasion, mostly during the first dozen years after he died. On *Transfiguration* she wrote about her piece "One For The Father": "In reality, this music exemplifies my fond remembrance of the father, John Coltrane; and at such time of remembering, I see the father, his three sons, and the Holy Ghost, or Nilakantha who is Lord Siva, the Destroyer Of Ignorance" [in the Hindu religion as practiced in India].

Elsewhere she often refers to John as Omnedaruth (compassion). She appears to see him as a significant spiritual figure in his own right. And she combines Christian and Hindu images together, and in other places, Egyptian mythology, into a personal vision that is an extension of what he began.

The Coltrane legacy will continue to grow. We can expect more music of Coltrane to be issued. Toward the end, Coltrane often had two master tapes made at his recording sessions and took one home to study in his home studio in Huntington. Therefore, even Impulse recording sessions that were never issued and eventually erased may still exist in Alice Coltrane's possession, and according to Michael Cuscuna there are plans to release them. There are also sessions that Coltrane recorded at his home studio. Then there are live recordings from his European tours that have never been issued. Saeeda and a musician who prefers not to be named have collections of Coltrane tapes that may someday be available to the public. Finally, a large number of tapes have been issued only as bootlegs and may be issued legally in the future.

Coltrane has become history. On U.S. 74, passing Hamlet, North Carolina, a historical marker reads "John Coltrane 1926–1967. Jazz saxophonist and composer: influential stylist. Work spanned bebop to avant garde. Born one block S.W." On the building facing Hamlet Avenue at the corner of Bridges Street—his place of birth—a plaque reads:

> JOHN COLTRANE
> "A Jazz Messiah"
> WAS BORN *HERE* 9-23-26
> DIED 7-17-67

The reconstructed red-brick building where he was born has a beauty parlor at one end. Besides the beauty parlor, the five-room building houses the Richmond County branch of the NAACP, Renee's Balloons, and Coltrane's Blue Room, a party rental place. In 1926 it was a two-story boarding house and Coltrane lived with his parents in an upstairs apartment over the current Blue Room. It was and is a black neighborhood, and the building, about one hundred years old, once housed N. C. Mutual Life Insurance, the largest black insurance company in the state. Dr. Fred McQueen Jr. bought it in the mid-1980s. It was falling down and had to be rebuilt for $60,000. He eventually wants to open a club for jazz students in one part of the building.[15]

In his boyhood home of High Point, another marker was erected in September 1996, describing him as "a world-renowned jazz legend whose warm and lyrical style influences generations of artists," directing people to the house on Underhill, and quoting Coltrane's statement that his music is "the spiritual expression of what I am."

Coltrane has become commercial. His image has become suddenly so fashionable that in 1994 it showed up in television ads for Honda vehicles and around that time in a music video by the rock band U2; his sound was heard in a television commercial for a realtor; the protagonist in the film "Mr. Holland's Opus (1996) named his son after the saxophonist.

Coltrane has become recognized by the U.S. government. In September 1995 a group of ten stamps were issued to commemorate jazz musicians, among them Coltrane. The image of Coltrane that was originally reproduced in the advance catalog showed him blowing fiercely into a soprano saxophone. Before it was issued, however, a decision was made to change to a portrait of Coltrane looking straight into the camera and holding a saxophone to the side. The face is a much better likeness than the original choice, but the top of the saxophone is a bit inaccurate; it looks something like an alto, but not exactly, nor does it appear to be a tenor or soprano saxophone. (The Congo issued a Coltrane stamp in 1973.)

As a fitting memorial, Coltrane has inspired good nonprofit works. In High Point, John Morton directs the John Cultural Workshop, a group that raises funds to help promising musicians in junior high and high school. In Philadelphia in 1979, Arnold Boyd founded the TraneStop Resource Institute, which presents educational jazz performances and lectures around the city.

Coltrane's favorite cousin, Mary Alexander, has been promoting his legacy at the house on Thirty-third Street in Philadelphia, where she resides. John had turned the house over to his mother; before she died she turned it over to Mary, who was like a daughter to her. In 1984 she and six other women formed the John W. Coltrane Cultural Society. By 1986 they succeeding in having the house designated a historic building, and in 1990 a marker was erected. The society primarily sponsors music workshops, concerts, and lectures for children at schools, libraries, and community centers citywide, involving an impressive variety of musicians and musical traditions. "In this way," says Mary, "I am sharing John's life with the children."[16]

Of course, the sad tinge to all this celebration is that these children will never get to meet John W. Coltrane. We are fortunate that he left behind such a rich and voluminous legacy. There is such power and reality in his music, such profundity and seriousness, yet it never sounds pompous or inflated or pretentious—perhaps that element of the down-home blues helps. Others can play his music, yet it is difficult to even approach the unbelievable emotional power he projected. And it's not a question of louder or faster—it's a combination of his tone quality and the melodic lines he improvises, the material he wrote and arranged, the musicians who became such an integral part of his sound. And it's his total lack of inhibitions. People are so different in the way they express emotion—there are plenty of wonderful instrumentalists in the world, but that total emotional openness is very rare, because it's so dangerous, so hard to be unafraid in front of hundreds of strangers. I'm convinced that that is a key to what creates monumental art of any sort.

Coltrane wanted his music to be a force for good, and I think it has been. One doesn't have to be religious to find Coltrane's expression of spirituality profoundly moving and important. Listen to "Dear Lord," recorded in May 1965 with Tyner and Garrison and Roy Haynes on drums. The theme that Coltrane plays on tenor begins with three notes going up a scale, each held for four measures with slight embellishments, floating over the support of the rhythm section. The very simplicity of it is daring. Somehow those three notes epitomize what so many people love about John Coltrane's music—the strength, the concentration, the purity, the aching directness of it. There will never be three notes quite like them.

Notes

Chapter 1

1. Boonville, to the north in Yadkin County, is so named because Daniel Boone is said to have camped at the site. Thanks to Jeff Coltrane, a descendant and historian of the white Coltranes, for all information on Boone.

2. The family was particular about their spelling of Bettie, which is incorrect in Thomas (7), Simpkins (4), and elsewhere.

3. Thanks to Michael Hill, a researcher with the Division of Archives and History in Raleigh, for checking the state senate lists and for the information about the backlash.

4. The Harlem Academy is no longer listed among Tampa phone numbers, so I assume it is defunct.

5. Thanks to Tynie Clemons for personally fetching a copy of the church history—from which these anonymous quotes come—and for answering my questions.

6. More details about the high school are given in Thomas (18–19) and in Gazelia Carter, "Memories of William Penn School Prevail," *High Point Enterprise,* February 10, 1982, 6A (courtesy High Point Museum). Further information is in Michael G. Pierce, *History of the High Point Public Schools 1897–1993* (High Point: High Point Public Schools, 1993). The Leonard St. School, a low U-shaped structure, was demolished in, I believe, the 1980s; a more recent addition still stands next to the site and is used for other functions.

7. Founded in 1901, St. Stephen became a Metropolitan church in the late 1920s and a new building was erected at the same address on Price Street. A larger parsonage house was built in the early 1930s. In the 1937 city directory the address is given as 207 Price. This address no longer exists; a highway cuts off Price after the first block off Leonard Street, around where 105 would have been. Tynie Clemons is certain the church was quite close to Leonard Street, so the high number must be deceptive; 105 must have been very close to 207. In 1967 the church was destroyed in a fire, and the current structure at 1012 Leonard (now Avenue) was completed toward the end of that year.

8. Other private high schools for blacks in the western part of the state were located in Concord and Sedalia.

9. The preceding details are according to Augusta Reid Austin, who attended Livingstone from 1925 through 1929.

10. On her college record her birth year is given as 1902 rather than the correct year of 1898, perhaps because she was embarrassed about being a bit older than the other students. The record of her graduation was written May 27, 1925. Dr. William S. Crowder shared Blair's records with me by fax on November 10, 1995. It was drawn partly from the *Livingstone College Annual Catalog of 1928–1929*.

11. Contrary to Simpkins, 2, they did not meet at Livingstone, and there is no record that Coltrane ever attended that institution. There is no marriage certificate for them in Hamlet, High Point, or Sanford.

12. It is not true, as reported in some sources, that the name Coltrane originated from the village of Culrain in Rosshire, Scotland. By the way, the popular singer Chi Coltrane is of Scottish descent; so is the actor Robbie, but Coltrane is his stage name, after the saxophonist. Thanks to Jeff Coltrane for all Coltrane details.

13. There are about 150 listed in North Carolina phonebooks, and a bit less than that in all other states combined, most of which have two or three such listings for the whole state.

14. A. M. Sperber, *Murrow: His Life and Times* (New York: Freundlich Books, 1986), 3.

15. Minnie Hohn Robertson and Jean Davis Swiggett (in *The Earth Abideth Forever: A Portrait of the Davis and Coltrane Families of Randolph County, North Carolina* [Welcome, NC: Wooten Printing Company, 1984], 17), state that the first hint of slave-owning in the family records is a reference in William Coltrane's will, dated November 4, 1814. He leaves several cows and pigs to "Amy and Jemima Huff." The authors feel these may have been slaves. But Jeff Coltrane's more authoritative research suggests the Huffs were probably grandchildren, not slaves.

16. Robertson and Swigget, *The Earth Abideth Forever*, 84. The 1900 census reports a few black Americans named Sandy Coltrane, including one born in April 1847 in Randleman, with a wife and five children. He could be a son or relation of "Uncle Sandy."

17. Sperber, *Murrow*, 4, 10. Thanks to Bill Kirchner for bringing this to my attention.

18. Simpkins incorrectly writes Hamlet Street and Bridges Avenue (3). His photo of the building as of 1972 (after p. 150) appears to show the entrance on Bridges Street. The current structure was rebuilt in the mid-1980s from demolished condition and only one floor remains, so I cannot recognize it from Simpkins's photo.

19. As the reader can see from the birth certificate, the time is unclear but appears to be either 3:00 or 5:00 P.M. Question 20 tells us that a previous infant died. Dr. J. S. Perry filled out and signed the document, but Simpkins is probably correct that the baby was delivered by a midwife (3). According to Dr. Fred McQueen, there was at most one black physician there at the time, and not named Perry. Typically a white physician would fill out the birth certificate. Unfortunately, Perry did a cursory job. He did not confirm their home address nor the birthplace of the father, and he lists the father's age as 30, which is probably too high. He may have simply guessed.

20. Interview by Blume, June 15, 1958. Thanks to Norman Saks for an initial copy of this tape; Blume himself sent me a tape once Carl Woideck located him for me. Blume was born in 1927, was in the navy from November 1944 through April 1946, and worked during the 1960s at promoting rock LPs. Blume said he had gone up to talk to Coltrane while he was with Miles Davis in Washington, D.C., and then invited Coltrane to Sunday dinner at his home in Baltimore. He surreptitiously taped their conversation, and at the end Coltrane noticed the recorder turning and shyly protested, saying "I was doing all right until I found this; I didn't think it was on at first." Blume volunteered to write it up for publication. When he sent a draft to Coltrane for approval, John modestly indicated that he wished he had more of substance to say. An edited section about Coltrane's performing experiences appeared in *Jazz Review,* January 1959; in this book those passages are taken verbatim from the tape. The balance, including the preceding passage, appears here for the first time.

21. I assume this because the signature on her birth certificate is not followed by "M.D."

22. Chris Harlos told me a member of his family met a nurse named Dorothy Coltrane in Philadelphia who seemed to be a relation of the saxophonist on his father's side, but I haven't been able to confirm this.

23. Thanks to the High Point Museum for sending me the relevant pages from this directory. City directories were issued before telephones were universal. They listed businesses by occupation (like the *Yellow Pages* today) and people by name and by street, with place of employment.

24. Commercial dry cleaning began as early as the mid-1800s in France, and new methods gained acceptance in the 1930s. See "dry cleaning," by Patricia Anderson, in *Grolier Multimedia Encyclopedia* (CD-ROM), 1993. Dry cleaners were listed in the 1940 city directory.

25. This is usually written as Underhill Street, but Floyd Phifer is certain that at that time it was Avenue. The house is still in use as a residence.

26. Mary Alexander, interviewed by Joel Dorn and myself, March 1, 1995, booklet to John Coltrane, *The Heavyweight Champion: The Complete Atlantic Recordings* (Rhino RZ 71984), 31.

27. The first quotation is from "John Coltrane: Une Interview," by François Postif, *Jazz Hot,* January 1962, 13; the second from liner notes to *Giant Steps* (Atlantic 1311; issued 1960).

28. The high school closed in 1968 and most of the buildings were later demolished. The photo in Simpkins (after p. 150) shows the auditorium building, the only part still standing.

29. Booklet to *The Heavyweight Champion,* 31.

30. Thanks to Barry Marshall and Greg Downing for information about stomach cancer. By the way, the name Coltrane continued to cause spelling problems; J. R.'s death certificate spells it "Coletrane," and even his tombstone, according to John Morton, reads "Coldtrane." On the certificate Alice said J. R. was 35, but this is not significant. The family evidently didn't keep track of ages since they are way off on all the certificates.

31. I think Mary is correct that some form of radiation treatment—at one time using

radium—was practiced that long ago. It is also worth noting that the death certificate, no. 88, was filled out with the help of Coltrane's mother, Alice. It lists the birth year of Mrs. Blair as 1870, which is eleven years too late.

Chapter 2

After I had selected this chapter title a book was published by the same name, about the problems of fatherless families in the United States.

1. Chronic asthma, if untreated and uncontrolled—and in those days they didn't know how to control it—can cause enlargement of the right side of the heart, which may lead to congestive heart failure. Dr. Louis Buzzeo, an internist in Tarrytown, New York, explained this to me by telephone on March 14, 1996.

2. It seems to me that Bettie was distraught when she filled out the death certificate, number 257: it was not written until November 4, and Goler's age is given as forty-two when he was actually about fifty-three. His parents' names are listed as unknown and the date and cause of death are omitted. The address mistakenly given is 110 Underhill, not 118.

3. Booklet to *The Heavyweight Champion,* 36.

4. Booklet to *The Heavyweight Champion,* 32. Simpkins incorrectly states that they did not take boarders (10), and Thomas is even farther off when he states that "one of his grandmothers and a few of her family" lived there (19). To be fair, I believe that both authors were given misleading information.

5. My interview with Alexander.

6. Cf. Simpkins, 17.

7. Michael Futch, "Theme from Hamlet," *Fayetteville Observer-Times,* August 11, 1995, sec. E: 8–9, 16.

8. This is Mary's account; she says neither Thomas (19) nor Simpkins (17) got this quite right.

9. Brower lived with his father, Thomas A. Brower, at 218 Underhill, and Kinzer lived with Flossie Kinzer at 305 Underhill. The addresses came from the city directories, for which I again thank the staff at the High Point Museum. Some of this information is also in Thomas, 5. Kinzer and Brower both contributed material to the opening chapters of Thomas and Simpkins. Nobody seems to know how to spell Kinzer's nickname, which sounds like "Poshay." Nor do they know its origin—Mary thinks it was his father's nickname.

10. Thomas mistakenly "corrected" the spelling to "Dorothea" (19).

11. Thomas states that Coltrane worked during his last two years of high school at Mrs. Drake's Confectionery Store in the Henley Hotel (10). The 1940 city directory lists Henley Apartments at 108 Underhill, near Washington, with beauty shops on both sides. But a confectionery called Drake's Place was located at 101 E. Washington. Simpkins states that Coltrane worked during his last semester, and that it was in the drugstore of Drs. (more likely they were pharmacists) Lemon and Greenwood (18); this was possibly the Washington Street Pharmacy at 731 East Washington. Perhaps he worked at both places.

12. Simpkins says May 31 (18), a Monday, but the 1942 school paper indicates that graduations occurred on Fridays.

13. Gazelia Carter, "Memories of William Penn School Prevail," *High Point Enterprise*, February 10, 1982, 6A. Courtesy High Point Museum. Annette Wright, a historian at the University of North Carolina (Chapel Hill), confirms that eleven grades was the rule in the state at that time.

14. Thomas states that he moved on June 11 (21). Simpkins says January 11, 1944 (19), but Brower himself wrote 1943 in a 1949 article (reproduced in figure 7) and Simpkins corrected his error in a letter to the editor of *Coda*, October 1976, 10.

15. The street name is Master, not Masters, as often listed.

16. Savannah Foods Industries, at 3600 South Darien Street, is listed under "sugar refining" in today's yellow pages, but I don't know if that's where Coltrane worked. Lee Lowenfish, "When the 'Trane Stopped in Philly," *Philadelphia Weekly*, December 13, 1995, 35 says he unloaded boxes at a Domino sugar plant, but I can't confirm this.

17. Mary told Lee Lowenfish that it was September 1943; Lowenfish, "When the 'Trane Stopped." Simpkins (21) and Thomas (27) say 1944.

18. See, for example, Betty Leach's story in Thomas (45); Leach is Jackson's former name.

19. Lowenfish, "When the 'Trane Stopped."

20. The company does not have any records that far back, but I thank Joan Berger of Campbell Soup for checking in February 1996.

21. Mary has them framed at the John Coltrane Cultural Society.

Chapter 3

1. For the North Carolina blues tradition, see Bruce Bastin's well-researched study, *Crying For the Carolines* (London: Studio Vista, 1971).

2. Thomas (7) states that he played for friends as well, but I trust Mary's account.

3. Alexander, booklet to *The Heavyweight Champion*, 33.

4. Coltrane's written responses to Leonard Feather's questionnaire, reproduced in Thomas (following p. 88) from the Institute of Jazz Studies collection.

5. Simon spoke on a radio tribute to Coltrane broadcast on *All Things Considered* on September 23, 1996, and probably recorded two days before.

6. Chris Sheridan, *Count Basie: A Bio-Discography* (Westport, Conn.: Greenwood Press, 1986), 1101 and 1105.

7. Thomas presents two interviews that support the claim that Coltrane first played alto horn (14). The recorded interview with Parker, by Marshall Stearns and James T. Maher, from 1950, was issued on Philology CD W57-2. A transcription is included in the booklet.

8. Thomas says Steele provided used instruments (15), but both could be true. They could have begun on Steele's instruments, then obtained their own.

9. From Postif. Here and elsewhere Coltrane is quoted as saying that he began the saxophone in 1943 or 1944. Perhaps he meant that he really became a musician at that time. In any case, he was always very casual about dates.

10. Contrary to what Ingram recalls, the song was not entitled "A Dream of Two Blue Orchids" and was never recorded by Artie Shaw, to my knowledge. The opening words are "I dreamed of two blue orchids."

11. *Student's Pen*, May 22, 1942, 3. Floyd Phifer, who graduated in 1942, confirms that the band started in his junior year, 1940–41. So both Thomas, who gives September

1942 (20), and Simpkins, who says it was John's junior year (15)—1941 to 1942—have placed the starting date too late.

12. See Eileen Southern, *Biographical Dictionary of Afro-American and African Musicians* (Westport, Conn.: Greenwood Press, 1982), 104–5. Thomas says Yokely was from Durham and had started in High Point in the fall of 1938, but left for further study at Michigan State University, then returned to High Point in September 1942 and started the band (19–20). Besides the fact that this is too late for the beginning of the band, I have trouble believing that the job was unfilled for three years. This may be a garbled account of something that could have happened—Yokely could have begun in 1938, started the band in 1940, then spent the summer of 1943 at Michigan State in East Lansing, because it so happens that at that time Dett had moved to Battle Creek, which is very near by. But this is just my guess.

13. "Coltrane," by Tom Steadman, *Greensboro News and Record.* September 22, 1991; page number missing from North Carolina Collection, University of North Carolina, Chapel Hill.

14. Paul D. Zimmerman, "Death of a Jazzman," *Newsweek,* July 31, 1967, 78–79.

15. This was the older brother of keyboardist Milt Buckner, not to be confused with trumpeter Teddy Buckner.

16. Forrell must have been Yokely's married name, because the first name is still spelled in that unusual way, and none of my informants remembered a different band director.

17. John's cousin Mary doesn't remember John's being in the mixed chorus, although he could have joined them in his last semester, after Mary had moved to Newark.

18. Simpkins tells a rather strange story about how the boys chorus was formed (17), but he does not indicate that Coltrane performed in that chorus. Thomas claims Coltrane enjoyed choruses but never sang in one (12).

19. Booklet to *The Heavyweight Champion,* 32.

20. Booklet to *The Heavyweight Champion,* 34.

21. Simpkins, 20, and Thomas, 27. Both authors refer to Coltrane's "applying" there and being "accepted," but my sense is that Ornstein was a typical nondegree music school where anyone could sign up for lessons and was assigned a teacher depending on one's level.

22. This brief biography is based on David Ewen, *American Composers: A Biographical Dictionary* (New York: G. P. Putnam's Sons, 1982), 484–85; *Baker's Biographical Dictionary of Musicians,* 8th ed., revised by Nicholas Slonimsky (New York: Schirmer Books, 1992), 1340; and my interview with Ornstein's colleague Isadore Granoff. Several apparent inaccuracies appear in the Ornstein entry in *The New Grove Dictionary of American Music* (London: Macmillan, 1986), 3:452.

23. This biography was adapted from Harry R. Gee, *Saxophone Soloists and Their Music, 1844–1985* (Bloomington: Indiana University Press, 1986).

24. Rastelli mentioned two other books to me whose names I could not make out (they sounded like "Bendrix" and "Aidken").

25. This should not be confused with other Schubert compositions: The same name, "Standchen," appears on a Schubert song to Shakespeare's "Hark Hark the Lark!" and on a four-voice setting of another poem.

Chapter 4

1. Advertisement in the *Philadelphia Afro-American.*

2. Lowenfish, "When the 'Trane Stopped," 6.

3. Golson attracted notice as early as June 25, 1949 (*Philadelphia Afro-American*, 7) in a group led by Philly Joe Jones.

4. Rice recorded a bit in the 1950s with Howard McGhee and others, toured and recorded with Chet Baker in 1964 and 1965, then left full-time performing to teach music in the public schools.

5. See Coltrane's written responses to Leonard Feather's questionnaire, reproduced in Thomas. I don't know what trio Coltrane meant. Cocktail lounges of the time included the MoonGlow Cocktail Lounge at 225–27 Market Street in Chester, "presenting the sensational trio 'Plink, Plank 'N Plunk'" (ad in *Philadelphia Afro-American,* October 6, 1945) and later featuring Arthur Davey and his trio (same newspaper, November 3, 1945). Other places that used the word *cocktail* in their name included the Simmons Grille and Cocktail Lounge, 5717 Girard Avenue, and the Hotel LaReve Cocktail Lounge and Grille, 821 W. Columbia Avenue.

6. Later his son, Jimmy Johnson Jr., had an even stronger reputation as a drummer and played in the New York recording studios.

7. The personnel listed for this band in Fujioka, 2, is a composite personnel as recalled by Benny Golson to researcher Kurt Mohr (*Jazz Hot,* January 1959, 11). It certainly does not represent the band at any one time or for any particular number of gigs. For instance, Ray Bryant does not recall ever having played with Johnson. A grainy photo of the Johnson band in an ad in the *Philadelphia Afro-American* on April 6, 1946 seems to include Bill Barron, a tenor saxophonist whom Vance Wilson identifies as Tony Mitchell, and probably Tommy Bryant, Ray's brother, on bass.

8. *Philadelphia Afro-American,* May 26, 1945, 10. The ad also notes that the Gillespie group had just been at the Three Deuces in Manhattan. In the booklet to *The Heavyweight Champion* (41) Jimmy Heath mistakenly remembered this as a JATP event.

9. Booklet to *The Heavyweight Champion,* 41.

10. Simpkins maintains that he took a job with the signal corps at the Naval Yard to avoid the draft (21), but I have found no evidence of this. Pianist James Forman worked at the signal corps as a typist for twenty-five years beginning May 1951. The signal corps was a branch of the military that sent messages (originally via pigeons, later via radar and radio-telephone). Forman knew Coltrane for years and says, "I have no knowledge of him ever working in the signal corps or even talking about it." The confusion may have arisen because his friend Brower is said to have worked there.

11. National Personnel Records Center, Military Personnel Records division. John William Coltrane's service ID number was 9851939. All previous writings give his dates of service as December 1945 through June or July 1946. This error arose from a misunderstanding of the response to Leonard Feather's question, "Have you ever worked overseas?" to which Coltrane wrote, "Only in the Naval Band in Hawaii, Dec. 1945 through June 1946" (see Feather's questionnaire in Thomas). Coltrane never said these were his dates of service, only that he was playing music overseas for these dates.

12. A strong movement to desegregate the armed forces was under way by 1948, but

Louis Lautier rated the navy as still the least hospitable to blacks at that time. The foregoing information came from Lautier's article, "Report Shows Lester Granger Still Has Soft Spot for Navy," *Philadelphia Afro-American,* September 14, 1948, 5; and from Samuel A. Floyd, Jr., "The Great Lakes Experience: 1942–45," in *The Black Perspective in Music* 3, no. 1 (spring 1975): 17–24, especially 18.

13. Floyd, "The Great Lakes Experience." Thanks to Hatton for his help with all navy details.

14. Details on the black band from the navy band newsletter *Leger Lines* 13, no. 1 (1981). Two photos in the article appear to show groups of different size. Thanks to Orin Hatton for sending this to me.

15. For example, *Leger Lines* 13, no. 1 (1981) reported that there was no record anywhere of the first all-black navy band in Chapel Hill.

Chapter 5

1. Golson LP *This One's for You, John,* Timeless 135, liner notes dated January 25, 1984.

2. Hodges had recorded that in a celebrated Lionel Hampton session for Victor in 1937, and as part of the Eddie Heywood trio in May 1944.

3. Golson, liner notes to *This One's for You, John.*

4. Phil Schaap, jazz historian, radio broadcaster, remastering engineer, and record producer, was playing Coltrane's recordings on WKCR-FM (Columbia University) one day when he received a call from a listener who assured him that Coltrane had recorded while in the navy and that somebody named Goldstein in West Hartford had this music. Schaap generously passed this lead on to me, and a few calls enabled me to locate Bill Goldstein and verify this valuable material. William Ruhlmann, ("Going to Extremes: John Coltrane on Record," *Goldmine,* June 23, 1995, 21) mistakenly assumes that these were commercial recordings. He also states that they are controlled by Coltrane's estate; this is only true in the sense that no Coltrane material may be issued legally without permission of the estate. The estate does not own or possess the original recordings.

5. The booklet to *The Last Giant,* Rhino Records, (R2 712 55) 5 and 23, mistakenly identifies this group as the Melody Masters, even though my notes, p. 12, contradict that. In any case, this six-man integrated bebop combo could hardly have been a segregated navy dance band!

6. The pianist, Norman Poulshock, a music teacher and composer in Tacoma, Washington, appears to be the only surviving member of the group. I tracked him down in a very unusual way. Goldstein guessed that Poulshock would be on the West Coast, and I asked my friend Don Manning, a drummer active with Claude Thornhill and others in the late 1940s and early 1950s, if he had ever run into Poulshock. Don did not know him but announced on his radio program on KBOO in Portland, Oregon, that we were trying to locate Poulshock, and he received a call from the pianist's son in response. Poulshock is not sure they had recording facilities at the radio station; he owned a disc recorder and may have brought it along.

7. This appears in *John Coltrane Speaks* (see the Bibliography), 23, but the original source isn't given and I can't locate it.

8. A short excerpt from Coltrane's "Koko" solo appeared in the *Miles Davis Radio Project* (1990), a series produced by Steve Rowland, and in the video *The World according to John Coltrane* (1991), produced by Toby Byron.

9. Ira Gitler, booklet to *The Last Giant*, 23.

10. This letter was read by the narrator in the *Miles Davis Radio Project*.

11. I do not agree with Thomas (52) that Coltrane didn't start at Granoff until 1951. All my sources agree that he completed at least four years of study, and he was simply not in town often enough after 1951 to have done this. Besides, it seems unlikely that he would have waited that long to take advantage of his veteran's tuition benefits. David Wild informed me that those benefits would have expired after five or so years.

12. I have no idea why Thomas believes that Granoff played in the premiere of Stravinsky's *Rite of Spring* in Paris in 1913 (52).

13. The accounts given in Thomas and Simpkins are mistaken. For instance, Simpkins says he received two scholarships, one for clarinet and saxophone, one for composition, and claims that he "graduated," and that he took "post-graduate" courses over a period of eight years (20). Granoff confirmed to me that his school, like most schools of this type, was not a degree-granting institution, and as such it did not offer scholarships or postgraduate courses.

14. Thanks to David Wild for help on the GI bill. Granoff sold the school and the name around 1972. At first Granoff remained as a part-time instructor but soon left. The new owners sold their interest to a group from California who opened a Granoff school there, and they in turn sold it to people in Canada. The student records cannot be located.

15. See Chris Popa's discography *Ray McKinley and his Orchestra* (Zephyrhills, Fla.: Joyce Music, 1979), 2–3. The date of 1939–40 given in the comprehensive jazz discography by Walter Bruyninckx is wrong (Sandole entry; p. S62 in latest edition); at that time McKinley was featured in Will Bradley's band.

16. During much of the 1950s he was involved in a writers' workshop along with James Moody, Benny Golson, Thad Jones, Art Farmer, and Al "Tootie" Heath. They would get together to play and discuss each other's compositions. Charlie Barnet recorded what Sandole calls his "three-part extravaganza," an altered blues entitled "Dark Bayou," on June 16, 1946, and Art Farmer and James Moody recorded his pieces in later years. Sandole and his younger brother Adolphe (1918–ca. 1981)—a composer who also played reed instruments and taught himself piano—recorded an LP entitled *Modern Music from Philadelphia* in 1955. At this writing Dennis is still active there in his private studio.

17. Steve Provizer, "Coltrane," transcript of an interview with Granoff conducted October 20, 1969, in *Kord Magazine*, Palo Alto, California (undated copy from Institute of Jazz Studies files): 3–6.

Chapter 6

1. Jimmie Brown column, "These Foolish Things," part 1 of a three-part series, the Jimmy Oliver Story, *Philadelphia Tribune*, October 22, 1955, 10. Further information came from Charlie Rice.

2. The ad for Webb appears in the *Philadelphia Afro-American*, September 14, 1946. (The Saturday paper was always issued on Friday.) Massey told Simpkins (30) that he

met Coltrane with Webb on South Broad Street, which confirms that this was the occasion. I'm unsure if Coltrane played at the Friday night dance or was hired the next day. Massey told Simpkins the band was rehearsing in the daytime before an audience, and he auditioned. In François Postif, "Cal Massey: Quarante-Deux Ans, Trompette" (*Jazz Hot* 264, September 1970, 22–23), he said it was in the wee hours of the morning, and that he sat in. It's unfortunate that Simpkins relied so much on Massey, an inconsistent witness. Worse, Massey constantly puts street language into Coltrane's mouth, which Simpkins quotes as though they were actual conversations.

3. I did find in the *Philadelphia Tribune* of March 31, 1945 an item saying that Joe Webb and "Maye Belle" played to a near-capacity house in Pensacola, Fla. *The Indianapolis Recorder* listed their touring schedules for that year but not for the following years.

4. *Indianapolis Recorder*, March 10, 1945, 2d sec., 5.

5. The existing photo of the band with Coltrane (Simpkins, following 150) when blown up suggests that Coltrane may have conked (straightened) his hair, a common procedure in those days, but if so this is the only time he is known to have done that. The trumpeter on the left might be Massey. Maybelle's age is given incorrectly in Simpkins as seventeen or eighteen. She must have been about twenty-two.

6. *Down Beat*, June 1942, cited in Albert McCarthy, *Big Band Jazz*. (New York: G. P. Putnam's Sons, 1974), 112.

7. *NJSO Jazz Journal*, fall 1995, 13.

8. In later years, through 1972, Kolax backed up such blues musicians as Otis Rush and Roosevelt Sykes on recordings.

9. Powell believes he was with Kolax from the summer of 1946, but it appears that Kolax was still with Eckstine through October 1946 and didn't start his own band until the end of that year. In general Powell's biography in the standard reference works seems to be a year early—instead of Kolax, Ernie Fields, and Lionel Hampton in 1946, 1947, and 1948 respectively, it should probably read one year later for each of these.

10. Miller now lives in Birmingham, Alabama. Kurt Mohr, a fine researcher, gave a personnel for this band in *Jazz Hot* 120 (April 1957), 14. But this was a speculative list that combined people from several years—for example he put Coltrane and Powell in the same band.

11. The recording was apparently never issued, if in fact it was intended for issue and not as a demonstration ("demo") disc. And a search of titles doesn't help, because this is so common a name that it is impossible to trace. BMI lists fourteen titles by that name; ASCAP, the other major music licensing organization, lists over a hundred. None of them are credited to Coltrane or Kolax!

12. Ira Gitler, *Swing to Bop*, (New York: Oxford University Press, 1985) 182. Coleman also says Coltrane decided that day to switch to tenor, but his account of this is clearly oversimplified.

13. See McCarthy, *Big Band Jazz*, 131–34.

14. Thomas says that first there were gigs with Mel Melvin's band featuring Coltrane, Bill Barron (probably the source of the report), and Jimmy Heath on saxophones; Percy Heath on bass; and Al Heath on drums (43). There are many reasons that I doubt this: He lists drummer Melvin as a trumpeter, Percy Heath wasn't playing professionally until at least 1947, and Al Heath was born in 1935. Finally, Jimmy Heath denies it. Since these

people all worked odd jobs with Melvin at various times, this is probably a conflation of many gigs.

15. Profile of Heath published in the column ". . . And Furthermore," by Violet Wilkins, *Philadelphia Tribune*, March 16, 1948.

16. He was later known as Rashid and died around 1994 in Los Angeles.

17. Bill Massey was profiled in *The Philadelphia Tribune*, November 5, 1960, 5, which states that he also plays piano and by that time was most active as an arranger for singers and shows. He was then leading the "Rock 'n' Blue orchestra that backs up [rock and pop] shows at the Uptown Theater." His wife, the former Jackie McLendon, had played drums professionally with Melba Pope; his daughter J'Neane was then seven months old.

18. *Jazz Hot*, January 1959, 11.

19. The photo is in Simpkins following 150, the booklet for *The Heavyweight Champion* (frontispiece), and Fujioka following 172.

20. This is apparently from the *Philadelphia Tribune*. All the microfilms that I found are missing the last half of 1948, so I have taken this from Simpkins (37), where he dates it only as from "the late 40s."

21. First quote from an interview with Ted Panken on WKCR, NY, July 16, 1987; the second from "Jimmy Heath" by Martin Richards, *Jazz Journal International*, May 1990, 7.

22. Golson, liner notes for *This One's for You, John*. Information on matinees from my newspaper research. There has been widespread complaint about the decline of such jams, which were a great learning experience. When I was a young player in the Bronx around 1972, there were many such sessions, but primarily in black neighborhoods, and I believe that they are still most common at local clubs in black neighborhoods and thus escape the notice of most critics and educators. However, it is probably true that there are fewer open jam sessions than there used to be.

23. Mary's comment in the booklet to *The Heavyweight Champion*, 34, seems to suggest that she was in favor of his drug use:

Mary: . . . When there were distractions, he still took care of business.
Joel Dorn: Distractions like what—drugs?
Mary: Yes, and that's when I knew he was going into something really big.

She was not sanctioning drugs. I was one of the interviewers; her meaning was that she knew he was going somewhere because he didn't let drugs hold him back and eventually managed to kick the habit.

24. The *Philadelphia Tribune* reported, "the all-out drive to rid the city of vicious dope peddlers and 'pushers,' and the hapless addicts, is being speeded up by police and Federal Narcotics agents" (anonymous front-page article, *Philadelphia Tribune*, January 25, 1955; continued on p. 3). Eighty-seven people had already been arrested, and over that weekend fifteen more "suspected traffickers were apprehended in their lairs and hauled before U.S. District Commissioner Hanry P. Carr and city magistrates." They included two musicians: James E. Heath, twenty-seven, of 1927 Federal Street near Twentieth, and Steve Davis, thirty-three, of Uber Street near Diamond. "Heath is one of the city's better known tenor and alto saxophone players and formerly was connected

with the Dizzy Gillespie band. Davis is a bass fiddler and has played with well-known local combinations." Heath was reported to have been "slated and held in bail." A very unhappy-looking photo of him is included. Davis was held for five thousand dollars bail, the highest amount given, which suggests that the charges against him were more serious. In 1960 he became Coltrane's bassist. Heath says he was busted on January 9. Ironically the *Tribune* of April 10, 1954, Frances E. Cauthorn's column "The Night Shift," had reported that "Those weedish habits from the narcotics beat has [*sic*] been beaten by smallish tenor sax blower, Percy Heath (currently working at Emerson's with organist Preston)." Obviously Jimmy is the person referred to, not the taller bassist Percy, and the article is congratulating him for having beaten the drug habit.

By the way, Simpkins 44 reports, via Cal Massey, that Coltrane did spend a night in jail in 1954 under the vague charge of "corner lounging"—basically loitering.

Chapter 7

1. All quotations from Jimmy Heath in this chapter, including the music examples, derive from an interview I conducted for the Smithsonian Institution Jazz Oral History Program on March 3 and 4, 1995. I thank Matt Watson and the Smithsonian for permission to use these excerpts.

2. For more on this, look up "transposition" in the index to Paul Berliner's massive and important study, *Thinking in Jazz: The Infinite Art of Improvisation* (Chicago: University of Chicago Press, 1994).

3. Jamey Aebersold Jazz, Inc. (New Albany, Ind.), series of play-along recordings with booklets, over 70 volumes to date.

4. Gillespie never recorded this arrangement commercially. It turned up on live recordings of the band from as early as January 1947, as on the LPs *Live at the Apollo,* various artists, Everybodys 3003; *Gillespie at the Downbeat Club,* Jazz Guild 1010.

5. Readers will be interested to know that Golson has compiled a large book about his experiences in jazz and his advice about writing, with numerous musical examples. As of this writing he is making plans for publication. He is also beginning work on his Second Symphony. His first was "really a concerto" called "Two Faces."

6. Forman is certain that a newspaper ad presented a photo of this group, but I haven't found it.

7. Coltrane appears to have purchased a clarinet—I assume his childhood clarinet had stayed in High Point, or in any case was not good enough to use professionally. Thomas says Coltrane would borrow Golson's tenor at one time (39). He puts this after the Vinson tour, which seems unlikely since Coltrane owned a tenor by then.

8. Squire Bryant column, "Thru the 'Spy' Glass," *Philadelphia Tribune*, June 19, 1948, p. 8.

9. Ramon Bruce column, "Ravin' with Ramon," *Philadelphia Afro-American*, June 19, 1948, 6. My book *Lester Young* (Boston: Twayne, 1985), is the fullest treatment of Young's music, with many notated examples. The book also includes a short biography and an extensive discography, both of which have been superseded by two books of Frank Büchmann-Møller, *You Just Fight For Your Life* (biography) and *You Got To Be Original, Man!* (discography and criticism), both Westport: Greenwood Press, 1990.

10. Oliver is still active in Philadelphia. The rumor that he is the nephew of legendary cornetist King Oliver, with whom Young once toured, is false, Heath says. The rumor derives from the fact that Oliver's brother, not a musician, was known as "King."

11. J. W. Woods, "Philly Sax Men Almost Blew Les Young Out of His Title," *Philadelphia Afro-American*, January 25, 1947, 11.

12. Brown's column, "These Foolish Things," 10.

13. Jimmie Brown's column, "These Foolish Things," part 3 of the Jimmy Oliver Story, *Philadelphia Tribune*, November 7, 1955, 5.

14. Ad for Jerome Ashford and his Quartette with Joe Jones at drums, Cafe Society, *Philadelphia Tribune*, June 15, 1946, 13; there are earlier ads as well.

15. Some discographers think both solos are from 1945. See the notes to the LP, *Hawk Variation* Contact ST 1004. I have heard it said that "Picasso" is based on "Body and Soul" or, according to Brian Priestley in his notes to the *Jazz Scene* (Verve 314 521 661–2), on "Prisoner of Love," but I am not convinced of either after numerous listenings. Other artists of that time, when invited to perform "free improvisation," generally came up with a blues or "Rhythm changes" (variations on the chords of Gershwin's "I Got Rhythm"). Perhaps we have been too quick to identify the Lennie Tristano recordings of 1949 as the first freely improvised jazz recordings—Hawkins was already there.

16. Byas said, in Art Taylor's *Notes and Tones* (self-published, 1977), 54, that Coltrane used to attend his performances, but that was in the 1960s.

17. Both quotations from Barbara Gardner, "Jazzman of the Year: John Coltrane," in *Music 1962, Down Beat Yearbook* (Chicago: Maher Publications, 1961), 66–69.

18. Leonard Feather, "Stan Getz: Before and After," *Jazz Times*, June 1990, 8.

19. With Carl-Erik Lindgren, issued on *Miles Davis and John Coltrane Live in Stockholm 1960* Dragon LP 90/91, misdated March 26.

20. For more on this, look up "sound" in the index to Berliner, *Thinking in Jazz.*

Chapter 8

1. This explanation is given in several places; for example, Larry Birnbaum, "Eddie 'Cleanhead' Vinson," *Down Beat*, October 1982, 29.

2. Franks, mentioned by the *Philadelphia Afro-American*, was apparently not a musician; he may have been someone who traveled with the band as a driver and valet. Thanks to Johnny Coles for this suggestion.

3. Vinson says so in Birnbaum, "Eddie 'Cleanhead' Vinson," and also in "Just Call Me Cleanhead," by Herb Nolan, *Down Beat*, May 8, 1975, 29. In the latter Vinson says he just happened to arrive at the union when Coltrane was playing. This is possible, but Vinson's memory was sometimes unreliable.

4. Anonymous, *Philadelphia Afro-American*, March 12, 1949.

5. Lowenfish, "When the 'Trane Stopped."

6. Squire Bryant, "Philadelphia Story," *Philadelphia Tribune*, July 9, 1949, says James Young is at the Cotton Club.

7. Thomas, probably from Jesse Powell, says Powell recommended Heath and Heath brought Coltrane to the audition (46), but that is incorrect.

8. Though the article is unsigned, Brower identifies himself as its author in Thomas (45). Brower moved to New York City and went to work for the postal service, later went back to Philadelphia, and has since passed away.

9. Pat Harris, *Down Beat,* January 13, 1950, 8–9.

10. Gillespie, *To Be or Not . . . to Bop: Memoirs* (Garden City, N.Y.: Doubleday, 1979), 356.

11. Jimmy Heath interview conducted by Howard Mandel on June 26, 1990, for *The World according to John Coltrane,* a film produced by Toby Byron. Courtesy Avalon Archives.

12. The sheet music lists Garner as composer and Gil Fuller as arranger; the recording adds a co-composer credit by Gillespie. The supposedly complete LP issue of Gillespie's RCA titles (French RCA PM 42408) accidentally omitted "Minor Walk" and instead had "Swedish Suite" twice.

13. Forman says Gillespie had used the name "Hen Gates" as a pseudonym when he played the piano introduction on the original Parker recording of "Billie's Bounce" in 1945. Forman learned that solo by memory. When Gillespie heard Forman play it, he dubbed him the new "Hen Gates."

14. Unsigned article, "Profile of a Vocalist: Billy Valentine Began Career as a Pianist," *Philadelpia Afro-American,* August 12, 1950, 9.

15. Gillespie, *To Be,* 357. He writes that they broke up at the Silhouette Club in Chicago, but I believe he was conflating this with the story that begins the next chapter. Nor does Thomas seem to be correct in stating that the band broke up on New Year's Day of 1950 (50).

Chapter 9

1. Coltrane dated this in 1949, Davis (on page 134 of his autobiography) says it was 1950, and Sonny Rollins agreed, saying there were actually "a few memorable gigs" in 1950 (Thomas, 73). Rollins later told Fujioka (19) it was 1952. Ken Vail came up with the 1951 ad, the only documented date.

2. Most of the titles with solos have been issued on two bootleg LPs, Oberon 5100 and Original Broadcasts 009. "Good Groove" is also released legitimately on *The Last Giant.*

3. Sometimes broadcasts are transferred to LP at wrong speeds; therefore, I am assuming that the key of E-flat minor, as heard on the LP, is an accident, since "A Night in Tunisia" has been recorded scores of times and always in D.

4. "'Trane on the Track," *Down Beat,* October 16, 1958, 16–17.

5. Unpublished Odean Pope interview with radio producer Steve Rowland, 1990. See also De Sayles Grey, "John Coltrane and the 'Avant-Garde' Movement in Jazz History," Ph.D. diss., University of Pittsburgh, 1985, 59–72.

6. *Philadelphia Afro-American,* unsigned press notice, November 24, 1945, 11.

7. The notes to the Rhino reissue list the piece as an ASCAP composition, which is incorrect. Hale Smith is a BMI artist. Smith, born in Cleveland in 1925, was playing jazz piano in nightclubs as early as age fourteen and has gone on to a distinguished career in classical composition. He was also a close associate of Eric Dolphy and got to know Coltrane in the 1960s.

8. The personnel for the Crosse recordings is still unknown, and that given in Fujioka is incorrect. Alvin Jackson told me he did not play bass (Fujioka, 18); Smith says the usual trumpeter was Edward Harris, and Oliver Jackson did not play drums. He does confirm that John Lathan was the regular bassist (Fujioka, 17).

9. See page 11 of Doug Ramsey's essay in *John Coltrane: The Prestige Recordings.*

10. Bostic had been hospitalized due to an auto accident in early December 1951 and resumed touring on April 1, 1952, with a new group, so this must be when Coltrane started with him.

11. I base this on several factors: Coltrane was in the band for recording sessions in April and August 1952 but not on the sessions of December 17 and after. Also, Bostic completed a tour in early December, and beginning December 19 he would go out again on tour, so this would be the place for Coltrane to leave. Confusing the issue, the *New York Amsterdam News* printed a photo of the band including Coltrane, and identifying him in the caption, on December 20, 1952 and again on January 30, 1954. Based on the above evidence, I must assume that Bostic's managers were using old publicity materials after Coltrane left the band.

12. Ira Gitler, "Trane on the Track," *Down Beat,* October 16, 1958, 16–17.

13. Frances E. Cauthorn, "Night Shift" column, *Philadelphia Tribune,* July 29, 1952, 12: "Elaine 'Coltrane' reports that her man, John is still holding over with the Earl Bostic group in San Francisco." She was inviting everybody over to attend a "mad party" given by friends in New York.

14. *The New Information Please Almanac* 1965 (New York: Simon and Schuster, 1964), 325.

15. "Jazz Fans Gather at Home of a Giant," by Daniel Rubin, *Philadelphia Inquirer,* June 14, 1992, Section A, 1.

16. *Philadelphia Tribune,* February 10, 1953.

17. Thomas, 56, presents a slightly different version of this story.

18. Especially in Postif.

19. Jimmie Brown column, "These Foolish Things," *Philadelphia Tribune,* May 16, 1953, 12.

20. In the published version of the Blume interview Coltrane says that he did this after Bostic, but on the tape there is absolutely no sequence indicated. Also, please note that the photo in Fujioka (24) which is identified as Coltrane with two friends from the Hep Cats in 1953 cannot possibly be from that year. Coltrane's appearance unmistakably dates the photo from around 1947.

21. Wilson toured nationally with the Chris Powell band from around 1950 through 1956 and was there throughout Clifford Brown's tenure with the group and on Brown's first recordings.

22. A Philadelphia paper of April 11, 1953, describes Golson as "formerly with Bull Moose Jackson."

23. "Woody" McBride column, "Wandering with Woody," *Philadelphia Tribune,* April 20, 1954, 13.

24. The personnel listed in Fujioka 24 is from Mohr's article in *Jazz Hot,* January 1959, probably based on a Golson interview. Hodges had enlarged his band for a similar tour in August and September 1951, without Coltrane.

25. *This One's for You, John.*

26. The back of the LP Norgran MGN-1009 contained the only known photos of the band with Coltrane.

27. Thanks to saxophonist Arun Luthra for this observation.

28. Jack Cooke, "Chasin' the Trane," *Wire*, April 1991, 32.

29. Coltrane said he'd known Dolphy since about 1954, but I don't know if it's true that he was stranded and needed money. Johnny Coles told Simpkins that he and Coltrane were both in Bostic's band and were stranded in Los Angeles in 1952, but since Coles was with Bostic in 1955 and 1956 this appears unlikely. See Simpkins's letter to the editor in *Coda*, October 1976, 10.

30. Jimmy Brown column, "These Foolish Things," *Philadelphia Tribune*, September 18, 1954, 9.

31. Panel discussion about Philadelphia jazz on Terry Gross's program "Fresh Air," at that time on WUHY-FM, broadcast June 6, 1979.

32. Gillespie, *To Be*, 291.

33. This information is confirmed by the marriage license. Jamal Dennis couldn't remember the town's name. Simpkins repeats Naima's claim that she was over a year younger than Coltrane (46), when in fact she was nine months older. Thomas says she was born in Philadelphia (68), and he calls her the sister of Earl Grubbs, when she is his cousin. Davis also calls her Naima Grubbs (196); she may in fact have used that name at one time. But Saeeda told me that Grubbs was Naima's mother's maiden name, and that name was passed on through her mother's brother to Naima's cousins, musicians Earl and Carl Grubbs. Carl has a daughter named Naima Grubbs, which may have added to the confusion.

34. The name "Toni's Dance," after Antonia, is found as a rejected title for "Slow-trane" in some older discographies.

35. Marriage license 54587, Docket 1955, Folio 100, Circuit Court for Baltimore City. Franklin filed a certificate on October 5, confirming that he did indeed wed the couple on October 3. See also Davis with Troupe, *Miles*, 196.

Chapter 10

1. Chambers I, 214, claims that during this time Coltrane was dismayed to read a "newspaper article" reporting that Rollins would be with the group. The only such report I know is in "Miles" by Nat Hentoff (*Down Beat*, November 2, 1955: 13), which was written earlier but only came out when Coltrane was already with the band. In any case Coltrane knew Rollins was unavailable; that's why Davis was looking for a tenor!

2. Kirby Kean, "The Pope Gets Serious," *Down Beat*, June 1996, 39.

3. This comes from Ken Vails generally reliable *Miles' Diary* (see Bibliography). Contrary to Chambers (*Milestones*, 1:215), the twenty-eighth was not a Monday, the gig did not begin at 9:00 A.M., and the club was not the Anchors Inn.

4. All the Davis quotes are from Davis with Troupe, *Miles*, 195–97.

5. Nat Hentoff, in *Down Beat* of May 16, 1956.

6. Edgar Jackson, *Melody Maker*, June 7, 1958, 14.

7. *Melody Maker*, December 6, 1958, 13.

8. Chambers (253–54) says this was during the next Jazz City engagement, in 1957, but by then people surely would have known that Coltrane was in the band, and one of the Prestige albums was already released.

9. Davis with Troupe, *Miles,* 195.

10. "John Coltrane, Un Faust Moderne," by Jean-Claude Dargenpierre, *Jazz Magazine* 78 (January 1962), 24.

11. Gardner, "Jazzman of the Year," 67.

12. "John Coltrane Talks to *Jazz News,*" unsigned article by Kitty Grime, assistant editor of this London publication, December 27, 1961, 13.

13. Davis fans got the joke when Davis said nearly this same thing on a Honda motorcycle ad aired on television in 1986.

14. I have heard CD reissues of Dean Martin and of Elvis Presley from this same period that include studio chatter, but I don't know if the originals included that.

15. A more detailed history of this arrangement appears in Barry Kernfeld, *What to Listen for in Jazz* (New Haven: Yale University Press, 1995), 81–85.

16. This title is often referred to as "Woodyin' You" or even "Wouldn't You." These are totally incorrect—Gillespie always made it perfectly clear that this piece was written for Woody Herman's band, thus "Woody and You" or "Woody 'n You" for short.

17. The last-named title, an Ellington item, is often listed incorrectly as "Squeeze Me," which is an unrelated Fats Waller–Clarence Williams song. Incidentally, Jamal's trio with guitar had also recorded "Poinciana" in 1955, nearly three years before the much better known version with drums.

18. Tomlinson, "Cultural Dialogics and Jazz: A White Musicologist Signifies," *Black Music Research Journal* vol. 11, no. 2 (Fall 1991): 229–64.

19. Bret Primack, "John Coltrane: A 65th Birthday Salute from his Friends, Peers and Disciples," *Jazz Times,* October 1991, 16, 18. McLean says he was with Mingus, but I know of no engagement pairing Mingus and Davis, whereas the April 1957 gig is the right time period. McLean was certainly with Blakey at the time, as he recorded with the Messengers on April 8.

20. Thomas reports that Monk told Coltrane not to put up with that and to come work with him (85). *Miles* (207) gives the same story, but dates it as October 1956. Unfortunately, this book must be used with caution; in compiling it Troupe combined his interviews of Davis with material from other publications—uncredited—so it is hard to tell whether Davis actually told this to Troupe or whether Troupe took it from Thomas. But the wording is different enough to suggest that Davis did say it. (The Miles autobiography is most useful where it presents unique information that is clearly from Troupe's own interviews.) Orrin Keepnews, Monk's producer, does not believe any of this happened. In any case, the date of October 1956 makes less sense since Monk was barred from working at nightclubs in New York during that period and had no work to offer Coltrane.

21. Davis with Troupe, *Miles,* 209.

22. For more details about these events, read Chambers, *Milestones I: The Music and Times of Miles Davis to 1960* (Toronto: University of Toronto Press, 1983), particularly 249–57.

23. Rollins had been with the Max Roach quintet (with Kenny Dorham replacing the late Clifford Brown) at least through April 20, 1957, when they performed at Town Hall in Manhattan. *Down Beat* also announced on May 30 that trombonist Curtis Fuller left Yusef Lateef's group to join Davis, so it's possible that Fuller filled in until June 17, when Rollins arrived.

24. McCoy Tyner in Len Lyons, *The Great Jazz Pianists* (New York: William Morrow, 1983), 238, from an interview conducted August 16, 1977.

25. Bret Primack, "The Real McCoy," *Jazz Times,* January–February 1996, 30–32. Tyner says it was 1955 and he was seventeen, but from other details of his story it sounds to me that this was 1957. However, from other Tyner interviews it seems he met Coltrane in 1955, also with Massey, as noted before.

26. Davis with Troupe, *Miles,* 223.

27. Simpkins credits bassist Reggie Workman with convincing Coltrane to quit (57), but Workman did not confirm this to me. John Gilmore, in *Down Beat* (December 20, 1973, 38) credited Sun Ra. It seems clear that Coltrane himself had made the resolve—a resolve that, after all, only he could make.

28. Gardner, "Jazzman of the Year," 67.

29. Liner notes to *A Love Supreme.*

30. Published in Gleason's notes to Prestige 24014 in 1972. Toby and Jean Gleason, son and widow of Ralph, were kind enough to provide me with a tape of the interview from May 2, 1961 that provided material for that LP, for the notes to *Olé,* and for Gleason's column in the *San Francisco Chronicle,* July 15, 1961. This quotation is not on the tape, so the Prestige notes appear to be drawn partly from another one, probably later since Gleason mentions Coltrane's 1963 TV taping.

31. Gitler, "'Trane on the Track." Ellipses in the original.

32. Gene Lees, in "Consider Coltrane," *Jazz,* 7, writes that at the November 1962 recording session for the *Ballads* album, Coltrane's saxophone case was full of cigars.

33. This was wrong in my notes to the Monk/Trane CD.

34. Cooke, "Chasin' the Trane," 32.

35. This doesn't negate Copeland's observation that Coltrane was nodding off—but he may have simply been exhausted. I believe he'd already quit heroin by this time.

36. The dates and personnel were unearthed by researcher and writer Peter Keepnews, who is working on a biography of Monk, from the files of Joe Termini, former co-owner of the Five Spot. *Down Beat* (July 25, 1957) announced that Monk's "trio" would begin on the nineteenth; Keepnews is more reliable.

37. Ware's defense is that he rushed from the *Mulligan Meets Monk* recording date that afternoon to the Five Spot, put his bass on the bandstand, and told Coltrane, who was already there, "I'm going to go around the corner to get a sandwich; I'll be right back." He got a tuna sandwich and felt so sick that he took a cab home and called another bassist to fill in. He claimed Joe Termini encouraged Monk to fire him for being unreliable (National Endowment for the Arts Jazz Oral History Project, conducted by the Smithsonian Institution, housed at the Institute of Jazz Studies, Ware transcript, December 18, 1977, p. 79). Ware did not work again with Monk until 1969 and 1970.

38. The preceding is based on Keepnews' research, with his kind permission.

39. Ira Gitler, "The Remarkable J. J. Johnson," *Down Beat,* May 11, 1961, 19.

40. Johnson is certain that Shadow Wilson was not on the drums the night he attended. It could have been the week Philly Joe played, or some one-night replacement.

41. Postif and Guy Kopelovicz, "Coltrane en Tete du Peloton des Ténors," *Jazz Magazine* 40 (August–September 1958): 32–33. This article also presents a French translation of a career summary that Coltrane had sent to Postif, which makes for an interesting

comparison with the one Coltrane sent to Leonard Feather. Postif no longer has Coltrane's original letter.

42. LeRoi Jones, "The Acceptance of Monk," *Down Beat,* February 27, 1964, 21.

43. These were not issued until 1961. Naima taped some nights at the club, but those tapes appear to be lost. A live recording that has been issued appears to be from 1958 and will be discussed later.

44. Gitler first used the term in his notes on the back of the *Soultrane* album (Prestige LP 7142) recorded February 7, 1958, and released later that year.

Chapter 11

1. *Down Beat,* December 12, 1956.

2. Blume; this part was garbled in the published version of the interview.

3. I can't quite place its origin. Thanks to Phil Schaap for trying, and to Carl Woideck for offering that it may not be any particular Parker tune and that it is suggestive of Ornette Coleman's first records a few years later.

4. This excludes a radio broadcast with Davis on December 8, 1956. Contrary to Nisenson (40), this gap in Coltrane's studio activity does not indicate that he was "depressed." Recording opportunities came and went and were unpredictable at this stage in Coltrane's career. Besides, he was still with Davis and had not been fired, as Nisenson assumes.

5. Postif, 13. Simpkins also credits this to Coltrane (62)—I don't know his source.

6. Quoted by Hentoff, liner notes to *Giant Steps.*

7. Gardner, "Jazzman of the Year," 67.

8. Woideck points out that the Pilgrim Travellers, a gospel group, recorded a song by the same name in 1955. It appears to be unrelated musically, but the title may have stuck in John's mind. By the way, vocalist Lenore Von Stein has recorded her own lyrics to Coltrane's "Straight Street" on her CD *Love Is Dead.*

9. Interview with Michel de Ruyter, London, November 11, 1961. Transcribed from the original tape.

10. John S. Glenn (born June 8, 1930) told me he had picked it up from Curtis Porter (also known as Shafi Hadi), a tenor saxophonist from Detroit who recorded with Charles Mingus in 1957. Porter came to Philadelphia in 1955 or 1956 and taught the technique to Glenn. Glenn had started on the saxophone around 1948; he specializes in baritone sax and tenor and has worked as a saxophone repairman, too.

11. Paul Berliner discusses this process extensively in *Thinking in Jazz;* see, for example, chap. 4.

12. Harris confirmed that he met with Coltrane; see Reppard Stone, "The Peregrination of Slonimsky's *Thesaurus of Scales and Melodic Patterns,*" in *Jazz Research Papers 1989* (Manhattan, Kans.: National Association of Jazz Educators Publications, 1989), 240. Harris has since taught hundreds of musicians and published a videotape and book set of his insights. See also references to Harris in the index to Berliner, *Thinking in Jazz.* Thanks to Steve Bloom for explaining Harris's approach to me.

13. See Gunther Schuller, "Sonny Rollins and the Challenge of Thematic Improvisation," *Jazz Review,* November 1958, 6–11, reprinted most recently in Schuller's book,

Musings: The Musical Worlds of Gunther Schuller (New York: Oxford University Press, 1986), 86–97. Lawrence Gushee, responding to Schuller, pointed out that Schuller was wrong to analyze Rollins's entire solo as a variation of one idea; it makes more sense to hear Rollins as returning to a unifying idea. To me, "Blue Seven" is far from being one of Rollins's most exciting solos, and Rollins himself reportedly was fed up with all this analysis of his music—but Schuller's piece is still worth reading.

14. David Baker catalogs ii–V–I formulas of Coltrane in *The Jazz Style of John Coltrane*, 69–81, and Don Sickler discusses this practice and indicates examples on each transcription in *The Artistry of John Coltrane* (see especially 8–11).

15. Gitler, "'Trane on the Track." Few people are aware that James Moody (born in 1925) was even more daring than Coltrane at this time. On his 1955 "Jammin' with James" (Prestige OJCCD-1780-2) his solo sometimes goes right into a different key than the rhythm section! Coltrane only did that much later on. As with so many other things, Parker had paved the way. For example, on "Lester Leaps In" and "The Rocker" (second version), live at the Rockland Palace on September 26, 1952, he plays a phrase and then transposes it up a third (major on the first, minor on the second) while the rhythm section stays in key. (See also Woideck, *Charlie Parker*, 189 and 198.) Another experimenter, one who was better known for this kind of bitonality, is altoist Lee Konitz (born in 1927).

16. Gardner, 68.

17. See Krin Gabbard, "The Quoter and His Culture," in *Music in Mind*, ed. Steven Wieland (Detroit: Wayne State University Press, 1991). Thomas Owens says Coltrane also liked to quote "All This and Heaven Too." See his *Bebop: The Music and Its Players* (New York: Oxford University Press, 1995), 89. A general discussion of Coltrane's style and favorite licks appears on 88–98.

18. I think the word "serious" is more appropriate than the common stereotype that minor is "sad."

19. Leonard Feather, "Honest John—the Blindfold Test," *Down Beat*, February 19, 1959, 39; *Melody Maker*, August 14, 1965.

20. Booklet to *The Heavyweight Champion*, 52.

21. John Glenn, panel discussion, John Coltrane Cultural Society, May 19, 1992. Thanks to Tim Blangger for the tape.

22. Valerie Wilmer, "Conversation with Coltrane," *Jazz Journal*, January 1962. Woideck suggests to me that Postif may have inadvertently omitted a word: Perhaps Coltrane said ". . . extremely hard reeds with a number nine mouthpiece." That would be a very open mouthpiece requiring a lot of air—a number four mouthpiece would require less effort.

23. The Mark VI is distinguished from the older models by an "S" on the octave key (at the top of the instrument) and by connected (as opposed to separate) covers for the lowest keys at the bottom. In the booklet to the *Heavyweight Champion*, the photo on p. 25 is clearly not from 1962, as suggested, but from about 1959—the saxophone tells us this, as well as Coltrane's suit and face.

24. Interview with Howard Mandel conducted June 26, 1990, for the video, *The World according to John Coltrane*. Courtesy Avalon Archives.

25. Currently available on CD as Verve 815.150-1.

26. See Carl Woideck's essay in *John Coltrane: The Prestige Recordings,* 26, and Cuscuna's note to *The Ultimate Blue Train.*

27. Gillespie recorded another version in December 1957, and Coltrane's former idol Sonny Stitt used some pentatonic patterns in his solo.

Chapter 12

1. Most sources say December 1957, and Ruhlmann, "Going to Extremes," 32, says Coltrane rejoined on Christmas Eve at the Sutherland Hotel in Chicago through New Year's Eve. This would be from Tuesday, December 24, 1957, through the following Tuesday, December 31. But the research of Peter Keepnews places Coltrane at the Five Spot though January 1. So I would assume the Sutherland gig was with Adderley only, although it is possible that even though Coltrane was hired to play at the Five Spot, he left in order to play with Davis. Coltrane himself wrote to François Postif that he rejoined Davis in November 1957, which is surely too early. See Postif and Guy Kopelovicz, "Coltrane en Tete du Peloton des Ténors," *Jazz Magazine* 40 (August–September 1958), 32–33.

2. March 11, 1958, 12, by Nat Middleton Jr.; primarily about Louis Jordan's new band members from Philadelphia.

3. The matching of scales to chords was espoused by Lennie Tristano and George Russell during the early 1950s. Before that time, players were already doing that by ear, as we've seen.

4. "Coltrane Par Coltrane," *Jazz Hot* 265 (October 1970), 9. No editor is listed for this compilation from European interviews but the source is suggested to be an interview by Björn Fremer probably done on March 22, 1960, and published in Swedish. This is my translation of the French version of the Swedish publication.

5. "Trane on the Track."

6. A full set of this material was issued in 1992. (Coltrane's words suggest several sets, but this is all that has turned up to date.) The tape was undated, and in my notes to the CD, I assumed it was from the 1957 Five Spot engagement. But after it was released, Peter Keepnews found an entry in the Five Spot records indicating that Coltrane played there with Monk on September 11, 1958, instead of the usual tenorist at that time, Johnny Griffin. In two unpublished interviews, one with François Postif and one with Fujioka, Griffin has maintained that this couldn't have happened since he only missed one day—a Tuesday (September 11 was a Thursday)—in all the time he was with Monk. But I would tend to trust the written records of the club from that time over anyone's memory thirty-seven years later. Besides, Griffin seems to have taken this personally, thinking that he was being blamed for not showing up. It could have been a planned event, which would explain why Coltrane was prepared to tape it. This also explains why drummer Roy Haynes ended up on the recording; it was difficult to justify Haynes's presence in 1957 when he was with busy touring with Sarah Vaughan and was not known to have played with the Monk quartet. In 1958 he was Monk's regular drummer.

Another point: Ahmed Abdul-Malik told me he considered using Coltrane for an album but used Johnny Griffin instead. His one album with Griffin, *Jazz Sahara* (Riverside label) dates from October 1958. So it could be that he had thought of Coltrane after playing with him again in September, but that Coltrane was too busy touring with Davis to commit. So, while this date is not by any means proven, it makes sense to me as the best guess we have. I sent this information in time for it to be included in the complete Monk on Blue Note boxed set.

7. Unpublished interview with radio producer Steve Rowland, 1990. Used by permission.

8. Interview with Howard Mandel, June 26, 1990. Courtesy Avalon Archives.

9. Wilmer, "Conversation with Coltrane."

10. Gardner, 68, cites these but doesn't provide the sources.

11. *Down Beat,* August 7, 1958, 16.

12. "Trane on the Track," *Down Beat,* October 16, 1958.

13. She and Greenlee were together seven years, living at several addresses. She was still known as Mary Greenlee in 1967 but was living alone by then.

14. In the 1960s, Coltrane was booked by Milt Shaw's corporation.

15. The contract details are based on Nisenson, 79, Ruhlmann, "Going to Extremes," and my talk with Orrin Keepnews, who had hoped to sign Coltrane for Riverside Records.

16. Shorter interview for Rowland and elsewhere; also Chambers book.

17. Panel discussion at University of Virginia, February 21, 1993; thanks to producer Reggie Marshall for the tape. Valerie Wilmer notes that Coltrane was not quite so serious as his photographs suggest; he was reluctant to smile because he was self-conscious about the poor condition of his teeth; see *As Serious As Your Life* (London: Quartet Books, 1977), 44. A photo inside the *Ascension* album (Impulse A-95) gives a hint of his dental condition.

18. Heath had gotten out of prison—remember, he'd been arrested in January 1955 for heroin possession—in May 1959. He was soon back on the scene. In fact, during the same time that the Davis band was at the Blackhawk, Heath was performing starting Monday, June 15, in "The new, exciting Kenny Dorham, Jimmy Heath Quintette" (so announced an ad in the *Philadelphia Tribune*) at the Diamond Horseshoe Bar (Sixth and Germantown Avenue) in Philadelphia, with matinees Mondays and Saturdays.

19. Quincy Troupe interview of Heath for Steve Rowland. Used by permission.

20. The Heath episode in Chambers, 312, is wrong.

21. University of Virginia tape, February 21, 1993.

22. March 15, 1960, 5 (Sue O'Hara National Grapevine column).

23. On January 21, *Down Beat* had announced that Davis had turned down a proposed European tour, probably because he was having so much trouble getting the right personnel. My thanks to Fujioka for the program booklet and to Vince Pelote for the Montgomery story.

24. Charles Estienne in the *France-Observateur* (date not given), reprinted, along with several other reviews from 1960, in the booklet to the CD release of the concert, *Miles Davis En Concert Avec Europe 1* (4 CD set, Trema 710455), issued in 1994.

25. Ian Carr reports a rumor that Davis angrily cut short one of their German concerts when the audience booed Coltrane. Carr is a fine musician, but his book *Miles Davis: A Biography* (New York: William Morrow, 1982, 120) has many errors, and I

haven't been able to confirm this. On the same page, Carr says that Coltrane refused an invitation to jam with Stan Getz for European television—if so, what a shame!

26. Issue 154, 28–29. The above title is from the table of contents; the article itself is headed "Controversy around Coltrane." Please remember, as stated in the preface, that all translations from French are my own, and that I choose to be literal even when it reads a bit stiffly.

27. Notes by trumpeter Kenny Dorham to Henderson's LP *Page One* (Blue Note BST–84140).

28. Gleason, *Celebrating the Duke* (New York: Dell Publishing, 1975), 139.

Chapter 13

1. Priestley, letter to the author, September 14, 1995.

2. Conversation with the author, 1996.

3. See Walt Weiskopf and Ramon Ricker, *Coltrane: A Player's Guide to His Harmony* (New Albany, Ind.: Jamey Aebersold, 1991), 11–12. This forty-eight-page book has many useful suggestions and etudes for performers.

4. When Leonard Feather gave Coltrane a "blindfold test" ("Honest John," *Down Beat*, February 19, 1959, p. 39), he played for John the 1956 recording of "Miss Jones" by Tatum and saxophonist Ben Webster. From Coltrane's reaction it's clear that he knew the song—". . . it's a good tune"—but not the recording. Woideck also wrote to me about another popular song that uses thirds, but one that Coltrane is less likely to have known: "Are you aware of the similarities between the verse [introduction] of Jerome Kern's 'Till the Clouds Roll By' and the first part of 'Giant Steps?' Beginning at measure 12 of the verse, the progression is: E-flat, F-sharp⁷–B, D⁷–G, B-flat⁷–E-flat⁷ and then Fm–B-flat⁷ to lead into the chorus (E-flat)." Will Friedwald also heard third relations in a 1940 song entitled "Fifth Avenue."

5. I gleaned this from the summary abstract of Richard Cohn's paper, "Weitzmann's Regions and Cycles: An Early Group-Theoretic Approach to Triadic Progressions," given at the national conference of the American Musicological Society, Baltimore, November 10, 1996.

6. Conversation with the author, 1996.

7. Demsey, "Chromatic Third Relations in the Music of John Coltrane," *Annual Review of Jazz Studies* 5 (1991): 153–54.

8. This is no relation to the blues "Countdown" (or "Count Down") by Wilbur Harden that Coltrane recorded with him in March 1958. That was not released until 1976, so Coltrane need not have worried about any confusion over the title.

9. Thanks to Woideck for helping me to clarify this discussion.

10. Taylor recorded about fifteen minutes of the rehearsal, but the tape has never been located. Thanks to Phil Schaap for this lead.

11. Baker presented this idea at the symposium, "Coltrane in Carolina," University of North Carolina, Chapel Hill, February 28, 1997.

12. Andy LaVerne, "Twelve Steps to Giant Steps," *Keyboard*, November 1996, 56–75.

13. See David Demsey, "Chromatic Third Relations," and his *John Coltrane Plays Giant Steps* (Milwaukee: Hal Leonard, 1996) for further discussion of possible origins. Demsey published a short summary of his article in *Down Beat*, July 1995, 63. Barry

Harris is rumored to have introduced Coltrane to the Slonimsky book, but he denies this. See Reppard Stone, "The Peregrination . . . ," 240.

14. Lateef, *Repository of Scales and Melodic Patterns* (Amherst, Mass.: Fana Publishing, 1981), unnumbered frontispieces (credited in Acknowledgments). These appear to be the same drawing in two different stages. The keys of the circle of fifths are boxed; next to each one is circled the key up and down a half step from it, and missing notes are filled in. So the keys C and F are indicated this way: (B)–C–(C-sharp) (D–E-flat) (E)–F–(F-sharp). Then Coltrane has indicated that five complete twelve-note scales are formed as one goes around the circle.

15. Marcello Piras, "I Passi da Gigante," *Musica Jazz* 13, no. 6 (June 1987): 31–34.

16. Wayne Shorter, taped interview, June 26, 1990, by Howard Mandel for *The World According to John Coltrane*. Courtesy Avalon Archives.

17. Mentioned in Mark Levine, *The Jazz Piano Book* (Petaluma, Calif.: Sher Music, 1989), 244.

18. Thanks to Carl Woideck for reminding me to include this.

19. Jerry Coker et al., *Patterns for Jazz* (Lebanon, Ind.: Studio P/R, 1970), and Ramon Ricker, *Pentatonic Scales for Jazz Improvisation* (Lebanon, Ind.: Studio P/R, 1975).

20. For the whole solo, see Demsey. Both master takes are also in Coans.

21. This was dated as April 1 on its first issue, but research in the Atlantic files for *The Heavyweight Champion* uncovered the new date.

22. Joel Dorn located two additional takes from this session for release in 1995.

23. Interview with Robert Palmer, August 13, 1990. Courtesy Avalon Archives.

24. *Jazz Hot* (December 1963), 10–11. As stated in the preface, I have done literal translations so as not to be interpretive.

25. The only Coltrane-led session without Chambers was on August 16, 1957, with Earl May on bass. At that time Coltrane was with Monk and Chambers may have been busy with Davis.

26. Recorded interview in Stockholm, March 22, 1960, released on Dragon Records.

27. This varies from one version to another; sometimes the turnaround is only played at the end of the B section.

28. See, for example, Harold S. Powers, "Three Pragmatists in Search of a Theory," *Current Musicology* 53 (1993), esp. 13–15.

29. Barry Kernfeld, "Adderley, Coltrane, and Davis at the Twilight of Bebop: The Search for Melodic Coherence (1958–59)," Ph.D. diss., Cornell University, 1981, 128–74.

30. Nat Hentoff, "An Afternoon with Miles Davis," *Jazz Review*, December 1958.

31. There has been so much inane criticism of West Coast jazz that people seem to have forgotten how much interesting writing was going on there. True, there was not as much hard blowing, and of course the West Coast sound eventually became commercial, resulting in so many "cute" versions of Broadways show tunes. But one misses some fascinating music if one neglects to look at the whole picture.

32. In Davis with Troupe, *Miles*, 223, and in a 1986 interview with Ben Sidran transcribed in *Talking Jazz: An Illustrated Oral History* (San Francisco: Pomegranate Artbooks, 1992), 4, Davis said that he had given these ideas to Coltrane, telling him, for example, that he could move up in thirds. He told Sidran: "I would give him five chords to play in one chord, and I would tell him he could play either way."

33. The album is said by Chambers (*Milestones,* 1:305) to have been produced by composer and saxophonist Teo Macero—who was important in many of Davis's later albums—but it seems that Macero was just starting to produce at Columbia. He may have been present, but on the tapes of the recording session Davis can clearly be heard addressing producer Irving Townsend.

34. The reader may have noticed that Davis reportedly had a pattern of claiming other people's tunes as his own, such as Vinson's "Tune-Up" and "Four," as well as Jimmy Heath's "Serpent's Tooth" and guitarist Chuck Wayne's "Solar." But in Davis with Troupe, *Miles,* 234, he denied that Bill Evans was a "co-composer" of the album. It seems clear that Bill and Gil had the input I've mentioned; that still leaves the lion's share of credit for Davis. See the late Conrad Silvert's notes to Milestone M-47034 (LP), where Bill Evans says that at most Davis suggested two chords for "Blue in Green." Davis told Nat Hentoff in *Jazz Review* (December 1958) that he wanted to write a ballad for Coltrane using two chords, and this may have been the kernel of "Blue in Green." On Evans's own recording of it in December 1959 he received coauthor credit with Davis. On the session tapes for *Kind of Blue,* Davis suggests that Evans play his four-bar introduction twice, and he may have had other input as well. It is said that Davis improvised the melody, but he plays it basically the same on several incomplete takes, suggesting he is reading. As for the Gil Evans preface to "So What," I know it's written because Bill and Paul Chambers can be heard reading through it several times on the tapes.

35. Concerning another piece from this album, the reader will be interested to know that "Freddie the Freeloader" was a real person in Philadelphia. The *Philadelphia Tribune,* August 2, 1960, 5 (Art Peters, "Off the Mainstem"), reported that "'Freddy the Freeloader,' the popular barkeep formerly employed at Tubby Norrington's Nitelife Cafe, has quit his job following a dispute with the boss. He is now employed at Yancey's bar on South St., near Broad."

36. "An Afternoon with Miles Davis."

37. At the end of the master tape of "So What," someone—I think Chambers—jokingly sings the phrase "With A Song in My Heart" as the bass plays the last note. Of course the issued cut fades out before this.

38. See Simpkins, 89. On the original LP the titles of "All Blues" and "Flamenco Sketches" were interchanged in the list of pieces and in the notes by Bill Evans. (I think they were correct on the LP label.) This led to confusion in Chambers (1:308) and in some editions of Mark Gridley's *Jazz Styles.*

39. Berliner's *Thinking in Jazz* is the most detailed examination of how this process is mastered.

40. Valerie Wilmer, "Conversation with Coltrane," *Jazz Journal,* January 1962, 2. On the back of the album *Olé* he says he was "advised," but doesn't name Davis.

41. Interview with Michel de Ruyter, November 11, 1961, England, transcribed from the tape.

42. In pianist Zita Carno's notebook of Coltrane's music, there were two versions of "Fifth House." One is quite similar to the one in his workbook; the other, under the title "You Tell Me," has a few extra passing chords thrown in, and has a much simpler melody, a little two-note riff repeated at different levels. Thanks to David Demsey for reminding me about this.

Chapter 14

1. Ian Carr, apparently from drummer Jimmy Cobb, says that the last gig with Davis was in Philadelphia after they returned (*Miles Davis,* 120). Perhaps Cobb was remembering one of the gigs from just before the European tour.

2. An ad appeared in the *Village Voice* on May 4, and Termini's files don't show the exact date of the opening, but *Down Beat* listings show that acts usually opened on Tuesdays at that club, and Ken Vail agrees.

3. Notes by trumpeter Kenny Dorham to Joe Henderson's LP *Page One* (Blue Note BST–84140).

4. On September 20, 1947 the *Philadelphia Afro-American* printed an ad for Tenor Sax Man Joe Sewell appearing at the Cafe Holiday with his "Quartette" that included Chas. (Dolo?) Coker on piano, Bill Green on drums, and Steve Davis on bass. Trumpeter Calvin Todd was added on weekends.

5. June 9, 1960, 10. *Down Beat* was often about two months behind events due to its publication schedule.

6. Quotes are from Kuhn's interview with Frances Moore and Jason Varano on April 27, 1995, unless otherwise noted.

7. Thomas writes that Coltrane auditioned several pianists, not just Kuhn, and that Kuhn knew Coltrane's music best (116). Kuhn believes Coltrane did not audition others.

8. Don Nelsen, "Trane Stops in the Gallery," *New York Daily News,* Sunday paper, May 15, 1960; "Jazz Gallery, N.Y.," review signed by "Bill," *Variety,* May 25, 1960, 66. Neither Kuhn, LaRoca, or Termini recall the incident from Simpkins 110, about a man wearing only a loin-cloth, who ran up to the side of the stage shouting "Coltrane!"

9. Carno inadvertently left her notebook in the garage of her house when she moved some years ago. It was acquired by unknown persons who recopied and published some of its contents in *Compositions of John Coltrane and Wayne Shorter* (no author, publisher, or date), thus preserving the pieces just discussed. With the help of my readers, I hope to locate the notebook and return it to Carno.

10. Michael Ullman, "Jazz Profile: Steve Kuhn," *New Boston Review* (July–August 1981), 8.

11. Kuhn interview cited above from April 1995.

12. Both items from Fred Norsworthy's New York column, *Coda,* June 1960, 20.

13. Notes by trumpeter Kenny Dorham to Joe Henderson's LP *Page One* (Blue Note BST–84140).

14. Lyons, *The Great Jazz Pianists,* 238.

15. Dargenpierre, 25.

16. Lyons, *The Great Jazz Pianists,* 238.

17. Postif, *Les Grandes Interviews de Jazz Hot* (Paris: Editions de L'Instant, 1989), 133–34. Originally in *Jazz Hot.*

18. The photographs of Coltrane with Higgins and Steve Davis (Tyner not visible) in the booklet to *The Last Giant,* 40 and 43, are from September 1960, not from 1962 as listed.

19. LaRoca began law school in the late 1960s and practices entertainment law and several other areas. He still performs—brilliantly—around New York.

20. Postif, "Dossier John Coltrane," in *Nota Note* (Toulouse, France), 3 (April 1996), 15.

21. Quoted in Nat Hentoff's liner notes to *Coltrane "Live" at the Village Vanguard.*

22. Both quotes from Gardner, "Jazzman of the Year."

23. Anonymous, "Finally Made," *Newsweek*, July 24, 1961, 64. Coltrane says 1959, but as usual his dates are off. The article identifies the friend as someone who "left the music business to become a newspaperman." Bayen is named in Leonard Feather, "Coltrane Shaping Musical Revolt," *New York Post*, October 18, 1964, 54.

24. Goldstein e-mail to the author, January 17, 1997. Goldstein says Philly Joe Jones had recently recorded his Dracula imitation; since that was cut on September 17, 1958, and would have been released a few months later, this early 1959 date fits.

25. Davis with Troupe, *Miles*, 223–24.

26. Mike Hennessey, "Coltrane: Dropping the Ball and Chain from Jazz," *Melody Maker*, August 14, 1965, 6.

27. Anonymous, "Steve Lacy: The Man Who Explained it to Coltrane," *Melody Maker*, July 24, 1965, 6.

28. As Brian Priestley pointed out in his letter to me of September 14, 1995.

29. In "Coltrane and Dolphy Answer."

30. Thanks to Ed Hazell for this perceptive observation.

31. Lyons, *The Great Jazz Pianists*, 246.

32. Priestley notes (41) that the opening of Coltrane's solo on the title piece presages Chick Corea's "La Fiesta." Tyner says Davis may have sat in on October 8, 1963.

33. Gardner, "Jazzman of the Year."

34. Dargenpierre, 25.

35. Gleason interview from May 2, 1961, by permission of Jean and Toby Gleason.

36. I corrected Postif's dates—he wrote 1959 for the Davis tour, and "two years later."

37. "Coltrane and Dolphy Answer."

38. Gardner, "Jazzman of the Year."

39. John Tynan, "Take 5" column, *Down Beat*, November 23, 1961, 40.

40. Frank Kofsky, "John Coltrane: An Interview," *Jazz and Pop*, September 1967, 23–31. Reprinted in *Black Nationalism and the Revolution in Music* (New York: Pathfinder Press, 1970), 242.

41. "Coltrane and Dolphy Answer."

42. "'I'd Like to Play Your Clubs,' John Coltrane Tells Bob Dawbarn," *Melody Maker*, November 25, 1961, 8.

43. Letter by Archie Cotterell from *Melody Maker*, November 25, 1961; Cooke, "Chasin' the Trane," 32.

44. Other than Grime, among the few English writers who defended Coltrane were Tony Hall and Ronald Atkins. Atkins absolutely raved—"overwhelming . . . breathtaking . . . the most exciting *group* I have heard" (John Coltrane and Dizzy Gillespie in Britain," *Jazz Monthly*, February 1962, 11–12).

45. [Grime], "John Coltrane Talks," 13.

46. Hartman had toured and recorded with Gillespie before Coltrane had joined the band, and he appeared on the same bill as Gillespie in March 1950, during Coltrane's stint with the band.

47. Kofsky, 237; also see 235.

48. *Jazz Times,* October 1991, 18. Also Steve Rowland interview with Thiele, 1990 (unpublished).

49. Thiele in *Jazz Times,* October 1991, 18. Quotes from liner notes to the LP.

50. Mialy recalled the dialogue and published it as "On the Road," *Jazz Hot* 265 (October 1970), 22; and again but with different surrounding text as "Interstellar Space," *Jazz Hot* 491 (July–August 1992), 47. Carl Woideck gave me helpful comments on my translation, which was then reviewed by Mialy himself.

51. Wilmer, "Conversation with Coltrane." In the United States another guitarist, Grant Green, also sat in, perhaps after this tour (Thomas 135).

52. Jean Clouzet and Michel Delorme, "Entretien avec John Coltrane," *Les Cahiers du Jazz* (an annual formerly put out by *Jazz Magazine*) 8 (1963): 6. Jimmy Heath expressed surprise to me that Coltrane never considered hiring Freddie Hubbard, the sensational trumpeter he'd worked with in 1958.

53. Davis later struggled with emphysema for a long time and passed away in 1987.

54. Interview by De Sayles Grey, November 2, 1977, in "John Coltrane and the 'Avant-Garde' Movement in Jazz History," Ph.D. diss., University of Pittsburgh, 1985, 116.

55. Unsigned caption under photo, *Philadelphia Tribune,* July 10, 1956, 5.

56. Garrett in Gardner, "Jazzman of the Year." Coltrane and Dolphy in Wilmer, *Jazz Journal.*

57. This mysterious tape of under three minutes is an excerpt of an interview that I date as November 23 (or possibly 21), 1961 (not July 1961 as sometimes listed). The Swedish interviewer is said to be the late Claes Dahlgren, who spent much time in New York and wrote for *Orkester Journalen.*

58. According to "John Coltrane," in *Jazz Masters of the Fifties* by Joe Goldberg (New York: MacMillan, 1965), 206, the main reason things didn't work out was that Coltrane didn't give Davis enough advance notice of gigs, but Davis says this was not a key factor: "There were cases where he did call the last minute but not always. That was John's nature—not maliciously. Other times, he gave advance notice."

59. Clouzet and Delorme, "Entretien avec John Coltrane," 9.

60. At that time the draft took men up through age twenty-five. Workman has continued to do marvelous work in jazz and has also been teaching since about 1986 at the New School for Social Research in Manhattan.

61. There is no page number on this clipping in the Institute of Jazz Studies files. Judging from other clippings of *Disc,* its deadline was close to publication; for example, the review of the November 11 performance was published on November 18. So this could have been recent news.

62. Don Heckman, "Jimmy Garrison after Coltrane," *Down Beat,* March 9, 1967, 18.

Chapter 15

1. Nat Hentoff's notes to *Coltrane "Live" at the Village Vanguard.*

2. [Grime], "John Coltrane Talks."

3. Bill Coss, "Cecil Taylor's Struggle for Existence," *Down Beat,* October 26, 1961, 21. Thanks to John Szwed for leading me to this.

4. Transcribed by myself and Carl Woideck from the original tape, provided by Michel Delorme. French version published by Benoit Quersin as "Entretiens: La Passe Dangereuse," *Jazz Magazine* 90 (January 1963), 40.

5. First quote from notes to Atlantic SD-1384; second from Atlantic SD-1317.

6. See Jost, *Free Jazz*, chap. 3, for more on Coleman's music. Also see Schuller's essay from *A Collection of the Music of Ornette Coleman*, ed. Schuller (New York: MJQ Music, 1961).

7. Peter Watrous, "John Coltrane: A Life Supreme," *Musician* 105 (July 1987), 106. It was typical of Coltrane to go out of his way to pay people when they didn't expect it.

8. "Rehearsing with Ornette," *Metronome*, December 1961; reprinted in *Jazz Masters in Transition, 1957–69* (New York: MacMillan, 1970; reprinted by Da Capo, 1980), 54.

9. Peter Watrous, 106.

10. [Grime], "John Coltrane Talks."

11. Cooke, "Chasin' the Trane," 32.

12. Clouzet and Delorme, "Entretien avec John Coltrane," 6–7.

13. Feather, "Coltrane Shaping Musical Revolt," October 18, 1964.

14. Kofsky, 234.

15. Kofsky, 235.

16. Kofsky, 232–33.

17. Simpkins calls the book *200 Negro Spirituals;* it has been republished several times, but I am not familiar with it under that title. I used the 1977 Da Capo reprint of the 1969 edition, which brings together both of Weldon's books of spirituals, with piano arrangements by his brother J. Rosamund Johnson, as *The Books of American Negro Spirituals.*

18. Tape of de Ruyter interview, November 11, 1961.

19. Dargenpierre, 24.

20. This corrects Thomas (199), who says they first met in 1965, and Simpkins (114), who says Shankar came to the Jazz Gallery in 1960. Shankar's book *My Music, My Life* (New York: Simon and Schuster, 1968), 90, confirms that he toured the United States from late 1961 through 1962.

21. Bauer found the Indian recording accompanying Tom Manoff's textbook, *Music: A Living Language* (New York: W. W. Norton, 1982), but it derives originally from a Folkways LP, I believe *Religious Music from India*, Folkways 4431. Ahmed Abdul-Malik told me he gave Coltrane the idea for "India"—perhaps he played him the Folkways recording. The Columbia LP is *Spanish Folk Music*, vol. 15 of the Columbia World Library of Folk and Primitive Music, last issued as CSP 91A-02001; it and the Folkways item may commonly be borrowed from public libraries. George Avakian, who was then a producer at Columbia, told Loren Schoenberg, as broadcast on WBGO-FM, Newark, on November 27, 1996, that he had given the Spanish album and others in order to help Evans get ideas for an album of "international music" that never came off as planned but became *Sketches of Spain.* (In the interview he misidentified "Saeta" as deriving from a Portuguese singer's LP.)

22. In the Japanese scale on the second staff Coltrane omitted the flat on the A. This sounds to me like the "in" scale, which should have an A-flat. See, for example, Titon et al., *Worlds of Music*, 2d ed. (New York: Schirmer Books, 1992), 322.

23. Clouzet and Delorme, "Entretien avec John Coltrane," 12–13.

24. Hentoff's notes to *Coltrane "Live" at the Village Vanguard.*

25. Clouzet and Delorme, "Entretien avec John Coltrane," 14.

26. This song was well known so Coltrane might have heard it from several sources; the Weavers used to sing it—it's on their Carnegie Hall concert album of 1955—among other groups. An arrangement by Fernando Obradors shows up in classical vocal recitals—more recently Elly Ameling recorded it on an LP (Philips 412-216-1, from 1983). This is not related, however to "El Viti," which was in Duke Ellington's repertory in 1966 and has been attributed either to Ellington or to Gerald Wilson.

27. Gleason's taped interview of Coltrane, May 2, 1961, by permission of Toby and Jean Gleason.

28. *The Real McCoy* by Bret Primack, from *Jazz Times,* January/February 1996, pp. 30 (col. 2, para. 2)–32.

29. Clouzet and Delorme, "Entretien avec John Coltrane," 10.

30. Gleason interview, May 2, 1961; used by permission.

31. It says "best," which is clearly a misprint.

32. [Grime], "John Coltrane Talks."

33. Swedish interview of November 1961.

34. "Coltrane: Next Thing for Me—African Rhythms," by Ray Coleman, *Melody Maker,* July 11, 1964, 6.

35. "Requiem For Trane: Another Kind of Soul," in Phyl Garland, *The Sound of Soul* (Chicago: Henry Regnery, 1969), 223.

36. On *Sunship* (Impulse AS 9211), released in 1971. There is obviously an edit after the last word, since the band starts instantly. One photo in the album shows Tyner looking at some music, but it appears to be a published song with words—besides, the photo might be from another session.

37. Clouzet and Delorme, "Entretien avec John Coltrane," 14.

Chapter 16

1. Putschogl's entire dissertation, *John Coltrane Und Die Afroamerikanische Or-altradition,* was published in German, but with a substantial English summary, as *Jazzforschung/Jazz Research* 25 (Graz, Austria, 1993).

2. Panel discussion, University of Virginia, February 19, 1993.

3. *Baker's Biographical Dictionary* provided some data on Gould and Ravel. The common claim that "Impressions" (and sometimes "Chasin' the Trane") comes from Debussy is due to writers who confuse him with Ravel—and who never heard of Morton Gould.

Priestley also reports that Pete La Roca used "Impressions" nine months before Coltrane as "Why Not." But here he is mistaken. True, saxophonist Rocky Boyd did record "Why Not" in February 1961, and it does use the second theme of Gould's "Pavanne." But for the bridge Boyd simply plays the same theme again in the new key. And Coltrane had already been performing his piece as early as the summer of 1960, according to Steve Kuhn and La Roca, so Boyd must have heard it. Finally, LaRoca, the drummer on the date, says he did not write that tune. He says since the piece was based on a theme that was not actually by Coltrane, perhaps "Rocky just felt he could do his version and put another name on it. I was there when Rocky Boyd played it and I might have been in on the thought process, underlying naming and all the rest of that, but if they have me listed as the writer, that's because of something Rocky said after I wasn't there any longer. . . . It's a false attribution."

4. Elvin Jones, in Taylor, *Notes and Tones.*
5. Clouzet and Delorme, "Entretien avec John Coltrane," 6.
6. "Coltrane and Dolphy Answer."
7. Quoted by Ralph Gleason in the notes to *Olé.*
8. [Grime], "John Coltrane Talks."

Chapter 17

A different version of this chapter appeared in the *Journal of the American Musicological Society,* fall 1985.

1. Interview by Michel Delorme and Jean Clouzet, Hotel Claridge, Paris, November 1, 1963, in the late afternoon before the concert. I thank Delorme for allowing me to transcribe this from the original tape.

2. "John Coltrane," in *Jazz Masters of the Fifties* by Joe Goldberg (New York: Mac-Millan, 1965), 210.

3. This portion of the interview, from the same date as the above, is credited to Delorme alone, and was published as "Coltrane 1963: Vers la Composition" in *Jazz Hot,* December 1963, 10–11. It does not appear on the surviving tape.

4. First part, before the ellipsis, from Paul D. Zimmerman (with Ruth Ross), "The New Jazz," *Newsweek,* December 12, 1966: 108. Second part, apparently from the same 1966 interview, quoted posthumously in Paul D. Zimmerman, "Death Of A Jazzman," *Newsweek.* July 31, 1967: 78–79. The first part also appears in that posthumous article but is reedited and abridged; unfortunately that is the version often cited. Thanks to Bill Kirchner for showing me the original and more authentic 1966 source.

5. Max Hoff spotted an error in the CD issue, GRD 155: Where Coltrane wrote, "His way is through love, in which we all are," the booklet states, "His way is in love, through which we all are."

6. The photo was not shot especially for the album; it had been used in *Impulse* magazine ads for at least a year beforehand.

7. Michel Delorme (with Claude Lenissois for the interview portion), "Coltrane, Vedette D'Antibes: 'Je Ne Peux Pas Aller Plus Loin," *Jazz Hot* 212 (September 1965), 5–6. This from page 6.

8. I hear the b-flat' and a-flat' of measure 3 as a changing tone leading to the a-natural', and this obviously is unstable itself and going to a-flat'. Alternatively, one might hear the notes e-flat , a-flat' and f' as most important, which would also tie in with the cell, in inverted form.

9. Delorme (with Lenissois), 6.
10. Delorme (with Lenissois), 6.
11. This is the only such recitation known. Coltrane reportedly based the opening recitative of his "Alabama" on some words by Martin Luther King, but I have studied two speeches sent to me by Woideck and have not found a connection. Max Hoff feels there are words to "After the Rain" (1963), but Coltrane's embellishments make this

doubtful. A vague resemblance between "Welcome" (1965) and "Happy Birthday" is also unconvincing. A related technique was used by Duke Ellington in his 1957 composition, "Such Sweet Thunder," where four sections are based on the fourteen-line sonnet form. Although Coltrane's recitation has not been analyzed anywhere else, some listeners have been aware of it. Simpkins wrote in 1975 that "he plays the words of a poem . . . which he wrote" (180). The earliest reference that I know of is by Gary Giddins, in Dan Morgenstern, editor, *The Sax Section* (exhibition booklet, New York Jazz Museum, 1974). Giddins writes that the last movement is "improvised entirely from the syllabic content of a poem he had written."

12. Jeff Titon, "Tonal System in the Chanted Oral Sermons of the Reverend C. L. Franklin," paper delivered at the Annual Meeting of the Society for Ethnomusicology, Wesleyan University, October 17, 1975. My thanks to Titon for allowing me to study it. It is no accident that we find similar general principles of chant in other cultures. After all, Christian psalmody goes back to ancient Jewish chant and in turn was passed on to black Christian churches such as Franklin's. For example, see the instructions in the *Liber Usualis* on principles of Gregorian chanting, which follow the same shape of ascent, recitation, and descent.

13. Thanks to Joshua Rifkin for this observation as well as for general help with this chapter in 1980.

14. Bob Thiele as told to Bob Golden, *What a Wonderful World* (New York: Oxford University Press, 1995), 127.

15. Michel Delorme, "Coltrane, Vedette D'Antibes," 6.

16. There is one other moment of editing, pointed out to me by Bob Belden, a saxophonist, composer and producer, and confirmed to him by Ravi Coltrane. At the end of "Resolution," the long high note that begins the last eight-bar statement blends into the following note, because it was dubbed in by Coltrane to replace a note that didn't speak properly.

17. David Wild reported in his Coltrane discography that there was a second recording of the entire suite, but that was an error.

Chapter 18

1. Postif's preface to the 1961 interview in *Jazz Hot.*

2. Gardner, "Jazzman of the Year."

3. Graham Lock, "Trane Talk," *Wire* 86 (April 1991), 42–43.

4. Interviewed by Grey, "Coltrane and Avant-Garde," 105.

5. Heath, interviewed by Mandel. Courtesy Avalon Archives.

6. Booklet to *The Heavyweight Champion*, 36.

7. Postif, preface to 1961 interview.

8. Cooke, "Chasin' the Trane," 32.

9. "Coltrane: Next Thing for Me—African Rhythms," by Ray Coleman, *Melody Maker*, July 11, 1964, 6.

10. Mike Hennessey, "Dropping the Ball and Chain from Jazz," *Melody Maker*, August 14, 1965, 6.

11. Letter to the author, June 1996, a rewrite of a passage in Wilmer's *Mama Said There'd Be Days Like This.*

12. Davis with Troupe, *Miles*, 212.

13. Mike Hennessey, *Melody Maker,* August 14, 1965, 6.

14. Mialy's comments were made to me. The dialogue with Coltrane is from Mialy, "On the Road," *Jazz Hot* 265 (October 1970), 22; reprinted with different surrounding text as "Interstellar Space," *Jazz Hot* 491 (July–August 1992), 47; my translation, with help from Carl Woideck and Mialy himself.

15. Mialy, "Interstellar Space."

16. The first book is probably Richard H. Popkin and Arum Stroll, *Philosophy Made Simple* (recent edition, New York: Doubleday, 1993). The other book is A. J. Ayer, *Language, Truth, and Logic* (1936, 2d ed., 1946). It introduced many philosophers in the English-speaking world to the ideas of logical positivism.

17. Taped interview in Japan, 1966, issued on LP. Transcription printed in *Jazz & Pop,* March 1968, 23, and in the booklet to the CD issue. During the issued portion of the Japan interview, Coltrane remarks that they got him talking for hours. I pursued this lead but discovered that the original tapes—over four hours!—had been kept in an archive and eventually destroyed during the 1970s. Thanks to Ernie Carmichael for tracking down this information. Fujioka has not found any copy of the tapes.

18. Clouzet and Delorme, "Entretien avec John Coltrane," 7–8. Again, I offer a literal translation.

19. Kofsky, 227–28.

Chapter 19

1. Gardner, "Jazzman of the Year," 68–69.

2. Mike Hennessey, *Melody Maker,* August 14, 1965.

3. Thiele, *What a Wonderful World,* 128.

4. *The Music of John Coltrane* (Milwaukee: Hal Leonard, 1991), 12. No editor is listed but Alice Coltrane is thanked in the introduction for suggesting chords.

5. David Such, *Avant-Garde Jazz Musicians: Performing "Out There"* (Iowa City: University of Iowa Press, 1993), 55–59.

6. Martin Johnson, "Pharoah's Return," *Down Beat,* April 1995, 22.

7. Elizabeth van der Mei, "Pharoah Sanders," in *Coda,* June–July 1967, 4.

8. Van der Mei, 5.

9. Kofsky, "An Interview . . . ," 234. Michel Delorme mentions Antibes in "Trane," *Jazz Hot* 265 (October 1970), 11. Delorme says it was Ayler at Judson Hall, but I believe the only such recording is from September 1965; perhaps it was the Town Hall concert Ayler recorded on May 1, 1965; it may have been just issued or Coltrane could have had an advance copy.

10. Hentoff's notes to *Om* (Impulse A-9140, released late 1967). Frank Kofsky reviewed *Om* before it was released (*Jazz and Pop,* December 1967, 42), stating that Coltrane had decided to withhold it and encouraging readers to press for its issue. If he is correct, it must have been pretty far along before Coltrane made that decision, since Hentoff specifically discusses the album with Coltrane in his notes, and the LP actually was released before the end of 1967.

11. According to four reliable sources, speaking off the record.

12. Anonymous, "New and Views," Down Beat, December 2, 1965, 12.

13. Anonymous news item, *Down Beat,* March 10, 1966, 8.

14. Valerie Wilmer, *As Serious As Your Life* (London: Quartet Books, 1977), 42. It is unclear whether Wilmer did this interview herself, or if she is quoting a publication she cites earlier (Tony Cummings, "Tyner Sells In," *Black Music,* March 1975).

15. Thierry Pérémarti, "McCoy Tyner: 25 Apres J.C.," *Jazz Hot* 491 (July–August 1992), 37.

16. Lyons, *The Great Jazz Pianists,* 239.

17. *Down Beat,* March 10, 1966, 8.

18. The two quotes are from *Down Beat,* March 10, 1966, 8.

19. Comment about Elvin in Randi Hultin, "I remember Trane," *Down Beat Music '68* (yearbook), 104–5; last quote from *Down Beat,* March 10, 1966, 8.

20. Radio interview broadcast by Alan Grant shortly after John's death in 1967.

21. David N. Baker, Lida M. Belt, and Herman C. Hudson, eds., *The Black Composer Speaks* (Metuchen, N.J.: Scarecrow Press, 1978), 83.

22. Kofsky, 232; Hentoff, notes to *Coltrane/Live at the Village Vanguard Again!*

23. Rashied Ali, taped interview with Howard Mandel conducted on June 26, 1990 for *The World according to John Coltrane.* Courtesy Avalon Archives.

24. Martin Johnson, "An Easy Marriage of Styles: McCoy Tyner and Michael Brecker," *Down Beat,* January 1996, 18.

25. Mary adds, "No one's heard from them for years." Sheila may have married and changed her name.

26. Kofsky, 236.

27. Thanks to Ravi Coltrane for this information. The balance of this paragraph was drawn partly from the program book of the 1990 John Coltrane Festival, p. 12, produced in Los Angeles under Mrs. Coltrane's auspices, and from "The Evolution of Alice Coltrane," a radio documentary produced by Delores Brandon, broadcast February 29, 1988 on WBAI-FM, Manhattan, which includes an interview of Alice Coltrane, probably taped in September 1987.

28. "Evolution of Alice Coltrane." According to the program book of the 1990 John Coltrane Festival, p. 12, Alice played with Sonny Stitt, Duke Ellington, Ornette Coleman (probably referring to occasions with John, and to a later album of hers for which Coleman wrote arrangements), Lucky Thompson (in Europe), Terry Gibbs, and Yusef Lateef. It also says "She collaborated with such musical greats as Bud Powell, Terry Pollard, and Oscar Pettiford" (who moved to Europe shortly before his death there in 1960). It notes that she progressed by "studying classical music and concertizing" in New York, but no details are given.

29. "Evolution of Alice Coltrane."

30. There were other recordings with Gibbs afterward, as well as a session for SESAC, a transcription service not for sale to the public.

31. Leonard Feather, *The Encyclopedia of Jazz in the Sixties* (New York: Bonanza Books, 1966), 209.

32. Alice Coltrane, taped interview by Robert Palmer conducted on July 31, 1990, for *The World according to John Coltrane.* Courtesy Avalon Archives.

33. I confirmed the legal details of the preceding paragraph with George Weissblum, a lawyer in Bronxville, N.Y., in a conversation of January 12, 1996.

34. "Requiem for Trane: Another Kind of Soul," in Phyl Garland, *The Sound of Soul* (Chicago: Henry Regnery, 1969), 227.

35. Reggie Workman, interviewed by Ted Panken on WKCR-FM, May 9, 1990.

36. Goldberg adds that the harp at that time was a rental; "John Coltrane," in *Jazz Masters of the Fifties*, 211.

37. First quote from Dargenpierre, 25; second from Bob Dawbarn, *Melody Maker*, November 25, 1961, 8.

38. Interview with Robert Palmer, 1990, heard as a voice-over in *The World according to John Coltrane*. Courtesy Avalon Archives.

39. Francis Davis, "Take the Coltrane," *Village Voice*, February 18, 1992, 73.

40. Interview with Robert Palmer, courtesy Avalon Archives. Part of this appears as a voice-over in the film. My sources do not agree with Simpkins (211–12) that the gig lasted three nights, or that Coltrane lost his temper.

41. Quoted in Graham Lock, "Trane Talk," *Wire* 86 (April 1991), 43.

42. Hennessey, *Melody Maker*, August 14, 1965.

43. Interview with Mandel, courtesy Avalon Archives.

44. "John Coltrane," in *Jazz Hot*, August–September 1967, 5. Berger's column is dated July 19, 1967. Cecil Payne's report in Thomas, 194, accidentally dates this as summer 1965.

45. Robert Palmer, "Alice Coltrane's First Concerts Here in 7 Years," *New York Times*, September 21, 1984.

46. See also Jost, *Free Jazz*, 94.

47. Jost, *Free Jazz*, 99–100.

48. In October 1995 a CD of previously unissued quartet recordings from the week before was issued under the title "Stellar Regions." All the pieces had been untitled, and Alice Coltrane devised the titles, apparently not knowing that the title cut, which appears in two versions, is in fact "Venus." I noticed this when I was sent a preview tape, but it was a week before the album's release, too late to correct the error. However, the information was given to some of the reviewers. The notes also omit that Coltrane plays alto on both takes of "Tranesonic."

49. *Melody Maker*, October 15, 1966; Simpkins, 235.

50. Kofsky, 233.

51. *Pittsburgh Courier*, May 20, 1967.

52. See also Thomas (204). Simpkins says March 1968 (240), but Olatunji's own typescript, distributed by its author and found at the Institute of Jazz Studies, gives this date.

53. Kofsky, 230. Yoruba detail from Rich Scheinin.

54. *NJSO Jazz Journal*, fall 1995, 13.

55. "Requiem for Trane: Another Kind of Soul," in Phyl Garland, *The Sound of Soul* (Chicago: Henry Regnery, 1969), 227.

56. Zimmerman, *The New Jazz*, 108. See also Kofsky, 243.

57. Frank Kofsky, "The New Wave: Bob Thiele Talks to Frank Kofsky about John Coltrane," *Coda*, May 1968, 6, 8.

58. So writes Andrew White from "a very reliable source (unnamed)" in *Trane 'n Me (A semi-autobiography): A Treatise on the Music of John Coltrane* (Washington, D.C.: Andrew's Musical Enterprises, 1981), 53.

59. Alice in "Requiem for Trane," 228. Mary in "Jazz Fans Gather at Home of a Giant," by Daniel Rubin, *Philadelphia Inquirer*, June 14, 1992, section A, 1.

60. Obviously Simpkins (241) means July, not June.

61. "Requiem for Trane," 228.

62. Davis with Troupe, *Miles,* 285.

63. *Jazz Hot,* August–September 1967, 5.

64. Dr. John Morgan, chair of the Department of Pharmacology at City University of New York Medical School, talked over this and other medical details with me.

65. The following report is summarized from the National Cancer Institute's Physicians Data Query, a service available on Compuserve and other computer services. The article is entitled "Adult Primary Liver Cancer (for Health Care Professionals)" and it is an updated version from August 1995. Thanks to Allison Chestnut (January 7, 1996) and to Marlene Shapiro (January 9, 1996), who corresponded with me on the cancer forum of Compuserve.

66. Thanks to Dr. Morgan for the preceding information.

67. Recorded message from Dr. Weiser to the author, December 29, 1995.

68. Kofsky, 241.

Chapter 20

1. The following information is from his probate file 445 A 1967 in Suffolk County, Long Island, New York.

2. Thanks to George Weissblum and Herb Cohen, CPA for helping me to interpret these documents.

3. Interview with Robert Palmer, July 31, 1990. Courtesy Avalon Archives.

4. From Alice Coltrane, cited in "Living with the Spirit and Legacy of John Coltrane," by Darlene Donloe, in *Ebony,* March 1989, 46, 48, 50. The article has numerous errors on career matters but seems reliable on family matters such as this.

5. Gene Kalbacher, "Tenor Saxophonist Ravi Coltrane Respectfully Sidesteps the Shadow of a Titan," *Hot House,* November 1995, 22.

6. Barry Witherden, "Blowin' into History," *Wire* 86 (April 1991), 41.

7. There are many good examples of this in Ramon Ricker, *Pentatonic Scales for Jazz Improvisations* (Lebanon, Ind.: Studio P/R, 1975).

8. Robert Palmer, "Alice Coltrane's First Concerts Here in 7 Years," *New York Times,* September 21, 1984. I corrected his statement that Coltrane "studied informally with" Shankar.

9. Ralph Fasanella, conversation with the author, ca. 1991.

10. Tyner in Wilmer, *As Serious As Your Life,* 44 (possibly reprinted from a periodical). Jones in a radio interview broadcast by Alan Grant shortly after John's death in 1967.

11. See "Trane's Widow Sues Church" by Robert Bruce, *Down Beat,* April 1982, 12; also, *Notes on People* column (anonymous), "Coltrane's Widow Sues," *New York Times,* October 24, 1981, 26. For more on the church, see *Image* (March 6, 1988, 17–20); *Wall Street Journal* (July 20, 1993); *Boston Globe* (December 6, 1996, D1); *Wire* (September 1995, 10); *Life* (December 1992, 21, anonymous column "Our Times"). David G. Schwartz, in his senior thesis, *Reflections in Blue: Jazz and Messianic and Quasi-Religious Movements* (University of Pennsylvania, March 1995), discusses the church as well as Coltrane's own beliefs.

12. "The Evolution of Alice Coltrane."

13. 1978, Warner Brothers 2-WB-3218.

14. The preceding sentence and some of the information that concludes this paragraph are drawn from the Donloe piece in *Ebony,* where Alice also discusses how she has seen and spoken with John since his death. The town is given as Agoura, but my map says Agoura Hills.

15. All this from Futch, "Theme from Hamlet," and my visit with Dr. McQueen.

16. The Society may be contacted at 1511 N. 33rd Street, Philadelphia, PA, 19121; phone (215) 763-1118.

Chronology

This is an annotated listing of all known performances and recorded interviews of John Coltrane. Even though there is much new information here, there are still many gaps—one may assume that Coltrane was performing somewhere just about every week from, say, 1949 on, even if nothing is listed here. Recordings (in studios, at performances, from radio broadcasts, and from interviews) and television broadcasts known to survive are prefaced with asterisks. Those that have been fully issued to the public on audio or video have two asterisks, even if they are currently out of print. I also count a session as fully issued if the only unissued items are short, incomplete takes that do not contain Coltrane solos, or tapes that were probably erased. If only some of the recorded material has been issued, the prefix is *(*). Please note that the single-asterisk items are not available to the public at this writing and in some cases appear to be lost—they are included for completeness. (Recordings that were definitely destroyed are not asterisked.) Also remember that this is a list of performances; if there is no asterisk, there are no known surviving recordings of the performance.

When the dates for an engagement are given, note that there was often at least one night off each week, usually Monday; until the mid-1950s clubs were also closed Sunday in many states because of blue laws (laws that enforced the Christian Sabbath as a day of rest). Often, I have only an advertisement from the middle of the week that says "Now appearing," but where possible I have extrapolated the probable week's dates from that information; these instances are preceded by *Ca.* I can do this with some certainty when I know the booking policies—for instance, I know that the Apollo Theater at one time booked from Friday through the next Thursday, while many nightclubs booked Tuesday or Wednesday through Sunday. In some cases I know the first date of an engagement, but not whether it was for one week or several weeks. When exact dates are unknown, I have placed the gigs in their known order; when even the order is unknown, I have placed them in a cluster. When not even the year is known, the performance is listed in its probable year with an annotation. Gigs that may not have happened or may not have included Coltrane are given in parentheses.

Through the 1960s it was typical for more than one band to perform at a club or concert; they took turns on the bandstand. I have in many cases listed the bands that played on the same bill, because it is of great historical interest. I have not always listed the exact order of the billing, but as a rule the groups that Coltrane played in, even Gillespie's and Miles Davis's, were second- or third-billed until about 1959. Please keep this in mind, in order to have a realistic picture of Coltrane's career.

To save space, my sources are not indicated in every case. Newspapers are key sources for this type of research. I used primarily the *Philadelphia Afro-American* (PAA), *Philadelphia Tribune* (PT), *New York Post, New York Amsterdam News, Village Voice, Chicago Defender,* and *New York Times.* (I thank German researcher Franz Hoffman for sending me his self-published collections of "jazz ads" from the last four of these.) When quoting from them I have not corrected spelling or punctuation. I also used the magazines *Down Beat* (DB), *Metronome, Jazz Hot* (France), *Melody Maker* (England), *Coda* (Canada), and *International Musician,* among others, for concert reviews and gig listings. The listings in magazines are less reliable because they cannot take into account late changes. For example, *Down Beat* will often report that Coltrane is scheduled to perform a gig but not that it was later canceled.

Other sources included interviews that I conducted (especially with Jimmy Heath), the Simpkins and Thomas books, the Chambers book on Davis, the Davis autobiography (*Miles*), and many other books, especially *Miles' Diary* by Ken Vail (London: Sanctuary, 1996), a Davis chronology (Vail). I have been able to date some undated or incorrectly dated items by collating itineraries of several musicians and listings in several sources. Research is still needed in local newspapers around the United States, in California, Cleveland, Detroit, and so on, and I welcome and will acknowledge all information.

The Fujioka discography was, of course, an important source. He conducted many interviews of his own. Since I was an assisting author of that work, the reader may be surprised to discover many differences between that listing and mine. That is primarily because much of my own research for this listing was conducted after that book went to press. In many cases it has been necessary for me to correct the Fujioka discography, but it would have been impractical to do so in every case. Rest assured that wherever a gig listed there has been redated or omitted, the change was intentional. For details of studio recordings, Fujioka remains the definitive source.

1926 to 1944

Fall 1939. High Point, N.C. Begins first training in community band; unknown performances, if any.

Fall 1940. High Point, N.C. Joins newly formed high school band; unknown performances.

May 24 (Sunday), 1942. High Point, N.C. Performance with high school band.

Late May 1943 (week before graduation). High Point, N.C. Performance in dance band for high school party (Thomas, 21).

1945

Ca. early to mid-1945. Philadelphia. First professional work with cocktail lounge combo. Occasional jobs with Jimmy Johnson big band.

August 6, 1945 through August 11, 1946. In the navy. In naval band on Oahu from December on.

1946

Through July. Oahu, Hawaii. Continues in navy band.

*(*)July 13. Oahu, Hawaii. Privately records eight titles with navy colleagues. "Hot House" issued on *The Last Giant*. Bit of "Cherokee" used on radio and in soundtrack of video *The World according to John Coltrane*. Others unissued.

August 11. Discharged from navy, begins to freelance around Philadelphia, including several gigs over a period of perhaps six months (into 1947) with Ray Bryant and bassist Gordan "Bass" Ashford, at Joe Pitt's Musical Bar (one day a week), and weekends at Caravan Republican Club.

September 13 (Friday). Philadelphia. Elate Ballroom. Joe Webb and his Decca Recording Orchestra with Big Maybelle. The "5 Sharps of Rhythm" and Miss "Bronze" Philadelphia also on bill. Coltrane may have played this gig, or was hired the next day to go on tour.

Joe Webb tour with Coltrane (*Indianapolis Recorder,* Nov. 16, 1946, sec. 2, p. 4)

Ca. September 20–November 15 (eight weeks). Jackson, Miss. Flame Club.

November 16 (Saturday). Cannonsburg, Penn. Colored Elks Club.

November 17–21. Various one-nighters in Pennsylvania and Michigan.

November 22–ca. December 5. Probably Pittsburgh. Chez Paree club. (Kansas City had a Chez Paree club, but the notice suggests Pittsburgh.)

After December 5. Albany, Georgia, and other stops. Unknown locations. Massey leaves in Albany.

Mid-December through early January (three weeks). New Orleans. Unknown location. (This and the preceding reported by Massey in Simpkins, 32.)

1947

February–April. On tour with King Kolax band.
        Ca. February 17–23 (Monday–Sunday). Los Angeles. Kolax band (at Key Hall?).
        February 19. Los Angeles. Reportedly meets Charlie Parker at a recording session.
        March 28. Pensacola, Fla.
        March 31. Orlando.
        April 1. Tampa.
        April 2. West Palm Beach.

Ca. summer 1947; or right after navy in 1946. Philadelphia. A gig at the Showboat with Johnny Coles, Ray Bryant, Sugie Rhodes, possibly unknown drummer. (See photo section.)

Sometime in 1947. Philadelphia. In the "projects" where Bill Cosby later was born. Golson, Ray Bryant, Tom Bryant; Coltrane on sax and clarinet.

May 16 (Friday). Millsboro, Del. "Jimmy Heath and His 16 Piece Orchestra" play for dancing at Rosedale Beach, featuring Calvin Todd, trumpet; Walt Dickerson, vibraphone; Jimmy Thomas, vocalist. Price $1 before 10:30, 1.25 after (PAA, May 10, 1947, 20).

June 27 (Friday). Philadelphia. Met Ballroom, Broad and Poplar Streets. "Jimmy Heath and His Orchestra" played second bill to Johnny Moore's 3 Blazers (guitar-playing brother of Oscar Moore, known from the Nat King Cole trio). Admission $1.50 including tax; "dancing 9 until ?" (PAA, June 21, 1947, 5).

Ca. fall 1947–July 1948. Philadelphia. Every Saturday night at midnight at Elate Club, in Johny Lynch quintet with James Forman, Stanley Gaines (possibly replaced at one point by another bassist), Specs Wright.

November 14 (Friday). Philadelphia. "By Popular Demand Club Emanon presents an Autumn Swing Session featuring Jimmy Heath and his 17 Piece Orchestra plus [including] Johnny Lynch (Trumpet) James "Sax" Young (Tenor Sax) John Coltrane (Alto Sax) Jimmy Heath (Alto and Baritone Sax) Jimmy Thomas (vocalist)" at O.V. Catto Auditorium, 16th and Fitzwater Streets. Dancing 9:00 until 2:00; admission 75 cents before 10:00—85 cents after. Heath says Specs Wright's brother Ike Wright, who ran that club, passed away in 1995. (Poster reproduced in *Heavyweight Champion* booklet p. 45 without year.) In PT ("And Furthermore," by Violet Wilkins, Mar. 16, 1948) it said, 'He [Heath] will long remember his engagement at the O.V. Catto on Thanksgiving [1947?] as his most successful." O.V. Catto was the Elks Lodge no. 20. Heath doesn't remember one exactly on Thanksgiving. It may have been the one above.

November 16 (Sunday). Philadelphia. Jimmy Heath, baritone sax, Johnny Coltrane, alto sax, Reds Garland, piano, Percy Heath, bass, and Charlie Rice, drums were among those at the Jazz Guild's swing concert at the Elate Ballroom, attended by several hundred music lovers. They seem to have comprised the house band backing up the featured players such as Jimmy Oliver and Johnny Lynch (James H. Brown, "Jazz Guild Show 'Real Great,'" PT, November 22, 1947; it says the event was "last Sunday").

December 7 (Sunday), 6:30–9:30 P.M. Philadelphia. Heath "and his band" with Coltrane appeared at a benefit at the Elate Club (or Ball Room) at 711 S. Broad St. "for little Mary Etta Jordan, who is 6 years old and lost both of her legs in a recent trolley accident. This show, sponsored by Philly's own Beryl Booker, who is the pianist with the Slam Stewart Trio, was the finest name-packed show seen in the old town of Philadelphia in a long, long time." The article reports that 2,500 people attended to hear Heath, Charlie Parker (photographed with Heath's band while Coltrane watched with a lit cigarette), Max Roach (who also played with the band), Booker and the Slam Stewart Trio, Earl Bostic, and many local players such as Jimmie Oliver and ["Philly"] Joe Jones (Ramon Bruce, "Ravin' with Ramon," PAA, December 13, 1947, 7). "Kid Swingster" in PT, December 13, 1947, 12, estimates the crowd at 3,000 and says the Heath band (16 pieces) played three selections and sounded "better than ever before." A PT story (December 9, 1947, 1 and 8) concurs that the official figure was 3,000 and says another 2,000 were turned away.

(December 31, 1947. Philadelphia. May have included Coltrane: Tropical Garden, New Year's Eve Floor Show featuring Johnny Lynch and His Quintette plus dancers, a singer, a comedian—for members only [PAA].)

1948

(February 6 [Friday]. Philadelphia. The Club Evounce hosted a party at the Elate Ballroom featuring dancing to Jimmy Heath and his Sextette, probably with Coltrane. A piece in PT [or possibly PAA] February 21, 1948 says four members of the sextet sang "Ooh Bop a Lop" and the crowd joined in.)

February and maybe March. Camden, N.J. As of February 10, Jimmy Heath's group were the regular Sunday night "musicites" at Raymond White's Embassy Ballroom, 1400 Broadway. "The 'Heath mob' is naturally a group of young Philadelphians who can play anything . . . from a wild Hampton Ride to a smooth Ellington riff."

February 13 (Friday). Philadelphia. Club Quadrigas hosted a dance "Februa(?) Fantasia" at Mercantile Senior Ballroom, featuring Jimmy Heath and his Band with Jimmy Thomas on vocals. Awards were given to the club presidents.

Late February–March. Philadelphia. "Jimmy Heath and his 16-piece band are really going places. They are at the Elate Club every Tuesday night, with Jimmy Thomas as vocalist" (Ramon Bruce column, PAA, February 28; confirmed March 6 and 16).

Ca. one week before April 3. Philadelphia. "All the boys in Jimmie Heath's band" went to see Gillespie's group (PAA, April 3, 1948).

June 17. Philadelphia. In the audience for Lester Young at Emerson's on Thursday, "I saw Percy Heath and his beard [girlfriend], Marty—Martin, Johnnie Coltraine and Joan Smithers" (PT, June 19, 1948).

Note: International Musician, November, 17, says "Trumpeter Howard McGhee has formed a seventeen-piece orchestra." McGhee actually took over Heath's sixteen-piece group and added himself.

October, for a week. Chicago. Regal Theater. Howard McGhee big band.

Note: Heath says it is possible the band also played a week at the Howard Theater in Washington, D.C. He also recalls talk of a gig in Kansas City on a bill with Billie Holiday, but he believes that gig never happened.

Probably late October, for a week. Manhattan. Apollo Theater. Howard McGhee big band, as part of a show. Coltrane said this was before Detroit (Simpkins, 37).

Probably November 5–11. Detroit. Paradise Theatre. Howard McGhee big band, on bill with Illinois Jacquet and Sarah Vaughan. (This date comes from the Jacquet-Vaughan tour itinerary; but another listing puts them elsewhere at this time.)

Note: By late November McGhee was with Jazz at the Philharmonic (a touring show) on the West Coast, and on December 15 he was to open in Manhattan with a quintet including the Heath brothers, followed by other gigs.

Eddie Vinson Tour with Coltrane

November 20	Charleston, W.V.
November 21	Monessen, Pa.
November 24	Kimball, W.V.
November 25	Kinston, N.C.
November 26	Lumberton, N.C.
December 5	Miami, Fla.

December 6	Jacksonville, Fla.
December 11	Beckley, W.V.
December 12	Ft. Wayne, Ind.
December 17	Ann Arbor, Mich.
December 18	Decatur, Ill.
December 19	Davenport, Iowa
December 20	Kansas City, Kans.
December 24	South Bend, Ind.
December 25–26	St. Louis, Mo.
December 27	Paducah, Ky.
December 28	Paris, Tenn.
December 29	Jackson, Tenn.
December 31	Louisville, Ky.

1949

Eddie Vinson Tour with Coltrane, *continued*

Note: The PAA lists Vinson in New York City on January 2–21. But Charlie Rice says they were never there; it is possible that they were playing around New York state during that time, including the Newark gig listed next.

January 15	Newark, N.J.
January 22	Wilmington (Del., I assume, based on their direction of travel)
January 23	Washington, D.C. Red Garland says Buddy Johnson's band was in the audience (liner notes to Prestige 24090).
January 24	Newport News, Va.
January 25	Winston-Salem, N.C.
January 26	Atlanta
January 27	Birmingham, Ga. (Coltrane may have missed the next gig due to a toothache. See Thomas, 41.)
January 28	Albany, Ga.
January 31	Shreveport, La.
February 5	Vicksburg, Miss.
February 6	Hattiesburg, Miss.
February 7	Greenwood, Miss.
February 8	Cleveland, Miss.
February 9	Grenada, Miss.
February 10	Bogalusa, La.
February 11	Tallulah, La.
February 12	Greenville, Miss.
February 18	Florence, Ala.
February 19	Evergreen, Ala.
February 20	New Orleans
February 21	Montgomery, Ala.
February 22	Jackson, Miss.
February 23	Yazoo City, Miss.

March 10	Marshall, Tex.
March 12	Wichita, Kans.
March 14	Junction City, Iowa
March 15	Des Moines
March 16	Omaha
March 18	Grand Rapids, Mich.
March 19	Inkster, Mich.
March 20	Indianapolis
March 25	Youngstown, Ohio
March 26	Gary, Ind.
March 27	Detroit. Donald Byrd says he met Coltrane at this time.
March 28	Lorain, Ohio
March 29	Cleveland. This may be when Coltrane played alto (still his pre-ferred instrument) at a matinee jam session at Lindsey's Sky Bar. Tony "Big T" Lovano (born September 21, 1925) was playing tenor with the house band. He believed that Coltrane was in town with the "Hot Sauce" Williams blues band; if so, this would have been in the early 1950s. (Reported by Tony's son, saxophonist Joe Lovano.)
April 1	Toledo, Ohio
April 2	Buffalo, N.Y.
April 15	Richmond, Va.
April 16	Beckley, W.V.
April 17	Kimball (I assume W.V.)
April 18	Winston-Salem, N.C.
April 19	New Bern, N.C.
April–May	Simpkins says Coltrane visited Greensboro, N.C. (39), so it would likely be around this time.

(There is a gap in the newspaper listings here.)

| May 28 | Logan, W.V. |
| May 30 | Stroudsburg, Pa. |

Note: There is another gap here. However, Coltrane may have left at this time since this brought the band back to the area of Philadelphia and New York, where Vinson had made his ill-fated plans to record. The PT of July 9 ("Philadelphia Story" by Squire Bryant) says James Young, who was in the band with Coltrane, is at the Cotton Club in Philadelphia.

End of Vinson Tour

Opening July 25 (Monday). Philadelphia. Jo Jones (remember, this is "Philly" Joe) and His All Stars at Ridge Point Cafe (PAA, July 16, 6), with Coltrane. Golson was the tenor in this band in an ad of June 25 (Norris Hotel and Musical Bar), and Coltrane could have joined before July 25.

(*Note:* Bullmoose Jackson worked at the Showboat in Philadelphia for two weeks starting around August 8 with his Buffalo Wild Cats. Coltrane could have joined the
group.)
Probably sometime around here. Philadelphia. Coltrane did several gigs with guitarist
Billy Butler and Philly Joe Jones (told by Butler to violinist Andy Stein).
Ca. September 10 (Saturday), probably for one week. Philadelphia. Ridge Point Cafe
proudly presents ["Philly"] Jo Jones and his All Stars featuring John Coltrane and
His Sax; Percy Heath on bass; William Langford at Piano and Jo Jones on Drums.
9:00–2:00 A.M.; jams Monday and Thursday 4:00–7:00, Saturday 4:00–closing
(PAA, September 10; by September 17 Jimmy Oliver was performing instead of
this band).

Dizzy Gillespie Big Band Tour with Coltrane

Note: See also list of undated performances placed in 1950.
September 16–22. Baltimore. Royal Theater. Gillespie band on bill with Billie Holiday,
comedians Lewis and White, and dancer Derby Wilson. Coltrane probably joined
just in time for this gig.
September 24 (Saturday). Probably Gary, Indiana. Miramar Ballroom. (The ad in the
Pittsburgh Courier doesn't specify the city but there was a Miramar in Gary.)
October 4 (Tuesday). Xenia, Ohio. Wilberforce University. Jones Auditorium. Gillespie
band played to twelve hundred fans. Jimmy Heath was definitely in the band by
this time.
Around here. St. Louis, Mo. According to Forman and Heath.
October 17. Manhattan. Gillespie and his thirteen Be-Boppers appeared at Carnegie Hall
Horizons in Jazz concert in honor of George Shearing, who played last. Gillespie
played first at 9 P.M. with "Summertime," "Taboo," "Manteca," "and his other
familiar bop numbers, temporarily relieved by vocal refrains of his latest vocalist,
Tiny Irvin of Pittsburgh. Miss Irvin, who has been with the band for the past four
weeks, sang 'Dreamer with a Penny' and 'Where Are You?'" (PAA, October 29,
1949, 7; review by Conrad Clark). Over three thousand people attended.
Beginning Friday, October 21, for one week. Philadelphia. Earle Theater, on bill with
Dinah Washington, the Ravens, others, and a movie.
Early November. Los Angeles. The band must have been in LA if the following session is
correctly dated.
*(*)November 7. Los Angeles. Billy Valentine recording session, with small group,
released on Mercury 78 RPM. One title, "Beer Drinking Baby," was issued in 1996
on CD: *The Mercury Blues 'N' Rhythm Story* (Mercury 314-528-292-2). Outakes
also exist. Coltrane solos. (Phil Schaap believes these are from March 1, 1950, in
New York City, which would change the preceding session as well.)
Probably November. Buffalo. James Forman says the band was stranded in a snowstorm.
He soon left the band, so it had to be around here.
**November 21. Manhattan. Gillespie band. Capitol recording session. No Coltrane
solos.
Possibly late November–mid-December. Manhattan. Bop City. Don Manning was in
the audience. Thomas says this was the last big-band job and that it was for six

weeks from Thanksgiving week to New Year's (50). He is wrong on both counts, but I don't have correct details. He may have confused this with the gig at San Francisco's Bop City—see October 1950.

Probably December, for one week. Chicago. Club Silhouette (reviewed in DB on Jan. 13, 1950).

Opening December 23, for one week. Manhattan. Apollo Theater. On bill with the Orioles featuring their hit "What Are You Doing New Year's Eve?" (a Frank Loesser song from 1947). A photo from this gig that includes Coltrane is in Fujioka, 8, and in Gillespie's *To Be Or Not To Bop.*

1950

**January 9. Manhattan. Gillespie band, Capitol recording session. Probably two Coltrane solos.

Undated performances reported by Jimmy Heath (late 1949 and early 1950):

Peoria, Ill. "It was the first gig on a big-band tour. We played there for dancers and we had to play 'Manteca' every night and they didn't dance really until we started playing it."

Wichita, Kans.

Maybe Iowa, several days, separate shows for white and for black.

Dayton, Ohio, at a theater, second bill to Sugar Chile Robinson.

Little Rock, Ark. "We outnumbered the audience; they wanted dance music. A very racist area."

Symphony Ballroom, Boston.

Holyoke, Mass.

Milwaukee. "We played at the Riverside Theater. We opened the week after Jimmy Dorsey. We went to hear his closing night. He played very well but he was drunk as he could be." Saxophonist and educator Bunky Green places this in 1950 and says Coltrane and Heath were practicing Bird solos, or Bird-like at least, during intermission (Thomas, 45–46).

Other undated performances with Gillespie:

Revere, Mass. Rollaway *(sic?)* Ballroom (reported to me by Herb Pomeroy).

Jefferson City, Mo. Possibly Lincoln University (reported to me by Ira Gitler). (*Note:* A former student, Ed Coleman, said that saxophonist Andy McGhee told him he saw the Gillespie band at a club that sounded like "Remo Plama"—maybe "Rainbow Plaza"?)

Opening March 24 (Friday), for one week. Manhattan. Apollo Theater. Nellie Lutcher, Gillespie, vocalist Johnny Hartman (beginning his career as a single while on the same bill as his former employer Gillespie), and others, as well as the Humphrey Bogart film "Chain Lightning."

Ca. April 3–9. Philadelphia. Club 421.

Ca. May. Winston-Salem, N.C. Armory. Betty Leach, a High Point neighbor, reports this in Thomas (45), adding that Coltrane invited all the musicians to his mother's house afterwards. (His family still owned the house but was renting it out.)

June 20. Sewickley, Penn. Willie Cook says this was the last big-band gig with Gillespie.

Apparently Gillespie didn't work much or at all that summer, and Coltrane freelanced. (*Note:* Bullmoose Jackson was at Club 421 in Philadelphia around July 31 for one week and Coltrane could have worked with him.)

August, for approximately the whole month. Philadelphia. Lou's Crystal Bar proudly Presents Harry Polk formerly with King Cole Trio and his Polka Dots, Featuring John Coltrane on the sax, formerly with Dizzy Gillespie. (PAA, August 5 and 12, 1950. Charlie Rice says Polk was an excellent guitarist, now deceased.) The PAA of August 26 says Club Bill and Lou's presents Harry Polk and the Five Polka Dots featuring Johnny Coltrane and Charlie ["Specs"] Wright formerly with Dizzy Gillespie; Herb Gordy was also on the bill.

Gillespie Tour Resumes Primarily with a Sextet

Opening August 31, for one week. Manhattan. Apollo Theater. Gillespie may have put together a sizeable group for this. Billy Eckstine was also on the bill and Heath remembers that a small string section was added to the band when they accompanied his singing.

(*Note:* The Gillespie sextet recorded September 16, 1950 in Manhattan for Prestige. Coltrane was ill and was replaced by Jimmy Oliver.)

Undated performances (late 1950) reported by Jimmy Heath:

"We went heading West; we went down through Texas and definitely played in Albuquerque and New Mexico."

Minneapolis. Heath believes that Gillespie wrote "Birk's Works" while there (or possibly "Con Alma," but that wasn't recorded until 1954).

Mid-October. Los Angeles. Oasis nightclub.

*Mid-October. Los Angeles. Television broadcast from the Hollywood Palladium, with the Gillespie "Quintet," Ray Anthony big band and Helen Forrest, and Art Tatum performing solo. No copy of this program is known.

Late October. San Francisco. Jimbo's "Bop City," probably for several weeks. A photo of Gillespie, Kenny Dorham, Miles Davis and Heath from that engagement appears in *Miles* as photo 39. (The date of 1951 on the photo doesn't jibe with the known itinerary and could have been written in much later.) Gillespie and Specs Wright took a break to fly back to LA to do a record with Johnny Richards on Tuesday, October 31, and Wednesday, November 1.

Around here. Detroit.

*Late November–early December, probably for one week. Chicago. Silhouette Club. Gillespie (*To Be or Not to Bop,* 357) mistakenly says he broke up the big band at this time. Coltrane does solo. One of the numbers is "Nice Work If You Can Get It," which had been recorded without Coltrane on September 16. Strangely, there is a train passing at several points during the tape. Perhaps the club was located near a train, and the recording was made through a window or from speakers outside the club—the poor sound quality would support this. Or when it was dubbed onto cassette, did the person leave a window open while trains were passing?

Opening December 11 (Monday) for two weeks. Philadelphia. Club Harlem. On bill with Slam Stewart and Miss Sepia Philadelphia for the first week, and opposite George Shearing from December 18 on.

Probably December 25–31. Toronto (or possibly Montreal; see *Coda,* July 1963, 7). Seville Theatre. On bill with with Bill Farrell, who sang "You've Changed" (had a hit with it in 1949). Last week for Heath. Specs Wright had already been replaced by Kansas Fields on drums.

1951

Probably January 4–February 7. Manhattan. Birdland, on bill with other groups. Radio broadcasts survive and many songs contain Coltrane solos:

> **January 6. Gillespie at Birdland. Radio broadcast.
> *(*)January 13. Gillespie at Birdland. Radio broadcast.
> *(*)January 20. Gillespie at Birdland. Radio broadcast.
> *(*)February 3. Gillespie at Birdland. Radio broadcast.

Ca. March 1, perhaps for one week. Detroit. Club "Juana" (according to Kenny Burrell).
**March 1. Detroit. Gillespie Septet recording session. One Coltrane solo.
Ca. March 1. Bassist Alvin Jackson recalls Coltrane stopping in at an after-hours place called the West End which was frequented by Kenny Burrell, Yusef Lateef, and Tommy Flanagan, possibly during this engagement. Jackson was the house bassist every weekend and the house drummer was Hendell Butts or Oliver Jackson or Leon Rice, and sometimes Elvin Jones!
March 11 (Sunday), 1951, 3 p.m. Manhattan. Audubon Ballroom. Miles Davis dance job with Coltrane, Sonny Rollins, Bud Powell, Art Blakey (or, according to Rollins, Kenny Clarke), and unknown bass. Jackie McLean told Fujioka that he played also. (Peter Pullman informs me that Powell was in mental institutions from September 1951 through February 1953, which limits the possible timing of this engagement.)
During this time period: "Big Nick" Nicholas remembers Coltrane jamming with him on Gillespie's nights off at Birdland, and at the Paradise in Harlem. These could have also happened during Gillespie's previous visit to Manhattan beginning August 31, 1950.
March 15–21. Manhattan. Birdland. Parker was at Birdland from March 22, so the photo of him with Gillespie and Coltrane (see Thomas after p. 88, and elsewhere) is likely from this engagement.
*(*) March 17. Gillespie at Birdland. Radio broadcast.
Possibly around this time. New York. Lonnie (L. G.) Slappey (not Slappery) and His Band. He was a pianist from Philadelphia—mentioned in *Blue Train* notes.
March 19–ca. March 29. Philadelphia. Club Harlem. In the PAA of April 7, 6 ("Midnight Mirror," Dick Banks) the personnel listed are "John Calertrape, tenor sax" (!), and J. J. Johnson, Milt Jackson (piano and vibraphone), Percy Heath, Kansas Fields.
(*Note:* Gillespie appeared with Parker at Birdland from March 29. He opened at the Apollo in Manhattan on Friday April 6. Both gigs were without Coltrane, I believe.)

End of Gillespie Tour

Opening April 9 or 10, through early June (possibly with some weeks off). Philadelphia. Zanzibar. Dizzy Gillespie Alumni Band, led by Heath. The PT of April 7 reported,

Dizzy Gillespie's alumnua *(sic):* Train, Jimmy Heath, Forman and Rex all to appear in an all-star act at Zanzibar next week. PT of April 14: [Drummer] Coatesville Harris, visiting with Jimmy Heath and his boopers *(sic)*, including: John Coltrane, tenor, Specs Wright, drums; Tom Bryant, bass, and James Forman, piano. PT of May 8: Jimmy Heath and his Dizzy Gillespie Alumni-Orch at the Zanzibar. PT of June 2: "Jimmy Heath and his Bop All-Stars are still displaying their temperamental brand of Gillespying. It sounds more pleasing to the ears since they partially altered their song renditions."

Ca. June 4–10. Philadelphia. Club Harlem. "Jimmy Heath's Band, formerly with Dizzy Gillespie, Featuring 'Coaltrain,'" on bill with Herb Lance, Wini Brown, and and a shake dancer. "Club Harlem is featuring those Dizzy Gillespie All-Stars led by little Jimmy Heath and his alto-boperoos. Remember, this column recently reviewed the groups' 'new sounds' and was awarded by the patrons of their jive-style, that it was pleasing to the ear, and sporting a fine-thread of the melodic for a change" (PT, June 5, 12). Heath's band at Club Harlem presenting "the new innovation with dance privileges" and "have done a swell job" (PT, June 9, 12). PAA, June 9, 7 says "Jimmy Heath and his crew, all former Dizzy Gillespie sidemen, take the bandstand honors with the spotlight on 'Coaltrain.'"

(*Note:* Heath says this band also performed in Wilmington, Del. and Clifford Brown sat in, but he is certain Coltrane was not at that gig.)

(*Note:* Bullmoose Jackson came to Club Harlem around June 16, and Coltrane could have played with him.)

Around here. Snake Bar in Philadelphia (see Thomas, 56).

(*Note:* Gay Crosse and his Good Humor Six played at the Showboat in Philadelphia. June 25 through July 11. It is possible that Coltrane joined them this early.)

1952

*(*)January 19. Philadelphia. Gay Crosse recording session.

*(*)Unknown dates. Nashville, Tenn. Recording sessions by Christine Kittrell and Gay Crosse; Gay Crosse and His Good Humor Six; Charles Ruckles and His Orchestra. No solos appear to be by Coltrane.

Probably around here. Philadelphia. Home recording of Bill Barron, Coltrane, and pianist Hasaan Ibn Ali, about twenty minutes. Appears to be lost.

Maybe around here. Philadelphia. Jam session at Woodbine Club with Coltrane, Hasaan Ibn Ali, drummer Donald Bailey, and others. (Reported by Odean Pope to Steve Rowland.) There were surely many such sessions going back to the late 1940s.

Earl Bostic Tour with Coltrane

April 1. Bostic tour begins.

**April 7. Cincinnati. Bostic recording date. No Coltrane solos.

Ca. June 2. Winston-Salem, N.C. (says Simpkins, 43, and Mary Alexander). Bettie Lyerly, Coltrane's aunt, dies June 2, and Coltrane is in the area.

June 7. Philadelphia. Reynolds Hall. "Earl Bostic whose style was tersely described by little Jimmy Heath as 'desperate' will be on hand" (Jimmie Brown, "These Foolish Things," PT, June 7, 12).

Ca. June 14, probably for a week. Philadelphia. Club 48.

PT, June 14, 9, says Bostic is booked all but two nights through July 31.

Mid-July, for three weeks or more. San Francisco. Possibly the Blackhawk. Elaine "Coltrane" reports that her man, John is still holding over with the Earl Bostic group in San Francisco (PT, July 29, 12). Thomas implies that this stint was three weeks (or more) and that at least part of it was at the Blackhawk (61).

Mid-August, for at least a week. Los Angeles.

**August 15. Los Angeles. Bostic recording. No Coltrane solos.

Late August. Thomas, 60 suggests that possibly Midlands, Tex. was the next gig.

October 6–12. Philadelphia. Pep's, Broad and South St.

Opening October 31, for one week. Manhattan. Apollo Theater, on bill with Lloyd Price.

Ca. November 14. Dayton, Ohio. Farm Dell Night Club. Bostic held a contest there for lyrics to his instrumental hit "Velvet Sunset."

PT of December 9 says Bostic just completed a "swing through the midwest."

Note: Probably Coltrane left here as he's not on the next Bostic record date of December 17.

End of Bostic Tour

1953

Most of February. Philadelphia. Spider Kelly's. Specs Wright band. "Specs Wright and his smooth riding drums has developed a fine stylized brand of Boperooing. The group are smooth and rhythmic, and not bad on the listeners, despite the difficulty of boppers being commercial riders . . . Specs' Special arrangement by piano (sic) man Coletrain titled 'Sambo Blues' is fine" (PT, Feb. 10). (None of my informants had heard of "Sambo Blues.") Bettye Logan will be singing at Spider Kelly's "for the next week . . . [including 3:00 P.M. matinees on Monday, Friday, and Saturday] She is backed by Specs Wright and His All Stars with John Coltrane, former Bostic sideman on the tenor, Mike Jefferson, who feels like 'the gent from Virginny' on piano, James 'Sugie' Rhodes plunking the bass and 'Specs' on drums. Their musical offering has made them one of the top groups in the city. Bop does it" (PT, Feb, 21, 9). Heath doesn't know what the "Virginny" joke is, but recalls that "Jefferson was a little ahead of us musically." He played Arnett Cobb, and Dinah Washington's "Evil Gal Blues" (1945) for Heath. Rice says Jefferson was a "single" piano player, not really a jazz player; perhaps he means more of a cocktail player. (The paper of March 7 lists the Stanley Gaines all stars with Logan, not Coltrane.)

Sometime in 1953, or even in 1955. Wildwood, on the tip of New Jersey. Coltrane was out there with Daisy Mae at Club Esquire

(Note: The PAA of August 8 lists Bullmoose Jackson's band of that time, and Coltrane is not in it.)

(Note: Coltrane may have joined Johnny Hodges as early as the end of 1953.)

1954
Johnny Hodges Tour with Coltrane

(January 18–28. East St. Louis, Ill. Terrace Lounge [cocktail lounge]. Coltrane may have joined this early.)

Most of March. Hodges toured with a ten- or twelve-piece band in a show that included Billy Eckstine, Ruth Brown, and the Clovers.

Early March. Pittsburgh. (PT, Mar. 13, says they were in Pittsburgh earlier.)

Undated engagements with the Hodges large group:

> Ohio, on date with a harpist added for certain numbers to accompany a vocalist who had a current ballad hit (reported by Benny Golson).
>
> Baltimore (reported by Gary Bartz on Ted Panken's radio show).

March 23 (Tuesday). Philadelphia. Academy of Music, two shows.

From April on, Hodges toured with a septet:

Probably April 12–18. Philadelphia. Emerson's. (This was possibly April 5–11; PT of April 20 may have been behind as it also says Hodges had a record date "last Friday"—that was April 9, an all-star date without Coltrane.)

After the above, for one week. Buffalo. Colonial Tavern ("Woody" McBride, "Wandering with Woody," PT, April 20, 13).

May 4–9. Detroit. Crystal cocktail lounge (DB, May 19).

Undated engagements with Hodges:

> Chicago. Chico Hamilton (on tour with Lena Horne) saw the Hodges band with Coltrane at a place in Chicago with a bar under the stage. Doesn't remember Coltrane soloing.
>
> Washington, D.C. (reported by guitarist Bill Harris; Thomas, 134).

Sometime in June through at least early August. Los Angeles. Unknown location(s).

**June. Los Angeles. Hodges taped in performance. Coltrane does solo.

**July 2. Los Angeles. Hodges recording date for Norgran, now Verve. No Coltrane solos.

**August 5. Los Angeles. Hodges recording date for Norgran, now Verve. No Coltrane solos.

Mid-August. (East) St. Louis, Mo. (reported by trumpeter Conte Candoli).

August 30–September 5. Cleveland. Loop cocktail lounge (DB, Sept. 8). *Note:* It is not certain that Coltrane was still with Hodges at this point.

End of Hodges Tour

Note: Naima says she heard Coltrane "backing up a name singer" in Philadelphia in July 1954. Could be with Big Maybelle in early September? (Thomas, 69).

Ca. September 18, for at least one week. Philadelphia. "Mop Dudley and his Collates still at Pitts' Musicalounge, 13th and Poplar Streets. Featured on tenor sax is John Coltrane" (Jimmy Brown, "These Foolish Things," PT, Sept. 18, 1954, 9).

Undated engagements:

> Maybe 1954–55. Philadelphia. Pickup band with Miles Davis and Jimmy Forman (says Forman). Occasional gigs, perhaps at the 421 Club.

December 1954 or February 1955. Philadelphia. Blue Note. If Coltrane did work
here as a leader opposite Parker, it would have to have been during one of these
Parker gigs: December 13–18, 1954, or February 21–27, 1955 (dates from Vail's
Bird's Diary).

Maybe 1954. Philadelphia. Walking the bar at Point Bar, Snake Bar, maybe Diamond Shoe.

Maybe 1954–55. Cleveland. With Big Maybelle and Steve Davis. If so, this could be
when Coltrane heard Art Tatum and Oscar Peterson at a private jam session.

Maybe 1954–55. Manhattan. Birdland. Some Monday night sessions (according to
Billy Taylor in Thomas, 70–71).

Late 1954 through 1955. Philadelphia. Bill Carney's "Hi-Tones."
December 31. Vineland, N.J. Ted Curson group.

1955

(February. See December 1954 re Parker.)

Undated engagements:

Philadelphia. Bill Carney's "Hi-Tones," various locations including Club Zel-mar
(also known as Zelmar back in 1947) at 37th and Market, and Spider Kelly's (1
S. Mole St.)

*1955. Philadelphia. Bill Carney's "Hi-Tones" taped at a club with Coltrane.

New Jersey. Bill Carney's "Hi-Tones."

Buffalo, several times. Bill Carney's "Hi-Tones."

June 15. Niagara Falls, American side (Simpkins, 258). This may be the polka band gig
with bassist Jymie Merritt in upstate New York (see Simpkins, 42). Or this could
have been with the "Hi-Tones."

(*Note:* Miles Davis appeared July 18–24 with Bud Shank on alto and a local rhythm
section at the Blue Note in Philadelphia. It is possible that James Forman was on
piano and that Coltrane was added on tenor for at least part of the gig.)

(*Note:* September 5–10. Philadelphia. Blue Note. Miles Davis. Davis probably tried out
John Gilmore on tenor this week [Vail]. Coltrane may have played as well; George
Avakian remembers seeing Davis and Coltrane in Philadelphia before they
recorded.)

Ca. September 19–25; possibly beginning September 12. Philadelphia. "Mr. Organ"
Jimmy Smith and trio at Spider Kelly's with matinees at 4:00 on Monday, Friday,
Saturday. (The gig continued with Odean Pope on tenor after Coltrane joined
Davis.)

Miles Davis Tour with Coltrane

September 27 (Tuesday)–October 2. Baltimore. Club Las Vegas (Vail).
October 5–10. Detroit.
Possibly October 11–12. Philadelphia. Andy's Log Cabin. DB of November 16 says
Davis was recently there.

October 13–26. Manhattan. Birdland. On bill with Terry Gibbs Quartet and vocalist Jeri Southern (Vail).

(*Note:* Chambers, 217—copied in *Miles*, 195—says the group was at the Sutherland in Chicago, opening October 12, then at Peacock Alley in St. Louis, and then Cafe Bohemia in New York, but all this appears to be incorrect.)

October 15 (Saturday), 8:30 P.M. Manhattan. Carnegie Hall. Jazz for Israel (Red Cross Benefit), on bill with Tito Puente, Steve Allen, Art Blakey, many others. Probably played at Birdland later that night.

October 27–November 9. Manhattan. Cafe Bohemia.

*(*)October 27. Manhattan. Davis recording for Columbia. From now on Coltrane solos on most of his recording sessions.

**November 16. Hackensack, N.J. (original location of Rudy van Gelder studio). Davis recording for Prestige.

November 18–19 (Friday–Saturday). Manhattan. Basin Street. On bill with Erroll Garner, Johnny Smith.

**November 18. Manhattan. Basin Street. (*Note:* The date October 18 given in Fujioka is wrong.) About ten minutes was broadcast live on Steve Allen's NBC-TV program. Only the audio has been issued. The visual program was destroyed years ago simply because NBC needed to clear off some shelf space. (Thanks to Steve Allen for this information.) It is remotely possible that another copy exists. On the audio portion, Allen asks Davis what's wrong with his voice, to which Davis replies, "Operation." Apparently this was shortly after the time when Davis was hospitalized to remove nodes on his vocal chords. This operation is usually given as February 1956 in Davis's autobiography and elsewhere but must have been shortly before this broadcast. (DB, Oct. 17, 1957, reported that Davis had had surgery around late August–early September 1957; that must have been something different.)

November 21–27. Washington, D.C. Olivia Davis's Patio Lounge.

December 5–10. Philadelphia. Blue Note (DB, December 14).

*One night during the above gig. Philadelphia. Blue Note. Newly discovered tape from within the club, about 90 minutes in all. The repertory places the tape in this time period. The drummer is clearly announced as Arthur Taylor.

December 21–January 3, 1956. Chicago. Birdland (formerly Beige Room), on bill with a Calypso dance team and exotic dancer.

1956

(All gigs are still with Davis except for those otherwise listed.)

(*Note:* Chambers, 231 says a Toronto gig for early 1956 was canceled.)

January 6–19. Los Angeles/Hollywood. Jazz City (Vail).

January 24–Feb. 5. San Francisco. Blackhawk (Vail).

February, for two weeks. Los Angeles. Jazz City again (from Sy Johnson; Chambers, 253, says this was in 1957 but Johnson says it was their first time there, which was 1956).

**March 1 or 2. Los Angeles. Paul Chambers Quartet recording.

March 7–27. Chicago. Show Lounge (formerly Beige Room), on bill with Sun Ra and Johnny Guitar Watson.

April 9–15. Quebec (Quebec City?). Oyster Barrel (DB, April 18). *Note:* This may be the gig mentioned in *Miles* 213. It may have been Quebec City, as there is no evidence of them having performed in Montreal.

April 16–22. Boston. Storyville (Vail).

**April 20. Cambridge, Mass. Paul Chambers Sextet recording.

May 3–9. Manhattan. Cafe Bohemia (Vail).

**May 7. Hackensack, N.J. Elmo Hope Sextet recording for Prestige.

**May 11. Hackensack, N.J. Davis Quintet recording for Prestige.

**May 24. Hackensack, N.J. Sonny Rollins and John Coltrane recording for Prestige (one number, "Tenor Madness," only).

May 25–June 10. Manhattan. Cafe Bohemia, in celebration of the club's first anniversary (DB, June 27).

*(*)June 5. Manhattan. Davis Quintet recording for Columbia.

June 19–July 7. Chicago. Crown Propellor Lounge (DB, June 13).

July 13–21. St. Louis, Mo. Peacock Alley (DB, July 11).

**July 14. St. Louis. Peacock Alley. Radio broadcast.

**July 21. St. Louis. Peacock Alley. Radio broadcast.

August 31–September 27. Manhattan. Cafe Bohemia (DB, Aug. 8), opposite Bud Powell.

**September 7. Hackensack, N.J. Prestige All Stars recording.

*(*)September 10. Manhattan. Davis Quintet recording for Columbia.

*September 15. Manhattan. Cafe Bohemia. Short radio broadcast.

*(*)September 21. Hackensack, N.J. Paul Chambers Sextet recording for Blue Note.

*September 29. Manhattan. Cafe Bohemia. Short radio broadcast.

October 1–7. Boston. Storyville, opposite Australian Jazz Quintet (Vail).

October 5 at 8:30 P.M. Manhattan. Carnegie Hall. Salute to Sammy Davis, benefit for Fellowship House, on bill with Bud Powell, others. Davis may have driven down for this while Coltrane and the others continued in Boston.

October 6. Boston. Storyville. Radio broadcast aired but never found.

October 15–31. Manhattan. Cafe Bohemia. Coltrane was out for part of this gig.

(*Note:* There was no broadcast on October 27 as listed in discographies.)

Possibly around here. Long Island, N.Y. Unknown club. A tape is rumored of Davis with Coltrane and Rollins, but it has never been found. (Not 1957 as in Fujioka, 85.)

**October 26. Hackensack, N.J. Davis recording for Prestige.

(*Note:* Davis was in Europe for most of November. DB, November 28 said he would be at the Marina—possibly Olivia Davis's upstairs jazz parlor—in Washington, D.C., for two weeks in November, but this must have been canceled.)

Probably around here. Philadelphia. Jimmy Garrison plays with Tommy Monroe big band and Coltrane appeared as guest soloist.

**November 30. Hackensack, N.J. Tadd Dameron Quartet recording for Prestige.

Ca. December 4–9, or longer. Philadelphia. Davis Quintet at the Blue Note. (Vail is wrong to put Davis at Olivia's in Washington, D.C. opposite Max Roach. It is well documented that Lester Young was at Olivia's, and Roach was at Cafe Bohemia in Manhattan. In fact both of them broadcast after Davis on December 8; see next listing.)

**December 8 (Saturday), 8–8:15 p.m. Philadelphia. Blue Note. Short radio broadcast. (Vail is wrong to put this in 1955. The broadcast is definitively dated by Art Zimmerman, and is from a series that only aired on Saturdays beginning in 1956.)

December 21 (Friday)–27. Chicago. Crown Propellor Lounge. (*Note:* They were not at the Sutherland, as sometimes listed.)

1957

All gigs are still with Davis except for those otherwise listed.

January 5–21. Los Angeles/Hollywood. Jazz City (second annual visit, says DB, Jan. 23). (*Note:* Reported from anywhere around this time is a tape of Coltrane with the Lighthouse All Stars. See Fujioka, 369.)

January 25–February 7. San Francisco. Blackhawk, on bill with Dave Brubeck (Vail).

Feb. 15. Pittsburgh. Syria Mosque. Concert with Ted Heath band from England also on bill (Vail).

March 6 (Wednesday)–19. Chicago. Preview's Modern Jazz Room, featuring "John Coltran." Vocal trio also on bill. (DB Feb. 20 gives the date as Feb. 27–March 10, but the ads confirm the above.)

**March 22. Hackensack, N.J. Prestige All Stars recording.

March 26–April 1. Baltimore. Comedy Club. Local drummer Owen Pinkney filled in the first night because Philly Joe Jones was a day late (DB 5/16).

Ca. April 2–4 (Tuesday–Thursday). Pittsburgh. Midway (DB 4/18).

April 5–28. Manhattan. Cafe Bohemia, first weekend on bill with Art Blakey's Jazz Messengers (including Johnny Griffin and Jackie McLean), then a week with Ronnell Bright, and last two weeks with Lee Konitz Quintet.

*(*)April 6. Hackensack, N.J. Johnny Griffin recording for Blue Note, with Blakey.

*April 13. Manhattan. Cafe Bohemia. Short radio broadcast. (Concerts with Davis, Gillespie and others at Town Hall were announced for April 13 and 20 but later Davis was removed from the bill.)

**April 16. Manhattan. Thelonious Monk recording for Riverside.

**April 18. Hackensack, N.J. Prestige All Stars recording.

**April 19. Hackensack, N.J. Mal Waldron recording for Prestige.

**April 20. Hackensack, N.J. Prestige All Stars recording.

End of Davis Tour

**May 17. Hackensack, N.J. Mal Waldron recording for Prestige.

**May 17. Hackensack, N.J. Paul Quinichette/John Coltrane recording for Prestige.

One Sunday, spring 1957. Manhattan. Cafe Bohemia. Art Farmer reports that Coltrane filled in for ailing Hank Mobley.

Probably May. Philadelphia. Red Rooster. Coltrane Quartet with Tyner, Garrison, and drummer Al Heath or (says John Glenn) Eddie Campbell.

Probably May. Philadelphia. House of Jazz. Coltrane Quartet.

**May 31. Hackensack, N.J. John Coltrane recording for Prestige.

Sometime in June. Brooklyn. (Blue) Coronet. Coltrane group (according to Nellie Monk).

**June 25. Manhattan. Thelonious Monk recording for Riverside.

*(*)June 26. Manhattan. Thelonious Monk recording for Riverside.

July 18 through late August. Manhattan. Five Spot. Monk quartet.

**Between July 18 and August 11. Manhattan. Thelonious Monk recording for Riverside.

**August 16. Hackensack, N.J. John Coltrane recording for Prestige.

**August 23. Hackensack, N.J. John Coltrane recording for Prestige.

Last week of August to early September. Manhattan. Monk replaced at the Five Spot by the Donald Byrd-Lou Donaldson group; Coltrane freelances elsewhere?

Early September–November 6. Manhattan. Five Spot. Monk quartet. *Note:* Naima told T. S. Monk Jr. there were many hours of tape from the Five Spot, but they apparently no longer exist. The issued tape is probably from Sept. 11, 1958, q.v.

*(*)September 1. Hackensack, N.J. Sonny Clark recording for Blue Note.

*(*)September 15. Hackensack, N.J. Coltrane recording for Blue Note; *Blue Train.*

**September 20. Hackensack, N.J. Prestige All Stars recording.

**October. Manhattan. Oscar Pettiford All Stars recording for Bethlehem.

October 11. Manhattan. Five Spot. Joe Termini, owner of the Five Spot, rigged a birthday celebration for Monk, and Oscar Pettiford showed up to m.c. the impromptu party. Every patron got a piece of Monk's cake (DB, Nov. 14).

October 27 (Sunday), afternoon. New York. Palm Gardens ballroom. Coltrane with Donald Byrd, Art Taylor, Tommy Potter, and Red Garland (DB, Nov. 28). Coltrane played with Monk that night.

November 3 (Sunday), 3:00–7:00 P.M. Philadelphia. "The Soul Sisters of Bal De Tete Presents Their 2nd Rhythm & Jazz Concert of '57" at Times Auditorium, 309 S. Broad at Spruce St. "Guest Star John Coltrane, Sax Sensation, Formerly with Miles Davis—Currently with Thealonius *(sic)* Monk; Calvin Massy's *(sic)* Cotillion (QV.) Band, plus many others." Coltrane probably played that night in New York with Monk.

Between November 7 (Thursday) and 20 (Wednesday). Manhattan. Unknown location. Coltrane reportedly performed with the Red Garland quintet with Donald Byrd. Sahib Shihab and Oscar Pettiford were at the Five Spot during this time. Monk was slated to appear at Cafe André in Montreal as a guest, I suppose with someone else's group (DB, Oct. 3).

**November 15. Hackensack, N.J. Red Garland recording for Prestige.

November 21–December 26. Manhattan. Five Spot. Monk quartet.

November 29. Two shows, 8:30 P.M. and midnight. Carnegie Hall. Benefit for the Morningside Community Center (122nd St.). "Miss Billie Holiday. Gillespie; Monk Quartet with John Coltrane (Courtesy 5 Spot Cafe); Introducing in Concert the Brilliant Sonny Rollins. Chet Baker/Zoot Sims Qtt. Special attraction Ray Charles." Voice of America was supposed to record this, but there is no tape in the V.O.A. collection at the Library of Congress (see also Fujioka, 81, bottom) (reviewed by Whitney Balliett, *New Yorker*, December 7, 1957). Uncertain if they played at all at Five Spot that night.

**December 13. Hackensack, N.J. Red Garland recording for Prestige.

**December. Manhattan. Art Blakey Big Band recording for Bethlehem. Coltrane may be heard joking about balance problems before "Pristine" Take 6. His voice also seems to be barely audible at the end of "El Toro Valiente" Take 1.

(*Note:* Coltrane did not lead a quartet at the Five Spot from December 17–23, as listed in Fujioka. That was my error—correct details are below.)

**December 20. Hackensack, N.J. Ray Draper recording for Prestige/New Jazz.

December 27–January 1, 1958. Manhattan. Five Spot. Coltrane quartet. Peter Keepnews notes, from Joe Termini's notes, that the group appears to have continued without Monk; no pianist is listed for Friday, December 27, and from December 28 through January 1, Red Garland replaced Monk. Keepnews notes that Monk had reportedly at times taken a night or part of a night off during this long stint and he may have simply not shown up on the twenty-seventh. DB, Feb. 6, 1958, reported that Monk was to play at the Five Spot at least for New Year's Eve; perhaps he did.

(*Note:* Based on the above it seems that Coltrane was not with Davis at the Sutherland in Chicago from Dec. 25 through Jan. 1.)

(*Note:* The Davis jam session listed here in Fujioka, 85, probably took place around October 1956—q.v.—if it ever happened at all.)

1958

Davis tour resumes. All gigs are with Davis except for those otherwise listed.

January 2–15. Manhattan. Birdland, opposite Johnny Richards Orchestra (Vail).

**January 3. Hackensack, N.J. Gene Ammons All Stars recording for Prestige.

**January 10. Hackensack, N.J. Coltrane recording for Prestige.

January 21–26. Brooklyn. Continental.

**February 4. Manhattan. Davis recording for Columbia.

**February 7. Hackensack, N.J. Coltrane recording for Prestige.

February 10–15. Pittsburgh. Copa (DB, Mar. 6).

February 16 (Sunday), 8:00 P.M. Philadelphia. Miles Davis Quintet *(sic)* "World's Greatest Jazz Trumpet" and D. Staton, H. Silver, Joe Pauline Qtt featuring Red Rodney, also Lee Morgan, Sonny Stitt, others, at Cavalcade of Jazz, Town Hall, Broad and Race Streets. Backing up Davis were "John Coltran, Cannonball Adderly, Paul Chambers, Philly Jo Jones" (piano not listed); so it's the sextet.

*(*)March 4. Manhattan. Davis recording for Columbia.

**March 7. Hackensack, N.J. Kenny Burrell recording for Prestige. (*Note:* Saxophonist Greg Wall pointed out to me that "Freight Trane" is the same theme played on a tune called "Drummer Man" on a Dinah Washington 1949 session. The composer is unknown. Tommy Flanagan told me that he did not write "Freight Trane," although he is listed as composer. Kenny Burrell wrote to me on May 6, 1996 that this tune was played around Detroit, but "we did not know the composer.")

**March 13. Hackensack, N.J. Wilbur Harden recording for Savoy.

**March 26. Hackensack, N.J. Coltrane recording for Prestige.

April 5, 8:30 and 11:30. Manhattan. Town Hall. Village Voice presents a tribute to W. C. Handy (he died March 28) with the Davis group, Gillespie, J. J. Johnson, Stan Getz, others.

*Around this time. At least two tapes remain of Coltrane practicing solo; he always practiced with a tape recorder, but I believe he usually recorded over the same tape.

Easter evening and the next night. Manhattan. Five Spot. Carl Grubbs believes that Coltrane was there but did not attend and doesn't know what band it was.

April 25–May 18. Manhattan. Cafe Bohemia, on bill with Jimmy Giuffre. Bill Evans joins on piano.

*May 3. Manhattan. Cafe Bohemia. Short radio broadcast.

(*Note:* There was a broadcast on May 10 but no tape is known. It has sometimes been placed at Storyville in Boston, but must have been at the Bohemia.)

May 12–18. Manhattan. Cafe Bohemia, opposite Phineas Newborn.

**May 13. Hackensack, N.J. Wilbur Harden recording for Savoy.

**May 17. Manhattan. Cafe Bohemia. About twenty-minute broadcast.

May 20–25, including Sunday matinee May 25 at 4:00. N.J., near Philadelphia. Red Hill Inn. Jimmy Cobb replaces Jones.

**May 23. Hackensack, N.J. Coltrane recording for Prestige.

*(*)May 26. Manhattan. Davis recording for Columbia.

Ca. May 27–June 1 or the following week. Detroit. Blue Bird Inn (DB, June 26).

Note: There exist several hours of practice tapes, mostly solo, from Coltrane's visits to Detroit in the period around 1958. These would be from the above and other dates.

June 10–15. Washington, D.C. Spotlite Lounge. (Blume calls it "Cecilia's.")

*June 15, before the gig. Taped interview with August Blume in Baltimore. Some published in *Jazz Review,* the rest in this book.

Ca. June 17–22. Manhattan. Black Pearl (around Seventy-second and Second Ave.) (according to pianist Walter Davis Jr. and DB, July 24).

June 24–29. Manhattan. Small's Paradise.

**June 24. Hackensack, N.J. Wilbur Harden and Curtis Fuller recording for Savoy. I don't know why Vail gives August 25 for this.

*June 25. Manhattan. Michel Legrand recording for Columbia.

**July 3. Newport, RI. Newport Jazz Festival. Live recording for Columbia.

**July 11. Hackensack, N.J. Coltrane recording for Prestige.

July 22–August 3. Manhattan. Village Vanguard, on bill with Ethel Ennis.

August 5–10. Washington, DC. Spotlite Lounge.

*August 9. Washington, DC. Spotlite Lounge. Short radio broadcast. (Sometimes wrongly dated as June 30.)

August 12–17. Baltimore. Comedy Club.

August 23. New York. Randall's Island jazz festival. Coltrane appeared twice—with Davis, and with an all-star "Dream Band."

**September 9. Manhattan. Plaza Hotel, Persian Room. Live recording for Columbia. Coltrane also participated in a jam session, not recorded.

**September 11. Manhattan. Five Spot. Thelonious Monk quartet with guest John Coltrane. Audience tape, issued on Blue Note.

**September 12. Manhattan. George Russell recording for Decca; "Manhattan."

Opening September 15, for at least one week. Philadelphia. Showboat. (Wayne Shorter said that Abbey Lincoln sang with Davis; thanks to Avalon Archives for making this interview available to me.)

Ca. September 23–28. Detroit. Unknown location. This may be Coltrane's date leading his own group with Yusef Lateef. (Fujioka, 137, gives this as 1959, which is possible, but Lateef moved to New York before October 1959, probably over the summer.)

*September 25. Detroit. Tape at private house of Joe Brazil. Jam session with Joe Henderson and others.

*(*)October 13. Manhattan. Cecil Taylor recording for United Artists.

October 17–23; midnight show on Saturday. Manhattan. Apollo Theater, on bill with Sarah Vaughan, the Wailers, Johnny Richards.

October–December. Newark, N.J. Wayne Shorter recalls a gig for one night with Lee Morgan and Coltrane. (This goes here, not in 1959 as in Fujioka, because Shorter said he had just left the army, which was in late 1958.)

October 29–November 2. Washington, D.C. Spotlight Lounge.

**November 1. Washington, D.C. Spotlight Lounge. About twenty-minute broadcast.

**November. Manhattan. Ray Draper recording for Jubilee.

November 4–16 or possibly 23. Manhattan. Village Vanguard, on bill with Phineas Newborn (reviewed in *Daily News,* November 9, 8), and then with singer Ernestine Anderson (DB, Nov. 27). Bill Evans leaves at the end of this gig, and Garland returns for a bit.

(November 26 [Wednesday]. DB, November 13, reported Davis was "possibly set" for a Carnegie Hall concert that night. I haven't seen evidence that it happened.)

November 28 (Friday). Manhattan. Town Hall, two shows, on bill with Monk, Mulligan, Guiffre (reviewed by Balliett, *New Yorker,* Dec. 6, 1958).

December 12–18. Washington, DC. Howard Theater, on bill with Horace Silver, Jimmy Smith, Betty Carter.

**December 26. Hackensack, N.J. Coltrane recording for Prestige.

December 27 (Saturday). Manhattan. Town Hall, two shows (8:30, 11:30), on bill with Rollins, J. J. Johnson, Blakey, Anita O'Day. Philly Joe Jones subs for Cobb (Vail).

1959

All gigs are with Davis except for those otherwise listed.

January 1–14. Manhattan. Birdland (DB, Jan. 22), opposite Maynard Ferguson with Wayne Shorter.

**January 3. Manhattan. Birdland. About twenty-minute broadcast.

**January 15. Manhattan. Coltrane/Milt Jackson recording for Atlantic.

January 21–February 2. Chicago. Sutherland Lounge. Coltrane first performs on soprano saxophone.

**February 3. Chicago. Cannonball Adderley recording for Mercury.

Perhaps here. Philadelphia. Showboat (DB, April 2).

February 14. Chicago. Civic Opera House, two shows (8:00, 11:00) on bill with Monk, Mulligan, Sarah Vaughan (Davis now top bill).

February 17–22. San Francisco. Blackhawk.

**March 2. Manhattan. Davis recording for *Kind of Blue*, Columbia.

March 13–19; midnight show Saturday, March 14, only. Manhattan. Apollo Theater. Davis (top bill), Ruth Brown, Monk, and the Johnny Richards Band.

March 13 at midnight. Queens. Loew's Valencia (Jamaica and 165th), on bill with Jimmy Smith, Red Garland Trio, Betty Carter.

**March 26 (formerly thought to be April 1). Manhattan. Coltrane recording for Atlantic. Complete session reel issued in *The Complete Atlantic Recordings* (Rhino).

Likely the same week as above. Manhattan. Armory in Harlem. Kenny Dorham Quintet with Coltrane, Cedar Walton, Lex Humphries.

**April 2. Manhattan. CBS-TV broadcast (aired July 21, 1960). Video issued on Vintage Collection, vol. 2 (Warner).

April 16–29. Manhattan. Birdland, opposite Gil Evans band (Vail).

**April 22. Manhattan. Davis recording for *Kind Of Blue*, Columbia. (Also said to be April 6.)

*Late April or early May. New York. Fifteen-minute tape of Coltrane rehearsing "Countdown" at Art Taylor's mother's house; never found but Taylor (since passed away) told Phil Schaap and myself that it did exist. It was a duet, not quartet as listed in Fujioka, 136.

**May 4 and 5. Manhattan. Coltrane recording for *Giant Steps*, Atlantic.

May 6–18. Chicago. Sutherland Hotel Lounge.

(After the above, Simpkins, 90 mentions an undated gig at Storyville, Boston. Chambers, 2:6, is wrong to assume that gig goes here—it could even be 1956; cf. Chambers, 1:268.)

Possibly May 21–26 (or in March). Philadelphia. New House of Jazz. Coltrane quartet (a pick-up group just for this gig, personnel unknown).

May 29–June 18. San Francisco. Blackhawk (see Simpkins, 89–90).

(*Note:* DB, May 14, said Davis would be at the Shrine in Los Angeles at the end of June. I have no evidence that this occurred.)

July 1–5 or possibly through 12. Los Angeles. Jazz Seville. (Reviewed by John Tynan in DB, August 6, 32—says first West Coast appearance in over two years!?) Heath replaces Coltrane midway.

(*Note:* Davis played the following gigs without Coltrane:

Thursday, July 23. Toronto jazz festival with Jimmy Heath. Not July 22 as in Vail. Reviewed in *Coda*, August 1959; 13.

July 24–30. Chicago. Regal Theater with Jimmy Heath, on bill with Dakota Staton, Sonny Stitt, Jimmy Smith, Nipsey Russell.

August 2. French Lick Jazz Festival, Indiana, with Heath. Originally scheduled for July 31. [Vail].

August 7. Chicago. Playboy Jazz Festival with only Adderley on saxophone.

August 9. Lenox, Mass. Berkshire Music Barn.)

August 13–September 16 (but see below). Manhattan. Birdland, opposite Chico Hamilton for first two weeks. Coltrane is back (Vail).

Sunday, August 23. Randall's Island festival (off of Manhattan).

*August 26. According to *Miles*, 238, there was a Voice of America radio broadcast this night (a tape is reported). This is also the night that Davis was assaulted by a policeman. For the rest of the Birdland engagement Nat Adderley played where possible; sometimes they worked without a trumpeter.

Sometime during the Birdland gig above, one Sunday matinee and one Monday night. Manhattan. Birdland. All-star group with Wayne Shorter, Cedar Walton, Tommy Flanagan, George Tucker, Elvin Jones alternating with another drummer (reported by Wayne Shorter).

Somewhere around here. Atlantic City. Cotton Club. Byard Lancaster definitely saw the group here on two separate weeks right around this time, without Adderley. A gig had been scheduled ca. September 1–6. Vail writes that it was canceled, but maybe the band did play there and then returned to Birdland through September 16. A return to the Cotton Club could have followed.

October 4. Manhattan. Hunter College. Benefit for the NAACP, Davis sharing headline with Dakota Staton over many other groups.

October 11. Philadelphia. Academy of Music, on bill with Ray Charles, Horace Silver, Sonny Stitt and Philly Joe Jones with his own group (Vail).

October 16–22. Washington, DC. Howard Theater, on bill with Dakota Staton (top bill), Red Garland's trio, singer Leon Thomas, comedian Redd Foxx (Vail).

October 23–29. Brooklyn Paramount theater. The bill was, in order, Basie featuring Joe Williams, Dakota Staton, the Davis group, George Shearing sextet, Lambert, Hendricks and Ross, Don Adams, Symphony Sid, and the film *The Young Land.*

Possibly October 30–November 4. Manhattan. Birdland (DB, Nov. 12).

November 5–25. Manhattan. Birdland, opposite Johnny Smith, then Harry Edison, whose group possibly included Elvin Jones.

**November 24. Manhattan. Coltrane recording for Atlantic.

Friday, November 27, 9 P.M. to 3 A.M. Manhattan. St. Nicholas Arena (Sixty-sixth St. and Columbus Ave.), on bill with Tito Puente's and a warmup band.

November 28, two shows. Manhattan. Town Hall. Coltrane Quartet (personnel unknown), on bill with Ornette Coleman, Monk, Cecil Taylor, the Jazztet, Lee Konitz, singer Ernestine Anderson, Count Basie (Fujioka, 140, top).

**December 2. Manhattan. Coltrane recording for Atlantic.

December, one Friday or Saturday. Unknown club, Tottenville Beach, Staten Island. Teddy Kotick Trio with guest Coltrane (reported by pianist Don Friedman).

December 25–31 at midnight. Chicago. Regal Theater, on bill with Blakey, Stitt, Betty Carter, Jesse Powell (who worked with Coltrane in Gillespie's band), others, and a film. (All other sources are wrong to list this as the Sutherland Hotel.)

1960

All gigs are with Davis except for those otherwise listed.

(*Note:* Chambers, 2:6 says Davis played at the Village Vanguard early in 1960, but the source he cites only mentions the Cafe Bohemia from previous years.)

January. San Francisco. Masonic Auditorium (see Fujioka, 141; this may be from late February, when Davis was in California).

Friday, January 15–21. Manhattan. Apollo Theater, top billing over Dakota Staton and James Moody.

Feb. 11–21. Chicago. Sutherland Lounge. They were advertised to open Feb. 10 but couldn't due to a snowstorm in Chicago; their plane was routed to Indianapolis, from where they took a bus to Chicago; meanwhile Chambers was stranded in New York (DB, Mar. 17).

Ca. February 22–26. Philadelphia. Showboat (see DB, Mar. 3 and 17).

*February 24. Philadelphia. Showboat. Coltrane group. Since Davis is not listed on this private audience tape, he must have been absent for one or more sets during this week. The tape box says March 24, which must be wrong.

February 27. Los Angeles. Shrine Auditorium. Davis Sextet with Buddy Montgomery (vibraphone), and Modern Jazz Quartet, Paul Horn, Jackie and Roy (reviewed by John Tynan in DB, April 14, 42).

(*Note:* A tape of this group doing "So What" is rumored to exist.)

Around the same time as above. San Diego. Unknown location, on bill with Paul Horn and possibly the others.

March 3. San Jose. Unknown location. Montgomery still in the group (Vail).

March 4. San Francisco. Civic Center. Montgomery still in the group (Vail).

March 5. Oakland Auditorium Arena. Montgomery still in the group (Vail).

(*Note:* DB, Mar. 17 says Coltrane was scheduled to join the Mal Waldron Trio at the Five Spot March 1 and then have his own combo ready for Mar. 8–22; DB, March 31 says Coltrane would be opposite the Kenny Dorham group with Steve Kuhn for the latter period through March 21. Probably because Coltrane agreed to the European tour with Davis, all this was canceled, and Ornette Coleman's group appeared instead.)

March 7–13 and/or 14–20. Philadelphia. Showboat. Coltrane group, unknown personnel.

**March 21. Paris. Olympia, on bill with Oscar Peterson and Stan Getz groups; the same bill was on all of the following. Most of the indicated tapes are from radio broadcasts.

**March 22, two shows. Stockholm. Konserthuset.

**March 22, between shows. Stockholm. Konserthuset. Taped interview, issued on LP and CD.

March 23. Oslo, Norway. Njårdhallen.

**March 24. Copenhagen. Tivoli Konsertsal.

March 25. Hanover, W. Germany. Niedersachsenhalle.

March 26. Oldenburg, W. Germany. Weser-Ems-Halle.

March 27. West Berlin. Sportpalast.

March 28, two shows. Munich. Deutsches Museum.

March 29. Hamburg. Musikhalle.

*March 30. Frankfurt. Kongresshalle.

March 31. Milan. Teatro Dell Arte.

*April 1 (not 4 as listed elsewhere). Dusseldorf, Germany. Rheinhalle. Coltrane and rhythm section. (Davis was out.)

April 2. Cologne, W. Germany. Messehalle.

April 3. Munich. Deutsches Museum.

April 4. Karlsruhe. Unknown theater.

April 5. Ulm, W. Germany. Donauhalle.

April 6. Vienna. Stadthalle.

April 7. Nürnberg (Nuremberg), W. Germany. Messehalle.

**April 8. Zürich, Switzerland. Kongresshaus.

**April 9, 8:15 P.M. Scheveningen, Netherlands. Kurhaus.

April 9, midnight. Amsterdam, Netherlands. Concertgebouw.

April 10, two shows. Stuttgart, W. Germany. Liederhalle.

From now on all gigs are led by Coltrane unless otherwise noted.

April 16. Manhattan. Town Hall. Vocalist Chris Connor, top billing, followed by Dizzy Gillespie, Oscar Peterson, Coltrane (with unknown personnel), Jackie McLean "and others."

Tuesday May 3–Sunday July 3, with Mondays off (nine weeks in all). Manhattan. Jazz Gallery. Coltrane quartet alternated sets with Chico Hamilton's Quintet (equal billing as "East vs. West Coast Jazz"), May 3–22. Atilla Zoller played part of the gig with Hamilton, and Philly Joe Jones subbed when Hamilton fell ill. Coltrane continued May 24–29 with singer Al Hibbler getting top billing, then Gillespie getting top billing (May 31–June 12), then Monk getting top billing (June 13–July 3). At first Coltrane was only announced through May 15, which has led to some errors in other books, but his engagement was extended.

*June 10. Manhattan. Jazz Gallery. Audience tape, about 90 minutes.

(*Note:* Somewhere in here, Coltrane went to the Showboat in Philadelphia to see the opening night of Davis's new quintet with Sonny Stitt in his place. The Showboat opened on Mondays, Coltrane's night off at the Jazz Gallery. "Miles shocked everyone by *speaking* from the bandstand" to acknowledge Coltrane [DB, July 7, 1960, 46].)

*June 27. Manhattan. Jazz Gallery. Audience tape.

**June 28. Manhattan. Coltrane and Don Cherry recording for Atlantic.

(*Note:* Coltrane was listed in advance ads for Thursday, June 30 at the Newport Jazz Festival, and he was finally scheduled for Monday, July 4 as in Fujioka 141, along with Gunther Schuller, Ornette Coleman, and Bill Evans. But the festival was canceled after Sunday afternoon's concert, due to rioters and other problems, and Coltrane did not appear, which is why the reviews do not mention him. The festival almost went out of business altogether that year; see the reports in *Down Beat*, August 18, 1960, 18–23, 44.)

*July 1. Manhattan. Jazz Gallery. Audience tape.

July 5–17. Manhattan. Small's Paradise (not in Conn. as in Fujioka, 141).

**July 8. Manhattan. Coltrane and Don Cherry recording for Atlantic.

July 18 (Monday)–24. Philadelphia. Showboat.

*July 19. Philadelphia. Showboat. Audience tape.

*July 21–24. Philadelphia. Showboat. Audience tapes from each night.

Possibly July 26–31. Pittsburgh. Crawford's Grill.

August 3–14, except August 8–9. Chicago. Sutherland Hotel Lounge. Billed as "Quintette," but that was probably an error. (Originally scheduled to begin July 20, but apparently postponed; does not appear to be July 26–Aug. 14 as in Fujioka, 141.) During this period "Coltrane on Coltrane" was prepared for DB, to be published September 29 (Thomas, 130 has this wrong),

Saturday, August 20. New York. Randall's Island jazz festival, last billing after Ellington, Monk, Dakota Staton, MJQ, Adderley, and Chico Hamilton.

Probably August 23–28. Detroit. Minor Key.

September 1–11. Los Angeles. Zebra Lounge. Billy Higgins on drums.

*September 8. Los Angeles. Recording for Roulette.

Probably September 13–25. San Francisco. Jazz Workshop. (Thomas, 139, has references to social encounters on September 16 and 22, but since no location is given I must assume these were in San Francisco.)

September 24, afternoon. Monterey, Calif. Monterey Jazz Festival, on bill with Ornette Coleman and others. (Orrin Keepnews tells me there are no tapes of Coltrane at Monterey.)

Possibly September 27–28. Denver. Sonny's Lounge. Elvin Jones joins.

Ca. September 29-October 9. Manhattan. Birdland.

October 10 or 11 through November 6. Manhattan. Half Note.

**October 21. Manhattan. Recording for Atlantic, including "My Favorite Things."

**October 24 (Monday). Manhattan. Two recording sessions for Atlantic.

*October 26. Manhattan. Recording for Atlantic.

November 9–20. Chicago. Birdhouse. (*Note:* Not "Bird House.")

(*Note:* Bobby Hutcherson says he saw the band with Jones and Steve Davis at the Jazz Workshop in San Francisco. If so, it had to be around here.)

1961

Early January. Manhattan. Probably at Village Gate.

Ca. January 17–February 5. Manhattan. Half Note.

(*Note:* Steve Davis says he left after a Philadelphia gig, around here. Thomas, 135.)

Friday, March 17–23. Manhattan. Apollo Theater. Top bill is Miriam Makeba, followed by Coltrane, Oscar Brown, Jr., Machito and Sabu.

*March 20. Manhattan. Davis recording for Columbia; "Someday My Prince Will Come."

*March 21. Manhattan. Davis recording for Columbia.

*Perhaps somewhere in here. Chicago. Sutherland Hotel Lounge. Two tapes, possibly from broadcasts as the Sutherland's radio broadcasts began on October 8, 1960. These tapes cannot be from October 61 as shown in Fujioka, 174. Coltrane added a second bassist—Donald Garrett—and a second drummer for part of a Sutherland gig! (Reported by Gary Goldstein.) After the last set, Coltrane sometimes jammed at Garrett's place with Andrew Hill and others, according to Hill.

April 25 through May 7. San Francisco. Jazz Workshop. During this gig Fujioka, 161 reports that Coltrane played a benefit concert for a thousand sit-ins at the University of California in Berkeley. But it never happened, writes Kofsky (221–22).

*May 2. San Francisco. Taped interview with Ralph Gleason. Mostly published in liner notes.

Probably May 9–14. Los Angeles. Zebra Lounge (*Coda,* June, 14).

**May 23. Englewood Cliffs, N.J. (new location of Rudy Van Gelder studio). Recording for Impulse.

**May 25. Manhattan. Recording for Atlantic.

Somewhere in here. Andrew White recalls seeing the quartet (with Art Davis on bass) in Baltimore.

**June 7. Englewood Cliffs, N.J. Recording for Impulse.

*(*)Saturday, July 1, 8:00 P.M. Newport, RI. Newport Jazz Festival.

July 11–23. Manhattan. Village Gate; second on bill is Aretha Franklin.

*July 22. Manhattan. Village Gate. Audience tape.

*July 23. Manhattan. Village Gate. Audience tape.

July 24–29. Philadelphia. Showboat.

*July 24. Philadelphia. Showboat. Audience tape.

*July 26. Philadelphia. Showboat. Audience tape.

Note: Some of the titles listed in Fujioka, 162 may also be from this week.

August 7. Detroit. Unknown location. Thomas, 144 suggests the Adderleys were on the same bill.

August 8–September 3. Manhattan. Village Gate. First week bills Coltrane first, followed by Blakey and Horace Silver; second week lists Blakey, Coltrane, Silver; third week lists Blakey, Olatunji, then Coltrane. According to Bob Rusch, Roland Kirk sat in with Coltrane on August 17.

August 20 (Sunday). Lenox, Mass. Berkshire Music Barn. Coltrane and Blakey bands, probably in afternoon so they could be at the Village Gate that night.

August 25. New York. Randall's Island Jazz Festival.

Perhaps around here. Andrew White recalls that Coltrane played for a week at the Bohemian Caverns, Washington, D.C.

(September 19–24. San Francisco. Jazz Workshop, with Wes Montgomery. It is possible that Coltrane played here except for the night at Monterey shown below, then continued as shown below.)

September 22. Monterey, Calif. Monterey Jazz Festival, with Wes Montgomery in the band. (Orrin Keepnews tells me there are no tapes of Coltrane at Monterey.)

Probably September 26–October 1. San Francisco. Jazz Workshop, with Wes Montgomery in the band.

*One night between September 26 and October 1. San Francisco. Jazz Workshop. Audience tape of one set.

October 3–8, possibly longer. Los Angeles. The Renaissance, on bill with Carmen McRae.

Note: Coltrane was scheduled to play at the Sutherland Lounge in Chicago October 11–15 or until the twenty-second, but the gig never happened. *Coda,* October, 14, explains that the Sutherland's main lounge closed on September 12 and that Coltrane's date was canceled. Coltrane appears to have stayed in California, as Thomas confirms he was in San Francisco on October 16 (145). Perthaps he played another week, through October 15, in Los Angeles. (The tapes listed in Fujioka must be from earlier this year, q.v.)

October 16–22. Philadelphia. Showboat.

*October 21. Philadelphia. Showboat. Audience tape. (Some of the ones listed in Fujioka, 162 might also be from this week.)

October 24–November 5. Manhattan. Village Vanguard.

**November 1–3. Manhattan. Village Vanguard. Live recordings for Impulse.

(*Note:* Fujioka 179 is in error. There was no concert on November 4. They were still at the Vanguard, according to David Wild.)

**November 5. Manhattan. Village Vanguard. Live recording for Impulse.

*November 10. Manhattan. Television "PM West" broadcast; Carmen McRae with Norman Simmons trio on same program. No copy has been found.

November 11, two shows. London. Gaumont State Theater, Kilburn; on bill with Gillespie, as on all of the following. Most of the indicated tapes are from radio broadcasts.

*November 11. London. Taped interview with Dutch radio producer Michiel de Ruyter. Coltrane practices his tenor briefly as well.

November 12, two shows. Birmingham, U.K. Hippodrome.

November 13. Glasgow. St. Andrews Hall. (This may be the 14th.)

November 14. Newcastle, U.K. City Hall. (This may be the 13th.)

November 15. Leicester, U.K. De Montfort Hall.

November 16. Brighton, U.K. The Dome.

November 17, two shows. London. Granada theater, Walthamstow.

**November 18, two shows. Paris. Olympia.

As above. While in Paris Coltrane was interviewed by Radio-Beromunster, but no tape appears to exist. The same day he was interviewed for print publications by Marc Crawford (he died in 1995 and I don't know if he taped it), François Postif (he made a tape but it was erased) and J. C. Dargenpierre (aka Zylberstein; he made a tape but it no longer exists)!

November 19. Scheveningen, Netherlands. Kurhaus.

November 19, 11:00 P.M. Amsterdam. Concertgebouw.

**November 20. Copenhagen. Falkonercentret.

November 21, two shows. Göteborg, Sweden. Koncerthuset.

*November 22, two shows. Helsinki. One show was broadcast; the tape exists.

**November 23, two shows. Stockholm. Konserthuset.

*Probably November 23 (but possibly 21). Interview fragment tape (less than three minutes), credited to Claes Dahlgren.

**November 24. Baden-Baden, W. Germany. Television studio. Half-hour TV broadcast, issued on video, *The Coltrane Legacy.*

November 25, two shows. Hamburg. Musikhalle.

November 26. Copenhagen. Falkonercentret. Mel Lewis on drums (Jones had left his passport in Hamburg). Jam session at a club after the concert, possibly including Coltrane.

*November 27. Frankfurt. Kongresshalle.

*November 29. Stuttgart. Liederhalle.

November 30. Nuremberg, W. Germany. Lessingtheater.

December 1. Munich. Deutsches Museum.

*December 2. West Berlin. Freie Universitat. Tape of one title exists.

*Around this date. Unknown location. Undated tape of "Impressions" and "Blue Train." Fujioka, 198 (bottom) puts it in 1962, but Coltrane only performed "Blue Train" around the time of his European tour of 1961.

Possibly December 19–24; more likely the week before. Detroit. Minor Key. (Cf. next item.)

*December 21. Probably Englewood Cliffs, N.J. Recording for Impulse. (Cf. previous item. One of these has the wrong date.)

December 31. Manhattan. Carnegie Hall. On bill with Monk, Rollins, Nina Simone. DB, January 18, 1962 says Stan Getz was there too.

Undated engagements:
Thomas, 144 says Coltrane also performed in Washington, D.C. (Olivia's Patio Lounge) and the Cotton Club in Cleveland.

1962

Ca. January 2 (Tuesday)–14. Manhattan. Jazz Gallery, on bill with Stan Getz quartet.

January 22–28. Detroit. Minor Key.

Ca. February 6–18. Manhattan. Birdland, opposite Bill Evans Trio. Evans's drummer Paul Motian sits in with Coltrane one night, probably for one set.

**February 9. Manhattan. Birdland. Radio broadcast.

*February 16. Manhattan. Birdland. Radio broadcast.

February 24. Manhattan. Kaufman Concert Hall of Ninety-second Street Y, on bill with Betty Carter, Clara Ward. (Not November 4, 1961 as in Fujioka.)

February 28–March 5. Detroit. Minor Key.

March 7–18, except March 12–13. Chicago. McKie's.

March 20–25. Manhattan. Village Gate, on bill with flamenco artist Sabicas (top bill) and blues artist Sam "Lightnin'" Hopkins (after Coltrane).

Ca. March 26–April 8. Philadelphia. Showboat.

*(*)April 11. Englewood Cliffs, N.J. Recording for Impulse.

*April 12. Englewood Cliffs, N.J. Recording for Impulse, unissued; may no longer exist.

May 1–20. San Francisco. Jazz Workshop. DB, July 5 says Dolphy, Wes Montgomery and violinist Michael White sat in during the last day, when there was a matinee and possibly a final evening show as well.

Ca. May 29–June 3, maybe longer. Manhattan. Birdland.

*(*)June 2. Manhattan. Birdland. Radio broadcast; Kai Winding also on bill.

*Somewhere around here. Short taped interview by Benoit Quersin at a club. Published in *Jazz Magazine* (France), January 1963.

*(*)June 19. Englewood Cliffs, N.J. Recording for Impulse.

*(*)June 20. Englewood Cliffs, N.J. Recording for Impulse.

*(*)June 29. Englewood Cliffs, N.J. Recording for Impulse.

July 8. Newport Jazz Festival, Rhode Island. Local television stations WJAR and WPRI shot footage that night; I don't know if they filmed Coltrane, and the current location of the films is unknown.

Sometime in July. Manhattan. Village Gate. (*Coda* August 1962 says Monk and Horace Silver were there too, perhaps sharing the bill.)

Note: Thomas, 153 says Coltrane did not perform ca. August 1–7.

August 15–26. Chicago. McKie's.

Ca. August 27–September 2. Cleveland. Leo's.

**September 18. Englewood Cliffs, N.J. Recording for Impulse.

**September 26. Englewood Cliffs, N.J. Duke Ellington and Coltrane recording for Impulse.

October 12–13 only. Westbury, N.Y. Cork 'n Bib. Perhaps this was the gig attended by educator and trombonist Tom Everett, when reedman Charles Davis played, and Jones had his jaw wired due to an injury. Freddie Hubbard may have appeared also.

October 15–21. Philadelphia. Showboat.

*October 19. Philadelphia. Showboat. Audience tape.

*October 20. Philadelphia. Showboat. Audience tape.

Undated engagements:

Rochester, N.Y. (Simpkins, 145).

Buffalo, NY. Either at the Red Garter or Bon-Ton (Jazz Workshop); *Coda* December 1962 says it was during the past three months.

Blue Coronet, Brooklyn (Simpkins, 156).

*(*)November 13. Englewood Cliffs, N.J. Recording for Impulse.

*November 17, two shows. Paris. Olympia. Most of the indicated tapes from this European tour are from radio broadcasts.

**November 17, between shows. Paris. Olympia. Short taped interview by Benoit Quersin (see photo section). Published in *Jazz Magazine* (France) January 1963.

November 18, early morning. Paris. Blue Note club. Jam session.

*Probably November 18, early morning. Paris. Blue Note club. Somebody taped Coltrane talking on the phone (just his side of the conversation) for three minutes, apparently without his knowledge (cf. Fujioka, 368; not from 1960 as listed there).

**November 19, two shows. Stockholm. Konserthuset.

*November 20. Helsinki. (Tape recently discovered.)

November 21. Oslo. Njårdhallen.

*(*)November 22, two shows. Copenhagen. Falkonercentret.

November 23. Düsseldorf, W. Germany. Robert Schumann Saal.

November 24. Unknown location, W. Germany.

November 25. Hamburg. Musikhalle.

November 26. Unknown location, W. Germany.

November 27. Vienna. Konzerthaus.

**November 28. Graz, Austria. Stefaniensaal.

November 29. Unknown location, W. Germany.

November 30. Zürich. Konzertsaal des Volkshauses.

*December 1, 8:15 P.M. Scheveningen, Netherlands. Kurhaus. A taped interview fragment exists.

December 1, midnight. Amsterdam. Concertgebouw.

*December 2. Milan. Teatro dell' Arte. It is possible that some or all of this was filmed for Italian television, but only the audio is known to exist.

December 1962 or January 1963. New Orleans. Vernon's. During this engagement Ellis Marsalis ran a club called the Music Haven and was there with a quartet including saxophonist Nat Perrilliat. During a break the owner of Vernon's brought out Tyner and Coltrane to hear Marsalis. Coltrane and Perrilliat got to talking and Perrilliat brought Coltrane to Marsalis's house, where they jammed briefly. Earl Turbinton may have jammed with Coltrane also during this week.

December 19–30, except December 24–25. Chicago. McKie's, with Dolphy. Tyner missed the first day, as his wife, Aisha, gave birth then (DB, Jan. 31, 1963).

December 31. Manhattan. Philharmonic Hall.

1963

January 2–6. Chicago. McKie's.

January 7–13. Philadelphia. Showboat.

*January 8. Philadelphia. Showboat. Audience tape.

Probably January 18–27, or January 25–February 3 (a Friday through the following Sunday, including Monday). St. Louis. Gino's. (Reported by Bob Blumenthal.)

*Somewhere around here. Philadelphia. Vocalist Khadijah and John Coltrane (piano). Private home recording of the two.

February. Philadelphia. Showboat.

*February. Philadelphia. Showboat. Audience tape. Roy Haynes on drums.

Probably February 19–March 3, possibly longer. Manhattan. Birdland.

**February 23. Manhattan. Birdland. Radio broadcast, about 25 minutes.

**March 2. Manhattan. Birdland. Radio broadcast, about 23 minutes.

*(*)March 6. Englewood Cliffs, N.J. Recording for Impulse.

**March 7. Englewood Cliffs, N.J. Coltrane and Johnny Hartman recording for Impulse.

Around here. Washington, D.C. International Jazz Mecca, otherwise known as Abart's (reported by Andrew White and DB, May 9).

Tuesday, March 19–24. Los Angeles. Shelly's Manne-Hole (see flyer in *Jazz Critique* [Japan] No. 86, January 20, 1996, 278).

(*Note:* Posters were made for a concert at the Civic Theatre in New Orleans to be held March 20, 1963—see photo section—but as far as I can tell it never occurred.)

March 27 or 29–April 7. Detroit. Grand Bar.

April 9–21. San Francisco. Jazz Workshop.

Around this time. San Francisco and San Jose. Two concerts on a bill with Monk; Coltrane may have played with Monk on one occasion (reported by Nellie Monk).

April 27 and 28, one show each day. Chicago. Civic Opera House, benefit, on bill with Getz, Jack Teagarden, others, and on Sunday the twenty-eighth, Count Basie.

*(*)April 29. Englewood Cliffs, N.J. Recording for Impulse. Roy Haynes replaces Elvin Jones.

May 1–12. Chicago. McKie's.

Probably May 21–26, possibly through June 2. Manhattan. Birdland, on bill with Horace Silver and "The Group." Philly Joe Jones played drums at least on May 23 (Thomas, 162).

June. Cleveland. Jazz Temple.

June, for one week Monday matinee through Sunday. Philadelphia. Showboat.

*June, from Monday matinee of above week. Philadelphia. Showboat. Audience tape.

June 24 or 25 through July 6. Montreal. La Tete de L'Art. Haynes had to go to Newport early to perform with other groups, so he was replaced the last three days by Donald Bailey of Jimmy Smith's trio. (According to Len Dobbins in *Coda*, Coltrane had not been there since with Gillespie.)

*Probably during the above week. A tape exists of drummer André White sitting in with Coltrane.

**July 7. Newport Jazz Festival in Rhode Island.

July 8–14. Philadelphia. Showboat. Elvin Jones is back.

*July, from middle of above week. Philadelphia. Showboat. Audience tape.

July 18–31, or through August 4. Manhattan. Birdland, on bill with Terry Gibbs (including Alice McLeod).

Probably September. Buffalo, NY. Royal Arms.

Possibly September. Cleveland. Jazz Temple. Local drummer "Jacktown" filled in for Elvin Jones on the opening night (DB, Nov. 7).

Ca. October 1–13, possibly longer. Manhattan. Birdland; Joe Newman also on bill.

*(*)October 8. Manhattan. Birdland. Live recording for Impulse.

(October 20. Manhattan. Five Spot. Benefit for CORE with many groups. Coltrane quartet listed as unconfirmed so I don't know if they actually played; Don Friedman played and doesn't recall Coltrane.)

**October 22. Stockholm. Koncerthuset. Most of the indicated tapes from this European tour derive from radio broadcasts.

October 23. Oslo. Njårdhallen.

October 24. Helsinki. (*Note:* A tape is reported, but this very likely is from 1961.)

**October 25. Copenhagen. Tivoli Konsertsal.

October 25, after above concert. Jam session with Roland Kirk's band at Cafe Montmartre.

October 26, midnight. Amsterdam. Concertgebouw.

October 27–30. Probably other concerts in Europe.

October 31. Frankfurt. Kongresshalle.

*November 1. Paris. Salle Pleyel. Tapes exist. There is also a short taped excerpt of unknown origin that some believe is from this date (Fujioka, 235).

*November 1. Paris. Claridge Hotel. Taped interview (ten minutes) with Jean Clouzet and Michel Delorme, published in *Jazz Hot,* December 1963.

**November 2. West Berlin. Auditorium Maximum in Freie Universitat.

November 3. Munich.

*(*)November 4. Stuttgart, W. Germany. Liederhalle. The seventy minutes that remains unissued is among the most extraordinary of all Coltrane recordings.

Probably November 6–24. Philadelphia. Showboat.

*November 6. Philadelphia. Showboat. Audience tape.

*November 18. Philadelphia. Showboat. Audience tape.

**November 18. Englewood Cliffs, N.J. Recording for Impulse.

November 26–probably December 8. San Francisco. Jazz Workshop.

**December 7. San Francisco. "Jazz Casual" public television program produced by Ralph Gleason. (Broadcast in February 1964.) Video issued on *The Coltrane Legacy.*

Probably December 10–22. Los Angeles. Shelly's Manne Hole.

Possibly around here. Buffalo, N.Y. Royal Arms.

Late December. Manhattan. WKCR-FM, Columbia University. Coltrane and Dolphy were on the air, probably talking about the upcoming concert, shortly before December 31. Phil Schaap assures me the tape was erased back in 1966.

December 31, 8:00 P.M. Manhattan. Philharmonic Hall. Coltrane reunited with Dolphy (for the last time), on bill with Cecil Taylor group including Albert Ayler, and Blakey with Wayne Shorter, Freddie Hubbard, Curtis Fuller, Cedar Walton, Reggie Workman (plus Blakey's cousin singing) (reviewed by LeRoi Jones/Amiri Baraka, DB, Feb. 27, 1964, 34).

1964

Probably sometime this year: Tony Williams played one night when Jones was busy playing a drum exhibition. (See *DB*, March 25, 1965, 19.)

January, for two weeks. Manhattan. Half Note. One night Ornette Coleman sat in on trumpet. (This is not Feb. 19–27 nor did Coleman play saxophones, as listed in Fujioka, 242. See DB, Mar. 12, 8.) Gerald "Splivy" McKeever says Dolphy, Shepp, Ayler, Hubbard, and Sanders also sat in. (Interview, late 1973, broadcast on WBUR-FM, with Charlie Perkins.)

February 5–16, except February 10–11. Chicago. McKie's.

February 17–23. Montreal. Casa Loma.

Probably February 24–March 1. Toronto. Unknown location.

March 13–April 2. Manhattan. Half Note.

*April 16. Manhattan or Philadelphia. Audience tape from unknown location.

April 26 (Sunday), 4–8:00 P.M. Manhattan. Five Spot. Benefit for CORE, along with the groups of Sonny Rollins, Joe Farrell, Sheila Jordan. (It is not certain that all appeared.) Coltrane was not at the previous benefit on April 19, as was tentatively announced in DB April 23, but Chris Albertson, who hosted, confirms that he was at this one.

*(*)April 27. Englewood Cliffs, N.J. Recording for Impulse.

**June 1. Englewood Cliffs, N.J. Recording for Impulse.

Note: Simpkins, 172 says there are unissued takes of "Crescent" from one or both of the above sessions.

Note: Thomas says Coltrane canceled concerts planned for Cincinatti and Montreal during the summer of 1964 (174–75); this is confirmed in *Coda*.

*July. Manhattan or Philadelphia. Audience tape from unknown location.

July 15–26. Chicago. McKie's.

July 30–August 4. Manhattan. Birdland, on bill with Les McCann and singer Irene Reid.

August 6–18. San Francisco. Jazz Workshop.

August 21–27. Manhattan. Half Note.

Ca. September 15–19. Philadelphia. Pep's.

*September 18. Philadelphia. Pep's. Audience tapes.

September 24–October 4. Los Angeles. Shelly's Manne Hole.

October 6–18. San Francisco. Jazz Workshop. (DB, Aug. 27, said this would be from September 20–October 4, but the above from Fujioka looks more accurate.)

October 20–24. Chicago. Plugged Nickel.

November 2–8. Boston. Jazz Workshop.

November 10–15. Manhattan. Birdland, on bill with Mingus and comedian Flip Wilson. *Note:* Rashied Ali reports in Fujioka, 245 that he sat in with Coltrane at this time, but elsewhere he said that was in spring 1965 before the *Ascension* recording of June 28. Gerald "Splivy" McKeever claims Coltrane was writing the poem "A Love Supreme" on a napkin during breaks (interview, late 1973, broadcast on WBUR-FM, with Charlie Perkins).

November 20–December 3. Manhattan. Half Note.

*December 9. Englewood Cliffs, N.J. Recording for Impulse; *A Love Supreme.*

*December 10. Englewood Cliffs, N.J. Recording for Impulse; unissued outtakes of parts one and two of *A Love Supreme,* with Shepp, Art Davis and a percussionist added on part one only.

December 18–24. Manhattan. Half Note. There was a radio broadcast, probably on Dec. 18, but there is no tape.

December 27, 2:00 P.M. Manhattan. Village Gate. Benefit for civil rights periodical *Freedomways,* on bill with Max Roach, Abbey Lincoln, Dick Gregory, others.

1965

Probably sometime this year: Coltrane hosted a three-hour program on WBAI-FM, Manhattan. He introduced and played records of his choice, by invitation of program manager Chris Albertson. The show was not recorded.

January 4–10. Montreal. Le Jazz Hot. Opposite Pierre Leduc trio.

January 12–February 3. Manhattan. Half Note.

Probably February. Cleveland. Leo's Casino (DB, Jan. 14).

Possibly February. Philadelphia. Pep's (DB, Mar. 11).

*(*)February 17. Englewood Cliffs, N.J. Recording for Impulse.

**February 18. Englewood Cliffs, N.J. Recording for Impulse.

March 8–14. Boston. Jazz Workshop.

March 19–April 5. Manhattan. Half Note.

*March 19. Manhattan. Half Note. Long radio broadcast.

*Probably from March 26. Manhattan. Half Note. Radio broadcast, recently discovered.

*March 28, 3 to 8:00 P.M. Manhattan. Village Gate, Benefit for Black Arts Repertory Theater School. On bill with Cecil Taylor, Archie Shepp, Albert Ayler, Sun Ra, Betty Carter (singing with Ra, according to the ad), others. Coltrane probably played at the Half Note that night.

*(*)April 2. Manhattan. Half Note. Long radio broadcast.

April 7–18. Chicago. Plugged Nickel.

Note: A week at the Pink Poodle in Indianapolis was announced, but it "fell through" says DB, June 3. I believe it was rescheduled for another unknown time, because David Baker and Marion McPartland recall seeing the band there. Very likely the Pink Poodle was also known by another name and is one of the clubs shown for September 65.

May 4–9, no Sunday matinee. Manhattan. Half Note. Rashied Ali probably sat in at times.

**May 7. Manhattan. Half Note. Long radio broadcast.

**May 17. Englewood Cliffs, N.J. Recording for Impulse.

May 19–23. Washington, D.C. Bohemian Caverns.

**May 26. Englewood Cliffs, N.J. Recording for Impulse. Roy Haynes substitutes for Jones.

*(*)June 10. Englewood Cliffs, N.J. Recording for Impulse. *Note:* A blues (six minutes long) remains unissued from this session.

**June 16. Englewood Cliffs, N.J. Recording for Impulse.

**June 28. Englewood Cliffs, N.J. Recording for Impulse; *Ascension.*

**July 2, ca. 8:00 P.M. Newport Jazz Festival in Rhode Island, on bill with Monk, Carmen McRae, Gillespie, Blakey.

*Soon after recording *Ascension.* Excerpts of Coltrane talking, perhaps partly from on-air discussions with Alan Grant from the Half Note; later compiled and broadcast in posthumous tribute.

July 6–25, except Mondays. Manhattan. Village Gate; with Monk (top billing) through July 18. (*Note:* DB, July 17, says Half Note, which appears to be incorrect.)

**July 26–27. Antibes, France. Juan Les Pins Jazz Festival, on bill with Woody Herman and others. All the audio is issued. The performance was broadcast on television and the first twelve minutes survives; the master tape was reportedly erased.

**July 28. John Coltrane Quartet at Salle Pleyel in Paris.

**August 1. Comblain [La Tour], Belgium, on bill with Woody Herman and others. All the audio is issued; the complete television broadcast survives and an excerpt appears in *The World according to John Coltrane.*

(*Note:* Alain Corneau and Daniel Berger proposed to film a documentary of the preceding European tour but never got a straight answer from Harold Lovett or Coltrane. They expressed their frustration in "Letter Ouverte A John Coltrane," *Les Cahiers Du Jazz* 12 (1965), 106–11.)

*August 15 (Sunday), 8:00 P.M. Chicago. Down Beat Jazz Festival with Shepp added to Coltrane's quartet; on bill with Monk, Mulligan, Herman, others.

August. Cincinnati. Ohio Valley Jazz Festival, on bill with Blakey featuring Gary Bartz (Thomas, 194).

Ca. August 17–22. Cleveland. Possibly Leo's Casino. (See letter to Randi Hultin from August 21, reproduced in this book.)

**August 26. Manhattan. Recording for Impulse.

**September 2. Englewood Cliffs, N.J. Recording for Impulse.

August 31–September 12. San Francisco. Jazz Workshop.

(*Note:* Johnny Hartman was working across the street. Duke Ellington's band was in town from late August on, playing at Basin Street West and to present the first Sacred Concert on September 16; Ellington and some band members came to hear Coltrane one night.)

September. Indianapolis. Carousel Lounge.

September. Indianapolis. Chateau de Count et Eve.

*September. Unknown location. Audience tape; extra drummer performing. (The owner of this tape usually recorded in New York or Philadelphia, but he may have recorded this in California.)

Ca. September 21–26. Probably San Francisco. Possibly Jazz Workshop.

**September 22. Recording session later issued on Impulse.

**September 30. Seattle. Penthouse. Recorded live, later issued on Impulse.

*September 30. Seattle. Penthouse. Last 45 minutes was broadcast on radio; not issued.

**October 1. Lynnwood, Washington. Recording session later issued on Impulse; *Om*.

Early October. Probably Los Angeles. Unknown location, but possibly the It Club. Frank Butler may have been the only drummer on some nights.

**October 14. Los Angeles. Recording session later issued on Impulse.

(*Note:* Fujioka lists for October 10 [but see above] or sometime in November: Baltimore. Madison Club. Concert for Left Bank Jazz Society. This may be Oct. 10, 1966, q.v.)

October, ending October 31. Manhattan. Village Gate.

Ca. November 2–6. Philadelphia. Pep's. Warren McClinton added on drums.

November 10–14. Manhattan. Village Gate, on bill with Carmen McRae; Dick Gregory on Friday and Saturday. *DB,* Dec. 30, 44, says Coltrane played bagpipes and bass clarinet on November 10. The group would have opened on November 9 but that was the date of the massive electrical blackout.

November 15–21. Los Angeles. It Club. (DB, Dec. 2, 12, says it was for ten days, so there may have been three more days.) Frank Butler, Elvin Jones, and Donald Garrett added.

November 21 (Saturday night/Sunday), 2:00–6:00 A.M. Los Angeles. Kabuki Theatre, on bill with (or sitting in with?) singer Arthur Prysock.

**November 23. Englewood Cliffs, N.J. Recording for Impulse; *Meditations*.

November 30–December 5. Manhattan. Village Gate, with Gloria Lynne on bill Friday and Saturday.

Around here: Boston, for one week. Jazz Workshop. Jones and Ali on drums.

*During above engagement. Coltrane interviewed by Ed Rhodes on college radio. A tape exists but Rhodes doesn't have it.

Late December. Manhattan. Village Vanguard.

(*Note:* The Veteran's Day concert listed here in Fujioka, 248, was in 1966, q.v.)

1966

*Probably somewhere in 1966: Coltrane in rehearsal, taped on several occasions; "Lush Life" and other pieces.

January 23. Stamford Jazz Festival, Conn.

January 25–ca. February 6. San Francisco. Jazz Workshop. Monk also on bill. Garrison and Garrett on basses; Jones and Ali on drums. Beaver Harris replaced Jones from February 26 on.

**February 2. San Francisco. Recording session later issued on Impulse.

February. Detroit. Cobo Hall. Thomas says Coltrane's band was snowed in elsewhere and Coltrane played duets with Alice as well as sitting in with Monk's group (206)!

Undated engagement:

Madison, Wisc.; see photo section in Thomas (preceding 161).

*February 19. Manhattan. Philharmonic Hall, Lincoln Center; "Titans of the Tenor," on bill with Rollins, Hawkins, others. (Postponed from January 14 due to a transit strike; Shepp was removed from the bill and Zoot Sims added.)

Ca. March 2–6 (March 2 is a Tuesday but I believe they opened on a Friday). Chicago. Plugged Nickel. This is probably when Jack DeJohnette played drums along with Ali.

Around here. Los Angeles. Unknown location. Leonard Feather (*Melody Maker,* April 16) says he saw Coltrane "recently" with two drummers, not Elvin Jones.

Ca. March 6–8. Stanford University, Calif. One concert of the quintet plus Juno Lewis, Donald Garrett on additional bass, and Elvin Jones returning on additional drumset.

Ca. March 8–19. San Francisco. Jazz Workshop. Jones still on drums.

Note: A concert announced for March 20 at Loyola College in Montreal was canceled by a telegram on March 18 stating that John was ill (*Coda,* April–May, 1966, 15).

March 22–26. Philadelphia. Pep's. This seems to be the gig Odean Pope remembers with Garrison and a second bass, Jones, Ali and sometimes a third drummer. Jimmy Oliver says Rufus Harley sat in on bagpipes.

April 1. Atlanta. Pascal's La Carousel.

April 3. Austin, Texas. Disch Field. First Longhorn Jazz Festival.

*April 21. Englewood Cliffs, N.J. Recording for Impulse.

April 24, 3:00 and 7:00 P.M. Brooklyn. St. Gregory's Rectory, in the School Hall, on bill with Tyner, Roland Kirk, others. Elvin Jones plays with Coltrane. Shows at 3:00 and 7:00 P.M.

*April 28. Englewood Cliffs, N.J. Recording for Impulse.

May 20–29 including Sunday shows at 4:30 and 9:00 P.M. Manhattan. Village Vanguard, on bill with Clark Terry first two nights, Coleman Hawkins quartet from May 24 on. Byard Lancaster reports that he (on Dolphy's bass clarinet) and Shepp played on the night the album cover photograph was taken, probably Sunday, May 29. Cal Massey was present.

**May 28. Manhattan. Village Vanguard. Live recording for Impulse.

Around here. Detroit. The Drome. DB, August 11 says this was his first Detroit appearance in three years.

*July 2, 2:00 P.M. Newport Festival, Rhode Island, on bill with Horace Silver, Charles Lloyd, Bill Dixon. Silent footage, with an Impulse recording on the soundtrack, appears in the video *The World According to John Coltrane.*

July 9. Tokyo. Prince Hotel, Magnolia Room. Press conference and performance.

**July 10–11. Tokyo. Sankei Hall. Live recording later issued on Impulse.

*July 12. Osaka. Festival Hall. Audience tape exists of this and/or July 20.

July 13. Hiroshima. Kyoto Kokaido.

July 14. Nagasaki. Nagasaki Kokaido.

July 15. Fukuoka. Fukuoka Shimin Kaikan.

July 16, 6:30 P.M. Kyoto. Kyoto Kaikan.

July 16, 11:30 P.M. Osaka. Syochikuza.

*July 17. Kobe. Kokusai Kaikan. Audience tape.

July 18. Tokyo. Koseinenkin Hall.

*(*). July 18, afternoon. Tokyo. Taped interview; about eleven minutes was issued out of at least four hours; the balance was erased in the early 1970s and no copy appears to exist!

July 19. Tokyo. Koseinenkin Hall.

*July 20. Osaka. Festival Hall. Audience tape exists of this and/or July 12.

July 21. Shizuoka. Shizuoka Kokaido.

**July 22, 6:30 P.M. Tokyo. Koseinenkin Hall. Live recording later issued on Impulse.

July 22, 11:30 P.M. Tokyo. Video Hall. Jam session with Coltrane and Japanese jazz musicians.

July 23. Tokyo. Aichi Bunka Kodo.

July 24, midnight. Tokyo. Video Hall. Jam session with Coltrane and Japanese jazz musicians.

(*Note:* A short solo alto saxophone tape is said to be from the Japan tour but it is clearly not in Coltrane's style; it could be Sanders.)

Ca. July 27–August 7. San Francisco. Jazz Workshop.

August 12, 8:30 P.M. (Friday). Manhattan. Village Theatre (2nd Ave. at 6th St; later known by other names), on bill with Marion Brown, Jeanne Lee–Ran Blake duo. (Reviewed in DB, October 20, 1966.)

*Ca. August 14, 1966. Deer Park, Long Island, NY. Taped interview with Frank Kofsky; published in Kofsky's book, in Simpkins and elsewhere. The tape (about one hour) was broadcast on the Pacifica Radio in Berkeley, CA, I think in the early 1970s, and was sold in their catalog at that time.

Possibly early October. Newark, N.J. Front Room—canceled after one night, a Tuesday, according to Sonny Fortune and Byard Lancaster. (Simpkins 211 says three nights.) Lancaster reports that he saw the band there with organist Larry Young sitting in on piano and Sonny Johnson on bass. Fortune says (*Jazz Times,* October 1991, 35) he was to have joined the band if the gig had continued.

Possibly here instead of 1965. October 10. Baltimore. Madison Club concert for Left Bank Jazz Society.

(*Note:* Probably around here. Larry Young duet with Coltrane, probably at Coltrane's home on Long Island. Tape recording said to exist.)

October 30, 7:00 P.M. Manhattan. Village Gate, benefit for Cal Massey, on bill with Max Roach, Betty Carter, Kenny Dorham–Joe Henderson big band, Mel Lewis–Thad Jones big band, Billy Taylor, Shepp, many others.

Note: Coltrane was to go to Berlin November 5, and to England, the Netherlands, and elsewhere, but the tour was canceled. The Sonny Rollins trio with Max Roach and Jymie Merritt went instead.

Friday, November 11. Philadelphia. Temple University. Two altoists sat in, one named Steve Knobloch (confirmed by Francis Davis, Michael Cuscuna, and DB, December 29).

Around this time. Philadelphia. Church of the Advocate. Sonny Fortune sat in and says Coltrane gave a short speech (Thomas, 218, and Simpkins, 210).

November 18–19 (I think just for these nights). Manhattan. Village Vanguard.

December 2–3, possibly starting earlier in the week. Manhattan. Village Vanguard, on bill with Thad Jones–Pepper Adams group.

Somewhere around here. Cambridge, Mass. Massachusetts Institute of Technology. Quartet without Sanders (reported by Bob Blumenthal).

December 26, 8:30 P.M. Manhattan. Village Theatre, on bill with Ornette Coleman.

1967

**February 15. Englewood Cliffs, N.J. Recording for Impulse. Issued in 1995 as *Stellar Regions;* the correct title for that song is "Venus." Also, Coltrane plays alto on both takes of "Tranesonic."

**February 22. Englewood Cliffs, N.J. Recording for Impulse; duets with Rashied Ali.

*February 27. Englewood Cliffs, N.J. Recording for Impulse.

**March 7 (not 17). Englewood Cliffs, N.J. Recording for Impulse.

*March 29. Englewood Cliffs, N.J. Recording for Impulse.

(*Note:* According to Fujioka, around April 9, for one week, Coltrane was scheduled to give three concerts at universities in Chicago but these were canceled. However as shown below this may be from June.)

*(*)April 23, 4:00 and 6:00 p.m. Manhattan. Olatunji Center of African Culture. Last public performance. The first show was taped (one hour) but only a fragment has been issued, on *The Last Giant.*

(*Note:* The following bookings for April and May were canceled:
Ca. April 24–30. San Francisco. Jazz Workshop.
Early May. Baltimore. Concert for Left Bank Jazz Society.
May 14. Los Angeles Jazz Festival; Coltrane group plus strings.)

*May 17. Englewood Cliffs, N.J. Recording for Impulse.

(*Note:* The following last bookings of John Coltrane were canceled:
June. University of Chicago. See Thomas, 222.
June 13–25. Los Angeles. Lighthouse, and Hermosa Beach Club.
Coltrane was listed on advance press release, without a specific date, for the Newport festival on May 20; he was removed from the ads by June 24.)

(*Note:* Coltrane's funeral service, July 21, 1967, with performances by Albert Ayler and Ornette Coleman, was recorded and later broadcast by French radio on October 10, 1967.)

Bibliography

The notes to each chapter provide ample bibliographic information for most sources, and it would be wasteful to repeat that here. The following list gives details for those publications that are cited only by author, with some annotations. A few other items of interest have been added.

Bibliographies

The following two books contain lengthy listings of articles and reviews. Despite one or two errors in each, they are a convenient place to start. The Cole book, below, also has a lengthy bibliography.

Skowronski, JoAnn. *Black Music in America: A Bibliography.* Metuchen, N.J.: Scarecrow Press, 1981. Pp. 169–81. Lists articles from 1958 through 1979. See also "Miles Davis," pp. 183–85.
Gray, John. *Fire Music: A Bibliography of the New Jazz, 1959–1990.* Westport, Conn.: Greenwood Press, 1991.

The Jazz-Institut Darmstadt, directed by Wolfram Knauer, has an excellent search service; they will print out or e-mail a computerized bibliography for any artist, including Coltrane, that will be especially complete for European magazine articles from about 1957 to the present. The lists are free, but donations are welcome. They can also provide copies of the articles themselves if needed, but they will provide only a few of these and will bill for their cost.

Address: Bessunger Strasse 88, 64285 Darmstadt, Germany.
Phone: 49-6151-132877.
Fax: 49-6151-133418.
Home page: http://stadt.darmstadt.gmd.de/kultur/musik/jazz.html
e-mail: jazz@stadt.darmstadt.de

Discographies

Fujioka, Yasuhiro, with Lewis Porter and Yoh-Ichi Hamada. *John Coltrane: A Discography and Musical Biography.* Lanham, Md.: Scarecrow Press, 1995. This has superseded the discography by David Wild that was the previous standard (*The Recordings Of John Coltrane: A Discography* [Ann Arbor: Wildmusic, 1979], plus separately available supplements through 1982). Fujioka intends to keep this volume up to date, with the next edition out in 1998. The listings of issued and unissued recordings are definitive and supersede all other publications. The "musical biography" part consists of listings of gigs interspersed between recordings; this part of the book is not as reliable, and is replaced by my chronology. The book also contains over seventy-five rare photos, and hundreds of small photos of every LP and CD cover.

Ruhlmann, William. "Going to Extremes: John Coltrane on Record," *Goldmine,* June 23, 1995, 18ff. This lengthy article summarizes the biography of Coltrane as given in Thomas and Simpkins. More important, it presents release dates for most of Coltrane's albums, allowing one to see not only when they were recorded but when they were available to the public and began to have an impact. (Discographies give dates of recording, not of issue.) Detailed LP listing and album jacket photos.

Books

Listed in order of publication.

Thomas, J. C. *Chasin' the Trane: The Music and Mystique of John Coltrane.* Garden City, N.Y.: Doubleday and Company, 1975. This book offers many useful interview segments, though the surrounding text contains errors. No index. According to reviewer Ron Welburn in *Coda* (April 1976), Thomas played drums with Stan Kenton's band in the 1960s, had met Coltrane and was a longtime friend of Franklin Brower.

Simpkins, Cuthbert Ormond, M.D., *Coltrane: A Biography.* New York: Herndon House, 1975; reprinted in 1989 by Black Classic Press, with partial index added. This self-published work contains essential information from original interviews. (Unfortunately they are woven into the text in such a way that is often difficult to tell who is speaking, and there are some factual and typographical errors.) Simpkins also reprints numerous interviews, reviews, and rare newspaper clippings from Naima's collection. These are usually set off in small typeface. Twelve pages of Coltrane's music manuscripts are reproduced, as well as some of his prose.

Cole, Bill. *John Coltrane.* New York: Schirmer Books, 1976; reprinted New York: Da Capo, 1993. This book, based on Cole's Wesleyan University dissertation, includes excerpts from solos transcribed by Andrew White. The examples contain copying errors not present in White's originals, such as the incomplete measures on page 73. There is very little analysis of the music; examples are often accompanied by such general observations as "one can see his amazing symmetry and his knowledge of what he wanted to do where" (73). Cole primarily concerns himself with Coltrane's spiritual development, a very important matter, but he neglects to relate this development to the content of the music. Indexed, with lengthy bibliography.

Priestley, Brian. *John Coltrane*. London: Apollo Press, 1987. The author is a jazz pianist himself, and a thoughtful and careful researcher. There is not much new in this little book in the way of biography, but there are many original insights into the music. The discography has since been superseded by Fujioka.

Nisenson, Eric. *Ascension: John Coltrane and His Quest*. New York: St. Martin's Press, 1993; reprinted New York: Da Capo Press, 1995. This book is drawn entirely from secondary sources—mostly Simpkins and Thomas—and as such has no new research to offer. It is a relatively uncritical digest of what other books had to say. Its most interesting and original chapter is the last one, a discussion of the jazz scene since Coltrane died.

Fraim, John. *Spirit Catcher: The Life and Art of John Coltrane*. West Liberty, Ohio: GreatHouse Company, 1996. This self-published effort is basically a fan's overview of the literature and the recordings. I would warn the novice away from it because there are many errors due to Fraim's reliance on the other books and his lack of knowledge about music.

Woideck, Carl. *The John Coltrane Companion*. New York: Schirmer Books, 1998. This anthology will reprint notable articles and reviews about Coltrane, as well as interviews; two of the latter will appear in previously unpublished versions. Some of the contents are asterisked below.

There are also several foreign-language books, among them the following.

Daverat, Xavier. Editions du Limon, 1996. (*Note:* I don't know the title of this book but François Postif tells me it is quite interesting, with much discussion of Coltrane's French concert appearances. In French.)

Filtgen, Gerd, and Michael Ausserbauer. *John Coltrane: Sein Leben, Seine Musik, Seine Schallplatten*. Kempten, Germany: Oreos, 1989. A basic biography, and a discussion of such musical features as the "Giant Steps" changes; the bulk of the book is a discussion of recordings, album by album, with photographs. In German.

Gábor, Simon Géza. *John Coltrane Öröksége*. Budapest: Jazzforum, 1981. A bound photocopied work of about fifty-five pages from the jazz club of Budapest, this is basically an overview of Coltrane's life and career. In Hungarian.

Gerber, Alain. *Le Cas Coltrane*. Marseille, 1985. A detailed discussion of the Atlantic recordings. It is useful for the detail it brings to these works, and for quoting extensively from the French literature on Coltrane. In French.

Articles

The following are some of the publications containing statements by Coltrane. There are also many LP liners, some cited in the Notes, where Coltrane's comments appear. Those articles marked with an asterisk will be reprinted in the Woideck anthology listed above.

St. John's African Orthodox Church (the Coltrane church) has issued *John Coltrane Speaks* (San Francisco: Sunship Publishing, 1981; second edition 1993), a useful compilation of Coltrane's published words, indexed by topic but unfortunately not showing the source of each quotation. It is a pocket size paperback of about 85 pages. A new edition is planned.

Anonymous, "Coltrane Par Coltrane," *Jazz Hot* 265 (October 1970), 8–9, 36. This compilation from French interviews and from Swedish interviews by Björn Fremer (translated into French) includes material not elsewhere available.

The following are in date order:

*Gitler, Ira. "'Trane on the Track." *Down Beat,* October 16, 1958, 16–17.

*Blume, August. "An Interview with John Coltrane." *Jazz Review,* January 1959, 25. A revised version will be in Woideck.

*Feather, Leonard. "Honest John: The Blindfold Test." *Down Beat,* February 19, 1959, 39.

*Coltrane, John, with Don DeMicheal. "Coltrane on Coltrane." *Down Beat,* September 29, 1960, 26–27.

Postif, François. "John Coltrane: Une Interview." *Jazz Hot,* January 1962, 12–14.

*Wilmer, Valerie. "Conversation with Coltrane." *Jazz Journal,* January 1962, 1–2.

Dargenpierre, Jean-Claude. "John Coltrane: Un Faust Moderne." *Jazz Magazine,* January 1962, 21–25. A little-known article, buried in a series of reviews of Coltrane's November 1961 Paris concert, that includes quite a bit of interview with Coltrane.

*DeMicheal, Don. "John Coltrane and Eric Dolphy Answer the Jazz Critics." *Down Beat,* April 12, 1962, 20–23.

Clouzet, Jean, and Michel Delorme. "Entretien avec John Coltrane." *Les Cahiers du Jazz* 8 (1963): 1–14.

Michel Delorme (with Claude Lenissois for the interview portion), "Coltrane, Vedette D'Antibes: 'Je Ne Peux Pas Aller Plus Loin," *Jazz Hot* 212 (September 1965), 5–6.

Coltrane, John. Recorded interview, "Second Night in Tokyo" (Japanese Impulse YB-8508-10). Recorded in 1966, the LP contains about eleven minutes of excerpts from an interview that originally lasted all afternoon. The balance of the interview was later erased.

*Kofsky, Frank. "John Coltrane: An Interview." *Jazz and Pop,* September 1967, 23–31. Reprinted in *Black Nationalism and the Revolution in Music* (New York: Pathfinder Press, 1970), 221–43; citations in this book are to these pages. Also in Simpkins, 163–64, 175, and 212–31.

Magazine issues devoted to Coltrane.

Coda (May 1968), *Down Beat* (July 12, 1979), *Jazz Hot* (France: 265, October 1970; 491, July–August 1992; 492, September 1992), *Wire* (April 1991), *Musica Jazz* (Italy: June 1987) *Musica Oggi* (Italy: 17, 1997) and other magazines have had occasional special issues.

Here are a few authors who discuss the music using transcribed excerpts:

Berliner, Paul F. *Thinking in Jazz: The Infinite Art of Improvisation.* Chicago: University of Chicago Press, 1994. This 900-page work explains all the training and planning that go into jazz improvisation. It includes a score transcription of Coltrane and his rhythm section on "Softly, as in a Morning Sunrise" (1961, live at the Village Vanguard), with analysis, on pp. 689–708, and an analysis of the saxophonist's line on 588–91.

Block, Steven. "Pitch-Class Transformation in Free Jazz." *Music Theory Spectrum* 12/2 (Fall 1990): 181–202. Includes an analysis of Coltrane's playing on "Ascension" (mostly the first take and a bit of the second).

*Carno, Zita. "The Style of John Coltrane." *Jazz Review,* October 1959, 17–21, and November 1959, 13–17. The article's music examples include an arrangement of "Star Eyes," which Coltrane never recorded. Woideck asked Carno about this for me; she said she had heard this in concert.

Horenstein, Stephen. "L'Offrande Musicale de Coltrane." *Jazz Magazine* 283 (February 1980), 32–33.

Jost, Ekkehard. *Free Jazz.* Graz, Austria: Universal Edition, 1974; reprinted by Da Capo Press, 1981. Jost, an insightful and musically knowledgeable observer, pointed out some aspects of prearranged form in Coltrane's late recordings such as "Ascension," and drew attention to some of the influences that motivated new developments in Coltrane's music.

Kernfeld, Barry. "Two Coltranes." *Annual Review of Jazz Studies* 2 (1983), 7–66. Includes detailed analysis of solos from 1958 and 1959.

Logan, Wendell. "The Case of Mr. John Coltrane: A Compositional View." *Numus-West* 2/2 (1975), 40–45.

Pressing, Jeff. "Pitch Class Set Structures in Contemporary Jazz." *Jazzforschung* 14 (1983), 133–72. Includes a detailed analysis of "Offering" (1967).

Putschögl, Gerhard. *John Coltrane Und Die Afroamerikanische Oraltradition (Jazzforschung 25).* Graz, Austria: Akademische Druck-u. Verlagsanstalt, 1993. This 340-page volume of *Jazzforschung* is entirely devoted to this doctoral dissertation, in German with an English summary chapter and many musical examples. The first third is an analysis of black preaching and gospel styles; the remainder looks at Coltrane's way of preaching and "hollering" on the saxophone, as well as his harmonic and rhythmic devices and sense of form. "Out Of This World," "Impressions," "Transition," "Brasilia," and other works are treated in depth.

White, Andrew Nathaniel, III. *Trane 'N Me (A Semi-Autobiography): A Treatise on the Music of John Coltrane.* Washington, D.C.: Andrew's Musical Enterprises, 1981. An informal spiral-bound treatise that combines reminiscences with musical analysis.

Compositions of Coltrane:

The Music of John Coltrane (Milwaukee: Hal Leonard, 1991). No editor is listed but Alice Coltrane is thanked in the introduction. This is the best source for over one hundred compositions that Coltrane recorded from 1956 through 1967. For the later works a transcription of the opening of the recording is provided when no leadsheet exists.

Transcriptions of complete solos (all in B-flat key except the Watanabe):

Baker, David N. *The Jazz Style of John Coltrane: A Musical and Historical Perspective.* Lebanon, IN: Studio 224, 1980. Transcriptions with short text and analysis.

Coan, Carl. *John Coltrane Solos.* Milwaukee: Hal Leonard, 1995. Here are twenty-seven solos.

Demsey, David. *John Coltrane Plays Giant Steps.* Milwaukee: Hal Leonard, 1996. Transcriptions of every take issued in *The Complete Atlantic Recordings,* with a substantial and informative text.

Sickler, Don. *The Artistry of John Coltrane.* Ed. Bobby Porcelli. New York: Big 3 Music Corporation, 1979. Blue Note recordings only; leadsheets, accurate transcriptions, with short text and analysis.

Watanabe, Sadao, ed. *John Coltrane: Jazz Improvisation,* vols. 1 and 2. Tokyo: Nichi-on, 1975. Two books of solos in concert key, supervised by a noted jazz saxophonist.

White, Andrew. Library of about 600 transcribed Coltrane solos. Available individually from the author, at 4830 South Dakota Avenue, N.E., Washington, D.C., 20017. This is the largest source of transcriptions, and they are quite accurate.

Play-Along Recordings

Jamey Aebersold has issued two play-along recordings of Coltrane pieces played by a rhythm section, with a booklet by saxophonist David Liebman. In early 1997 he issued a double-CD set under the heading *Countdown to Giant Steps.* These feature all the pieces that use "Giant Steps" changes, performed and explained by Andy LaVerne.

Related Books on Miles Davis

Chambers, Jack. *Milestones I: The Music and Times of Miles Davis to 1960* and *Milestones II: The Music and Times of Miles Davis since 1960.* Toronto: University of Toronto Press, 1983, 1985; reprinted as one volume. Chambers presents a wealth of information here, of varying reliability. The books are based entirely on prior publications, and incorrect details are mixed in with accurate statements. Every recording session known at that time is discussed.

Davis, Miles, with Quincy Troupe. *Miles: The Autobiography.* New York: Simon and Schuster, 1989. A fascinating "must read," but also a confusing mix of original Davis interviews with quotes and paraphrases from earlier publications (none of which are credited).

Vail, Ken. *Miles' Diary: The Life of Miles Davis 1947–1961.* London: Sanctuary, 1996. A well-researched chronology, amply illustrated with photographs and clippings.

Recommended Boxed Sets

Coltrane's recordings are readily available, and complete information may be found in the Fujioka discography. The three sets listed below are comprehensive—the Rhino sets contain material otherwise unissued—and include informative booklets.

The Last Giant. Rhino Records (R2 71255). Two CDs and booklet. The only issue of one of the 1946 recordings, with rare items from 1951 through 1954 and from 1961 and 1967. The balance is a sampling from the issued recordings with Monk, his own *Blue Train* and the Atlantic works. The essay I wrote for the booklet is superseded by this book.

John Coltrane: The Prestige Recordings (16 PCD-4405-2). Sixteen CDs and booklet. Everything for Prestige except with Miles Davis—those are on the Davis set.

The Heavyweight Champion: The Complete Atlantic Recordings (Rhino R2 71984). Seven CDs and extensive booklet including the only interview his cousin Mary has ever allowed to be published as a free-standing article. The essay I wrote for the booklet is superseded by this book. Everything for Atlantic plus about eighty minutes of new material. The ads for this actually undersold it—they mentioned the sixty new minutes on the seventh CD but not the twenty new minutes included among the other CDs. The seventh is packaged in a reduced-size facsimile of the tape box that some of this material was found in. Not knowing they were going to use it, I wrote on that box "'Village Blues' or 'Mr. Day'," so my handwriting is included! (All involved in the production, including myself, were nominated for a 1996 Grammy in Best Historical Album category.)

All the Impulse recordings are still in print as individual CDs or as small sets of two to four CDs.

Index

(1946–48), 54–62; term avoided by Jimmy Heath, 59; Vinson's appreciation for, 73, 75

bebop (seventh) scales, constructed by Harris, 123, 130

Bechet, Sidney, 181

Beethoven, Ludwig von, 146

"Bei Mir Bist du Schön" (Chaplin), 271

Belden, Bob, 332n. 16

Berger, Daniel, 275, 290

Bernstein, Leonard, 103

"Bessie's Blues" (Coltrane), 232

B-flat saxophones, soprano and tenor as, 181

Bhagavad-Gita, 265, 274

big bands, 27, 35

Big Maybelle (Mabel Louise Smith), 55–56, 94, 310nn. 3, 5

"Billie's Bounce," 47, 314n. 13

"Billy Boy," 103

bitonality, 124, 320n. 15

"Bitter Sweet" (Smith), 89

Black, James Martin (cousin), 13

Blair (African-American family), 1–6, *figs.* 4, 7. *See also individual members by name*

Blair (white family), 1

Blair, Alice Gertrude (mother). *See* Coltrane, Alice Gertrude Blair

Blair, Alice V. Leary (grandmother), 2, 5, 6, 11, 14; death from breast cancer, 16, 291, 294, 303n. 32

Blair, Bettie (aunt). *See* Lyerly, Bettie Blair

Blair, Effie (aunt), 2, 5, 16

Blair, Ethel Wilson (aunt), 20

Blair, John (uncle), 2, 5, 6, 11, 20

Blair, Mary (aunt), 2, 5, 6, 20

Blair, Minnie (Minnie Fowler) (aunt), 2, 5, 293

Blair, Viola (cousin), 14, 293–94

Blair, William Wells (Bud), Jr. (uncle), 2, 5, 6, 293

Blair, William Wilson (grandfather), 2, 5–6, 14, 16

Blakey, Art, 86, 87, 96, 108, 110, 212;

Bobby Timmons with, 172; McLean with, 104, 317n. 19; Shorter with, 144

"Bless This House O Lord We Pray," *Meditations* theme as variation, 267

Bley, Paul (pianist), 205

"Blue in Green" (Bill Evans and Davis), 161, 325n. 34

Blue Note Records, 127–31

"Blue Orchids" (Carmichael), 29

blues, 25, 64, 75, 89, 184, 228 place in Coltrane's music, 25, 84, 115–17, 148, 216; minor, 79, 120, 124, 216, 235; in the 1960s, 25, 184–85, 190 *See also* rhythm and blues

"Blue Seven," 319n. 13

"Blues in the Night," 188

"Blues to You" (Coltrane), 190

"Blue Train" (Coltrane), 156

Blue Train (Coltrane album), 127–31, 157, 191

Blume, August, interview with Coltrane, 55, 86, 106, 137–38, 315n. 20; on association between Coltrane and Monk, 108, 109, 112–13; on interest in philosophy and religion, 256–59; on religious background, 11, 13, 303n. 21

Blumenthal, Bob, 254–55

"Body and Soul" (Green), 64, 70, 71, 147, 173

Bono (of U2), 296

Book of American Negro Spirituals, The (Johnson, editor), 206, 329n. 17

Bostic, Earl (alto saxophonist), 25, 90, 91, 315nn. 10, 11

Boyd, Arnold, 299

Boyd, James (boyhood friend), 27–28

Boyd, Nelson (bassist), 59

Boyd, Rocky (saxophonist), 330n. 3

Boy Scouts, in High Point, 27–28

Bradley, Will, 309n. 15

Braxton, Anthony, 252

Brazil, Joe (saxophonist), 180, 265, 266

"Brazilia" (Coltrane), 226

Lewis Porter (Ph.D., Brandeis, 1983) is Associate Professor of Music at Rutgers University in Newark, and Director of the Master's in Jazz History and Research. A leading jazz scholar, he is the author of several books and articles on jazz, a coauthor of the definitive Coltrane discography, and a consultant to record producers, publishers, and producers of jazz radio shows and films. Dr. Porter has been called by Thomas Owens "a shining light in recent jazz scholarship," and Dizzy Gillespie called his first book, a study of Lester Young, "a monumental work!" His second book was *A Lester Young Reader* (1991). Porter's views on jazz history may be found in *Jazz: From Its Origins to the Present* (1993, with Michael Ullman and Ed Hazell; formerly available on CD-ROM). An anthology of rare historical articles and his essays is entitled *Jazz: A Century of Change* (1997). He is now at work on the first Baker's Biographical Dictionary of Jazz (1999). Porter was one of five people nominated for a Grammy in 1996 for their role in producing the boxed set of Coltrane's Atlantic Recordings (under Best Historical Reissue). He has performed, primarily as a pianist, with Alan Dawson, Jimmy Lyons, Don Friedman, Harvie Swartz, Tom Varner, Hank Roberts, and others. He speaks and performs at colleges, jazz clubs, and radio stations in the United States and Europe.